A DEEP CRY

First World War
Soldier-Poets
killed in France
and Flanders

A DEEP CRY

First World War

Soldier-Poets

killed in France

and Flanders

EDITED AND INTRODUCED BY

ANNE POWELL

SUTTON PUBLISHING

First published in 1993 by Palladour Books

This edition first published in 1998 by Sutton Publishing Limited
Phoenix Mill · Thrupp · Stroud · Gloucestershire GL5 2BU

Reprinted 1998

A catalogue record for this book is available from the British Library

ISBN 0 7509 1987 6

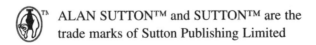 ALAN SUTTON™ and SUTTON™ are the
trade marks of Sutton Publishing Limited

Printed and bound in Great Britain by
Biddles Limited, Guildford, Surrey.

for JEREMY
With my love as always

... I sang to the long hope of my life
And the magic of the aspiration of youth;
The passion of the wind and the scent
Of the lightning of the path
Ahead were in my poem.
My muse was a deep cry
And all the ages to come will hear it,
And my rewards were grievous violence;
And a world that is
One long bare winter without respite...

Extract from 'The Hero' by 'Hedd Wyn'
(Private Ellis Humphrey Evans,
Royal Welch Fusiliers). Translated from the Welsh

... The whole earth is the tomb of heroic men;
and their story is not graven only on stone over
their clay, but abides everywhere, without visible
symbol, woven into the stuff of other men's lives.

Pericles' funeral oration from Thucydides.

The Land Occupied as British War Cemeteries in France is, by a Law of 29th December 1915, the Free Gift of the French People for the Perpetual Resting Place of those who are laid there.

The Land in Belgium Occupied as British War Cemeteries or Graves has been Generously Conceded in Perpetuity by the Belgian People under an Agreement made at Le Havre on August 9th 1917.

From the Commonwealth War Graves Commission's Cemetery and Memorial Registers.

CONTENTS

Maps 1 - 5 by David Goudge.
Map 6 by Jeremy Powell.

INTRODUCTION

Not far from the main gates of the Supreme Headquarters Allied Powers Europe (SHAPE) outside Mons in Belgium, a stone monument commemorates the date 22nd August 1914 when at 7.00 a.m. a squadron from the 4th Royal Irish Dragoon Guards fired the opening British shots of the First World War. Almost directly opposite, a bronze plaque on a wall of the Hotel Medicis, records: "the outpost of the 116th Canadian Infantry Battalion stopped at this very point upon the cease-fire on November 11th 1918." Three miles from here, on land originally given to the Germans to bury their own and the British casualties in August 1914, reputedly the first British soldier and the first officer to be killed, the first man to be awarded the Victoria Cross, and the last British soldier to die before the cease-fire, lie buried in the beautiful St. Symphorien Cemetery.

When we arrived at SHAPE in July 1975, the First World War evoked for me a vague jumble of dates and facts highlighted by the knowledge that my Grandfather, a Boer war hero, had been killed commanding his Battalion during the Battle of the Somme. However, over the next few months, although I was aware that the first and last British actions of this War had taken place near where we lived, I wanted to find out what had happened in the years in between; so playing truant from the ladies' lunch and coffee morning circuit my initial attempts to digest this catastrophic period were at the Musée de Guerre in Mons. Soon Jeremy and I were visiting local war-scarred places; the railway station at Nimy where Lieutenant Dease and Private Godley, of the 4th Battalion, Royal Fusiliers won their V.C.s; the sector round Obourg station where the 4th Battalion Middlesex Regiment's courageous fighting earned them a special memorial, erected at St. Symphorien by the Germans, who added the accolade 'Royal' to their name.

We gradually explored further afield; Verdun, Vimy, the built up areas round Ypres and Passchendaele, the lovely rolling country-side of the Somme, and became more and more appalled each time. Every visit produced a mixture of emotions - horror, grief, anger; and it did not take our senses long to assimilate not only the sheer magnitude of the maiming and slaughter, but the depth of suffering, in every corner of the world, which followed; the shadows linger today.

One Armistice day, using a copy of the description written in pencil three weeks after his death, we found the remote and peaceful cemetery where my Grandfather is buried. Subsequent pilgrimages followed, always leading to new discoveries. We visited cemeteries and memorials in towns, on the outskirts of villages, beside the main roads and at the end of rough country tracks. We tramped over many miles of battleground; in the Spring the chalk outlines of the trenches were clearly visible on the newly ploughed Somme battlefields. Here, too, we found rolls of barbed wire, rusty bayonets, waterbottles, helmets and quantities of ammunition of all different sizes; unexploded shells, we soon realised, remained a danger. During one picnic on the edge of a small copse with our three children, lunch was disturbed by our twelve year-old daughter saying, "What's this Daddy?" In one swift movement Jeremy took the unexploded hand grenade from her and disappeared into the trees.

When we returned to SHAPE in January 1982 we explored the battle areas again but this time in more detail with other members of a flourishing military history group; we researched some of the seemingly infinite number of names on the headstones and memorials; they represented every walk of life, irrespective of class, religion or culture; death, the ultimate equaliser, threw together the musician and coalminer, countryman, artisan, schoolteacher, barrowboy, writer, doctor, cobbler, tradesman, artist and barrister; they all had a story, and their civilian lives, or acts of courage on the field of battle, gave a new substance to the impersonal row upon countless row of rank and name.

Many survived the fighting but only a few were not physically or emotionally wounded. Over 80 years later there are still a number of surviving veterans, many of whom are cared for by organisations such as the Royal British Legion. In August 1982, thirty-five 'Old Contemptibles', the majority of whom had served in the Middlesex Regiment, returned to SHAPE for the annual Battle of Mons ceremonies. The wreath at the stone memorial was laid one morning by a Chelsea Pensioner who had been next to the man who fired the first shot of the war sixty-eight years previously. In the afternoon a joint German and British Service of Reconciliation was held at St. Symphorien Cemetery. The youngest among these veterans was 85 years old and the oldest almost 92. Straight-backed, sprightly and enthusiastic they recalled a rich assortment of harrowing and humorous anecdotes. On their last evening with us, singing 'It's a long way to Tipperary', all the emotion and pride rekindled by a week of pilgrimage and memories, overflowed in song and tears unashamedly.

By this time I was fascinated by the First World War literature; from the biographical details in Brian Gardner's anthology, *Up the Line to Death*, I realised that nineteen poets were buried in Northern France. The first of many requests to the Commonwealth War Graves Commission produced a list of the cemeteries where these men lie. During the next two years we visited all these poets, discovered many more and continued to walk over the ground on which they fought and died.

One very cold February afternoon Jeremy and I stood with three friends somewhere in No Man's Land at Newfoundland Park, Beaumont Hamel. We were examining a map and I was on the edge of the group. I suddenly became conscious of someone standing very still beside me. When I turned to speak there was no one there but the spiritual presence remained for some seconds. As it faded I was filled with a great sense of urgency – as if I had just been told something of vital importance – and must act on it immediately. It has taken me fifteen years to do so.

*   *   *   *   *

Over the last fifteen years I have researched the lives of more than eighty British soldier-poets for this book. My touchstone was that each one must have had a volume of war verse published, or to have appeared in an anthology, and that they all died on the Western Front. In the end twenty have been omitted because of scant information. Even so the biographical details for the sixty-six men included are uneven, although schools, families and various books have provided a range of information. Military details vary also. Regimental Histories produced a good over-all picture of particular events; in some cases Battalion Diaries proved comprehensive but in others facts were recorded sketchily – dependent on where and under what circumstances the Diaries were completed. Certain Battalion Diaries are untraceable.

A Deep Cry has been planned as a Literary Pilgrimage. Although the men are grouped chronologically under the year in which they died, 1915; 1916; 1917 and 1918, they are linked geographically on the maps, according to the location of their graves and memorials. In one instance two men who fell during the same battle, serving in the same Battalion, were buried miles apart; in other cases the graves of two soldier-poets will be found in the same cemetery although they were killed in different years. The men who have no known graves and are remembered on the Memorials to the Missing also span the four war years.

The reason for this paradox is that the cemeteries have been created and re-created over many years. Many of the dead still lie in their original graves dug by their comrades after an action; in Base Hospital cemeteries far behind the front line; and in cemeteries near the Main Dressing Stations and Casualty Clearing Stations where they died of wounds. In 1914, Fabian Ware, and his Red Cross unit, began to locate and record these crude graves. His register was recognised by the authorities, and in 1917 the Imperial War Graves Commission was established. At Ware's request Sir Edwin Lutyens went to France and realised that the graveyards were 'haphazard from the needs of much to do and little time for thought...'

After the War many thousands of the dead, some still unburied, some taken from original burial grounds and scattered graves, were reburied in cemeteries planned by the War Graves Commission. The Commission, in the face of much opposition, insisted that there should be no distinction between the graves of officers and men and that each headstone must be of identical design.

Over half a million Commonwealth and Foreign dead are buried in over 2,000 Commonwealth War Graves Commission cemeteries in Northern France and Belgium; on the Commission's twenty-six Memorials to the Missing in this region over 300,000 names are commemorated. The beautiful Cross of Sacrifice overlooks the rows of white headstones; the Stone of Remembrance, symbolising an Altar of Sacrifice, stands in a separate corner. At the gates of each cemetery, a Register gives short historical details of the men buried there.

Sir Edwin Lutyens believed there was 'no need for the cemeteries to be gloomy or even sad looking places. Good use should be made of the best and most beautiful flowering plants and shrubs...' Today, these lovely gardens of rest, even those on the edge of housing estates or close to motorways, radiate a sense of infinite peace. A wide variety of magnificent trees are grouped according to the size and shape of the cemetery; there are grassed paths between the rows of graves; the earth in front of the headstones is planted with shrubs, planned for every season of the year, spring bulbs and English cottage garden flowers. There is a profusion of colour and scent during the summer months and warm rich shades in the autumn. 460 Commission gardeners care for this 'mass multitude of silent witnesses' on the Western Front all the year round.

Almost 12,000 Commonwealth soldiers, the greatest number to be buried in any War Graves Commission cemetery, lie at Tyne Cot between Passchendaele and Zonnebeke in Belgium; here also, nearly 35,000 names are recorded on the Memorial to the Missing. The Cross of Sacrifice, commanding a view across what was once the Ypres Salient battleground of mud and massacre, was built on a large German blockhouse; behind the Cross, original graves remain as they were found at the end of the War. In Ypres, six miles away, over 54,000 names are inscribed on the vast Menin Gate Memorial to the Missing; every evening traffic is halted here and two buglers sound the Last Post. Apart from the period of the German occupation of Ypres, between May 1940 and September 1944, this short ceremony has continued unbroken since 11th November 1929.

In one of his Sonnets on death, Charles Hamilton Sorley wrote:

"... But now in every road on every side
We see your straight and steadfast signpost there..."

In Northern France these signs read like chapter headings from a children's storybook. 'Hawthorn Ridge'; 'Flat Iron Copse'; 'Caterpillar Valley'; 'Cuckoo Passage'; 'Pigeon Ravine'; 'Thistle Dump'; all are cemeteries. The great Thiepval Memorial to the Missing, commemorating over 72,000 British and Commonwealth soldiers who died during the Somme battles between July 1915 and March 1918 dominates the cemetery-strewn countryside for many miles. Not far from here a complete trench system has been well preserved at Newfoundland Memorial Park which stands in over 80 acres of land over which many bitter actions were fought.

The soldier-poets in this book are buried in thirty-nine cemeteries and are remembered on seven memorials; all but five lie within forty-five miles of Arras. The oldest to be killed was forty-two and the youngest just nineteen years of age; their military ranks at the time of death, spanned from private soldier to a twenty-three year old volunteer, who enlisted in August 1914, and, after gaining his commission, was promoted from Lieutenant to Lieutenant-Colonel in thirteen months. Seven were killed on the 1st July 1916, the first day of the Battle of the Somme. At all the hallowed places where they lie there are many poignant examples of the 'carnage incomprehensible' of the four tragic war years; a headstone of a member of the Chinese Labour Corps, who died far from home, inscribed with his number, date of death and the words 'A Good Reputation Endures Forever'; the sombre gravestones of a group of German soldiers remind that 'victor and vanquished are a-one in death' and that those who fought against each other often share the same resting ground; and the magnificent tree, white with blossom in the spring and laden with cherries in June, standing at the entrance to Agny Military Cemetery where Edward Thomas lies, immortalises his quatrain, a lament for all the sorrow and desolation of war.

*   *   *   *   *

It is difficult to appreciate, more than 80 years later, that the majority of the population in Great Britain were unaware of the true conditions and scale of the First World War. Until the casualty lists permeated the newspapers, few people at home realised the horror of what was happening across the Channel. There was neither radio nor television, and telephones were not in general use. Although telegrams were occasionally sent, letter writing was the principal means of communication for the fighting man. For the most part it was a quick way of maintaining contact; for those who were either wounded, illiterate, or had neither time nor inclination, there were official postcards, with printed headings against which a man could indicate his state of health etc. It was forbidden to keep a private diary at the Front, so these were written in secret and kept hidden. A vast amount of poems and rhymes were composed, sent home and printed in the daily newspapers and magazines and published in book form.

From the trenches, behind the lines, in hospitals and on leave, the soldier-poets wrote of the carnage, suffering and grim conditions they experienced. Some of these writers, who have become well-known, produced literature which will endure for ever; the lesser known may also influence and enhance our appreciation of war. The crude verse and impulsive description, written shortly before or after a terrible bombardment, are as important to understanding a soldier's feelings at that time as any of the finer poems and articulate prose.

The often hastily pencil-scribbled poems, letters and diaries cover a wide range of outlook and response to the brutal world of war. Every human emotion was shared and is evoked in unique language: vivid imagery, candid observation, lucid narrative, forceful accounts, straightforward comments and simple impressions. The philosopher, the underprivileged, the dreamer and the intellectual, expressed anger, fear, hope, humour, compassion, boredom, homesickness and despair in his own inimitable style. Common to each man was nostalgia for the way of life he once knew, love of his family, revulsion of violence, and anticipation of death.

The perceptive soon realised the futility of war. They were

cynical and critical of both Government policy and the military chaos around them. Officers acknowledged the difference between the relative comfort they enjoyed behind the lines compared to the conditions their soldiers were subjected to. The trenches were cruel and dangerous, mud-thick, rat-infested, places of filth and foreboding for all ranks. Hence out of brutality and bloodshed was born an extra-ordinary camaraderie; pain and fear and death bred sympathy, and tolerance towards comrades and the enemy.

Almost every Christian and Jewish soldier-poet struggled with the insoluble question as to where his God stood in the nightmare inferno of battle. The poems, letters and diaries constantly reveal the attempt to keep at least some form of belief in the sanctity of life and an all encompassing Goodness, in the scenario of hellfire and agony. Many men remained deeply committed to their religion, displaying absolute trust and an unshakeable conviction of their immortality; some one-time believers were driven to doubt and disillusionment; a few lost their faith completely.

A few miles behind the front, day-to-day life in France continued almost unchanged and the countryside remained undamaged, but the ground over which the battles were fought was devastated. Towns and villages lay in shattered ruins, trees were uprooted, fields and roads became a quagmire of mud, scarred with deep craters and shell-holes, the great desolation littered with mangled corpses. Nature, on the other hand, remained unaffected by all this; wild flowers grew on wasteland and wayside, larks flew and sang overhead. Bitter cold, torrential rain and intense heat caused endless discomfort; nevertheless the seasons could still provide occasional solace to the weary soldier when he found an isolated copse with the promise of green shoots and blossom, flowers amd soft fruit in a garden which had miraculously escaped destruction. A constant theme in the poetry and prose is the comparison between the very least of nature's wonders and man's relentless madness and destruction.

The soldier-poets came from many different backgrounds; from the working-class to the aristocratic. Only a small proportion were regular soldiers, working or professional men; the majority joined the Army straight from their public schools where the competitive spirit was all important. A few of these young men had a mature outlook from the start of the war and realised there would be neither glory nor splendour in the conflict ahead; others saw the challenge of the games field continued on the field of battle. This jingoistic fervour was crushed in the grim reality of actual warfare. A handful of the writers were virtually self-educated having left the local board school at the age of fourteen; the long working hours which followed made further education difficult, but they persevered in their few hours of leisure and ultimately produced some of the most remarkable writing of the war.

These sixty-six soldier-poets, remembered in grave-gardens over the Western Front, fought alongside and against a multitude of men. They represent the millions of combatants on the conflicting sides. Their underlying message of hope for reconciliation, tolerance and peace went unheeded. Their testimony of man's inhumanity to one another remains as clear and chilling in today's troubled world as it was then.

Anne Powell
Aberporth
1998

THE SOLDIER-POETS IN CHRONOLOGICAL ORDER
OF THEIR DEATH

Name and Rank	Regiment/Unit	Date of Death	Cemetery/ Memorial	Page
1915				
STERLING Lt., R.W.	1st Royal Scots Fusiliers	23 April	Dickebusch New Military Cemetery	2-5
LYON Lt., W.S.S.	9th Royal Scots	8 May	Menin Gate Memorial	6-9
PHILIPPS Capt. The Hon., C.E.A.	Royal Horse Guards	13 May	Menin Gate Memorial	10-14
GRENFELL Capt The Hon., J.H.F., DSO	1st Royal Dragoons	26 May	Boulogne Eastern Cemetery	15-27
SORLEY Capt., C.H.	7th Suffolk Regiment	13 October	Loos Memorial	28-39
LEIGHTON Lt., R.A.	1st/7th Worcestershire Regiment	23 December	Louvencourt Military Cemetery	40-45
1916				
FRESTON 2nd Lt., H.R.	6th Royal Berkshire Regiment	24 January	Bécourt Military Cemetery	48-52
HORNE Capt., C.M.	7th Kings Own Scottish Borderers	27 January	Mazingarbe Communal Cemetery	53-57
PITT 2nd Lt., B.	10th Border Regiment (Attached 47th Trench Mortar Battery)	30 April	Arras Memorial	58-68
STREETS Sgt., J.W.	12th York and Lancaster Regiment	1 July	Euston Road Cemetery	69-74
ROBERTSON Cpl., A.	12th York and Lancaster Regiment	1 July	Thiepval Memorial	75-80
WATERHOUSE 2nd Lt., G.	2nd Essex Regiment	1 July	Serre Road Cemetery No 2	81-86
FIELD 2nd Lt., H.L.	6th Royal Warwickshire Regiment	1 July	Serre Road Cemetery No 2	87-89
WHITE Lt., B.C. de B.	20th Northumberland Fusiliers (Tyneside Scottish)	1 July	Thiepval Memorial	90-95
RATCLIFFE Lt., A.V.	10th West Yorkshire Regiment	1 July	Fricourt New Military Cemetery	96-97

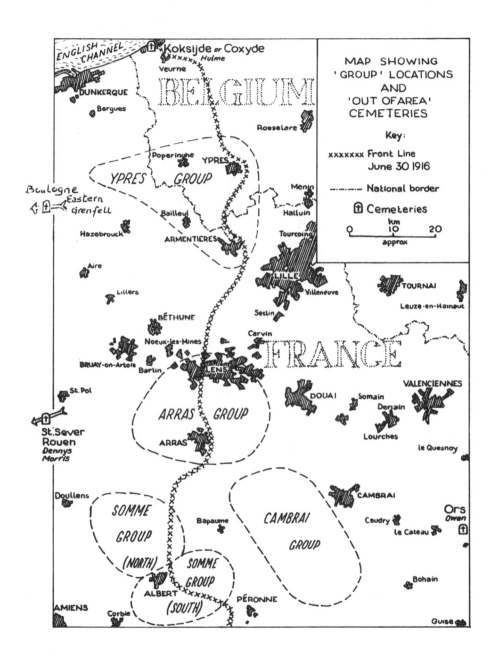

ENGLISH CHANNEL

Koksijde *or* Coxyde
xxxxxx Hulme
Veurne

BELGIUM

DUNKERQUE

Bergues

Roeselare

YPRES GROUP

Poperinghe   YPRES

Menin

Boulogne
Eastern
Grenfell

Bailleul

Halluin

Hazebrouck

ARMENTIERES

Tourcoing

Aire

LILLE

Lillers

Villeneuve

TOURNAI

BÉTHUNE

Seclin

Leuze-en-Hainaut

Noeux-les-Mines

Carvin

FRANCE

BRUAY-en-Artois   Barlin

LENS

VALENCIENNES

St. Pol

DOUAI   Somain

ARRAS GROUP

Denain

St.Sever
Rouen
Dennys
Morris

ARRAS

Lourches

le Quesnoy

Doullens

CAMBRAI

SOMME
GROUP

Bapaume

CAMBRAI
GROUP

Caudry

Ors
Owen

le Cateau

(NORTH)

SOMME
GROUP

ALBERT

PÉRONNE

Bohain

AMIENS

Corbie

(SOUTH)

Guise

MAP SHOWING
'GROUP' LOCATIONS
AND
'OUT OF AREA'
CEMETERIES

Key:

xxxxxx Front Line
June 30 1916

------- National border

⚔ Cemeteries

km
0   10   20
approx

1915

LIEUTENANT ROBERT WILLIAM STERLING

lst Battalion Royal Scots Fusiliers.

Born: 19 November 1893. Glasgow.
Educated: Glasgow Academy
          Sedbergh School.
          Pembroke College, Oxford.
Killed : 23rd April 1915. Aged 22 years.
Dickebusch New Military Cemetery, Belgium.

Robert Sterling gained a Classical Scholarship to Pembroke College, Oxford in 1912, and two years later won the Newdigate Prize with his poem 'The Burial of Sophocles'. Shortly afterwards War was declared and his career at Oxford ended. His love for Oxford is reflected in six out of the nine poems he wrote between 1913 and 1915 praising the University and his College:

TO PEMBROKE COLLEGE

Full often, with a cloud about me shed
Of phantoms numberless, I have alone
Wander'd in Ancient Oxford marvelling:
Calling the storied stone to yield its dead:
And I have seen the sunlight richly thrown
On spire and patient turret, conjuring
Old glass to marled beauty with its kiss,
And making blossom all the foison sown
Through lapsed years. I've felt the deeper bliss
Of eve calm-brooding o'er her loved care,
And tingeing her one all-embosoming tone.
And I have dream'd on thee, thou college fair,
Dearest to me of all, until I seem'd
Sunk in the very substance that I dream'd.
And oh! methought that this whole edifice,
Forg'd in the spirit and the fires that burn
Out of that past of splendent histories,
Up-towering yet, fresh potency might learn,
And to new summits turn,
Vaunting the banner still of what hath been and is.

2

Sterling was commissioned in the Royal Scots Fusiliers and sent to Scotland for training. He arrived in the Ypres area in February 1915 and the Battalion was in and out of trenches at St. Eloi. A few weeks later a close friend arrived unexpectedly at the billets at Reninghelst. Sterling wrote:

> As always we didn't know who was going to relieve us, and we were sitting in our quarters - what remained of the shell-shattered lodge of the chateau, playing cards by candle-light, awaiting events...

The two friends walked for an hour and a half in the chateau grounds with stray bullets from the firing-line whistling around them. Ten days later his friend was killed and Sterling recalled their last meeting:

> I had no idea I was afterwards going to treasure every incident as a precious memory all my life. I think I should go mad, if I didn't still cherish some faith in the justice of things, and a vague but confident belief that death cannot end great friendships.

LINES WRITTEN IN THE TRENCHES

I

Ah! Hate like this would freeze our human tears,
And stab the morning star:
Not it, not it commands and mourns and bears
The storm and bitter glory of red war.

II

To J.H.S.M., killed in action, March 13th, 1915.

O Brother, I have sung no dirge for thee:
Nor for all time to come
Can song reveal my grief's infinity:
The menace of thy silence made me dumb.

After six weeks at the front Sterling wrote:

I have had a comparatively easy time of it so far. My worst experience was a half hour's shelling when the enemy's artillery caught me with a platoon of men digging a trench in the open. On another occasion one of our trenches was blown up by a mine and lost us 60 men, but the Germans who attempted an attack at the time were quickly repulsed, and hardly any of them got back alive to their own trench.

THE ROUND

Crown of the morning
Laid on the toiler:
Joy to the heart
Hope-rich.

Treasure behind left;
Riches before him,
Treasur'd in toil,
To glean.

Starlit and hushful
Wearily homeward:
Rest to the brow
Toil-stain'd.

At the beginning of April 1915, Sterling was sent to hospital at Ypres suffering from influenza; this hospital and the subsequent one at Poperinghe, were shelled and he was sent on to Le Tréport.

The Second Battle of Ypres started on 14th April, 1915 and the town was completely destroyed during the German bombardment which continued for almost a month. Sterling rejoined his battalion and wrote to a friend on 18th April:

... I've been longing for some link with the normal universe detached from the storm. It is funny how trivial instances sometimes are seized as symbols by the memory; but I did find such a link about three weeks ago. We were in trenches in woody country (just S.E. of Ypres). The Germans were about eighty yards away, and between the trenches lay pitiful heaps of dead friends and foes. Such trees as were left standing were little more than stumps, both behind our lines and the enemy's. The enemy had just been shelling our reserve trenches, and a Belgian Battery behind us had been replying, when there fell a few minutes' silence; and I, still crouching expectantly in the trench, suddenly saw a pair of thrushes building a nest in a "bare ruin'd choir" of a tree, only about five yards behind our line. At the same time a lark began to sing in the sky above the German trenches. It seemed almost incredible at the time, but now, whenever I think of those nest-builders and that all but "sightless song", they seem to represent in some degree the very essence of the Normal and Unchangeable Universe carrying on unhindered and careless amid the corpses and the bullets and the madness...

In his *History of the Royal Scots Fusiliers*, John Buchan wrote of what happened to the 1st Battalion who had been in the Ypres Salient with the 28th Division "suffering much from mines and shellfire and mud:"

On 20th April the Division held the front from north-east of Zonnebeke to the Polygon Wood, with the Canadians on its left and the Twenty-seventh Division on its right. On the 17th, Hill 60, at the southern re-entrant of the salient, had been taken and held, and on the 20th there began a bombardment of the town of Ypres with heavy shells, which seemed to augur an enemy advance. On the night of the 22nd, in pleasant spring weather, the Germans launched the first gas attack in the campaign, which forced the French behind the canal and made a formidable breach in the Allied line. Then followed the heroic stand of the Canadians, who stopped the breach, the fight of 'Geddes's Detachment', the shortening of the British line, and the long-drawn torture of the three weeks' action which we call the Second Battle of Ypres. The front of the Twenty-eighth Division was not the centre of the fiercest fighting, and the 1st Royal Scots Fusiliers were not engaged in any of the greatest episodes. But till the battle died away in early June they had their share of losses. On 22nd April Second Lieutenant Wallner was killed in an attack on their trenches, and next day Second Lieutenant R.W. Sterling, a young officer of notable promise, fell, after holding a length of trench all day with 15 men...

LIEUTENANT WALTER SCOTT STUART LYON

9th Battalion Royal Scots.

Born: 1st October 1886. North Berwick.
Educated: Haileybury College.
            Balliol College, Oxford.
Killed: 8th May 1915. Aged 28 years.
Menin Gate Memorial to the Missing, Ypres, Belgium.

Walter Lyon graduated in Law at Edinburgh University in 1912 and became an advocate. *The Balliol College War Memorial Book* records that:

> ... he was extremely silent and reserved, and probably suffered a good deal from solitude... He is said to have been the first member of the Scottish Bar to fall in the war, and even the first advocate to fall in action since Flodden Field...

Lyon joined the Royal Scots before the War. He arrived in Belgium with the Battalion at the end of February 1915; after a few weeks behind the lines at L'Abeele and Dickebusch he went to trenches in Glencorse Wood, Westhoek near Ypres. On 9th, 10th and 11th April Lyon wrote two poems from 'Mon Privilège', his dug-out:

EASTER AT YPRES: 1915

The sacred Head was bound and diapered,
The sacred Body wrapped in charnel shroud,
And hearts were breaking, hopes that towered were bowed,
And life died quite when died the living Word.
So lies this ruined city. She hath heard
The rush of foes brutal and strong and proud,
And felt their bolted fury. She is ploughed
With fire and steel, and all her grace is blurred.

But with the third sun rose the Light indeed,
Calm and victorious though with brows yet marred
By Hell's red flame so lately visited.
Nor less for thee, sweet city, better starred
Than this grim hour portends, new times succeed;
And thou shalt reawake, though aye be scarred.

6

LINES WRITTEN IN A FIRE TRENCH

'Tis midnight, and above the hollow trench
Seen through a gaunt wood's battle-blasted trunks
And the stark rafters of a shattered grange,
The quiet sky hangs huge and thick with stars.
And through the vast gloom, murdering its peace,
Guns bellow and their shells rush swishing ere
They burst in death and thunder, or they fling
Wild jangling spirals round the screaming air.
Bullets whine by, and maxims drub like drums,
And through the heaped confusion of all sounds
One great gun drives its single vibrant "Broum."
And scarce five score of paces from the wall
Of piled sand-bags and barb-toothed nets of wire
(So near and yet what thousand leagues away)
The unseen foe both adds and listens to
The selfsame discord, eyed by the same stars.
Deep darkness hides the desolated land,
Save where a sudden flare sails up and bursts
In whitest glare above the wilderness,
And for one instant lights with lurid pallor
The tense, packed faces in the black redoubt.

In the early hours of the morning of 16th April 1915, during the
Second Battle of Ypres, Lyon wrote 'On a Grave in a Trench
inscribed " English killed for the Patrie"', and a few days later from
the trenches in Glencorse Wood he wrote 'I tracked a dead man
down a trench'.

ON A GRAVE IN A TRENCH INSCRIBED
"ENGLISH KILLED FOR THE PATRIE"

You fell on Belgian land,
And by a Frenchman's hand
Were buried. Now your fate
A kinsman doth relate.

Three names meet in this trench:
Belgian, English, French;
Three names, but one the fight
For Freedom, Law and Light.

And you in that crusade
Alive were my comrade
And theirs, the dead whose names
Shine like immortal flames.

And though unnamed you be,
Oh "Killed for the Patrie",
In honour's lap you lie
Sealed of their company.

I TRACKED A DEAD MAN DOWN A TRENCH

I tracked a dead man down a trench,
    I knew not he was dead.
They told me he had gone that way,
    And there his foot-marks led.

The trench was long and close and curved,
    It seemed without an end;
And as I threaded each new bay
    I thought to see my friend.

I went there stooping to the ground.
    For, should I raise my head,
Death watched to spring; and how should then
    A dead man find the dead?

At last I saw his back. He crouched
    As still as still could be,
And when I called his name aloud
    He did not answer me.

The floor-way of the trench was wet
    Where he was crouching dead;
The water of the pool was brown,
    And round him it was red.

I stole up softly where he stayed
    With head hung down all slack,
And on his shoulders laid my hands
    And drew him gently back.

And then, as I had guessed, I saw
His head, and how the crown -
I saw then why he crouched so still,
And why his head hung down.

At the beginning of May 1915 the 9th Battalion Royal Scots was alternately in trenches near Potijze Wood, south of the Menin Road, and in dug-outs only 200 yards from the firing-line inside the Wood. *The History of The Royal Scots* records:

> ... on the 8th May the heaviest bombardment we had ever experienced broke out... The shelling was terrific; from early morning till dark high explosives and shrapnel rained through the wood. Fine old trees fell torn to the roots by a coal-box; tops of others were sliced by shrapnel, and their new year's greenery died early: the whole wood became a scene of tragic devastation. Far worse than that, the stream of wounded became uninterrupted. We ourselves lost our first officer killed - Lieutenant Lyon...

CAPTAIN THE HONOURABLE COLWYN ERASMUS ARNOLD PHILIPPS

Royal Horse Guards.
Born: 11th December 1888. London.
Educated: Eton College.
Killed: 13th May 1915. Aged 26 years.
Menin Gate Memorial to the Missing, Ypres, Belgium.

Colwyn Philipps was the eldest son of Lord and Lady St. Davids. He was commissioned in the Royal Horse Guards in October 1908. Most of his light verse was written before the War.

Philipps arrived in billets at Verlorenhoek, in the Ypres Salient, on 4th November 1914; the Battalion was in support trenches at Hooge and Zwarte-Leen and then in the front line. In a letter home dated 10th November, Philipps wrote an account of his 'first battle':

... We were ordered to relieve some troops in the advanced trench. We rode about six miles, then dismounted, leaving some men with the horses, and walked about five miles to the trenches. As we went through the first village, we got heavily shelled by the famous Black Marias; they make a noise just like an express train and burst like a clap of thunder, you hear them coming for ten seconds before they burst. It was very unpleasant, and you need to keep a hold on yourself to prevent ducking - most of the men duck.

Most of the shells hit the roofs, but one burst in the road in front of me, killing one man and wounding four or five. However, once we got out of the village they stopped, and we arrived at the trenches in the dark of the evening. We filed quietly into them and waited in the darkness. We stayed there two days and nights, being shelled most of the time. The German trenches were about 1600 yards away, with Maxim guns. They never showed their noses by daylight, and the guns were miles away. We never fired a shot all the time. They only once hit the trench, wounding two men, but about fifty shells pitched within a few yards. They set fire to a large farm a hundred yards behind us that made a glorious blaze. The Frenchmen on our right and left kept up intermittent bursts of rifle-fire. This did no good and gave away the position of their trenches, so they got more shelled than we did. We have now come out and are billeted in a farm ten miles behind the trenches. We had dozens of guns behind our trenches, but they seemed to have little or no effect on keeping down the German fire. Now about tips. - Dig, never mind if the men are tired, always dig. Make trenches as narrow as possible, with no parapet if possible;

dig them in groups of eight or ten men, and join up later, leave large traverses. Once you have got your deep narrow trench you can widen out the bottom, but don't hollow out too much, as a Maria shakes the ground for a hundred yards and will make the whole thing fall in. Don't allow any movement or heads to show, or any digging or going to the rear in the daytime. All that can be done at night or in the mists of morning that are heavy and last till 8 or 9 a.m. Always carry wire and always put wire forty yards in front of the trench, not more. One trip wire will do if you have no time for more. The Germans often rush at night and the knowledge of wire gives the men confidence. Don't shoot unless you have a first-rate target, and don't ever shoot from the trenches at aeroplanes - remember that the whole thing is concealment, and then again concealment. Never give the order 'fire' without stating the number of rounds, as otherwise you will never stop them again; you can't be too strict about this in training. On the whole I don't think gun-fire is alarming, but from what I see of others it has an awfully wearing effect on the nerves after a time...

Philipps had leave in England in December 1914 and in February 1915. After he rejoined the Battalion in the Ypres Salient he wrote on 12th March, to his mother:

People out here seem to think that the war is going to be quite short, why, I don't know; personally, I see nothing here to prevent it going on for ever. We never attack the Germans, and simply do our utmost to maintain ourselves; when we seem to advance it is really that the Germans have evacuated the place. Someone once said that war was utter boredom for months interspersed by moments of acute terror - the boredom is a fact... Except for a belt of about twelve miles where the battle is being waged, the whole country shows hardly a sign of war. In many places the inhabitants return the day after the battle... We have had a lot of fighting all in trenches and look like having more... The other day we were evacuating some trenches and the question was if we could cross a piece of much-shelled ground safely - i.e., Was it under direct observation of their gunners? 'Send on one troop and see' was the order. I was first, and I saw the men's faces look rather long. I had no cigarettes, so I took a ration biscuit in one hand and a lump of cheese in the other and retired eating these in alternate mouthfuls to 'restore confidence'. We escaped without a shell, but I almost choked myself! It looks to me as if we shall have a busy time now...

On 26th April, twelve days after the start of the Second Battle of Ypres, Philipps wrote from Vlamertinghe:

This is a baby letter actually written in battle. Lord knows when it will be posted... I will write to you again when we finish this fight. We have just been moved up in support of the Canadians and may go into the line any time - a whole brigade of us is sitting by the road awaiting orders.

'Saddle up' has come - we are off.

On 29th April Philipps was billetted in a farm between L'Abeele and Steenvoorde:

For five days we have been riding round a most hotly contested battle, occasionally taking part - we have only lost half a dozen men and the crisis seems to be over... I am writing this in a farm a few miles back where we are in reserve. It is a most glorious spring evening, the air is heavy with the scent of bursting buds, and a great fat harvest-moon is roosting on the barn. It seems almost impossible to believe that the continuous rumble of distant thunder is caused by those damned guns.

The trooper is a curious animal - he will watch shells bursting 200 yards from him with perfect equanimity as rather adding interest to the view - then one comes really close and he huddles down miserably. Personally a shell within 200 yards impresses me as much as one at my feet. Another amazing and fortunate thing is the shortness of his memory - his best friend dies in agony at his side, and it depresses him for half an hour... The latest joke on the front is to call the cavalry the M.P.s, because they sit and do nothing.

On 12th May the Battalion received orders to take over trenches between the Ypres - Zonnebeke road and the Ypres - Menin road.

Sir John French's Despatch for the 13th May reported "the heaviest bombardment yet experienced broke out at 4.30 a.m. and continued with little intermission throughout the day." A Royal Horse Guards Trooper wrote five days later:

The regiment entered the reserve trenches almost on the outskirts of Ypres, on the night of the 12th, relieving the Middlesex Regiment. We proceeded to make ourselves as comfortable as we could, but about half-past two we were all disturbed by the Brigade Major ordering us all to move well along to our right, to allow a returned party of Essex Yeomanry from trench digging to get under cover. After a while we were somehow squeezed into the dug-outs again; it was pouring with rain and about 4 o'clock at the break of day the German Artillery commenced a violent bombardment. We still remained inactive despite the heavy firing. At about 6 - 8 a.m. (it was so hard to tell the time) we could see our people retiring in small batches from the second line of trenches, and when they reached our trenches we found they were the Life Guards, clean blown from the trenches and dug-outs and without a semblance of cover. After a short while Captain Bowlby, the Squadron Commander, called the Life Guards together, and they got back towards the firing line. All this time Captain Philipps was with us. I was in his troop. He was amusing himself by passing a loaf of stale bread and a tin of meat to Mr. Ward Price, and he told me to send the message that the kidneys were spoilt by cooking too much. He was as usual in the best of spirits and always on the look out. At about 10 o'clock we all made a move to our immediate right, I should think one and a half miles under shrapnel and bullet fire. Passing a large farm we were roughly called together and advanced in single file with a few casualties, then we had to extend again, as shrapnel was getting thick. Finally we reached the dug-outs held by the 1st Royal Dragoons. It was a complete cavalry movement acting as infantry. All this time we were receiving a terrible fire from the artillery. Most of us got into the remnants of the dug-outs, as the trenches in front were completely filled in by Jack Johnsons and were quite flat. At this time I was in conversation with Captain Philipps, who was explaining to me that to our left from 200 to 300 yards of the line was not held. I asked Captain Philipps what he expected to happen if the Germans got to know this, and he replied that he felt sure they knew, but were too chicken-hearted to attack. Just at that moment he was showing me a Catholic medal picked up at Ypres. We suddenly had an order to stand to and he slipped away without the medal.

From this moment commenced the most awful shell fire that God ever has allowed. We were ordered to advance. By clambering over the dug-outs we reached open ground affording excellent targets to the Germans. Captain Philipps inquired where Captain Bowlby was, and I told him I had seen him climb over just previously. Captain Philipps shouted to get over as quickly as possible and follow him. He climbed over and ran a distance of about thirty yards and then spread flat quite unhurt. I ran behind about half the distance. It is really impossible to give you the faintest idea of what was happening; it was as if we were in a terrific hailstorm, only lead instead of hail. Everything had been prepared on their front and we were not prepared. They had their machine-guns simply dealing out for all they were worth, and the artillery had the range beforehand. Seeing Captain Philipps to my front I got up to be as near as I could, knowing it would be a charge in a few seconds. I wanted to get a crowd together to support each other, and besides I had my Colt repeater, which was useless to me, as my rifle took all my time using, and I wanted to give it to Captain Philipps instead of his sword. In the morning he had been inspecting the Colt and told me to get hold of a German officer and pinch his cartridges.

Those were his words. However, on rising to rush forward I stopped one - it entered my thigh and passed right through. I dropped on the spot, and as I was dragged into a hedge and down an embankment I saw that our troops had all rushed forward again. This was the last I saw of Captain Philipps, and it was half-past two in the afternoon of the 13th. I crawled back towards Ypres, it taking me seven hours to do about three miles, and eventually I was picked up outside Ypres...

Colwyn Phillips was mentioned in despatches on 1st January 1916. When his kit arrived home his parents found the following poem in his notebook:

There is a healing magic in the night,
The breeze blows cleaner than it did by day,
Forgot the fever of the fuller light,
And sorrow sinks insensibly away
As if some saint a cool white hand did lay
Upon the brow, and calm the restless brain.
The moon looks down with pale unpassioned ray -
Sufficient for the hour is its pain.
Be still and feel the night that hides away earth's stain.
Be still and loose the sense of God in you,
Be still and send your soul into the all,
The vasty distance where the stars shine blue,
No longer antlike on the earth to crawl.
Released from time and sense of great or small
Float on the pinions of the Night-Queen's wings;
Soar till the swift inevitable fall
Will drag you back into all the world's small things;
Yet for an hour be one with all escaped things.

CAPTAIN, THE HONOURABLE JULIAN HENRY FRANCIS GRENFELL, D.S.O.

1st Battalion Royal Dragoons.

Born: 30th March 1888. London.

Educated: Eton College.

Balliol College, Oxford.

Died of Wounds: 26th May 1915. Aged 27 years.

Boulogne Eastern Cemetery, France.

Julian Grenfell was the eldest son of William and Ethel Grenfell. William Grenfell had been Liberal Member of Parliament for Salisbury between 1882 and 1886. A few years later he joined the Conservative party and became the Member for South Buckinghamshire from 1900 until he was created Lord Desborough in 1905. The same year Julian Grenfell became head of his house, Editor of *The Eton Chronicle* and *The Outsider* and was elected a member of Pop, the elite club, originally a debating society, which contributed to the government and discipline of the school.

Grenfell went up to Balliol in October 1906. During the Spring and Summer of 1909 he wrote seven essays. In these he attempted to highlight the conventions, values and fantasies which he considered would eventually lead society to ruin, and which oppressed any free thinking individual determined to lead his own life. He argued that conventionalism is nurtured by the competitive spirit found in the world of etiquette and social advancement.

> ... conventionality's terrible power consists perhaps chiefly in its grip on the cradles of our race. It's talons fasten relentlessly on the new-born infant... the very essence of conventionality is to force itself upon others, and the child is in duty bound to take all that is told him as the literal truth. He cannot see for himself what is black or white, right or wrong: None escape, except those hardy souls who refuse from the very first to believe that a gentleman is a man who wears a top hat...

Grenfell was commissioned in the Royal Dragoons in the summer of 1910 and arrived in India with the Regiment in November. It was stationed at Muttra, south of Delhi from where he wrote: "I shall begin polo and pig-sticking directly. I love the Royals, and the rich life of the soldier."

In October 1911 the Regiment left India and arrived in South

Africa two months later, where it was stationed at Roberts' Heights near Pretoria. Grenfell wrote to his family:

April 21st 1912... I went to Johannesburg on the 11th with our boxing men, trained up to the eyes, and when I got there found that I was the only Heavy-weight Officer entered! So I got the promoters to give a cup for a four-round contest, and a man who was in training for the Amateur Championship said he would come and fight me. He was a fire-man, called Tye; he used to be a sailor, and he looked as hard as a hammer. I quaked in my shoes when I saw him, and quaked more when I heard he was 2-1 on favourite for the Championship, and quaked most when my trainer went to see him, and returned with word that he had knocked out two men in a quarter of an hour. We went into the ring on the night, and he came straight for me like a tiger, and hit left and right; I stopped the left, but it knocked my guard aside, and he crashed his right clean on to the point of my jaw. I was clean knocked out; but by the fluke of Heaven I recovered and came to and got on to my feet again by the time they had counted 6. I could hardly stand, and I could only see a white blur in front of me; but I just had sense to keep my guard up, and hit hard at the blur whenever it came within range. He knocked me down twice more, but my head was clearing every moment, and I felt a strange sort of confidence that I was master of him. I put him down in the 2nd round, with a right counter, which shook him; he took a count of 8. In the 3rd round I went in to him, and beat his guard down - then crossed again with the right, and felt it go right home, with all my arm and body behind it. I knew it was the end, when I hit; and he never moved for 20 seconds. They said it was the best fight they had seen for years in Johannesburg, and my boxing men went clean off their heads, and carried me twice round the hall. I was 11 st. 4., and he was 11 st. 3., I think it was the best fight I shall ever have.

Grenfell went home on leave in September 1912 and returned to South Africa in April 1913. On 6th August 1914 he wrote to his mother:

Things have gone pretty quickly this last week, haven't they? There was hardly a breath of war here when I wrote last week. Then the next day we were called back in the middle of a big manoeuvre battle, post-haste, and told we must be ready to start at any minute. It is horrible being tucked away here at a time like this. We only get the merest driblets of news, and can only wait, knowing that the biggest battles of the world are going on at every and any moment... It must be wonderful in England now. I suppose the excitement is beyond all words...?

Julian Grenfell arrived in England with his Regiment on 20th September 1914; less than four weeks later they were in the Ypres Salient, involved in the First Battle of Ypres.

From billets at Wytschaete, Grenfell wrote on 15th October:

... The guns go on all day and most of the night - of course it is very hard to follow what is going on; even the squadron leaders know nothing; and one marches and countermarches without end, backwards and forwards, nearer and further, apparently without object. Only the Christian virtue of Faith emerges triumphant. It is all the most wonderful fun; better fun than one could ever imagine. I hope it goes on a nice long time; pig-sticking will be the only possible pursuit after this, or one will die of sheer ennui. The first time one shoots at a man one has the feeling of 'never point a loaded gun at anyone, even in fun'; but very soon it gets like shooting a crocodile, only more exciting, because he shoots back at you...

On 21st October the Battalion took over front line trenches at Zandvoorde, and Grenfell continued to send descriptive letters home:

October 24th 1914 ... We have had it pretty hot this last day or two in the trenches. We take to it like ducks to water, and dig much better trenches than the infantry and far quicker. We are all awfully well, except those who have stopped something. We have been fighting night and day; first rest today for four days. The worst of it is, no sleep practically. I cannot tell you how wonderful our men were, going straight for the first time into a fierce fire. They surpassed my utmost expectations. I have never been so fit or nearly so happy in my life before. I adore the fighting and the continual interest which compensates for every disadvantage..."

October 27th... We have been in the trenches for two days and nights since I started this, but no excitement except a good dose of shrapnel three times a day, which does one no harm and rather relieves the monotony... Our first day of real close-up fighting was Monday the 19th. We cavalry went on about a day and a half in front of the infantry. We got into a village, and our advance patrols started fighting hard, with a certain amount of fire from everywhere in front of us. Our advance patrols gained the first groups of houses, and we joined them. Firing came from a farm in front of us, and then a man came out of it and waved a white flag. I yelled '200, white flag, rapid fire,' but Hardwick stopped me shooting. Then the squadron advanced across the root fields towards the farm, and dismounted in open order, and they opened a sharp fire on us from the farm and the next field. We took three prisoners in the roots, and returned to the

17

houses again. That was our first experience of them, the white flag dodge. We lost two, and one wounded. Then I got leave to make a dash across a field for another farm where they were sniping at us. I could only get half way. My sergeant was killed and my corporal hit. We lay down. Luckily it was high roots and we were out of sight. But they had fairly got our range, and the bullets kept knocking up the dirt into one's face and all round. We just lay doggo for about half an hour, and then the firing slackened, and we crawled back to the houses and the rest of the squadron.

I was pleased with my troop under bad fire. They used the most filthy language, talking quite quietly and laughing all the time, even after the men were knocked over within a yard of them. I longed to be able to say that I liked it, after all one has heard of being under fire for the first time. But it is beastly. I pretended to myself for a bit that I liked it, but it was no good, it only made one careless and unwatchful and self absorbed; but when one acknowledged to oneself that it was beastly one became all right again, and cool.

After the firing had slackened, we advanced again a bit into the next group of houses, which were the edge of the village proper. I cannot tell you how muddling it is. We did not know which was our Front. We did not know whether our own troops had come round us on the flanks, or whether they had stopped behind and were firing into us. And besides, a lot of German snipers were left in the houses we had come through, and every now and then bullets came singing by from God knows where. Four of us were talking and laughing in the road, when about a dozen bullets came with a whistle. We all dived for the nearest door, and fell over each other, yelling with laughter, into a very dirty outhouse. James Leckie, the Old Old Man, said 'I have a bullet through my best Sandon Twillette Breeches.' We looked, and he had. It had gone clean through. He did not tell us till two days afterwards that it had gone through him too. None of us knew until he went to the Doctor on Wednesday, but it was like the holes you make to blow an egg, only about 4 inches apart.

We stopped there about two hours; then the Cavalry regiment on our right retired. Then we saw a lot of Germans, among the fires they had lit (they set the houses on fire to mark their lines of advance). They were running from house to house. We were told not to fire, for fear of our own people on the other side. I was the farthest troop out, in a house at the edge of the main village. Then came a lot of them shouting and singing and advancing down the street through the burning houses. One felt a peculiar hatred for them. I sent back word that I could not stay there, and the squadron retired without losing much. We heard afterwards that there had been a Division of German infantry in front of us. At first we thought there were only one or two patrols of them.   We retired about two miles, and dismounted for action.   Soon they began to come up from three sides of us, and we retired again.   They were pretty close, advancing higgledy-piggledy across the fields, and firing.   They shot abominably (nothing like the morning, from the houses, when they had all the ranges marked to a yard).   We lost only about 20 horse, no men killed...

The next day we went forward to another place and entrenched ourselves against a very big German force, with orders to hold out as long as we could.   But they took a long time deploying for attack, and we only had to face their guns...

Since that, we have been doing infantry work in the trenches.   We have been out-of-work in our trenches, only shrapnel and snipers.   Someone described this War as 'Months of boredom punctuated by moments of terror'.   It is sad that it is such an impossible place for cavalry.   Cavalry work against far superior forces of infantry, like we had the other day, is not good enough.   The Germans are dashed good at that house-to-house fighting business.   It is horrible having to leave one's horse.   It feels like leaving half oneself behind, and one feels the dual responsibility all the time.   Besides, it depletes our already small numbers, for horse-holders...

I adore War.   It is like a big picnic without the objectlessness of a picnic.   I have never been so well or so happy.   Nobody grumbles at one for being dirty.   I have only had my boots off once in the last 10 days, and only washed twice.   We are up and standing to our rifles by 5 a.m. when doing this infantry work, and saddled up by 4.30 a.m. when with our horses.   Our poor horses do not get their saddles off when we are in trenches.

The wretched inhabitants here have got practically no food left.   It is miserable to see them leaving their houses, and tracking away, with great bundles and children in their hands.   And the dogs and cats left in the deserted villages are piteous..."

November 3rd, 1914... I have not washed for a week, or had my boots off for a fortnight.   But we cook good hot food in the dark, in the morning before we start, and in the night when we get back to our horses;... It is all the best fun.   I have never never felt so well, or so happy, or enjoyed anything so much. It just suits my stolid health, and stolid nerves, and barbaric disposition.   The fighting-excitement vitalizes everything, every sight and word and action.   One loves one's fellow man so much more when one is bent on killing him.   And picnic-ing in the open day and night (we never see a roof now) is the real method of existence.

There are loads of straw to bed-down on, and one sleeps like a log, and wakes up with the dew on one's face.   The stolidity of my nerves surprises myself. I went to sleep the other day when we were lying in the trenches, with the shrapnel bursting within 50 yards all the time and a noise like nothing on earth. The noise is continual and indescribable. The Germans shell the trenches with shrapnel all day and all night; and the Reserves and ground in the rear with Jack Johnsons, which at last one gets to love as old friends. You hear them coming for miles, and everyone imitates the noise; then they burst with a plump and make a great hole in the ground, doing no damage unless they happen to fall into your trench or on to your hat. They burst pretty nearly straight upwards. One landed within 10 yards of me the other day, and only knocked me over and my horse. We both got up and looked at each other, and laughed. It did not even knock the cigarette out of my mouth... Our men are splendid, really splendid. One marvels at them. We shall beat those German swine by sticking it out...

We took a German Officer and some men prisoners in the wood the other day. One felt hatred for them as one thought of our dead; and as the Officer came by me, I scowled at him, and the men were cursing him. The Officer looked me in the face and saluted me as he passed, and I have never seen a man look so proud and resolute and smart and confident, in his hour of bitterness. It made me feel terribly ashamed of myself...

On 15th November the Battalion went to trenches north of Kleine Zillebeke; these were in a wood, very close to the enemy, who were in many places not more than 40 or 50 yards away. The following day Grenfell went out on an individual patrol behind the enemy's trenches; he later wrote a description of his action for which he was awarded the Distinguished Service Order.

... After a day of shells one's nerves are really absolutely beaten down. I can understand now why our infantry have to retreat sometimes; a sight which came as a shock to one at first, after being brought up in the belief that the English infantry cannot retreat.

These last two days we had quite a different kind of trench, in a dripping sodden wood, with the German trench in some places 40 yards ahead. Too close for them to shell us. Dead Germans lying all along the front. Most of the trees (fir trees) cut down by bullets and shrapnel, and piled along the ground with the branches sticking up over the ground.

We had been worried by their snipers all along, and I had always been asking for leave to go out and have a try myself. Well, on Tuesday the 16th, the day before yesterday, they gave me leave. Only after great difficulty. They told me to take a section with me, and I said I would sooner cut my throat and have done with it. So they let me go alone. Off I crawled through sodden clay and trenches, going about a yard a minute, and listening and looking as I thought it was not possible to look and listen. I went out to the right of our lines, where the 10th were, and where the Germans were nearest. I took about 30 minutes to do 30 yards, then I saw the Hun trench, and I waited there a long time, but could see or hear nothing. It was about 10 yards from me. Then I heard some Germans talking and saw one put his head up over some bushes about 10 yards behind the trench. I could not get a shot at him, I was too low down, and of course I could not get up. So I crawled on again very slowly to the parapet of their trench. It was very exciting. I was not sure that there might not have been someone there, or a little further along the trench. I peered through their loop-hole and saw nobody in the trench. Then the German behind put his head up again. He was laughing and talking. I saw his teeth glistening against my fore-sight, and I pulled the trigger very slowly. He just grunted, and crumpled up. The others got up and whispered to each other. I do not know which were most frightened, them or me. I think there were four or five of them. They could not trace the shot, I was flat behind their parapet and hidden. I just had the nerve not to move a muscle and stay there. My heart was fairly hammering. They did not come forward, and I could not see them, as they were behind some bushes and trees, so I crept back inch by inch.

I went out again in the afternoon, in front of our bit of the line. About 60 yards off I found their trench again, empty again. I waited there for an hour, but saw nobody. Then I went back, because I did not want to get inside some of their patrols who might have been placed forward. I reported the trench empty.

The next day, just before dawn, I crawled out there again, and found it empty again. Then a single German came through the woods towards the trench. I saw him 50 yards off. He was coming along upright and careless, making a great noise. I heard him before I saw him. I let him get within 25 yards, and shot him in the heart. He never made a sound. Nothing for 10 minutes, and then there was a noise and talking, and a lot of them came along, through the wood behind the trench about 40 yards from me. I counted about 20, and there were more coming. They halted in front, and I picked out the one I thought was the officer, or sergeant. He stood facing the other way, and I had a steady shot at him behind the shoulders. He went down, and that was all I saw. I went back at a sort of galloping crawl to our lines, and sent a message to the 10th that the Germans were moving up their way in some numbers. Half an hour afterwards, they attacked the 10th and our right, in massed formation, advancing slowly to within 10 yards of the trenches. We simply mowed them down. It was rather horrible. I was too far to the left. They did not attack our part of the line, but the

10th told me in the evening that they counted 200 dead in a little bit of the line, and the 10th and us only lost ten.

They have made quite a ridiculous fuss about me stalking, and getting the message through. I believe they are going to send me up to our General and all sorts. It was only up to someone to do it, instead of leaving it all to the Germans, and losing two officers a day through snipers. All our men have started it now. It is the popular amusement...

Grenfell was offered a staff job as ADC to General Pulteney which he refused "because we are now so woefully short of Officers." He thought it was "awfully good of Putty" but felt he was "doing far more good as a fighting-line soldier than I ever would on the staff... and should have to be clean and well mannered, which has now become a matter of impossibility to me." He was home on leave for a week at the end of December and returned to the Ypres Salient with three greyhounds on 6th January 1915. A few days later he took part in a boxing competition in the local Town Hall.

... Feeling war-like, I got them to issue a challenge (anonymous) to anyone in the room. The boxers had not been very good, and I hoped for a soft job. But a very large private in the A.S.C. immediately put up his gigantic hand, and said he was only too ready to fight! Imagine my chagrin and horror, especially when I was told that the man was a boxing pro, who had joined for the War! He closed my left eye right up in the first round, and they wanted to stop the fight, because it was bad. But I told them I was all right; and in the second round I caught him a beauty, and they had to carry him out to hospital. It was a terrific fight while it lasted. I had to make the pace, because I was so unfit. My eye is all right now, and a glorious colour. Purple shot with green. And the man is all right too...

On 8th February the Battalion went to trenches north of Kleine Zillebeke, slightly east of where it was in November. Grenfell wrote to his sister on February 19th:

... We had five days in the trenches, and only lost one man. We were within 30 yards of the Boches in one place. They started firing silly little sticks of nitro-picric-high-explosive-fire-and-brimstone-glycerine at us out of a trench gun. I was asleep, when suddenly there was a deafening crash, and half of the dug-out roof fell on to my face. I ran out, and found old Sammy being pulled by the legs from under the ruin of his dug-out, amid yells of ribald laughter. Then someone said

'Look-out', and another blasted stick came over like a rocketing pheasant. After that I started rapid fire with our rifle grenades, and, by great luck, pitched the first three plum into their trench. Then they stopped, by a sort of mutual agreement on both sides to remain inactive and comfortable, so long as each knew that the other side was able to retaliate if provoked...

From billets at Blaringhem in March Grenfell wrote "Prayer for those on the Staff."

PRAYER FOR THOSE ON THE STAFF

Fighting in mud, we turn to Thee,
In these dread times of battle, Lord,
To keep us safe, if so may be,
From shrapnel, snipers, shell, and sword.

But not on us, for we are men
Of meaner clay, who fight in clay,
But on the Staff, the Upper Ten,
Depends the issue of the Day.

The Staff is working with its brains,
While we are sitting in the trench;
The Staff the universe ordains
(Subject to Thee and General French).

God help the Staff - especially
The young ones, many of them sprung
From our high aristocracy;
Their task is hard, and they are young.

O Lord, who mad'st all things to be,
And madest some things very good,
Please keep the extra A.D.C.
From horrid scenes, and sight of blood.

See that his eggs are newly laid,
Not tinged as some of them - with green;
And let no nasty draughts invade
The windows of his Limousine.

When he forgets to buy the bread,
When there are no more minerals,
Preserve his smooth well-oiled head
From wrath of caustic Generals.

> O Lord, who mad'st all things to be,
> And hatest nothing thou hast made,
> Please keep the extra A.D.C.
> Out of the sun and in the shade.

At the beginning of April Grenfell had two days leave in Paris. He was captivated by the people and the city which he found "gloriously light and gay and beautiful... It was the biggest experience of New Things I have ever had in my life..." On the 14th April the Second Battle of Ypres started and on 22nd the first gas attack of the War was launched by the Germans north of Ypres. The following day the Battalion moved from billets at Thiennes to billets at Houtkerque near Watou, where Grenfell slept in a barn.

On the 29th Grenfell wrote in his diary:

Moved off 8 a.m. towards Pop. Brigade rested in field. Rested all day, and got back to our farm at 7.30 p.m. Pork chops for dinner. Wonderful sunny lazy days - but longing to be up and doing something. Slept out. Wrote poem - 'Into Battle'.

INTO BATTLE

> The naked earth is warm with Spring,
> And with green grass and bursting trees
> Leans to the sun's gaze glorying,
> And quivers in the sunny breeze;
> And Life is Colour and Warmth and Light,
> And a striving evermore for these;
> And he is dead who will not fight;
> And who dies fighting has increase.
>
> The fighting man shall from the sun
> Take warmth, and life from the glowing earth;
> Speed with the light-foot winds to run,
> And with the trees to newer birth;
> And find, when fighting shall be done,
> Great rest, and fullness after dearth.
>
> All the bright company of Heaven
> Hold him in their high comradeship,
> The Dog-Star and the Sisters Seven,
> Orion's Belt and sworded hip.

1915

The woodland trees that stand together,
They stand to him each one a friend,
They gently speak in the windy weather;
They guide to valley and ridges' end.

The kestrel hovering by day,
And the little owls that call by night,
Bid him be swift and keen as they,
As keen of ear, as swift of sight.

The blackbird sings to him 'Brother, brother,
'If this be the last song you shall sing
'Sing well, for you may not sing another;
'Brother, sing'.

In dreary, doubtful, waiting hours,
Before the brazen frenzy starts,
The horses show him nobler powers;
O patient eyes, courageous hearts!

And when the burning moment breaks,
And all things else are out of mind,
And only Joy of Battle takes
Him by the throat, and makes him blind.

Through joy and blindness he shall know,
Not caring much to know, that still
Nor lead nor steel shall reach him, so
That it be not the Destined Will.

The thundering line of battle stands,
And in the air Death moans and sings;
But Day shall clasp him with strong hands,
And Night shall fold him in soft wings.

On 9th May the Battalion moved further towards the front line and went to wooden huts a short way up the Brielen Road at Vlamertinghe. On the 11th Grenfell noted in his diary:

Moved off 7.30 to support trenches 27th Division wood next railway E of H in Halte, next field where we lost horses shelled. Walked through outskirts of Ypres blazing in summer night; stink, rotting horses and men. Drew rations on road and got into trench 11.30 p.m.

Detachments of Argyll and S's and Royal Fusiliers, dead beat, in our trench.

By the following day the Allied line had withdrawn to within two miles of Ypres. The First Battalion Royal Dragoons was in the second line of trenches between Hooge Lake and a railway line half a mile to the north. In the early hours of Ascension Day, 13th May, the Germans started a heavy bombardment of the trenches at Hooge and a small rise known as Railway Hill. During the morning Grenfell went up the hill, which he called 'the little hill of death', and was knocked down by a shell which tore his coat. He returned with the news that the Germans were outflanking the Royals and he volunteered to take the information to the Somerset Yeomanry in the trenches in front; later, Wilfrid Ricardo, one of their Company Commanders recalled Grenfell walking up to him under heavy fire and saying, "you once gave me a very good mount with the Belvoir Hounds." Grenfell returned with further messages and then went up Railway Hill again with the Brigade General. A shell landed a few yards from them and they were both hit. Grenfell had a splinter of shell in his head and was taken to No. 10 Casualty Clearing Station where he wrote a letter in pencil to his mother on blood stained paper.

Isn't it wonderful and glorious that at last after long waiting the Cavalry have put it across the Boches on their flat feet, and have pulled the frying-pan out of the fire for the second time? Good old 'iron ration'. We are practically wiped out; but we charged and took the Hun trenches yesterday. I stopped a Jack Johnson with my head, and my skull is slightly cracked. But I'm getting on splendidly...

Grenfell was moved next day to a hospital at Boulogne where Raymond Asquith's (qv) brother-in-law, Edward Horner, was recovering from a severe wound. Lord and Lady Desborough and their daughter, Monica, who was nursing nearby at Wimereux, arrived at the hospital and Billy was given a day's leave to visit his brother. Between the 15th and 23rd Grenfell underwent two operations and on the morning of the 25th May he said to his mother, "Hold my hand till I go". She wrote later in her *Family Journal*:

At 7.30 on Wednesday morning, May 26th, they thought that he was dying, but he lived on till 20 minutes to 4 in the afternoon. He knew them to the very end, and moved his mother's hand to his lips. At the moment that he died, he opened his eyes a little, with the most radiant smile that they had ever seen even on his face.

Julian Grenfell was buried on 28th May in the cemetery on the hill above Boulogne looking across to the battlefields. His parents, his sister and a few friends were there, but no one wore mourning. His mother wrote: "His grave was lined and filled with the wild-flowers from the forest and the green oak-leaves which had just come out... It was a very windy day, he had always loved the wind..." On the same day the announcement of his death and his poem 'Into Battle' were published in *The Times*.

CAPTAIN CHARLES HAMILTON SORLEY

'D' Company, 7th Battalion Suffolk Regiment.
Born: 19th May 1895. Aberdeen.
Educated: King's College Choir School, Cambridge.
　　　　　Marlborough College.
Killed: 13th October 1915. Aged 20 years.
The Loos Memorial to the Missing, Dud Corner Cemetery,
Loos, France.

At the time of his son's birth, Charles Sorley's father was Professor of Moral Philosophy at Aberdeen University; five years later he was appointed Professor of Moral Philosophy at Cambridge, and shortly afterwards became a Fellow of King's College.

Charles Sorley was the first member of his family to be educated at a public school; he loved the countryside around 'the little red-capped town' of Marlborough and referred to it in many of his poems. He left school at the end of the 1913 winter term having won a scholarship to University College, Oxford for the Autumn of the following year. It was decided that he should spend the interim months in Germany; he stayed first with a German lawyer and his family at Schwerin in Mecklenburg and then became a student at the University of Jena until the summer of 1914. During this time Sorley developed a deep affection and respect for Germany, her people and literature; he compared the German and his own country's culture and way of life, fiercely criticising the English public school system.

> ... At Marlborough we were always encouraged to despise and reject such as knew the first line of the Odyssey and the C.S., and to love, honour, and obey such as were better than us at hockey. Here the reverse... The immense relief of entire freedom from those warping artificial 'positions of responsibility' (that delightful phrase which the supporters of public schools use under the impression, I suppose, that only such people as they delight to honour have responsibility in a community)! What now seems to me such a pity was the way the public school atmosphere deliberately overdevelops the nasty tyrannical instincts. One is positively encouraged to confuse strength of character with petty self-assertion and conscientiousness with Phariseeism... Give me your German day-school that makes them so earnest and lemonfaced and pincenezed and unashamed of the pursuit of learning: and not the public school that makes one self-conscious,

ashamed of knowledge, always seeking to impress, and regarding all contemporaries as possible rivals...

Realising that war clouds were gathering Professor Sorley recalled his son.   On the way home, Sorley and a friend were arrested by the German military at Trier and imprisoned for a few hours. The war-fever and middle-class complacency which greeted Sorley on his return to Cambridge appalled him; his attitude to the War was perceptive and mature from the start and he wrote to a friend:

... But isn't all this bloody? I am full of mute and burning rage and annoyance and sulkiness about it. I could wager that out of twelve million eventual combatants there aren't twelve who really want it. And 'serving one's country' is so unpicturesque and unheroic when it comes to the point... Our friends and correspondents don't seem to be able to give up physical luxuries without indulging in emotional luxuries as compensation. But I'm thankful to see that Kipling hasn't written a poem yet.

TO GERMANY

You are blind like us. Your hurt no man designed,
And no man claimed the conquest of your land.
But gropers both through fields of thought confined
We stumble and we do not understand.
You only saw your future bigly planned,
And we, the tapering paths of our own mind,
And in each other's dearest ways we stand,
And hiss and hate. And the blind fight the blind.

When it is peace, then we may view again
With new-won eyes each other's truer form
And wonder. Grown more loving-kind and warm
We'll grasp firm hands and laugh at the old pain,
When it is peace. But until peace, the storm
The darkness and the thunder and the rain.

Charles Sorley was commissioned in the 7th Battalion Suffolk Regiment and was sent for training at Shorncliffe.

... So it seems to me that Germany's only fault... is a lack of real insight and sympathy with those who differ from her. We are not fighting a bully, but a bigot...

... England - I am sick of the sound of the word. In training to fight for England, I am training to fight for that deliberate hypocrisy, that terrible middle-class sloth of outlook and appalling 'imaginative indolence' that has marked us out from generation to generation. Goliath and Caiaphas - the Philistine and Pharisee - pound these together and there you have Suburbia and Westminster and Fleet Street. And yet we have the impudence to write down Germany (who with all their bigotry are at least seekers) as 'Huns', because they are doing what every brave man ought to do and making experiments in morality. Not that I approve of the experiment in this particular case. Indeed I think that after the war all brave men will renounce their country and confess that they are strangers and pilgrims on the earth...

In March 1915 Sorley wrote to his mother:

... After all, war in this century is inexcusable: and all parties engaged in it must take an equal share in the blame of its occurrence... I do wish also that people would not deceive themselves by talk of a just war. There is no such thing as a just war. What we are doing is casting out Satan by Satan...

ALL THE HILLS AND VALES ALONG

All the hills and vales along
Earth is bursting into song,
And the singers are the chaps
Who are going to die perhaps.
 O sing, marching men,
 Till the valleys ring again.
 Give your gladness to earth's keeping,
 So be glad, when you are sleeping.

Cast away regret and rue,
Think what you are marching to.
Little live, great pass.
Jesus Christ and Barabbas
Were found the same day.
This died, that went his way.
 So sing with joyful breath.
 For why, you are going to death.
 Teeming earth will surely store
 All the gladness that you pour.

1915

Earth that never doubts nor fears,
Earth that knows of death, not tears,
Earth that bore with joyful ease
Hemlock for Socrates,
Earth that blossomed and was glad
'Neath the cross that Christ had,
Shall rejoice and blossom too
When the bullet reaches you.
> Wherefore, men marching
> On the road to death, sing!
> Pour your gladness to earth's head,
> So be merry, so be dead.

From the hills and valleys earth
Shouts back the sound of mirth,
Tramp of feet and lilt of song
Ringing all the road along.
All the music of their going,
Ringing swinging glad song-throwing,
Earth will echo still, when foot
Lies numb and voice mute.
> On, marching men, on
> To the gates of death with song.
> Sow your gladness for earth's reaping,
> So you may be glad, though sleeping.
> Strew your gladness on earth's bed,
> So be merry, so be dead.

Charles Sorley arrived in France at the end of May 1915; the Battalion was first billetted in farmhouses in Acquin, a little hamlet not far from the front line, and then in Nieppe, a town "of single-line tramways and mean streets: four-foot square vegetable gardens, where plaintive lettuces wither: cobbles, tenements, and cats that walk on the tiles..."

From Acquin on 1st June 1915, Sorley wrote to Arthur Watts, who had been an English Assistant when Sorley was at Jena University.

... I have never felt more restful. We arrived at dawn: white dawn across the plane trees and coming through the fields of rye. After two hours in an oily ship and ten in a grimy train, the 'war area' was a haven of relief...

The other officers have heard the heavy guns and perhaps I shall soon. They make perfect cider in this valley: still, like them. There are clouds of dust along the roads, and in the leaves: but the dust here is native and caressing and pure, not like the dust of Aldershot, gritted and fouled by motors and thousands of feet. 'Tis a very Limbo lake: set between the tireless railways behind and twenty miles in front the fighting. Drink its cider and paddle in its rushy streams: and see if you care whether you die tomorrow. It brings out a new part of one's self, the loiterer, neither scorning nor desiring delights, gliding listlessly through the minutes from meal-time to meal-time, like the stream through the rushes: or stagnant and smooth like their cider, unfathomably gold: beautiful and calm without mental fear. And in four-score hours we will pull up our braces and fight. These hours will have slipt over me, and I shall march hotly to the firing-line, by turn critic, actor, hero, coward and soldier of fortune: perhaps even for a moment Christian, humble, with 'Thy will be done': then shock, combustion, the emergence of one of these: death or life: and then return to the old rigmarole...

From his billets in Nieppe Sorley wrote 'Two Sonnets' on 12th June.

I

Saints have adored the lofty soul of you.
Poets have whitened at your high renown.
We stand among the many millions who
Do hourly wait to pass your pathway down.

You, so familiar, once were strange: we tried
To live as of your presence unaware.
But now in every road on every side
We see your straight and steadfast signpost there.

I think it like that signpost in my land
Hoary and tall, which pointed me to go
Upward, into the hills, on the right hand,
Where the mists swim and the winds shriek and blow,
A homeless land and friendless, but a land
I did not know and that I wished to know.

1915

II

Such, such is Death: no triumph: no defeat:
Only an empty pail, a slate rubbed clean,
A merciful putting away of what has been.

And this we know: Death is not Life effete,
Life crushed, the broken pail. We who have seen
So marvellous things know well the end not yet.

Victor and vanquished are a-one in death:
Coward and brave: friend, foe. Ghosts do not say
'Come, what was your record when you drew breath?'
But a big blot has hid each yesterday
 So poor, so manifestly incomplete.
And your bright Promise, withered long and sped,
 Is touched, stirs, rises, opens and grows sweet
And blossoms and is you, when you are dead.

From the 16th June the Battalion was in and out of the trenches at Ploegsteert Wood; Sorley wrote to his mother on 10th July:

We have taken over a new lot of trenches and have been having a busy time this past week; our exertions have been those of the navvy rather than those of the soldier. And - without at all 'fraternizing' - we refrain from interfering with Brother Bosch seventy yards away, as long as he is kind to us. So all day there is trench duty broken by feverish letter censoring. No amount of work will break the men's epistolary spirit: I am qualifying for the position of either navvy or post-office clerk after the war. During the night a little excitement is provided by patrolling the enemy's wire. Our chief enemy is nettles and mosquitoes. All patrols - English and German - are much averse to the death and glory principle; so, on running up against one another in the long wet rustling clover, both pretend that they are Levites and the other is a Good Samaritan - and pass by on the other side, no word spoken. For either side to bomb the other would be a useless violation of the unwritten laws that govern the relations of combatants permanently within a hundred yards of distance of each other, who have found out that to provide discomfort for the other is but a roundabout way of providing it for themselves: until they have their heads banged forcibly together by the red-capped powers behind them, whom neither attempts to understand. Meanwhile weather is 'no bon': food, 'plenty bon': temper, fair: sleep, jamais.

Such is 'attrition', that last resort of paralysed strategy of which we hear so much...

At the end of July 1915 Sorley wrote again to Arthur Watts:

Herewith a jingle or two. I think you said "Send me anything you write"... We visit and return from the trenches with an almost monotonous regularity : we eat the fresh bread of the land and tramp over waste acres of tangled corn, self seeded from last year's ungathered harvest. The existence is incredibly peaceful: till suddenly some officer whom one had known and not disliked - dies: one wonders; and forgets about him in a week...

Do the Generals whom you no doubt associate daily with know what bloody fools they are all considered when they visit us with six pink-faced A.D.Cs, one Staff Officer to do their thinking and another to act as their megaphone? Being human, I suppose they do. The British private has this virtue: he will never be impressed...

> There is such change in all those fields,
> Such motion rhythmic, ordered, free,
> Where ever-glancing summer yields
> Birth, fragrance, sunlight, immanency,
> To make us view our rights of birth.
> What shall we do? How shall we die?
> We, captives of a roaming earth,
> 'Mid shades that life and light deny.
> Blank summer's surfeit heaves in mist;
> Dumb earth basks dewy-washed; while still
> We whom Intelligence has kissed
> Do make us shackles of our will.
> And yet I know in each loud brain,
> Round-clamped with laws and learning so,
> Is madness more and lust of strain
> Than earth's jerked godlings e'er can know.
> The false Delilah of our brain
> Has set us round the millstone going.
> O lust of roving! lust of pain!
> Our hair will not be long in growing.
> Like blinded Samson round we go.
> We hear the grindstone groan and cry.
> Yet we are kings, we know, we know.
>
> What shall we do? How shall we die?
> Take but our pauper's gift of birth,
> O let us from the grindstone free!
> And tread the maddening gladdening earth

In strength close-braced with purity.
The earth is old; we ever new.
Our eyes should see no other sense
Than this, eternally to DO -
Our joy, our task, our recompense;
Up unexplored mountains move,
Track tireless through great wastes afar,
Nor slumber in the arms of love,
Nor tremble on the brink of war;
Make Beauty and make Rest give place,
Mock Prudence loud - and she is gone,
Smite Satisfaction on the face
And tread the ghost of Ease upon.
Light-lipped and singing press we hard
Over old earth which now is worn,
Triumphant, buffeted and scarred,
By billows howled at, tempest-torn,
Toward blue horizons far away
(Which do not give the rest we need,
But some long strife, more than this play,
Some task that will be stern indeed) -
We ever new, we ever young,
We happy creatures of a day!
What will the gods say, seeing us strung
As nobly and as taut as they?

On the night of 31st July/1st August 1915 Sorley and his platoon were involved in a bombing expedition and a fellow officer wrote of the incident:

We were holding trenches just to the south of Ploegsteert wood. D Coy were on the left of the Battalion, about 100 yards from the Germans. That opposite Charles' platoon was, I think, the most interesting part of our line, as the Germans were working on it from the day we took over till the day we left. They seemed to be making a redoubt of some kind, and, as those were the days when shells were scarce, we couldn't ask the gunners to blow it up... C. knew the ground in front of this better than anyone in the company: where the ditches and disused saps ran; where the different shell-holes lay; where the beetroot met the clover, and where the clover ended in a strip of long thin grass up to the enemy's wire. C. had been out crawling often before, just for the fun of the thing... It was all planned out cleverly beforehand: C. and three other bombers to crawl up to within bombing distance, he leading and directing the show; four riflemen were to come up on the flank and cover their retirement... It was a dark night and everything went off splendidly up to the point when the bombs were to be thrown... The pins had all been taken out and the second signal was just being passed when the third bomber dropped his infernal machine. I think the others heard it thud and tried to get clear; at any rate he was stupid enough to fumble about in the long wet grass in an attempt to find it. There was a dreadful five seconds' suspense: then the thing exploded right under him. In the confusion C. and one of the other men managed to throw their bombs, and that and the fire of the riflemen, who opened up a steady burst immediately, saved the party somewhat. C. crawled to the man who had dropped his bomb and dragged him into the shell-hole... The shell-hole was his salvation. They had only just got into it when the Germans swept the ground with an absolute hail of rifle and machine-gun fire and lit up all around with Very lights... When the Germans had quietened down a bit, some more men came out and helped to get the wounded in. The one with C. was in a very bad way and died soon after. C. said every bone in the upper part of his body must have been broken - it was like carrying a piece of living pulp - and he never forgot the curious inarticulate cry of the man as he picked him up...

Next morning, a brilliant July day, I went round to pick up Intelligence and met C. on trench patrol. He had just come from breakfasting and was dressed in summer get-up; gum boots, breeches, shirt-sleeves, sambrown belt and pistol. He had a bandage round his head, but only a very slight scratch from a fragment of bomb. He was walking along, reading from his German pocket edition of Faust. He told me the whole story of the raid: rather sorry that his plans had been let down just when they might have been so successful; but he took it all in his happy careless fashion.

On 7th August Sorley wrote to his mother:

We are busy, very busy, with the pruning-hook however more than with the sword, as our part of the line is quietish. Our Major-General never sleepeth; and since his Division took over this part of the line, farms have been devastated and harvests ruined, and to be in reserve means work eight hours a day: but I think our piece of ground is now inviolable. Every day almost, one meets this tired, nervous, haggard, incredibly vivacious and sympathetic chief: who knows almost all the (300 odd) officers under him by name, and visits your part of the trench with the same apologetic agreeable air as an insurance agent assessing a private house: never interfering (on the spot) or directing, only apparently anxious to learn - till divisional orders come out!

Hard 'spade-work' (as school reports used to say) - 'curry' in the form of occasional skirmishes at night between patrols - still keep our days full and our nights unquiet. Armed with bombs and equipped with night one can do much raiding with extraordinary safety: much to the Bosch's annoyance, or to his amusement when with infinite care a bombing party creeps up to his wire and commences with deadly effect to bomb itself. Such has happened more than once. The unfathomable laboriousness of the people opposite, infinite and aloof! Working day and night, nor heeding us. Thorns in their side we are, often pricking ourselves more than them; till we get too close, too harmful, too informed one day - and then a whip of lead! We are the gnat that buzzes, hums and stings without ceasing: they the bee, undisturbable in toil till roused, and then a deep sting which remains. Who does the greater damage none can say. Both do enough to keep alive a spark of considerable mutual irritation which this year or next year must burst into flame...

At the end of August Charles Sorley was promoted to Captain and became second-in-command of 'D' Company. He wrote to Arthur Watts on 26th August:

... But out in front at night in that no-man's land and long graveyard there is a freedom and a spur. Rustling of the grasses and grave tap-tapping of distant workers: the tension and silence of encounter, when one struggles in the dark for moral victory over the enemy patrol: the wail of the exploded bomb and the animal cries of wounded men. Then death and the horrible thankfulness when one sees that the next man is dead: "We won't have to *carry* him in under fire, thank God; dragging will do": hauling in of the great resistless body in the dark, the smashed head rattling: the relief, the relief that the thing has ceased to groan: that the bullet or bomb that made the man an animal has now made the animal a corpse. One is hardened by now: purged of all false pity: perhaps more selfish than before...

On 17th September the Battalion Diary recorded that "Captain Sorley ... patrolled close to German wire and reported working party."

In spite of agreeing with his subordinates that the Loos - Lens area was unfavourable for a major attack to be launched, Sir John French consented to Joffre's plan for an autumn offensive in 1915, and the Battle of Loos was fought between 25th September and 13th October. Gas was used by the British for the first time. The initial assault was carried out by the six Divisions of I and IV Corps of the First Army under General Haig's command, with IX Corps as part of the general reserve under the command of Field Marshal

French.   In the event, Haig asked for this reserve early on the first day on finding his losses mounting considerably; but French unwilling to commit his inexperienced troops too soon, delayed their move forward. The appalling weather, the difficulty of fighting in the industrial terrain (slag heaps, mineshafts, factories and rows of houses), lack of supporting artillery ammunition, together with resolute German resistance, all combined to make the Battle a costly failure. The initial assault wave, consisting of twelve battalions 10,000 strong, lost over 8,000 officers and men in under four hours. The failure led to French being replaced by Haig.

On 26th September, the day after the Battle of Loos started, Sorley's Battalion left Ploegsteert Wood and reached Labourse, just south-east of Béthune, on the 29th where the billets were "insufficient and arrangements very bad." On 30th September the Battalion Diary recorded:

Marched to trenches. Great delay was experienced in obtaining tools from carts and proceeding over very difficult country to trenches. Wire and trenches continually delayed the march and the slippery chalk soil made walking very bad. Arrived in trenches four hours late and took over from Guards Brigade.

All the following day enemy bombardment was very heavy and working parties were sent out to the chalk pit nearby. On 5th October, Sorley wrote letters to the Master of Marlborough and to Arthur Watts:

... The chess players are no longer waiting so infernal long between their moves. And the patient pawns are all in movement, hourly expecting further advances - whether to be taken or reach the back lines and be queened. 'Tis sweet, this pawn-being: there are no cares, no doubts: wherefore no regrets. The burden which I am sure is the parent of ill-temper, drunkenness and premature old age - to wit, the making up of one's own mind - is lifted from our shoulders. I can now understand the value of dogma, which is the General Commander-in-Chief of the mind. I am now beginning to think that free thinkers should give their minds into subjection, for we who have given our actions and volitions into subjection gain such marvellous rest thereby. Only of course it is the subjection of their powers of will and deed to a wrong master on the part of a great nation that has led Europe into war. Perhaps afterwards, I and my likes will again become indiscriminate rebels. For the present we find high relief in making ourselves soldiers...

... I am bleached with chalk and grown hairy. And I think exultantly
and sweetly of the one or two or three outstandingly admirable meals
of my life. One in Yorkshire, in an inn upon the moors, with a fire of
logs and ale and tea and every sort of Yorkshire bakery, especially
bears me company. And yet another in Mecklenburg-Schwerin
(where they are very English) in a farm-house utterly at peace in broad
fields sloping to the sea. I remember a tureen of champagne in the
middle of the table, to which we helped ourselves with ladles! I
remember my hunger after three hours' ride over the country: and the
fishing-town of Wismar lying like an English town on the sea. In that
great old farm-house where I dined at 3 p.m. as the May day began to
cool, fruit of sea and of land joined hands together, fish fresh caught
and ducks fresh killed: it was a wedding of the elements. It was
perhaps the greatest meal I have had ever, for everything we ate had
been alive that morning - the champagne was alive yet. We feasted
like kings till the sun sank, for it was impossible to overeat. 'Twas
Homeric and its memory fills many hungry hours...

On 12th October the Battalion went into the front line trenches
near the Hohenzollern Redoubt, north of Loos. The following day
it advanced to attack two trenches, known as the Hairpin, south of
the Redoubt. During heavy machine-gun fire Sorley was shot in
the head and killed instantaneously.
   A sonnet, which was probably his last poem, was found in
Charles Sorley's kit after his death.

WHEN YOU SEE MILLIONS OF THE MOUTHLESS DEAD

When you see millions of the mouthless dead
Across your dreams in pale battalions go,
Say not soft things as other men have said,
That you'll remember. For you need not so.
Give them not praise. For, deaf, how should they know
It is not curses heaped on each gashed head?
Nor tears. Their blind eyes see not your tears flow.
Nor honour. It is easy to be dead.
Say only this, "They are dead." Then add thereto,
"Yet many a better one has died before."
Then, scanning all the o'ercrowded mass, should you
Perceive one face that you loved heretofore,
It is a spook. None wears the face you knew.
Great death has made all his for evermore.

LIEUTENANT ROLAND AUBREY LEIGHTON

1st/7th Battalion Worcestershire Regiment.
Born: March 1895.
Educated: Uppingham School.
Died of Wounds: 23rd December 1915. Aged 20 years.
Louvencourt Military Cemetery, France.

Roland Leighton's parents were writers; his father, Robert, was a literary critic, journalist and author of boys' adventure stories; his mother, Marie, wrote romantic novels.

At Uppingham Leighton was a friend and contemporary of Edward Brittain. Edward's sister, Vera, first met Leighton during an Old Boys weekend at the school in June 1913; she wrote in her diary on Sunday, June 29th, "I like him immensely, he seems so clever & amusing & hardly shy at all."

In January 1914 Leighton won a place at Merton College, Oxford and left Uppingham at the end of the summer term. At the outbreak of the War he volunteered for service but was turned down because of poor eyesight. He was accepted two months later and commissioned in the 4th Battalion Norfolk Regiment.

He applied to Major General Heath, a family friend, for a transfer so he could go to France. In March 1915 he was sent to the 7th Battalion Worcestershire Regiment two weeks before it went to the front.

On 17th April Vera Brittain received two letters from Leighton, the first of which was written from Armentières. She wrote in her diary:

He says he has not yet been afraid - although he has now been under fire... He is afraid of his imagination, afraid of being afraid - so am I. That is why he in the midst of the actual dangers fears & dreads nothing, while I far away from all sign of active warfare read of the perils he is undergoing & shudder and tremble... he wrote... that he was now actually in the firing line & was to take his platoon in the trenches at 7.0 that evening. The trenches run right into the town and he could hear the rifle-fire as he lay in bed. The Germans had been shelling the town two days before, but he saw nothing of it except one shrapnel that burst on their right as they marched in. The walls showed signs of former bombardment & were riddled with bullet-holes. (It has of course been the scene of a great deal of fighting ever since the war began). He & another subaltern were billeted in a small

40

house on the outskirts of the town facing a square called the Place Republique. It seems incongruous, he says, to find good shops & buildings & beds half an hour's walk from the trenches. They are to go in tonight & stay till Tuesday night - 48 hours - after which they will be relieved. An inexperienced regiment does not hold part of the line on its own at first, but is initiated by more experienced people into the mysteries of dug-outs, listening posts etc. "It is a beautiful sunny day today", he says, "and it seems a pity there should be such a thing as war. Summer & trenches don't go together somehow..."

Vera Brittain's Diary entry recorded that the second letter was written on Monday April 12th from the trenches:

... It is written in pencil, & there are very slight stains of mud on both the paper & envelope. He was sitting on the edge of his bunk in the dug-out which he was sharing with another officer. Firing was quiet as he wrote, but a German sniper was having chance shots at a traverse a few yards to the right of them. Some of the bullets skimmed over their roof, but these dug-outs are well covered with sandbags so that the danger inside is greatly minimised. The British artillery had been shelling a disused brewery behind the German lines all morning. The shells come straight over the trenches, & he describes them as a dull boom from the gun's mouth, a scream as they pass overhead & a crash when they burst. Of course you cannot put your head for a second over the parapet of the trench or you would get potted at once. But peering round the corner or through a periscope he watched the brewery. The smoke of the shells is mostly green from lyddite, but sometimes black, from howitzers, sometimes also tinged with red from falling brickwork. The regiment had just been ordered by telephone to keep under cover & so Roland was in the dug-out, which is a hut built into the rear part of the trench, about 7 ft square & 5 ft high, containing bunks for sleeping, shelves, a table & two chairs. For some unknown reason it was called "Le Château Germaine", & had a weathercock of wood & tin, fixed there by the bravado of a former occupant...

There is not much to do in the trenches, but officers have to go round every now & then to see that the men & sentries are in their places. They go round at night too, so don't get much sleep. They are not allowed to take their clothes off, & have to scrape as much mud as possible off their boots with a bayonet, tie up each foot in a sack so as to keep the mud out of their sleeping bags, & get in boots & all. They seldom have time to wash or shave properly. How I should like to see Roland in an unshaved & more or less unwashed condition...

... A little further down along the trench were three graves, marked only with a piece of board on which was scrawled "German grave.

R.I.P." Roland, 80 yards from the enemy & in danger of death from their bullets, at the sight of their graves is inspired by no bitterer thought than that "Somebody once loved the man lying there". On their way to the trenches they passed about thirty graves by the roadside - all of men of one regiment killed in these trenches...

On 24th April 1915 Roland Leighton "found the body of a dead British soldier hidden in the undergrowth a few yards from the path. He must have been shot there during the wood-fighting in the early part of the War. The body had sunk down into the marshy ground so that only the tops of the boots stuck up above the soil. His cap & equipment beside him were half-buried & rotting away. Roland ordered a mound of earth to be thrown over him, to make one grave more among the many in the wood."

The following day he wrote a villanelle:

> Violets from Plug Street Wood -
> Sweet, I send you oversea.
> (It is strange they should be blue,
> Blue when his soaked blood was red;
> For they grew around his head.
> It is strange they should be blue.)
>
> Violets from Plug Street Wood -
> Think what they have meant to me!
> Life and Hope and Love and You.
> (And you did not see them grow
> Where his mangled body lay,
> Hiding horror from the day.
> Sweetest, it was better so.)
>
> Violets from oversea,
> To your dear, far, forgetting land:
> These I send in memory,
> Knowing You will understand.

During his leave in England in August 1915 Roland Leighton and Vera Brittain became engaged. He returned to France and on 14th September Vera Brittain received a letter from him describing the conditions in the trenches near Hébuterne, north of Albert:

This afternoon I am very sleepy - almost too sleepy to write. It is partly the warm weather and chiefly perhaps not getting more than 4 hours' sleep at night and being too busy to get any rest in the day. I have been rushing round since 4 a.m., superintending the building of dug-outs, drawing up plans for the draining of trenches, doing a little digging myself as a relaxation, and accidentally coming upon dead Germans while looting timber from what was once a German fire trench. This latter was captured by the French not so long ago and is pitted with shell-holes each big enough to bury a horse or two in. The dug-outs have been nearly all blown in, the wire entanglements are a wreck, and in among [this] chaos of twisted iron and splintered timber and shapeless earth are the fleshless, blackened bones of simple men who poured out their red, sweet wine of youth unknowing, for nothing more tangible than Honour or their Country's Glory or another's Lust of Power. Let him who thinks that War is a glorious golden thing, who loves to roll forth stirring words of exhortation, invoking Honour and Praise and Valour and Love of Country with as thoughtless and fervid a faith as inspired the priests of Baal to call on their own slumbering deity, let him look at a little pile of sodden grey rags that cover half a skull and a shin bone and what might have been Its ribs, or at this skeleton lying on its side, resting half-crouching as it fell, supported on one arm, perfect but that it is headless, and with the tattered clothing still draped around it; and let him realise how grand & glorious a thing it is to have distilled all Youth and Joy and Life into a foetid heap of hideous putrescence. Who is there who has known and seen who can say that Victory is worth the death of even one of these?

In October the Battalion was in billets at Courcelles; during November and December Leighton wrote two poems, 'Hédauville' and 'Ploegsteert':

HEDAUVILLE

The sunshine on the long white road
That ribboned down the hill,
The velvet clematis that clung
Around your window-sill
Are waiting for you still.

Again the shadowed pool shall break
In dimples at your feet,
And when the thrush sings in your wood,
Unknowing you may meet
Another stranger, Sweet.

And if he is not quite so old
As the boy you used to know,
And less proud, too, and worthier,
You may not let him go -
(And daisies are truer than passion-flowers)

It will be better so.

PLOEGSTEERT

Love have I known, and dawn and gold of day-time,
And winds and songs and all the joys that are
Known once, and as a child that tires with play-time,
Leaped from them to the elemental dust of War.

I have seen blood and death, but all has ending,
And even Horror is but made to cease;
I am sickened with Love that lives only for lending,
And all the loathsome pettiness of peace.

Give me, God of Battles, a field of death,
A Hill of Fire, a strong man's agony...

In December Leighton's battalion was in reserve in the Hébuterne area. On Friday 17th December Vera Brittain received a message from her fiancé. "Leave from Dec. 24th - 31st. Land on Christmas Day." Ten days later she wrote in her diary:

Monday December 27th. I had just finished dressing when a message came to say that there was a telephone message for me. I sprang up joyfully, thinking to hear in a moment the dear dreamed-of tones of the beloved voice.

But the telephone message was not from Roland but from Clare; it was not to say that Roland had arrived, but that instead had come this telegram... Regret to inform you that Lieut. R.A. Leighton 7th Worcesters died of wounds December 23rd...

A few weeks before he was killed Roland Leighton became a Roman Catholic. After his death his parents received a letter from his Colonel and from the Roman Catholic Chaplain. On 2nd January Vera Brittain recorded the details of the two letters:

... At midnight on Dec. 22nd his platoon was preparing to repair the wire in front of their trench, and he went out first, before allowing his men to go, to see if all was safe, and to select the spots to be wired... the Germans... opened fire almost at once, with rifles previously trained on to that place. He fell, and his Company Commander, Captain Adam, and his platoon sergeant went out immediately and carried him back into the trench. The doctor was talking with the Colonel some distance off; he was sent for immediately and went to Roland as fast as he could go... In less than 6 hours he had Roland in the Hospital Clearing Station at Louvencourt, a distance of 10 miles away. Probably he could only be carried on a stretcher; at any rate he must have been for a few miles, till they got beyond the lines of the trenches. The doctor accompanied him to the hospital, which they reached about 6.0 in the morning. At 10.0 he had a severe operation; it could not be done before because he was suffering too much from shock. But there seems to have been scarcely any hope from the first... The Chaplain gave him Extreme Unction immediately after the operation while he was still unconscious - which shows that those who performed it knew that hope was practically over. He was visited twice again by the Chaplain in the afternoon, when he was recovering consciousness, made an "act of contrition" and received absolution. The Chaplain intended to visit him again and give him Holy Communion, as the doctors said he might last another 48 hours, but he died quite peacefully at 11 p.m...

... They buried Him on Sunday afternoon, Dec. 26th, in the little military cemetery at Louvencourt, the small village behind the lines, where the Clearing Station was to which they took him. Colonel Harman was at the service, the first part of which was in the church, and the last part by the grave-side. The Colonel says in his letter that as they carried His body out of the little church the sun came out & shone brilliantly...

VALE

And so, farewell. All our sweet songs are sung,
Our red rose-garlands withered;
The sun-bright day -
Silver and blue and gold -
Wearied to sleep.

The shimmering evening, like a grey, soft bird,
Barred with the blood of sunset,
Has flown to rest
Under the scented wings
Of the dark-blue Night.

1916

SECOND LIEUTENANT HUGH REGINALD (REX) FRESTON

3rd (Attached 6th) Battalion Royal Berkshire Regiment.

Born: 25th July 1891. Tulse Hill, Surrey.
Educated: Dulwich College.
               Exeter College, Oxford.
Killed: 24th January 1916. Aged 24 years.
Bécourt Military Cemetery, Bécordel-Bécourt, France.

Rex Freston initially planned to go into the Church but during his time at Oxford he abandoned this intention and was reading English when war broke out. He was commissioned in the Royal Berkshire Regiment in April 1915 and joined the 6th Battalion behind the line near Albert four days before Christmas 1915. During January 1916 the Battalion was in trenches at La Boisselle and Freston wrote a few poems:

THE MARCH

We were splashing along the muddy lanes:
And as I walked behind the long column,
I saw the men's shoulders swing to and fro;
And as they jolted along unevenly,
Marching at ease,
Their song came back to me on the wind;
And my heart sang with them.

When suddenly,
As the wind will sometimes cease at twilight,
Their song faded and died -

And then,
Looking round,
I saw, and in a glance understood -
We were passing the little graves...
Lonely and silent, I saw them side by side,
In the little new-made grave-garden:
There slept the soldiers of England;
There the heroes had found their peace.

1916

O FORTUNATI

O happy to have lived these epic days!
    To have seen unfold, as doth a dream unfold,
    These glorious chivalries, these deeds of gold,
The glory of whose splendour gilds death's ways,
As a rich sunset fills dark woods with fire
    And blinds the traveller's eyes. Our eyes are blind
    With flaming heroism, that leaves our mind
Dumbstruck with pride. We have had our heart's desire!
O happy! Generations have lived and died
    And only dreamed such things as we have seen and known!
Splendour of men, death laughed at, death defied,
    Round the great world, on the winds, their tale is blown;
Whatever pass, these ever shall abide:
    In memory's Valhalla, an imperishable throne.

TO THE ATHEISTS

I know that God will never let me die.
    He is too passionate and intense for that.
See how He swings His great suns through the sky,
    See how He hammers the proud-faced mountains flat.
He takes a handful of a million years
    And hurls them at the planets; or he throws
His red stars at the moon: then with hot tears
    He stoops to kiss one little earthborn rose.

Don't nail God down to rules, and think you know!
    Or God, Who sorrows all a summer's day
Because a blade of grass has died, will come
    And suck this world up in His lips, and lo!
Will spit it out a pebble, powdered grey,
    Into the whirl of Infinity's nothingless foam.

On 5th January Freston wrote to an editor who had asked for some of his poems for an anthology.

... I should rather like a piece I wrote called 'October 31st 1915' to go in, if it pleases you. Also one of the several poems I have written about Oxford... We are leaving billets tomorrow to go into the trenches so forgive this brief line - such a lot of packing to do!

49

On the whole I like being out here very much: but sometimes one gets awful home-sickness. Today has been fine and sunny, and I have just yearned for 'Oxford' all day long! Oxford in the summer time; the long glorious summer twilights on the river; with the spires all showing black against the sunset; the fields all grey with evening; the wistful stream; and the far-off murmur of the bells...

OCTOBER 31st, 1915

It is the last morning of October!
And the wind hisses among the ragged leaves;
The trees look shabby and cold.
The window-pane is splashed all over with raindrops;
And raindrops run down like tears on the ivy's face,
Pause a moment, and fall.

Where is everybody? What are they doing?
Are they walking about in the rain?
The sound of the church bells is blown about on the wind,
Now loud; now low;
Very far; suddenly, strangely near; and very far again:
A lot of people must be going to church -
I don't like the way people look at you as you go in,
It makes me feel so uncomfortable.

Out in France, a lot of men are standing in the trenches,
Most of them are wearing old caps.
And their unshaved faces are half hidden in dirty mufflers.
They all look very ugly, and are cursing the rain -
In a week or two I shall be out there with them -
What will happen if I never come back again?

It is most annoying that I shall not have time to express myself,
Owing to this war,
I shall not have time to make people angry with me for telling the
    truth,
O those respectable people! Those well-to-do, smug, self-satisfied
    men and women!
How daintily, finely they dress! Their voices are most refined.
But it would be splendid to take all their money away,
And make them live on eighteen shillings a week,
And work for it!

After I am dead,
And have become part of the soil of France,
This much remember of me:
I was a great sinner, a great lover, and life puzzled me very much.
Ah love! I would have died for love!
Love can do so much, both rightly and wrongly.
It remembers mothers, and little children,
And lots of other things.
O men unborn, I go now, my work unfinished!
I pass on the problem to you: the world will hate you: be brave!

TWO NIGHTS

I listened to the bugles, and I hearkened to the bells
    In old Oxford city, a night long, long ago:
O, the bells were full of music like the sound of fountain wells,
    But the others played a music, I never thought to know.

There's a lilt of martial music and a cry of fountain wells
    In the barrack square to-night beneath the lonely tree:
And I laugh to hear the bugles, but I weep to hear the bells,
    For I know the bells of Oxford will ring no more for me.

Between the 14th and 22nd January 1916 the 6th Battalion was
in billets at Albert and then relieved the 10th Essex in the trenches
at La Boisselle. The weather was fine, and that evening and the
following day were very quiet.

ON GOING INTO ACTION

Now the weak impulse and the blind desire
    Give way at last to the all-conquering will.
    Love now must pause, and fancy cease, until
The soul has won that freedom born of fire.
Sing, then, no songs upon the sweet-voiced lyre:
    But choose some nobler instrument, whose shrill
    Nerve-bracing notes, my doubting heart shall fill
With a new courage, that will never tire.
Sing me the dead men's glorious deeds again!

> Tell how they suffered, died, but would not fail!
> Stir me to action! Let me feel their pain,
>> Their strength, their mystery: that at the tale
> I rise with such clear purpose in my brain
>> That even Hell's own gates should not prevail.

On the 24th January the enemy artillery and trench mortars were active all day. In the afternoon Freston went to inspect a dug out which had been heavily shelled. As he talked to some stretcher bearers more shells came over; Rex Freston was hit by one and killed.

CAPTAIN CYRIL MORTON HORNE

'A' Company, 7th Battalion King's Own Scottish Borderers.
Born: 1887.
Killed: 27th January 1916. Aged 29 years.
Mazingarbe Communal Cemetery, France.

When the war broke out Cyril Horne, who had written an opera, was working in the American theatre. He returned home and was commissioned in the 7th Battalion King's Own Scottish Borderers in March 1915, and went to France as their Transport Officer in the summer of 1915. A picture 'A Feather in her Cap' by Paul Kirschner was printed in *The Sketch* of 15th June 1915, and a copy was found in a dug-out in the firing line by six officers. It was at first the subject of impersonal admiration, but the personality of the picture obtruded itself in the dug-out; the only piece of femininity among six males, it soon became the chief topic of conversation. The different outlooks of the six men were put into verse by Captain Horne.

DOLORES

Six of us lay in a Dugout
　　At ease, with our limbs astretch,
And worshipped a feminine picture
　　Cut from a week-old 'Sketch'.
We gazed at her Silken Stockings,
　　We studied her Cupid bow,
And we thought of the Suppers we used to buy
　　And the girls that we used to know.
And we all, in our several fashions,
　　Paid toll to the Lady's charms,
From the man of a hundred passions
　　To the Subaltern child-in-arms.
Never the sketch of a master
　　So jealously kept and prized,
Never a woman of flesh and blood
　　So truly idealized.
And because of her slender ankle,
　　And her coiffure - distinctly French -
We called her "La Belle Dolores" -
　　"The Vivandière of the Trench."

THE CAPTAIN'S TRIBUTE

Laddies, I despise the female species,
   (Tho' they say that love-affairs are sweet),
So I dinna care about the picture,
   (Tho' she's awfu' neat about the feet).

While I have a verra easy conscience,
   Yet I find it hard to sleep o' nights;
P'r'aps it is that after sae much bloodshed
   I'm unnerved by lookin' at such sights.

So I'll gaze nae mair upon the picture
   Lest my thoughts from Righteousness should stray,
I shall just forget she's in the Dugout;
   Only - dinna tak' the lass away.

THE IRISH SUBALTERN

I'm wondering why I squirm and seethe
   Whenever I gaze awhile
At the girl with the perfectly ripping teeth
   And the deucedly topping smile.

She wears her clothes so devilish well,
   And she's such an attractive wench
That she could be all the world - Aw, Hell!
   I'm still in this blistered trench!

Her ankles angle so daintily,
   Under her sheath-like skirt -
Which in itself appears to me
   Divine, tho' distinctly - curt.

Her silk-shod foot to me heart, anew,
   Tender excitement brings,
And the lace of her petticoat peeping through
   Suggests such feminine things.

I'd like to ruffle her perfumed hair,
   With the hand of a connoisseur,
But as I'm in a trench and she' not there
   Perforce I must leave her - pure.

THE ENGAGED SUBALTERN

Amber eyes, amber eyes,
Opening up in shy surprise,
    Were you by
    Now, would I
Still remain so worldly-wise?

Conscience-free I can be
Tho' you gaze askance at me;
    Still, my dear,
    Were you here,
Would I then be conscience-free?

Harvest bare Virtue reaps -
Circumstance his vigil keeps;
    Could I reach
    You, my peach,
Which of us but virtue sleeps?

THE MARRIED MAN

When I turned about in the small Dugout
    My glance on the Picture tarried,
So I hied me away from the fair display
    Remembering I was married.

THE VERY JUNIOR CAPTAIN

The Captain paused at the Dugout door;
In his breathless way, he observed, "Oh, Lor',"
What a Pearl of a Girl, you chaps; my word,
I'd buy her a quart of the best, a bird,
A box at the Gaiety - Lor', what fun.
I'd do the thing as it should be done;
Supper at Murray's, a perfect floor,
And what could a fellow wish for more?
Sensuous music, a dreamy band
A delicate pressure of the hand;
And after a last liqueur or so

A whispered word in the Hall, what, ho!
I'd drive her home in the daylight drab
And trust to luck in the taxi-cab.

THE IDEALIST

I have known many loves, Dolores,
Fleeting and tender, grave and gay -
Each one absorbing in its fashion.
     I have known
Love and laughter and tears and passion,
Times I have watched the fairies dance
Heavenward; and too well, perchance,
I may have loved at times, 'tis true;
Yet I have dallied lightly, too -
Dallied to while the hours away.
I have known many loves, Dolores.

Bought kisses, bartered hearts,
Budding passions and base intrigues,
The infatuation that fatigues
     The mind and the heart;
Riotous nights when the wine was red,
When music rippled and laughter sped
Nimble-footed from lip to brain -
Flung wide to the winds of Heav'n again.
     All this was part
     Of the days long dead.
I have tasted it all, Dolores.

And now you come, and all the loves long ended,
   Sorrows too poignant and delights too sweet,
Dead till you came - have risen and are blended
   Into the Love I lay before your feet.

So shall I love you; I shall never touch your mouth,
   Nor shall my fingers through your tresses stray -
Your tresses, breathing of the Scented South
   Where wood-nymphs whisper and where fairies play.

Your slender limbs, in youthful animation
    Erstwhile that would have thrilled beneath my touch,
Shall rest in unawakened fascination
    Since I have loved too little - or too much.

Your blue-veiled eyes shall never droop coquetting,
    Nor shall you feel the surge of Passion swell;
You shall not know the sorrow of forgetting
    When you have loved - not wisely - but too well.

Aye, I have known full many loves, Dolores -
    Fleeting and lasting, feeble and intense;
And so, sure-footed, do I come, Dolores -
    Bearing the Master-gift - Experience.

The Battalion suffered heavy casualties on 25th September 1915, the first day of the Battle of Loos; two days later Horne took over command of 'A' Company and he was one of the few officers to survive the Battle unwounded. On 27th January 1916, during an intense artillery bombardment in Loos village, Horne and two fellow officers left their dugout to rescue a wounded soldier. A shell exploded killing Cyril Horne and Lieutenant Millar and severely wounding Lieutenant Penfield who died the next day.

SECOND LIEUTENANT BERNARD PITT

10th Battalion Border Regiment (Attached 47th Trench Mortar Battery).
Born: 1881. London.
Educated: Middlesex Council School, Isleworth.
            London University.
Killed: 30th April 1916. Aged 35 years.
Arras Memorial to the Missing, Faubourg-D'Amiens Cemetery, Arras, France.

Bernard Pitt trained as a teacher at the Borough Road Training College, London. He taught at various schools and from 1912 he held classes in English Literature at the Working Men's College, St. Pancras; he was Assistant Master at Cooper's Company School, Bow, when war broke out. He joined a volunteer corps and was commissioned in the 10th Battalion Border Regiment in April 1915. Before he left for France, Pitt wrote the following poem:

ALFRISTON, SUNDAY, 3rd OCTOBER, 1915

We paced the white road where the river leads;
Behind the sheer-scarped down died out the day
The village nestled by the water-meads,
And threads of evening smoke rose blue and grey.

And in our hearts was peace and great content
After long hours of moving through clear space,
And with locked arms we loitered as we went,
And with kind words and looks we blessed the place.

And then the bells, the bells of evensong,
Called softly to their folk, and through the haze
The nearer hamlets sent their chimes along,
And mellow tones rang through the leafy ways.

But our full hearts strained in too great delight,
And overflowed in tears, and darkness fell;
While in the valley there before the night,
Oh, Love and Death pealed from the changing bell.

Our days of dreaming passion, dear days past,
Our days of toil, our nights of sweetest ease,
Our home, our little children, and the last
Love of our land, and peril of all these

Flashed in our eyes and in our hearts beat loud,
As we, poor lovers, caught in War's keen blast,
Clung once, kissed once, and with calm looks and proud
Paced on, and knew England and we hold fast.

Bernard Pitt arrived in France in December 1915 as a trench mortar officer attached to the 47th Trench Mortar Battery in the Béthune area.   On 7th January 1916 he wrote:

...We are now in a village so shell-shattered that there is not a roof in the place, and very few ceilings in the lower rooms. Frightful slaughter occurred when the French took the place from the Germans in August last, and the cellars are mostly full of corpses. In what was the garden, behind our house, there is a great grave decorated with a German Iron Cross, made of crushed brick, chalk, and broken bottle glass, and railed in with barbed wire. So you see, chivalry is not extinct yet, and we respect good fighters. The village is full of our guns, and shattering explosions startle one every now and then...

I am back from seventy-two hours in the firing-line, and am very glad to get a wash and to change my long service boots, laced so tightly to exclude water, for slippers...   Up in the line we have been digging every kind of shelter for our guns, and men, and bombs, and stores. My back aches most pleasantly. I am sitting near a huge fire and watching the mice running and leaping about on the floor. We don't mind them, but rats are a nuisance. Attracted, no doubt, by a smell of fat, last night a hungry rodent bit our cook's nose as he slept!

What is life like in the trenches, well, muddy, and cramped, and filthy. Everything gets covered with mud; you can't wash, for water has to be fetched for a mile. There is no room, and if you walk upright in many of the trenches, you run grave risks; and you sleep, huddled together, unable to stretch. Of course one gets greasy and smutty, and the place smells bad, as you can imagine. All day long shells and rifle bullets go banging and whistling, and from dark to midnight the Huns fire rifle-grenades and machine-guns at us. In our dug-out we can hear the bullets coming whop against the roof and against the sand-bags round it. But nobody minds that; nobody is one penny the worse...

January 18th 1916... On the morning of January 17th I was eagerly awaiting orders from headquarters to fire off a goodly number of bombs at certain high mounds of chalk in front of us, where the Germans were constructing machine gun emplacements, dug-outs, mine-shafts, and other annoyances known or suspected. The artillery had been pounding away at these craters on and off for days, but with little result. It was now a task for us. My C.O. had had two guns 400 yards from the mounds, and I had one gun about 200 yards away. Both of us were to observe from the front line, some 100 yards from the Germans, and we were connected with our guns by telephone. So far as we knew the bombardment was to begin at noon and continue till 1 p.m. Covered by artillery fire we were to fire seventy-five bombs... The time dragged on, our heavy artillery firing leisurely shots and occasionally knocking off a bit of the mound, while we gnawed our nails in idleness. Presently the Huns began to exchange gifts. Their shells burst along our reserve trenches, and suspecting trench-mortar activity in the background, they pitched packet after packet at our emplacements... Things were getting pretty hot along our line... Still no order to fire, and it was one o'clock. My heart sank to think of our inaction, with all those grand bombs asking to be burst. At last! Half-past one, and I am half-frozen, when suddenly I see a bomb of ours travelling overhead. In an instant I hear the welcome 'boom' of my gun, and our first bomb goes up in a slow curve, and over, and into the crater. I peep through the loophole and see the flash and column of black smoke, and hear the 'crash' of the explosion. A correction is telephoned down the wire, and the next bomb bursts right on the target, removing a machine-gun emplacement, beams, sand-bags and all from the face of the earth. Our three mortars are booming away, and we often see three great bombs in the sky at once. They burst on the mound, over it, in the trenches in front, and chalk, and wire, and timber, and rags are thrown up into the air. Meanwhile our own guns are sending batches of racing whistling shells over our heads.

The Huns reply with all kinds of stuff; small shell, large shell, bombs from a catapult, 'sausages' from their trench-mortars, rifle-grenades, and even a few rifle bullets fired from some position outside the danger-zone. Bits of earth and bits of iron are flying everywhere; bases of shells go humming through the air, rifle-grenades squeak and burst. As I get up to the loophole to watch the effect of my bombs, the ground behind and before me erupts in smoke and flame. We cannot make the telephonist near the gun hear at all. My C.O.'s orderly appears and says the men have been ordered off the gun into shelter, and again I must not fire. For five minutes I fret and fidget, and then from one of the mortars there goes up a bomb. I can't wait; off I rush down the trench, and as I near the gun I see my bombardier hurrying along in front of me, alone, eager to get off another round or so. He, too, has heard or seen the other bomb, and he, too, will not be outdone by the other crews. He gets to the gun and corrects his aim. I shoulder a bomb and thrust the tail into the muzzle of the howitzer. "Flash! Bang!" Off she goes. Another! Another! And up came the rest of the team panting and eager to do their work. Off I go back to my observing post, running along the trench like a madman. And as I get back my C.O.'s orderly appears again and says, "You can fire if you like, sir!" Lucky I didn't wait for that permission, five rounds would have been wasted, for behind him comes my C.O. out of breath, to gasp "Cease Fire." The artillery have finished, and so must we. Why we should finish is not apparent to my feeble mind, still intent on fireworks; but there is no help for it. Reluctantly I return to my gun to find only three bombs undischarged. Twenty-two bombs, each containing sixteen pounds of high explosive, is not bad.

Down by the other guns the scene of action is interesting. The emplacements of both have been blown in, piles of earth encumber the trench and as we troop down into the officer's dug-out where a R.A.M.C. man is waiting for casualties, we all laugh over the bombardment together, sixty rounds have been fired, a record... I sit down, having some command of language, to write a report. My C.O. dictates a bit here and there, and the men chuckle to think of it all going before the General. I drive them out to feed and my C.O. dashes off to lay his report before the feet of the mighty... From the men's dug-out issued the sound of a mouth-organ and songs. They had consumed their rum.

January 27th 1916... As I walked into the village from La Bourse, where I had been drawing money for our men, I noticed with annoyance that my short cut across the fields to our shattered billet was closed by the guns firing across it. Among the houses, and out of the meadows, great pale flashes leaped, and leaped again; over a line of half a mile they sprang into the quiet afternoon, and the following reports marred the peace of descending twilight. And as I sat by the roaring wood fire in the dilapidated room that is our mess, and library, and orderly room and dormitory all in one, the guns shouted and clamoured around me. Still, as I sat and wrote to my lovers and friends, the horrible barking and bellowing of the cannon shook the house and jarred the candle flame awry. Evening passed into black night, and the inhuman clangour of the monsters redoubled in volume and ferocity. My nerves were jangling with the brutal yells of the guns. And in the emotional tension of the hour I lent to the tramp of feet in the road outside a meaning of battle. In the darkness I questioned men, who said that we had sprung five mines and were attacking opposite Hulluch; that a regiment had lost and retaken a trench farther to the left. I saw crowds of soldiers passing in the dark; orderly, silent. The strain on my nerves grew harder to bear. Was there danger to our line? Was there conflict of rifle and bayonet, of bomb and machine-gun, of trench-mortar and spring gun, rifle-grenade and mine, in my section of our front? Then there was my place, not here; there among the shell-splinters and the snipers' bullets, under the ghastly light of the flares that revealed and brought death with their illumination. But the experienced non-commissioned officers were calm; if I was wanted I should be sent for, they said. I dined. And then, a runner arrived; it had taken him hours, he said, to struggle by the troops who flooded the trenches, and his message, timed 7.30 was delivered at half-past nine. It was from my commanding officer, and called me with eight men to his assistance; the Germans were going to attack; all the afternoon our trenches had been heavily bombarded, at some time after 8 p.m. the rush was expected. In an instant wild excitement raged in our billet - in the cellars men were forcing on their boots and cheering; in the room above there was the hasty but considered compiling of the list of chosen soldiers. Ten minutes passed, filled to the brim with the bustle of preparation, and after gas helmets, field-dressings and water-bottles had been inspected, electric torches produced, my revolver loaded, leather jerkins donned, and some rations taken, we issued on to the muddy road and picked our way through the dark to the communication trenches. Slowly and steadily we passed along these slippery and narrow paths, seeing above our heads the blackness invaded by floods or flashes of light. There was not a mouse stirring, and as the noise of our own guns diminished behind us, the quiet made itself felt in our hearts. But, presently, other sounds arose; the bursting of enemy shell; the rattle of machine-gun fire; and then the crack of the rifle with the newly-released bullet reeling out a long string of sound as it went. And, as we drew nearer to the front, following the winding ravines of the trenches that yet led one so straight to the scene of action, we came upon dark lines of men clad in their long great coats, with the rifle and fixed bayonet in their hands, leaning against the chalky walls of the trench, or sitting on the firing platforms of other trenches that had now begun to cross our way at right angles. The noise of the afternoon had waned to a broken calm by this, and louder than the crash of rifle grenades was the mutter and murmur of the troops packed into dug-outs and shelters, crammed into the reserve trenches, crushed into bays and behind traverses.

We found the rest of the battery most comfortably nestled into a huge dug-out, floored with lumps of chalk, and filled with bombs, boxes of charges and sand-bags. In half-a-dozen dialects, the Balliol speech of my C.O., the Welsh accent of a Bombardier, the Cockney of a Gunner, the broad Yorkshire of another, the situation was explained, and opinions challenged, controverted, and revised. However, for the present there was nothing to do but wait. Oh, that comfortless night! Hips will not rest on a chalk floor, heads cannot sleep on a bomb, legs get cramped, feet grow cold, all turn, and toss, and grumble. Nobby Clarke spreads his overcoat around me and graciously accepts my ration of rum in return... A bombardier has brought up a bottleful, hoarded by our Sergeant-Major. All drink and all are soothed. Some sleep at length. I get up, and walk round the trenches. My own dug-out with a stretcher for a bed, and a waterproof sheet and a blanket is denied me. I wander to the back entrance, and the steps are full of snoring or chattering Dragoons. I wander to the front stair, and they, too, are encumbered with cavalrymen. What horrid and fuggy congestion reigns below I shudder to think! In another dug-out I find a pile of dry sandbags, and with these I return to the battery. A dozen under me, and the hardness of the chalk is mitigated; one drawn up over each foot and leg keeps some warmth in those members, half-a dozen folded up on a box of detonators makes a good pillow, and what I do not spread over me and tie round my loins I distribute to the men. And I sleep for two hours, and then again for an hour.

Morning comes and my detachment moves off to its two guns. My orders are to fire when possible. Good heavens! while we are preparing bombs, the Germans shell the trench! My detachment vanishes up the trench for a safe dug-out; one young fellow alone finding shelter near by in the bomb store. I dodge shrapnel and those fiendish rifle-grenades, and get into a narrow bit of the trench and crouch. Good Lord! How can one escape these infernal shells that burst and fling fragments around, and bring earth down on one's head and say to the inward ear, "Keep your head down; get up against the trench; say your prayers; and yet we'll hit you." But my disposition can not stand this for long. I rush back along the battered trench to the bomb-store, and say to the uneasy lad within, "Will you help me to fire five rounds? We must give them tit for tat". And we run crouching to our gun. Oh, the dirt round it! Nothing will move, all parts being full of chalk fragments. No clinometer, no ramrod, no sponge-cloth, no pulley... Off I must slither again up the trench to get them out of the boxes of stores. We wrench the gun into position, and somehow or other, staggering round it, we blaze off one bomb. While my ears are still ringing with the crashing of the cordite, the Huns reply. I knew they had found the gun last week! Can the Hun shoot? Something hits me on the boot; something whizzes by my cheek. Something hums round my head like a great bee. All the fireworks again, and just for us two and our gun. This is not my work at all to ram home the charge, to lift that sixty-pound bomb, to insert the tail in the muzzle, to fix the T-tube in the vent, to remove the safety-pin from the fuse, to hook the lanyard and pull with all my force until the charge is fired, and I recoil dazed as the howitzer bursts into flame and thunder and jumps upright on its bed. I ought to be up in the front line observing and sending telephonic messages back to the N.C.O. in charge of the gun. But this is far better fun, and my No. 2 grins all over an agitated and dusty face. Half the parapet falls on my back as I lift the third bomb into the gun. And all the time these damned shells go crashing over and above us. Can we fire five rounds? Yes, we can; we do, and have done... Honour is satisfied! And we sit down in the narrow trench and congratulate one another... The two of us crawl into the bomb store, but it is too small for two. As neither will go in and leave the other without shelter, we make a dash for the big dug-out, and running the gauntlet for twenty yards come into a quiet length of trench where men are frying bacon and drinking tea, and so to the rest of the battery. They, too, have fired a few rounds, and they, too, feel pleased with themselves. Their trench has been battered in too, and they too have some souvenirs.

After this the events of the forenoon seem dull. The furious officer who comes from Headquarters to know why we don't fire, and gets precious little change out of us... The cheery Lancers who give me some breakfast..., the Dragoon officer with whom I eat sardines and tongue for lunch, the four-pounder mortar officer who is having his shattered trench repaired; all these people move about as on a stage. Even the poor wounded Hussars, stricken and patient, even the two men whose faces pale, whose eyes roll, whose teeth show in the agonies of death, even those lose their significance to the man who has not slept well, and to whose brief burst of violent activity succeeds reaction. The early afternoon sees me walking into the village again while German shells crash into the already shattered houses. And evening finds me again in front of a wood fire, lighted by candles and writing again to my lovers and friends...

[29th]... Yesterday broke very misty and, as I went along the reserve trench, where I live, it occurred to me that the enemy could not see me. So I climbed into the field, which of course consists of shell holes, and had a look round. One is in an irregular bit of flat ground; across this stretches a line of demolished German barbed wire, and the whole is pitted with holes two feet to twenty feet across. Along by the high banks of the trenches thousands of tins are lying, bully beef, jam, soup, cigarette, sausage, etc. Bits of iron and bits of shell are everywhere, and here and there are the conical fuses, our own and the enemy's, since this ground was once in German hands. Well I collected some fuses and went off across the top to my men. I told them that the misty day would give us good opportunities for finding new gun emplacements, and that they were to clean all the guns, and not to go a-souveniring on top.

Then I went off, and souvenired all day. I found a dug-out that had got lost and took some crockery out of it. Corpses had been uncovered, and I had some men out to re-bury them. Every heavy shell hereabouts disturbs some wretched, half-decayed soldier. Then I went off hunting for fuses, and round again into the disused trenches, unutterably filthy, but not as full of rats and mice as our used ones are. The dug-outs had all been used by the Germans, smashed in by our artillery fire, ransacked by our men, lived in for a few weeks and then abandoned. On one there was an illegible German inscription ending, 'So cowardly English and French'. At the back of these were piles of smashed German and English rifles, German hand-grenades, torn equipment, English and German cartridges, and, of course, shells exploded or not, and fuses. Farther back on the other side of the German wire - all smashed to bits - there were a dozen dead men, two of them lieutenants. I got a party of men and buried the poor fellows. They were all blackened, and the hands were almost fleshless. Over each man's mound we stuck a rifle and bayonet; heaps were lying about; and his cap on the rifle butt. Everything about them was mouldering. Some have been buried before and torn up by the shell-fire. One officer who was souveniring found a German's prayer-book, and a bandolier of the Prussian Guard. In a great shell-hole I found six men. We had a great wash and a good feed. But this gives you a true idea of the surface of the earth here. On fine days larks sing overhead, and hawks hover.

Bernard Pitt was given command of 47th Trench Mortar Battery, north of Arras, in February 1916:

FEBRUARY IN THE FIRING LINE

I have watched the breast of the lark pale in the blue,
And the kestrel eagerly quartering over the plain.
I have seen the tender and humble grass win through
The abhorrent relics of war and the bones of the slain:
And the birds and the grass in Winter were so much gain.
But to-day as the red sun sank on a day too mild,
And the white horse ploughing a field shone noble and fair,
And among green blades of corn stood a mother and child,
As I looked at the trees that quivered and though yet bare
Were sighing their dreams and hopes in the pleasant air,
I was shaken through with doubt of my own man's heart;
For the Winter was passing away, and the rising year
Was astir in the sap and the blood; and each human part
Of my being trembled and yearned at my cry of fear -
"Oh! how can I be out of England when Spring is here?"

At the end of March Pitt wrote to a friend:

... I am now in a hilly wooded region, like the skirts of the Kentish Downs, with copses full of anemones and delicate periwinkles, and the sapling hazels and willows tasselled and downy with catkins and buds. A mile away is a village, shattered and wasted, and beyond that a sight more shocking than the ruin of human work, a ghastly wood where the broken trunks and splintered branches take on weird and diabolical forms. It is the Bois de Souchez. The ground round about is poisoned with human relics, limbs and bundles of clothes filled with rotten flesh, and even those poor remains of men which pious hands have buried are daily disinterred by plunging shells. Souchez itself is merely a heap of bricks and stones, and it reeks to heaven of mortality. Do you wonder that, reading Wordsworth this afternoon in a clearing of the unpolluted woodlands, and marking the lovely faded colours on the wings of hibernated butterflies, and their soft motions, I felt a disgust, even to sickness, of the appalling wickedness of war. Sometimes one has great need of a strength which is not in one's own power to use, but is a grace of God.

I have so far escaped injury, and have seen very heavy fighting in different parts of our line. I was recommended for the Military Cross, but my usual bad luck intervened to relegate me to 'mentioned in despatches' only. Now I am in command of a Trench Mortar Battery, and I find the work as interesting as any war-making can be. You know we all long for the war to end, whether by peace, or by that furious slaughter which must lead to peace. Verdun, no doubt, has shortened the war by months...

THE WOOD OF SOUCHEZ

The coppices by Aylesford are beautiful in Spring:
Anemone and primrose delay the careless breeze,
The throstles try their grace-notes while woodland freshets sing,
The dewy catkins glisten on virgin-slender trees,
And England, my dear country, has many walks like these.
No flower blooms in the ruins of this accursed wood:
Through writhen splintered branches the shrapnel bullets hiss,
There is no leafy nook where a bird may rear her brood,
The reek of rotten flesh taints the pools where water is.
But England, my dear country, shall know no wood like this.

On 28th April 1916, two days before he was killed, Bernard Pitt wrote:

I have earned a day of rest; and am sitting under a walnut tree on the edge of this half-ruined village, blossoming cherry and pear trees near me in the broken closes, a field of dandelions and daisies at my feet, with swallows wheeling across it... Our woodlands have been lovely this April. There have been anemones, violets, the periwinkle and the primrose, most beautiful flowers and refreshing to the eyes and to the soul. The magpies venture across from tree to tree high over the clearings, fluttering along with much display of black and white feathers, jays flash and wheel and perch, dressed in the brightest brown and blue, and rooks swoop and drift, yielding themselves to the winds of heaven. Gaudy butterflies fan themselves in splashes of sunlight, and bronze and black beetles creep about on their errands. Yet the woods are defiled by war...

This is a land of hills, and as one trudges up to the firing-line, or back to billets, there are glimpses of valleys and crests and upland copses to delight the eye... But on one's way to the line there is the ghastly slope where lines of German corpses lie unburied, naked bones, curls of hair clinging to bleached skulls, lipless teeth, boots which the spoiler has relinquished, so set are the stiffened legs and feet within them... And so to the village and wood of Souchez heaps of bricks and stones and charred rafters, smashed trees, shell-holes full of putrid water, a stench of rotten and half calcined corpses. The place lies open to hostile eyes and nothing can be done to cleanse it. I have looked at the wreck until my imagination is obsessed by it...

My men have planted daisies and wallflowers and violets, and, practical souls, rhubarb, in their quarters. They have made bedsteads of planks and wire netting, and mended the roof. They have constructed an elaborate cooking place of bricks, and washing bench and put up clothes lines. We are not badly off either. Now two martins are building in one room and delighting us with their pretty ways, their liquid whistling, and their trust in our kindness. Life is rather good at present. And I expect leave in ten days time.

Brigadier-General Spedding later wrote to Mrs. Pitt:

Your husband was observing his fire from the front trenches and had just sent the man with him back to his mortars, when the Germans exploded a mine close to the spot, and we have been unable to find a trace of him since... I was going to make him my staff officer. I took him out with me the other evening to make sure that he did not go up to the trenches out of his turn, as he was in the habit of doing. The place he fell is about 200 yards south-west of the five cross roads, half-way between Souchez and Givenchy, at 7 p.m. on 30th April... I have had no officer under me for whom I have had more admiration...

URBS BEATA

As when the sunset smites upon the vanes
    Of some far city, and a hundred fires
    Flicker and flash above its imminent spires
And red gleams waken in the window-panes,
Even so Love's valedictory splendour stains
    With what sad sunset of denied desires
    The town of healing that my heart requires,
That pearl-clear city of the blessed plains.
Ah, the late pilgrim finds the beaten track,
    And kindly folk to guide him to the shrine,
    And respite from his journey and his load;
But I may neither travel on nor back,
    Nor ever shall I reach that rest of mine;
    The sun is dead, and no man knows the road.

SERGEANT JOHN WILLIAM STREETS

'D' Company, 12th Battalion York and Lancaster Regiment.
(Sheffield City Battalion - 'The Sheffield Pals').
Born: 1885. Whitwell, Derbyshire.
Educated: Local Council School.
Killed: 1st July 1916. Aged 31 years.
Euston Road Cemetery, Colincamps, France.

Will Streets became a coalminer at the age of 14, and later had a book on coalmining published. Although he worked underground in grim conditions a friend wrote later "the secret of his whole life, was an untiring love of nature."

At the outbreak of the war he enlisted in the 12th (Service) Battalion York and Lancaster Regiment - also known as the Sheffield City Battalion and the Sheffield Pals. After training at Hurdcott Camp outside Salisbury during 1915, the Battalion went to Egypt and was then sent to France in March 1916. During April, May and June the Battalion was at Colincamps and in front line trenches west of the village of Serre, at a rest camp at Courcelles-au-Bois and in billets at Bertrancourt and in the Bois de Warnimont.

APRIL EVENING: FRANCE, 1916

O sweet blue eve that seems so loath to die,
Trailing the sunset glory into night,
Within the soft, cool strangeness of thy light,
My heart doth seem to find its sanctuary.

The day doth verge with all its secret care,
The thrush is lilting vespers on the thorn;
In Nature's inner heart seems to be born
A sweet serenity; and over there

Within the shadows of the stealing Night,
Beneath the benison of all her stars
Men, stirr'd to passion by relentless Mars,
Laughing at Death, wage an unceasing fight.

The thunder of the guns, the scream of shells
Now seem to rend the placid evening air:

Yet as the night is lit by many a flare
The thrush his love in one wild lyric tells.

O sweet blue eve! Lingering awhile with thee,
Before the earth with thy sweet dews are wet,
My heart all but thy beauty shall forget
And find itself in thy serenity.

From Colincamps on 2nd May 1916, Streets wrote the following poem:

SHELLEY IN THE TRENCHES

Impressions are like winds; you feel their cool
Swift kiss upon the brow, yet know not where
They sprang to birth: so like a pool
Rippled by winds from out their forest lair
My soul was stir'd to life; its twilight fled;
There passed across its solitude a dream
That wing'd with supreme ecstasy did seem;
That gave the kiss of life to long-lost dead.

A lark trill'd in the blue: and suddenly
Upon the wings of his immortal ode
My soul rushed singing to the ether sky
And found in visions, dreams, its real abode-
I fled with Shelley, with the lark afar,
Unto the realms where the eternal are.

Streets sent his poems from the trenches 'written on scraps of paper stained with mud' to his publisher with the explanation:

They were inspired while I was in the trenches, where I have been so busy I have had little time to polish them. I have tried to picture some thoughts that pass through a man's brain when he dies. I may not see the end of the poems, but hope to live to do so. We soldiers have our views of life to express, though the boom of death is in our ears. We try to convey something of what we feel in this great conflict to those who think of us, and sometimes, alas! mourn our loss. We desire to let them know that in the midst of our keenest sadness for the joy of life we leave behind, we go to meet death grim-lipped, clear-eyed, and resolute-hearted.

MATHEW COPSE (JUNE 1916)

Once in thy secret close, now almost bare,
Peace yielded up her bountiful largess;
The dawn dropp'd sunshine thro' thy leafy dress;
The sunset bathed thy glade with beauty rare.

Spring once wove here her tapestry of flowers,
The primrose sweet, the errant celandine;
The blue-bell and the wild rose that doth twine
Its beauty 'round the laughing summer hours.

Here lovers stole unseen at deep'ning eve,
High-tide within their hearts, love in their eyes,
And told a tale whose magic never dies
That only they who love can quite believe.

Now 'mid thy splinter'd trees the great shells crash,
The subterranean mines thy deeps divide;
And men from Death and Terror there do hide -
Hide in thy caves from shrapnel's deadly splash.

Yet 'mid thy ruins, shrine now desolate,
The Spring breaks thro' and visions many a spot
With promise of the wild-rose - tho' belate -
And the eternal blue forget-me-not.

So Nature flourishes amid decay,
Defiant of the fate that laid her low;
So Man in triumph scorning Death below
Visions the springtide of a purer day:

Dreams of the day when rampant there will rise
The flowers of Truth and Freedom from the blood
Of noble Youth who died: when there will bud
The flower of Love from human sacrifice.

There by the fallen youth, where heroes lie,
Close by each simple cross the flowers will spring,
The bonnes enfants will wander in the Spring,
And lovers dream those dreams that never die.

A SOLDIER'S FUNERAL

No splendid show of solemn funeral rite,
No stricken mourners following his bier,
No peal of organ reaching thro' his night,
Is rendered him whom now we bury here.

'Tis but a soldier stricken in the fight,
A youth who flung his passion into life,
Flung scorn at Death, fought true for Freedom's might,
Til Death did close his vision in the strife.

No splendid rite is here - yet lay him low,
Ye comrades of his youth he fought beside,
Close where the winds do sigh and wild flowers grow,
Where the sweet brook doth babble by his side.
No splendour, yet we lay him tenderly
To rest, his requiem the artillery.

A LARK ABOVE THE TRENCHES

Hushed is the shriek of hurtling shells: and hark!
Somewhere within that bit of soft blue sky -
Grand in his loneliness, his ecstasy,
His lyric wild and free - carols a lark.

I in the trench, he lost in heaven afar,
I dream of Love, its ecstasy he sings;
Doth lure my soul to love till like a star
It flashes into Life: O tireless wings

That beat love's message into melody -
A song that touches in this place remote
Gladness supreme in its undying note
And stirs to life the soul of memory -
'Tis strange that while you're beating into life
Men here below are plunged in sanguine strife!

SERENITY

Peace can be found in strife: artillery
Are belching forth this sweet, entrancing morn
Their projectiles of death: yet as in scorn,
Lost in the sky's clear, blue serenity
The larks in music sing their love new-born,
Trilling its joy, its natural ecstasy;
The butterfly along Life's drift is borne;
And seeking nectar drones the wand'ring bee.

Thus Nature is serene amid the strife:
And in the hearts of those who calmly stand
Here in the trenches ('mid Death's hail) un-mann'd,
Flinging at Death the treasure of a Life -
There is a peace unknown to those (deny!)
Who have not dared for Liberty to die.

By the summer of 1916, the Germans had constructed in the Somme area a comprehensive defensive system based on 9 fortified villages and 11 'Redoubts' with a series of strongly wired trenches giving a formidable defence in depth. At 9.00 p.m. on 30th June the 12th Battalion marched to assembly trenches behind John Copse and Monk Copse not far from Courcelles. At 7.30 a.m. on Saturday, 1st July, 1916, after a massive bombardment lasting five days, the combined British and French attack was launched. The British sector was on an 18 mile front running north from the river Somme. The 12th Battalion Yorks and Lancs attacked in three waves opposite the village of Serre, a few miles north of Albert, and immediately came under very heavy shell, rifle and machine-gun fire. By the time it had crossed No Man's Land, the Sheffield Pals had lost at least half their strength, and whole sections had been wiped out. The attack petered out.

Will Streets was wounded early in the day during the bitter fighting for Serre. He was returning for medical aid when he heard that a soldier in his platoon was too badly wounded to return to a Dressing Station on his own. Streets went to his assistance and was not seen again. Streets' twin brothers were serving with the 58th Field Ambulance unit at the time. Harry Streets wrote of the conditions at a Dressing Station in the basilica at Albert on 1st July:

Wounded flooded in on foot, or were brought by stretchers, wheelbarrows, carts - anything. Their wounds were dressed and then they were laid out on the floor to await evacuation. Soon the whole church was packed and we were ordered to stop any vehicle that passed and make them take wounded to the rear. I even put three cases in a general's staff car. Those who were not expected to survive were put on one side and left. It was very hard to ignore their cries for help but we had to concentrate on those who might live. We worked for three days and nights without rest. It was the bloodiest battle I ever saw.

COMRADES

Those whom I've known, admired, ardently friended
Lie silent there wrapp'd in a soldier's shroud;
Death broke their dreams, their aspirations ended,
These sanguine youth, noble, brave and proud.

Slowly they bear them 'neath the dim star light
Unto their rest - the soldiers' cemetery:
The chaplain chants a low, brief litany;
The nightingale flings rapture on the night.

Back to their Mother Earth this night return
Unnumbered youth along the far-flung line;
But 'tis for these my eyes with feeling burn,
That Memory doth erect a fadeless shrine -
For these I've known, admired, ardently friended
Stood by when Death their love, their youth swift ended.

CORPORAL ALEXANDER ROBERTSON

'A' Company, 12th Battalion York and Lancaster Regiment.
(Sheffield City Battalion - 'The Sheffield Pals').
Born: 12th January 1882. Edinburgh.
Educated: George Watson's College, Edinburgh.
Edinburgh University.
Killed: 1st July 1916. Aged 34 years.
Thiepval Memorial to the Missing, near Albert, France.

Alexander Robertson gained a First Class Honours Degree in History at Edinburgh University in 1906. He became Senior History master at his old school for three years and then taught English Literature at the Lycée in Caen. He gave up being a schoolmaster to continue studying and went as a Post Graduate to Oxford where the subject of his thesis was published as a biography - *The Life of Sir Robert Moray*, an eminent 17th century Scotsman, one of the founders of the Royal Society and a minister of King Charles II. Alexander Robertson also wrote the history of Sir William Lockhart of Lea, a 17th century soldier and diplomat.

In February 1914 Robertson was appointed Lecturer in History at the University of Sheffield, and six months later he had enlisted as a Private in the 12th Battalion York and Lancaster Regiment - The Sheffield Pals. In December 1915, the Battalion sailed with the British Mediterranean Force for Egypt, and was then sent to France in March, 1916.

ON LEAVING EGYPT

As men whose lives in pain and toil of hand
Have passed and have not known the high delight
Of Beauty's Day or Knowledge' star-lit Night;
Even such are we who leave this storied land
And have but knowledge of its dreary plains
Of sand bush-sprinkled, and its orient hills,
Its mid-day ardours and its midnight chills;
Yet have not seen the splendour of its fanes,
Upraised to Allah's glory, nor the tombs
Near Memphis city, nor the solemn glooms
Of ancient palm groves, nor the giant face

Inscrutable; and have not in some place
Of quiet and shadow by the shining Nile
Mused on long-vanished empires for a while.

    Alexander Robertson was ill in hospital with jaundice for a few
weeks after he arrived in France.

WRITTEN IN HOSPITAL, PROVENCE

The tent is opened to the breeze
And 'neath its swinging flaps one sees,
Though not their shadowy foliage dark,
The stems of fir-trees, with their bark
Of gray and red. A road goes by
Beyond a row of stakes, not high,
But sharply pointed, joined with wires.
And overhead I hear the choirs
Of birds that, while they sing, do build;
Even as in ages past a guild
Of masons some fair fane might rear
That so God's glory might appear
More dearly and yet chant the while
They chiselled in some rich-wrought aisle.
And just across the rising way
Are dark green bushes, whose leaves sway;
How cool and fresh and smooth they look!
Adown the road there winds a brook
Of sunlight with no babbling air,
But bridged by shadows here and there.
Ah, pleasant shade and pleasant green
And brook for one whose eyes have seen
The power of cruel seas of light
And vast unshadowed deserts white.

Sometimes the peasant folk will pass;
Perhaps a strong Provencal lass,
With ruddy face and merry tongue
And o'er her arm a basket slung;
Or women old in donkey cart
With vegetables for the mart;
And turbaned Hindoo soldiers march

With stately gait beneath the arch
Of trees; and, sometimes, up or down
Pass officers with stars or crown;
And horses, straining, on the road;
The great gray motor with its load, -
A small space for the eye to see,
Yet Nature and Humanity.

In June, Robertson rejoined his Battalion in trenches west of the
village of Serre. During the next four weeks he wrote the following
poems:

A CONVICTION

A night of chill, a station dim,
And many an ambulance
To carry forth a burden grim
Of smitten men from France

Slow to its halting came the train:
The ambulances passed
Along the archway, to regain
A shelter through the blast.

I could not see nor could desire
Those prostrate men to see,
Some only wishful to expire, -
So dread can living be.

And some, recumbent lives must lead
Through their remaining years,
And some have gained as valour's meed
But madness and its fears.

And some have lost their sight and some
No voice again will hear,
And some before their death are dumb,
And others - still more drear

Their fate - bereft of sight and speech
A soundless world endure.
But I tried to see the soul of each,
Whom fate did thus immure,

Whom death could save not from distress,
Whose reason still was whole, -
To such does life give no redress
For all their anguish' toll?

They have no guerdon of renown
And gratitude is weak
To counter old plans overthrown, -
What object can they seek?

What purpose to sustain the will?
How shall they soon forget
The horrors seen so late, which still
Their memories beset?

The mean alone and cruel cry
To such that all is well.
And yet, to live, each man must spy
Some pathway from his hell.

And Life pursuant of her goal
(And great that goal must be)
With strange hopes partly calms the soul
And softening memory.

THOU SHALT LOVE THINE ENEMIES

(On seeing the letters, cards, soldier's book
and prayer-book found on a dead German soldier).

They were not meant for our too curious eyes
Or our imaginations to surmise
From what they tell much that they leave untold.
Strangers and foemen we, yet we behold,
Sad and subdued, thy solace and thy cheer.
Even here we see thee as thou dids't appear, -
Tall, with fair hair, blue eyes. Heinrich the name
The Lord's anointed gave thee;   Rome did claim
The homage of thy spirit: thou wert young, -
All this we know who read thy mother-tongue,

As that a farm Thuringian was thine,
Thou dead defender of imperial Rhine.
Thou had'st a wife and children: on this card
They are depicted; on another, marred
And soiled and crushed, thy mother, too, we see.
And here are cards with rustic eulogy
Of scenes that thou did'st know, old woods of pine
Through which doth pass a sunlit railway line.
These letters of thy wife, oh warrior slain,
No anguish tell, they give no hint of pain,
Cheerful her words, although the heart did weep
In solitude, thy babes and hers asleep,
The while on winter nights the wind would roar
And send its chills along the flag-stone floor.
This was thy book of prayer, and underlined
The words that solaced most thine anxious mind;
- Prayers for thy home and for thy comrades dead,
Such as for thee by her thou loved'st are said.
For thou art gone and nevermore shalt sway
The flaming scythe in some broad field of hay
Or guide the plough or golden harvests reap.
Of thee, alas, thy children cannot keep
A single memory. But one doth pass
Oft to thy cenotaph and on the grass
In prayer doth kneel, still as memorial stone,
Too sad for tears, too proud by far to moan.

Alexander Robertson was in the same attack on the village of Serre as Will Streets (qv). His Company, with 'C' Company, was the first to move forward at 7.30 a.m. on the 1st July. They were met with severe shell, rifle and machine-gun fire; Robertson was killed and his body was never found. A few men of 'A' and 'C' Companies managed to enter the German trenches on the right of the attack and remained there and in shell-holes until they could get back under cover of darkness. The failure of the attack was attributed, among other factors, to the wire being insufficiently cut; consequently, successive waves of men were struck down and did not arrive at the enemy front line wire in anything like sufficient strength for the attack to be pressed home.

LINES BEFORE GOING

Soon is the night of our faring to regions unknown,
There not to flinch at the challenge suddenly thrown
By the great process of Being - daily to see
The utmost that life has of horror and yet to be
Calm and the masters of fear. Aware that the soul
Lives as a part and alone for the weal of the whole,
So shall the mind be free from the pain of regret,
Vain and enfeebling, firm in each venture, and yet
Brave not as those who despair, but keen to maintain,
Though not assured, hope in beneficent pain,
Hope that the truth of the world is not what appears,
Hope in the triumph of man for the price of his tears.

SECOND LIEUTENANT GILBERT WATERHOUSE

2nd Battalion Essex Regiment.

Educated: Bancroft School.

Killed: 1st July 1916.

Serre Road Cemetery No. 2., Beaumont Hamel and Hébuterne, France.

Gilbert Waterhouse was commissioned in the 2nd Battalion, the Essex Regiment in May 1915. The Battalion went into action on the first day of the Battle of the Somme with a strength of 24 officers and 606 other ranks. They were part of the 4th Division's attack to the south of the village of Serre. The German defences were very effective, and the attacking troops so diminished by the retaliatory fire that they found themselves isolated, unsupported and running short of ammunition. The account from 'Essex Units in the War 1914 - 1919', continues:

... At the same time, the German batteries behind Serre placed a barrage along the British front trench, which effectively prevented the advance of supports to those who had broken through the German front defences. The ground between the support trench and the Munich trench was pitted with craters caused by the British bombardment, and using these as a protection, the German counter-attack developed rapidly. Working forward from front and flanks, the Germans ran from crater to crater, gradually forcing back the invaders, most of the fighting being with hand grenades. The British, the German account admits, defended themselves throughout with remarkable obstinacy and courage, barricading themselves at every step and showing fight to the last. Without supports, however, their supply of bombs and ammunition ran short and they were compelled to withdraw to the Heidenkopf crater by midday. Hand-to-hand fighting in the crater continued throughout the afternoon and it was not until dusk that the Germans succeeded in regaining the line of their front trench...

The Battalion, commanded by Sir George Stirling, Bart., who was wounded, was reduced by the evening to 2 officers and 192 other ranks. Gilbert Waterhouse was amongst those who were missing, presumed killed.

RAIL-HEAD

Someville is the Rail-head for bully beef and tea,
Matches and candles, and (good for you and me)
Cocoa and coffee and biscuits by the tin,
Sardines, condensed milk, petrol and paraffin.
Truck-load and train-load and lorries by the score,
Mule-cart and limber, "What are yer waitin' for?"
Dusty and dirty and full of noisy din,
"If 'e fights upon 'is stomach, this 'ere army oughter win!"
Someville is the Rail-head, full of noisy din,
Full of men and horses and mules and paraffin,
Frozen meat and apricots and peaches-a-la-tin,
Shunting up and down, across, and round and out and in.
But down beyond the Rail-head and village of that name,
Are green woods, where the cuckoo is calling just the same,
As he used to call in April, in the years before the war,
And he calls the same as ever now and doesn't care a straw,
Down the green and leafy lanes, where Jean and his Marcelle
In Spring-time would wander, their loving vows to tell.
But petite Marcelle now is up, and working on the farm,
With only the memory of Jean's encircling arm,
Only comfort, chilling comfort, can little Marcelle draw,
And cuckoos are calling, and never care a straw;
And Tommy says that girl Marcelle, indeed she is "no bonn,"
Because Marcelle "no promenade" with any mother's son;
Because petite Marcelle, he says, is always cross and sad,
When cuckoos are calling and all the woods are glad.
And madame, the mother of dark-eyed, sad Marcelle,
She ain't what yer'd call now a petite demoiselle,
"Gor blimy, she ain't, no!" says Tommy. "She's narpoo!
A-scoldin' 'er daughter, an' makin' such terdoo!"
But mother and daughter, tho' Tommy doesn't see,
Are held by the bond of a common memory,
A husband, a father, a lover, and a son,
The war barely started, and all were up and gone,
And mother and daughter now work upon the farms,
With only the memory of those encircling arms.

Someville is the Rail-head for tea and bully beef,
Dusty and dirty, with all the woods in leaf
In April, sweet April, and all the world at war,
And cuckoos a-calling and never care a straw.

MINNEWERFERS

Where I sit and tune my song,
In the valley all day long,
Ding-a-dong and ding-a-dong,
I hear the guns a-strafing -
And a bird of green and red,
In the branches o'er my head,
Keeps a-tapping, like the dead -
And like a ghost a-laughing -

Tap-a-tap and tap-a-tap,
Pecking wood devoid of sap,
Blasted by the guns mayhap,
Or dead and old and rotten -
Red and green and gold is he,
Tap-a-tapping ceaselessly,
But his laugh has little glee,
Aye, little mirth has gotten.

Pied with cowslips was the dell
Where the minnewerfers fell,
And the blackbird's mellow throat
Rang as loud as any bell.
Frail anemones did sprout,
And a chaffinch sang as well,
And a bee who boomed about,
Seeking honey in the dell -
Ere the minnewerfers fell.

But the minnewerfers fell,
And the blackbird ceased his song,
And the place became a hell,
Rang with curses loud and long -
Blackbird, chaffinch, bumble-bee
Fled away upon the wing -
Where they sang so merrily
Other messengers now sing -
Bumble-bee is busy still,
Blackbird and the chaffinch sing
In another faery dell,
By the village on the hill;

But a devil out of hell,
Tossing high explosive shell,
Gambols in the flowery dell
Where the minnewerfers fell.

BIVOUACS

In Somecourt Wood, in Somecourt Wood,
The nightingales sang all night,
The stars were tangled in the trees
And marvellous intricacies
Of leaf and branch and song and light
Made magic stir in Somecourt Wood.

In Somecourt Wood, in Somecourt Wood,
We slithered in a foot of mire,
The moisture squelching in our boots;
We stumbled over tangled roots,
And ruts and stakes and hidden wire,
Till marvellous intricacies
Of human speech, in divers keys,
Made ebb and flow thro' Somecourt Wood.

In Somecourt Wood, in Somecourt Wood,
We bivouacked and slept the night,
The nightingales sang the same
As they had sung before we came.
'Mid leaf and branch and song and light
And falling dew and watching star.
And all the million things which are
About us and above us took
No more regard of us than
We take in some small midge's span
Of life, albeit our gunfire shook
The very air in Somecourt Wood.

In Somecourt Wood, in Somecourt Wood,
I rose while all the others slept,
I seized a star-beam and I crept
Along it and more far along
Till I arrived where throbbing song

Of star and bird and wind and rain
Were one - then I came back again -
But gathered ere I came the dust
Of many stars, and if you must
Know what I wanted with it, hear,
I keep it as a souvenir
Of that same night in Somecourt Wood.

In Somecourt Wood, in Somecourt Wood,
The cuckoo wakened me at dawn.
The man beside me muttered, "Hell!"
But half a dozen larks as well
Sang in the blue - the curtain drawn
Across where all the stars had been
Was interlaced with tender green,
The birds sang, and I said that if
One didn't wake so cold and stiff
It would be grand in Somecourt Wood.

. . . .

And then the man beside me spoke,
But what he said about it broke
The magic spell in Somecourt Wood.

THE CASUALTY CLEARING STATION

A bowl of daffodils,
A crimson-quilted bed,
Sheets and pillows white as snow -
White and gold and red -
And sisters moving to and fro,
With soft and silent tread.

So all my spirit fills
With pleasure infinite,
And all the feathered wings of rest
Seem flocking from the radiant West
To bear me thro' the night.

See, how they close me in,
They, and the sisters' arms,
One eye is closed, the other lid
Is watching how my spirit slid
Toward some red-roofed farms,
And having crept beneath them, slept
Secure from war's alarms.

SECOND LIEUTENANT HENRY LIONEL FIELD

6th Battalion Royal Warwickshire Regiment.
Born: 2nd May 1894. Edgbaston, Birmingham.
Educated: Marlborough College.
            Birmingham School of Art.
Killed: 1st July 1916.   Aged 22 years.
Serre Road Cemetery No. 2, Beaumont Hamel and Hébuterne,
France.

Henry Field enlisted at the outbreak of War and was commissioned in the 6th Battalion Royal Warwickshire Regiment in September 1914. During his training he wrote 'Carol for Christmas 1914', but left the last line unfinished.

CAROL FOR CHRISTMAS 1914

On a dark midnight such as this,
Nearly two thousand years ago,
Three kings looked out towards the East,
Where a single star shone low.

Shepherds were sleeping in the fields,
When the hosts of heaven above them sang:
"Peace upon earth, goodwill towards men",
And the deeps in answering cadence rang.

Low in the manger poor and cold,
Lay Mary with her new-born child,
Scarce sheltered from the bitter blast
That whistled round them shrill and wild.

Be with them Lord in camp and field,
Who guard our ancient name to-night.
Hark to the cry that rises now,
Lord, lord maintain us in our right.

Be with the dying, be with the dead,
Sore-stricken far on alien ground,
Be with the ships on clashing seas,
That gird our island kingdom round.

Through barren nights and fruitless days
Of waiting when our faith grows dim
Mary be with the stricken heart,
Thou hast a son, remember him.

Lord Thou hast been our refuge sure,
The Everlasting Arms are wide,
Thy words from age to age endure,
Thy loving care will still provide.

Vouchsafe that we may see, dear Lord,
Vouchsafe that we may see,
Thy purpose through the aching days,

*   *   *   *   *   *   *   *   *   *

Field joined the Battalion in trenches at Fonquevillers in February 1916. He wrote to his mother:

... I am much happier than I ever thought I should be in the Army. After all, I am in my destined place, and doing or about to do what I should be doing or about to do. In some way or another, home seems nearer, and thank God I don't flinch from the sound of the guns...

At 10.30 p.m. on the night of 30th June 1916 the twenty-four officers and 626 men of the 6th Battalion marched from Mailly-Maillet to assembly trenches.   The History of the Battalion recorded the terrible events of the following day.

July 1st - Ill-fated day. Wounds and death were the fruit of it, and to those who outlived it an accursed memory of horror. Imperishable courage inspired every fighting man, but, where, where was Victory? Only the bare facts of that day are describable to those absent, the few who passed through it require no description.

At 7.30 a.m. the first wave of the 11th Brigade (the 8th Royal Warwickshire Regiment) leapt forward from the front line. Seven minutes later and the four Companies of the 6th Battalion were following them over No-Man's Land. Already we were decimated by shells and venomous machine guns that nothing could silence. The 8th ahead took what was left of the German front and support lines; together the two Battalions reached the third line and the near edge of the grisly quadrilateral. On the left the 31st Division were hung up below Serre. Munich Trench on the right was unattainable to the rest of the 4th Division. The Battalion made good its objectives, the quadrilateral and the cutting beyond. By 11.00 a.m. 2nd Lieutenant J.G. Cooper was the only officer of the Battalion untouched, and a dwindling handful of men of the 6th and 8th was left among heaps of dead and dying to man the quadrilateral against counter-attacks from both flanks and the pitiless cross fire of the German machine guns. It was useless to remain, impossible to go forward. In the evening they were ordered to withdraw to our old lines. Four Companies of heroes by sunset were reduced to the strength of two weak platoons...

At the end of the day Henry Field was one of the 520 men from the 6th Battalion who had been killed; a further 316 were wounded.

> Above the shot-blown trench he stands,
> Tall and thin against the sky;
> His thin white face, and thin white hands,
> Are the signs his people know him by.
> His soldier's coat is silver barred
> And on his head the well-known crest.
> Above the shot-blown trench he stands,
> The bright escutcheon on his breast,
> And traced in silver bone for bone
> The likeness of a skeleton.

LIEUTENANT BERNARD CHARLES de BOISMAISON WHITE

20th (1st Tyneside Scottish) Battalion Northumberland Fusiliers.

Born: 9th October 1886.   Harlesdon.
Educated: By tutors at home.
Killed: 1st July 1916. Aged 29 years.
Thiepval Memorial to the Missing, near Albert, France.

Bernard White was a direct descendant of the Ophthalmic Surgeon to Louis XVI, who was given the title and estates of Boismaison after he had successfully operated on one of the King's eyes; after the Revolution Boismaison came to England and settled in Chichester.

In 1909 Bernard White worked for a London printer for a year and then joined Hutchinsons, the publishers, for two years. He became a sub-editor and wrote for their two serial publications *The Wonders of the World* and *The Marvels of the Universe*; he also edited a collection of parodies and imitations. In 1912 he went to the publicity department of the Marconi Company where he was responsible for sending the daily news to ocean liners. He became Assistant Editor of the *Wireless News* and wrote a novel *A Pawn in the Game*.

In September 1914 he joined the Officers Training Corps of London University. In December 1914 he wrote a translation in verse of Henri Lavisse's speech delivered at the Sorbonne in December 1914, and a parody of 'Struwwelpeter'.

VERSE TRANSLATION

And all our sufferings and all our pains
Were worth the throes they cost us.
        Look you now,
We were a race, a people, when the sun,
Which set behind the broken walls of Rome,
Wak'd us to empire. We, whose heart and hand
Ne'er failed us in our purpose; we, who yet
With all our faults - and more than one dark stain
Corrodes the golden blazon of our tale -
Always, upon the hour of human need,
Spake no uncertain sound, made good our word,

And gave the world our national genius.
We, makers of fair marbles and fine verse,
Makers of Giants in the Scholiast Age,
And still the leaders of Philosophy:
We, who for Science hewed the pathway plain,
Who tested Social Creeds for social weal
- Witness the dynasties of early kings,
The spacious lordship of Le Grand Monarque,
Republican and Democratic rules -
We, who, in fine, have taught the world at large
The dignity and price of personal worth;
Who treated nations, small or great, as folk
Worthy consideration; and ourselves,
By force of arms restored to equity
Germany of old time, whenas her peace
Was by her princelings made a patchwork of
To fit an hundred thrones. For, to this day
These puppet-kings would ape the splendid role
Of mighty Louis with a broken state
Trained to be servile to their mockery,
Had not we come and set the earth a-quake,
And such disordered things in order new.

We saw the birthday of America's
Fair Unity; and Greece and Belgium,
Italy, and the states on Danube's shores
Had us for witness when they waked to life.

We are the hope of them that are oppressed,
We stand to all the World for Liberty:
To-day this question touches us: - Shall we
Allow our heritage to be despoiled,
Ourselves in turn to be Oppression's slave,
And France, the Nobler France, to be - a Name?

PARODY

Let us see if William can
Make war like a gentleman,
Let us see if he can fight
Like a true and noble knight;

See him with deceitful eyes
Pay blood-money to his spies;
Only to his own disgrace.
William, then, to save his face,
Catches at the Press; but, Lor!
He has played that game before
On unheeding ears they fall,
Mock-heroics, lies, and all;
Europe treats him scant o' grace
And sends him to - his proper place!

After he was gazetted to the 11th Battalion York and Lancaster Regiment in February 1915, White transferred to the 20th Battalion Northumberland Fusiliers (The 1st Tyneside Scottish) and went to France in January 1916. After a month at the Front he wrote a letter to his brother on 23rd February:

War is the most horrible, inconceivable, inhuman sacrifice it is possible to imagine. The homesteads in ruins, the quiet country lanes turned into pandemonium, the high roads broken up by shell-holes and swilled with the grey, slushy mud, the crosses dotted here, there and everywhere over the countryside, the thick clusters of them in the trenches themselves, and lastly the huddled forms of dead men that lie unretrieved between the two lines of trenches. These are all signs and tokens of the great, appealing cry that goes up dumbly: 'How long, O Lord, how long?...'

On 3rd March 1916 he wrote to a friend:

Fate and the hour are auspicious and I think that with luck I shall be able to finish you a letter ere nightfall. I am seated on a biscuit tin and am trying to take full advantage of the light percolating through the half-open door of the hut. The hut itself has a tarpaulin cover which reaches across to wooden walls two feet high. This is to make it as inconspicuous as possible. It's none so bad a residence now, but a week ago in the snow it was positively damnable. The ingenuity of the sub. has rigged up some sort of a stove, so that half the smoke finds its way outside, the other half helps to fumigate the interior.

Outside lies the camp, one hopeless quagmire; the field, formerly ploughed loam, has been trodden into soft, squelching mud that is undrainable, and the streams which surround the four sides of the field have so swollen with the rains and melted snow that bridges are necessary to connect us with the outside world.

We are here for a short rest before going into the trenches again. 'Rest' is a military term meaning 'out of danger from anything but long-range fire and aerial bombs'; but it does not necessarily mean ease. There are kit inspections, anti-gas helmet inspections, ration inspections, rifle inspections, foot inspections to be arranged. Also route marches, bathing parades, laundry parades, working parties (arranged for the sublime and impudent slackers that accompany us).

The most surprising thing to my mind in regard to our work is that we are supposed to be semi-specialists in all branches of army work. Infantrymen have to do a large part of the Engineers' work in the construction and repairing of trenches; they must be able to build bridges, load and unload transport (in its way quite technical work), and be able to read signal messages. Now each infantry company has its own machine-guns; and the infantry officer must know how to carry one. Every platoon commander is by force of circumstances his own medical officer, and has to bandage or supervise the bandaging of the wounded. Every garment issued to his men passes through the hands of the platoon commander; he reports on the quality of the oil for rifle cleaning, the quality of the men's food. If he is to be any good, he must be able to buy hay, straw, etc., for his men, whom he pays in the field. He is responsible that proper precautions are taken against gas, that the wire entanglements in front of his part of the trench are in good repair.

Moreover he has always some specialist duties assigned to him. He is either signalling officer, machine-gun officer, transport officer, sniping officer, scout officer, billeting officer, assistant adjutant, assistant quarter-master, bombing officer, etc., so that a platoon commander's life is not an idle one.

To take a particular instance, I am battalion engineer officer, billeting officer and company scout officer. When I am in the trenches, it is my duty to 'advise' on the work of repairing, reconstructing and improving the parapet, dug-outs and drainage of the part of the line held by the battalion, to arrange for stores from the Engineers and to see that these are brought up. This is by no means an easy job, for all stores have to be brought up at night, and all the time one is working under fire - not direct fire, but from snipers and machine-guns, or stray bullets, with a chance of shell-fire; for one is too far back to get protection from the trenches. Then, too, plugging along in the darkness over uneven ground, most of which is muddy, dropping into shell-holes and similar pitfalls make the work tiring, and the stuff we tackle, which is dumped by the transport some mile and a half from the firing-line, is heavy and awkward to carry.

As billeting officer, which is my work when out of the trenches, I get a chance of picking up French and generally seeing something of a country which is quite interesting. My French stands me in good stead, and, to tell the truth, I am the best linguist in the battalion. It is fortunate, for I have never once been able to have the assistance of the interpreter, and as on more than one occasion I have had to buy straw, coal and wood for the battalion from the natives I should have been badly 'landed' if I had been unable to understand or make myself understood. I am often commissioned to purchase other things, such as elastic, safety pins and scarlet cloth. Then I have to interview the mayors of the various towns we have visited, and the keepers of the estaminets (wine shops) with regard to serving the troops with liquor. I have to arrange for beds for the officers and stabling for the horses.

Since we came out as a brigade and have worked our way up country to the firing-line, we have seen much more life than do the drafts, which are sent direct to one spot and stay there. I am not the least sorry I transferred to this regiment, though by doing so I lost my seniority and may have to wait the devil of a time before I get another 'pip'. Really, I am the most junior officer in the battalion, and should, by rights, still be at the depot at Alnwick; but a platoon was found for me, I think because I was useful.

Trench warfare is monotonous, but fairly safe. Snipers do the most damage, although shell-fire is worse when it is unexpected. Given a little warning, one can get under cover from these veritable machines of iniquity; but if one comes plump into a billet, then it is sure to take its toll of life, for its ravages are widespread.

A post that we were holding when in support was so shelled; but on that occasion no one was hurt. The telephone was blown into the operator's stomach, but it only winded him, and before the next shell came everyone got away. The telephone, by the way, was consumed in the fire that ensued; for the farmhouse was burnt to a cinder.

Next day the adjutant received a peremptory inquiry as to the whereabouts of the said telephone. He replied that it was in bits. Next came a message that 'the bits' were to be collected and sent immediately to Brigade Headquarters. Consequently a search party was sent out, which returned after some hours with a solitary trophy of the hunt; a cinder about the size of a walnut, which might have been part of a telephone. This was duly wrapped in cotton-wool and tissue paper, and sent with proper ceremony to Headquarters. I presume it is now resident at the War Office. Perhaps that is what a War Office is for...

On 1st July 1916 the 20th Battalion was in the front line trenches opposite the village of La Boisselle. In the assault it suffered appalling casualties, including the Commanding Officer,

Lieut-Colonel Sillery, 16 other officers killed or missing and ten wounded. The battalion diary reveals that 'Not a single officer who went forward escaped being a casualty'. Of the Other Ranks, 329 were killed or missing and 305 wounded. Bernard White was amongst those killed. One of his brother officers, Lieutenant Frederick Nixon wrote later:

> His platoon was the first to leave the trenches, and he himself was responsible for the direction of the attack. He led his men right across 'No Man's Land' - here eight hundred yards broad - and was last seen standing on the parapet of the German trenches throwing bombs. He then disappeared, and for a short time was missing. Then his body was found and buried, with one or two other officers, who fell beside him ... His death has left a very empty place in my life, for he was an exceptional man in many ways, so brilliant and full of life...

LIEUTENANT ALFRED VICTOR RATCLIFFE

10th Battalion West Yorkshire Regiment.
Born: 1st February 1887.   London.
Educated: Dulwich College.
            Sidney Sussex College, Cambridge.
Killed: 1st July 1916. Aged 29 years.
Fricourt New Military Cemetery, France.

Alfred Ratcliffe, who was training to be a barrister, had a book of poetry published before the war. He was commissioned in 1914 and joined the Battalion in billets at Armentières at the end of March 1916.

On 1st July 1916 the 10th Battalion West Yorkshire Regiment was one of many committed to the Somme offensive.   From the front line trenches at 7.30 a.m. the Battalion went 'over the top' in four waves to attack the German-held village of Fricourt.   Once near the German front line the troops found themselves trapped in the open between two enemy trenches on a slope in full view of the German machine-guns two hundred yards away in the ruins of the village. By 9 a.m. the Battalion had been virtually anihilated apart from one officer and twenty men. Of the 710 casualties nearly 60 per cent were killed, amongst whom was Alfred Ratcliffe. The 10th Battalion West Yorkshire Regiment suffered more casualties than any other Battalion that day.

AT SUNDOWN

The day put by his valiant shield,
And cast him down.
His broken sword lay o'er a field
Of barley brown
And his bright sceptre and his crown
Were sunken in the river's heart.

His native tent of blue and gold
Was gathered in.
I saw his torn flags o'er the wold;
And on the whin
High silence lit, and her near kin
Fair twilight spread her firefly wings.

The birds like secret thoughts lay still
Beneath the hush
That held the sky and the long hill
And every bush.
And floated o'er the river's rush
And held the windlets in her hand.

OPTIMISM

At last there'll dawn the last of the long year,
    Of the long year that seemed to dream no end;
Whose every dawn but turned the world more drear,
    And slew some hope, or led away some friend.
Or be you dark, or buffeting, or blind,
We care not, day, but leave not death behind.

The hours that feed on war go heavy-hearted:
    Death is no fare wherewith to make hearts fain;
Oh, we are sick to find that they who started
    With glamour in their eyes come not again.
O Day, be long and heavy if you will,
But on our hopes set not a bitter heel.

For tiny hopes, like tiny flowers of Spring,
    Will come, though death and ruin hold the land;
Though storms may roar they may not break the wing
    Of the earthed lark whose song is ever bland.
Fell year unpitiful, slow days of scorn,
Your kind shall die, and sweeter days be born.

LIEUTENANT WILLIAM NOEL HODGSON, M.C.

9th Battalion Devonshire Regiment.

Born: 3rd January 1893. Thornbury, Gloucestershire.
Educated: Durham School.
            Christ Church College, Oxford.
Killed: 1st July 1916. Aged 23 years.
Devonshire Cemetery, Mansel Copse, Mametz, France.

Noel Hodgson's father was the Vicar of Thornbury, and later became the first Bishop of St. Edmondsbury and Ipswich. Noel was the youngest of four children all of whom were talented. He won a scholarship to Durham School and to Christ Church College, Oxford to read Classics, and he gained a First in Classical Moderations in 1913.

In September 1914 Hodgson was commissioned in the 9th Battalion, the Devonshire Regiment, where he was affectionately known as 'Smiler'. The Battalion arrived in France at the end of July 1915 and was sent to the trenches near Festubert. In August Hodgson composed a poem during a route march:

REVERIE

At home they see on Skiddaw
His royal purple lie
And Autumn up in Newlands
Arrayed in russet die,
Or under burning woodland
The still lake's gramarye.
And far off and grim and sable
The menace of the Gable,
Lifts up his stark aloofness
Against the western sky.

At vesper-time in Durham
The level evening falls
Upon the shadowy river
That slides by ancient walls,
Where out of crannied turrets
The mellow belfry calls.
And there sleep brings forgetting

And morning no regretting,
And love is laughter-wedded
To health in happy halls.

But here are blood and blisters
And thirst as hard as sand
An interminable travelling
Interminable land;
And stench and filth and sickness
And hate by hardship fanned.
The haunt of desolation
Wherein a desperate nation
Writhes in the grip of murder's
Inexorable hand.

Above the graves of heroes
The wooden crosses grow,
That shall no more see Durham
Nor any place they know,
Where fell tops face the morning
And great winds blow;
Who loving as none other
The land that is their mother
Unfaltering renounced her
Because they loved her so.

The Battalion was in trenches at Vermelles on 25th September 1915, the first day of the Battle of Loos. Under heavy enemy fire Hodgson, three other young officers and a hundred men held a captured trench for 36 hours without reinforcements or food. Hodgson was awarded the Military Cross.

BACK TO REST

(Composed while marching to Rest Camp
after severe fighting at Loos).

A leaping wind from England,
The skies without a stain,
Clean cut against the morning
Slim poplars after rain,

The foolish noise of sparrows
And starlings in a wood -
After the grime of battle
We know that these are good.

Death whining down from Heaven,
Death roaring from the ground,
Death stinking in the nostril,
Death shrill in every sound,
Doubting we charged and conquered -
Hopeless we struck and stood.
Now when the fight is ended
We know that it was good.

We that have seen the strongest
Cry like a beaten child,
The sanest eyes unholy,
The cleanest hands defiled,
We that have known the heart blood
Less than the lees of wine,
We that have seen men broken,
We know man is divine.

During February and March 1916 the Battalion was in front line trenches at Fricourt and in billets at Méaulte. From February 1916, under the pseudonym 'Edward Melbourne', Hodgson wrote regular articles for T*he Spectator, Saturday Review* and *Yorkshire Post*, giving vivid, honest and sometimes humourous accounts of trench life. In March 1916 he wrote of his batman under the title 'Pearson':

He is my servant, and if he were Commander-in-Chief the war would be over in a week. But I should get no baths, so I'm glad he isn't. And I doubt whether he would care to be, himself; at present he is supreme in his own sphere, and knows it and knows that the other servants know it. The only thing he does not know is his own limitations - nobody else does either - they have never been reached.

For example. We had taken over some new trenches, which were in a very filthy condition, and one day I discovered to my dismay, that I was becoming as Samson - a host in myself. Pearson was summoned. "Pearson," said I, "I'm lousy."

Pearson looked serious, but not at all surprised. "You must have a bath, sir, and a change of clothes." I smiled gently, and said that if he called a taxi I could go to the Jermyn Street Baths and call at my tailors on the way.

Pearson gave an accommodating laugh, and promised to see to it; and I returned to my work, trying to forget.

To my amazement, when I again entered my dug-out there was a little pile of underclothing on my table.

"Where did those come from?" I inquired.

"Medical officer, sir. I knew as he always carried a lot of stuff on his cart, so I seen his servant about it. But you mustn't put it on yet"; and with that the clean change was swept away from my ken. I acquiesced, as I have learnt always to acquiesce in all that Pearson does; and during the night I thought of Job and envied him his potsherd. Next morning while doing my irritable duties about the trench, enter Pearson, who remarks without a blush: "Your bath is ready in your dug-out, sir." Speechless with amaze, I hurried away to verify, and found an iron boiler half-full of boiling water, reposing on a bed of bricks. On the table were my clean clothes - or rather the Doctor's - a towel, soap, sponge, etc.

As I wallowed, Pearson told me all about it. It appeared that by bribery or force, one of the cooks had been persuaded to throw in his lot with Pearson. Together, under cover of darkness, they had quitted the trenches and gone to an old factory behind our line. No trenches ran near the factory and no one habited there, for the sufficient reason that by day the Boche placed fat shells there, and by night he larded it with machine-gun fire. Here the two knaves found the boiler, and hauled it back in safety to the company cook-house, where it was filled with water - and I suspect the water came from the next door company's supply store - I was careful not to ask. The theft of firewood is child's play to Pearson, but the compulsion of the cooks to boil the huge tub must have needed his supremest skill. Anyway, the whole great epic was accomplished and I had my bath.

Pearson subsequently hid the tub in an old cemetery, where he could find it again in case of need. He is of a thrifty temperament.

A good soldier servant is one of the greatest marvels of our modern civilisation. To possess one is better and cheaper than living next door to Harrods. Do you want a chair for the Mess? You have only to mention it to Pearson. Are you starving in a deserted village? Pearson will find you wine, bread and eggs. Are you sick of a fever? Pearson will heal you. From saving your life to sewing on your buttons he is infallible.

Perhaps Pearson was at his best in the Affair of the Mess Carpet. It came about in this way. When the regiment was in a village, not-to-be-named, behind the line, Headquarter Mess was in an empty house, the main room of which made a very creditable Mess Room, except for the extreme coldness of the stone floor, which was in no way counteracted by the warmth of the pictures left on the walls by the outgoing Mess. The Doctor, who does Mess President, was commenting on this to me one evening as we sat making toast over a brazier. "Look here, Adjer," said he, "if we want to be comfortable in here we must have a carpet."

"Well, tell Pearson to get one," was my off-handed reply.

"Rot! the boy isn't a conjurer."

"Bet you five francs he gets one."

"Done - by when?"

"This time to-morrow."

"Right - done with you - and if I win it'll be a bargain at five francs."

Thus the Doctor secure in the anticipation of five francs or a carpet for his Mess; for me I was not so content. Great as was my belief in Pearson's genius, I hardly saw how he was to obtain a carpet at twenty-four hours' notice. However, I called him; "Pearson," I said, "we want a carpet for the Mess by tea-time to-morrow."

"Very good, sir."

"There's a bet on it, Pearson."

"I'll see to it, sir," and off he went.

Next morning, as I was returning from the Orderly Room, Pearson met me.

"Please, sir, will you give me a pass to EXYZED?"

Now EXYZED is the remains of a town that became uninhabited very suddenly, and is still attended to daily by the German gunners. It is out of bounds for troops.

"Sorry, Pearson, I can't."

Pearson looked disappointed. "The carpet, sir——" he ventured.

"Have to give it a miss," said I.

Pearson shook his head and moved sorrowfully away.

Shortly before tea, the door of the Mess Room was violently agitated, and Pearson entered in a stream of perspiration, bearing on his shoulders a carpet and two rolls of linoleum.

"Good Lord," said the Doctor, "where did those come from?"

"EXYZED, sir;" then, turning to me, "you didn't tell me not to go, sir."

"Pearson," I said, "you're a bally marvel."

He gave an apologetic smile. "I could not let you lose a bet, sir, for the sake of a little trouble."

There are many like him, I am sure, though I prefer to think of him as supreme. But when next a soldier friend boasts of his servant - as they always do - sooner or later, remember that he is not always such a liar as he appears."

During April 1916 the Battalion was in front line trenches opposite Mametz and in billets at Bray-sur-Somme. At the beginning of May the men were in training behind the lines near Méaulte, and on 8th June Hodgson wrote:

DURHAM CATHEDRAL

Above the storied city, ringed about
    With shining waters, stands God's ancient house,
Over the windy uplands gazing out
    Towards the sea; and deep about it drowse

The grey dreams of the buried centuries,
    And through all time across the rustling weirs
An ancient river passes; thus it lies,
    Exceeding wise and strong and full of years.

Often within those dreaming aisles we heard,
    Breaking the level flow of sombre chords,
A trumpet-call of melody that stirred
    The blood and pierced the heart like flaming swords.

Long years we learned and grew, and in this place
    Put on the harness of our manhood's state,
And then with fearless heart and forward face,
    Went strongly forth to try a fall with fate.

And so we passed and others had our room,
    But well we know that here till days shall cease,
While the great stream goes seaward and trees bloom,
    God's kindness dwells about these courts of peace.

Four days before the start of the Battle of the Somme, between
26th and 30th June, the Battalion was in bivouacs in Bois des
Tailles, a wood about three miles behind the line. On 29th June, as
he waited here, before moving up to assembly trenches, Hodgson
wrote his last poem:

BEFORE ACTION

By all the glories of the day
　　And the cool evening's benison,
By that last sunset touch that lay
　　Upon the hills when day was done,
By beauty lavishly outpoured
　　And blessings carelessly received,
By all the days that I have lived
　　Make me a soldier, Lord.

By all of all man's hopes and fears,
　　And all the wonders poets sing,
The laughter of unclouded years,
　　And every sad and lovely thing;
By the romantic ages stored
　　With high endeavour that was his
By all his mad catastrophes
　　Make me a man, O Lord.

I, that on my familiar hill
　　Saw with uncomprehending eyes
A hundred of Thy sunsets spill
　　Their fresh and sanguine sacrifice,
Ere the sun swings his noonday sword
　　Must say good-bye to all of this;-
By all delights that I shall miss,
　　Help me to die, O Lord.

On 1st July 1916, the Battalion had orders to attack German
trenches south of the village of Mametz. Although some men
reached the enemy lines, the 8th and 9th Devons suffered very
heavy casualties as they left their forward trench to attack. They
were at first sheltered by a small hill and the trees of Mansel Copse;
but when they came over the top and moved downhill they were in
full view of the enemy who had placed a machine-gun in the base

of a shrine on the edge of Mametz 400 yards away. The crew of this, and other machine-guns positioned on the high ground around the village, opened fire catching the Devonshires on the exposed slope. Hodgson, the Battalion's Bombing Officer, was taking a fresh supply of bombs to his men in the captured trenches, when he was killed by a bullet in the throat.

At the end of the day the bodies of 159 men, including Noel Hodgson were found. The body of Hodgson's batman was lying at his side. The men of the 9th Battalion were buried in their Mansel Copse trench, and a notice above the trench read: "The Devonshires held this trench. The Devonshires hold it still."

LIEUTENANT DONALD FREDERIC GOOLD JOHNSON

2nd Battalion Manchester Regiment.

Born: 6th March 1890. Saffron Walden.

Educated: Caterham School.
Emmanuel College, Cambridge.

Killed: 15th July 1916. Aged 26 years.

Bouzincourt Communal Cemetery Extension, France.

Donald Johnson wrote poetry before the war and while at Cambridge he became a Roman Catholic. In 1914 he won the Chancellor's Medal for English Verse with 'The Southern Pole', a 14 stanza poem on Captain Scott's expedition.

The year after he graduated Johnson planned to make a special study of Chaucer but at the outbreak of the war he abandoned this idea and was gazetted to the 2nd Battalion, Manchester Regiment. He went to France at the end of 1915 and joined the Battalion at Sailly-Laurette, a village on the Somme a few miles east of Amiens.

YOUTH AND WAR

Among the windy spaces
The star-buds grow to light;
With pale and weeping faces
The day-hours bow to night;
Where down the gusty valleys
A blast of thunder dies,
And in the forest alleys
A startled night-bird cries.

Not pain but bitter pleasure
Surrounds my spirit here,
For life's supernal treasure
Is garlanded with fear;
Bright trees delight the garden
About my love's glad home
But all the flower-roots harden
Under the frost of doom.

Like the bright stars above me
My youthful hopes were set;
Yearning for lips that love me;
O how can I forget
The boyish dreams that brought me
To the high azure gate
Of heaven, where beauty sought me,
And love was satiate?

Now honour lets me dally
No longer with desire,
But goads me to the valley
Of death, and pain, and fire;
Not love but hate constraining
The soldier in the field,
Honour alone remaining
Of virtue for a shield.

Yet who dare doubt, resigning
The joys that mortals prize -
Beyond the heart's repining,
Behind the sightless eyes -
For all the tears and anguish,
The piteous dismay -
True love at length shall vanquish,
And crown the dawning day?

REIMS

Thy altars smoulder, yet if Europe's tears
Can stay the doom of malice, they are thine
To quench the fires that lick thy sacred shrine,
And scar the treasures of thy glorious years.
And nought can salve the heart's despairing fears
That knows its Head dishonour'd, while rapine
Thunders upon His citadel divine,
Till all its ancient splendour disappears.
But courage, tho' no hand can raise again
Thy perish'd glories, garlanded by Time,
The arm yet faileth not that ruleth all,
And God Himself the guilty shall arraign,

Bidding them answer their inhuman crime
Before His everlasting doom shall fall.

Between January and July 1916 the 2nd Battalion Manchester Regiment was either in the front line at Authuille, on the river Ancre just north of Albert, or in billets near Henencourt and training at St. Gratien and Contay Wood. The Battalion was in action during the first few days of the Battle of the Somme, and was then to be in reserve for an attack on Ovillers-la-Boisselle on the 6th July. On the 8th the Battalion's Commanding Officer recorded that "Sausage and Mash Valleys were littered with the dead and wounded from the attack which failed."

After a successful operation on the 10th July, the Battalion returned to Bouzincourt until it was in the line again at Ovillers on the 14th. The Battalion Diary records:

On night of 14th/15th July during the attack on the village of Ovillers a bombing party was sent forward to ascertain enemy strength. The party came under heavy fire and 25 casualties were sustained forcing them to retire...

It was sometime during the action to take Ovillers that Johnson was killed holding a trench against an enemy counter attack. The village was finally taken two days later.

BATTLE HYMN

Lord God of battle and of pain,
Of triumph and defeat,
Our human pride, our strength's disdain
Judge from Thy mercy-seat;
Turn Thou our blows of bitter death
To Thine appointed end;
Open our eyes to see beneath
Each honest foe a friend.

Give us to fight with banners bright
And flaming swords of faith;
We pray Thee to maintain Thy right
In face of hell and death.

1916

Smile Thou upon our arms, and bless
Our colours in the field,
Add Thou, to righteous aims, success
With peace and mercy seal'd.
Father and Lord of friend and foe
All-seeing and all-wise,
Thy balm to dying hearts bestow,
Thy sight to sightless eyes;
To the dear dead give life, where pain
And death no more dismay,
Where, amid Love's long terrorless Reign,
All tears are wiped away.

CAPTAIN RICHARD MOLESWORTH DENNYS

'A' Company, 10th Battalion Loyal North Lancashire Regiment.
Born: 17th December 1884. London.
Educated: Winchester College.
Died of Wounds: 24th July 1916. Aged 31 years.
St. Sever Cemetery, Rouen, France.

Although 'Dick' Dennys graduated from St. Bartholomew's Hospital in 1909 he decided against a career in medicine and turned to the world of arts. A pianist, painter, actor, writer of prose and poetry, Dennys was described by his friend Desmond Coke, Adjutant of the Regiment, who survived the war and later became a writer, as:

> ... A dreamer... an essential amateur; not in the vile modern sense but in the fine old meaning of that terribly ill-treated word. Beauty in every form he loved, and his whole life was beautiful in a degree that could never be communicated to any one who had not known him, nor is it easy to explain in what way he impressed one as possessing, far beyond those of more elaborate performance, the spirit and the splendour of rare artistry. He was a man above all to know, and to be thankful for having known...

At the outbreak of the war Dennys was in Florence working with Gordon Craig in his school for the improvement of the Art of the Theatre and Stage Production. He returned home and after an unsuccessful attempt to enlist in the Royal Army Medical Corps, he was commissioned in the Loyal North Lancashire Regiment. He was promoted Temporary Captain before the end of 1914, and arrived at Hazebrouck with his Battalion in August 1915. He became a Company Commander a few months later. Desmond Coke wrote:

> I was astonished, because it did not seem possible beforehand that a dreamy nature, so full of spiritual tenderness and the true love of beauty, should make anything except a grudging patchwork job of the rough practical, ugly business of war; but I was not surprised, because I knew of old the rugged strength, the moral courage, the force of the ideals, which lay beneath that outward gentleness... No Company Commander, as I can testify, was more constant in inquiries as to rations, straw, rum, or any comfort that could possibly be screwed out

of Head-quarters for his Company; and the men, always shrewd in an estimate, very quickly grew to ignore the characteristic reserve, that he never managed to subdue, and loved him all the more because they had first learnt to respect him..."

Richard Dennys wrote a few poems from Belgium and France:

WAR

To end the dreary day,
The sun brought fire
And smote the grey
Of the heavens away
In his desire
That the evening sky might glow as red
As showed the earth with blood and ire.

The distant cannons's boom
In a land oppressed
Still spake the gloom
Of a country's doom,
Denying rest.
"War!" - called the frightened rooks and flew
From the crimson East to the crimson West.

Then, lest the dark might mar
The sky o'erhead,
There shone a star,
In the night afar
O'er each man's bed,
A symbol of undying peace,
The peace encompassing the dead.

BALLADS FROM BELGIUM (I)

High in the sunny sky
    In summer weather
Man a butterfly
    Over the heather;
Down on the dusty road,
    Singing a song,
Many a soldier-man
    Marching along.

Ah! happy butterflies
    Poised in your flight,
Few are the hours of sun
    Ere it is night;
Light-hearted soldier-men
    Passing to-day,
Laugh while the daylight lasts,
    Sing while you may.

BALLADS FROM BELGIUM (II)

Last night within the crowded trench
    I and a friend lay side by side,
Waiting through fitful dreams for dawn
    To bring the flood of battle-tide.

To-night upon the moon-drenched plain,
    'Mid those who did not fear to die,
The friend I loved is lying still,
    His wide eyes staring at the sky.

For there, laid low by cruel war
    Ere manhood's day was scarce begun
Is many a strong and gallant lad
    Who will not see to-morrow's sun.

We who await another day
    For aching limbs brief respite find.
A moment's thought - a moment's prayer
    For the brave dead we leave behind.

BALLADS FROM BELGIUM (V)

Oh! toll of pillaged villages
    Left smouldering in the aggressor's track,
And ravaged farms and smitten fields
    And ruins desolate and black.

Oh! pitiful the little groups -
    Their homes in ashes left behind,

Who hopeless seek, poor stricken souls,
   The shelter that they cannot find.

Dumb, battered women-folk who pass
   Across a devastated land,
And aged men and little ones
   Too young as yet to understand.

Earth's precious peace is cast away,
   Fierce hate unloosed across the world,
With nation against nation ranged
   And army upon army hurled.

Hunger and lust and blood and pain
   And misery and crime and tears -
Is it for this God made mankind?
   For this the passage of the years?

Ah! moon across the trampled fields,
   Hanging low in a stifling sky,
Is it for this that we have lived?
   Is it for this that we must die?

In June 1916, three weeks before the opening bombardment of the battle of the Somme, the Battalion was at Bienvillers. Dennys wrote to Coke who was in hospital suffering from trench fever:

Billets again and a bit of a rest, but we've been having a fairly lively time in the trenches - two raids on the Boche by people close on our left with resulting bombardments on their part. Unpleasantly warm! My head-quarters dug-out was smashed to pieces the day before we took over, and during the 2nd bombardments the other to which I had repaired was buried in debris. A shell burst just near the door and you never saw such a mess! Bed a foot deep in earth, door blown in and utter confusion of all papers and things. Two shells through the mess kitchen and others in profusion all round. They have got Company H.Q marked all right! Yes, we are full of activities. There is much in the wind. You should have news of this part of the world at no distant date...

On 6th July the Battalion moved in buses to Albert and took over trenches in Tara Redoubt on Usna-Tara Hill. There were orders to push forward strong patrols, and try to occupy a line of trenches

running from the north-west corner of Contalmaison. The patrols
'pushed forward vigorously' but did not make much progress as the
front line was being heavily shelled. Dennys was seriously
wounded on the 12th and taken to the British General Hospital at
Rouen where he died twelve days later.

Better far to pass away
    While the limbs are strong and young,
Ere the ending of the day,
    Ere Youth's lusty song be sung.
Hot blood pulsing through the veins,
    Youth's high hope a burning fire,
Young men needs must break the chains
    That hold them from their heart's desire.

My friends the hills, the sea, the sun,
    The winds, the woods, the clouds, the trees -
How feebly, if my youth were done,
    Could I, an old man, relish these!
With laughter, then, I'll go to greet
    What Fate has still in store for me,
And welcome Death if we should meet,
    And bear him willing company.

My share of fourscore years and ten
    I'll gladly yield to any man,
And take no thought of "where" or "when",
    Contented with my shorter span.
For I have learned what love may be,
    And found a heart that understands,
And known a comrade's constancy,
    And felt the grip of friendly hands.

Come when it may, the stern decree
    For me to leave the cheery throng
And quit the sturdy company
    Of brothers that I work among.
No need for me to look askance,
    Since no regret my prospect mars.
My day was happy - and perchance
    The coming night is full of stars.

SECOND LIEUTENANT ROBERT HAROLD BECKH
12th Battalion East Yorkshire Regiment
Born: 1st January 1894. Great Amwell, Hertfordshire.
Educated: Haileybury College.
 Jesus College, Cambridge.
Killed: 15th August 1916. Aged 22 years.
Cabaret-Rouge British Cemetery, Souchez, France.

Robert Beckh planned to become a clergyman and work in India if he survived the War. The Battalion arrived in France in March 1916 and went to trenches near Bertrancourt. That month Beckh wrote the following poem:

THE SONG OF SHEFFIELD

Shells, shells, shells!
 The song of the city of steel;
Hammer and turn, and file,
 Furnace, and lathe, and wheel.
 Tireless machinery,
 Man's ingenuity,
Making a way for the martial devil's meal.

Shells, shells, shells,
 Out of the furnace blaze;
Roll, roll, roll,
 Into the workshop's maze.
 Ruthless machinery
 Boring eternally,
Boring a hole for the shattering charge that stays.

Shells, shells, shells!
 The song of the city of steel;
List to the devils' mirth,
 Hark to their laughters' peal:
 Sheffield's machinery
 Crushing humanity
Neath devil-ridden death's impassive heel.

A week before he was killed there was a Battalion order 'A Patrol will leave tonight to examine gap in German wire at C15 b 8.2'. Beckh wrote 'No Man's Land' after reading the order:

NO MAN'S LAND

Nine-Thirty o'clock? Then over the top,
And mind to keep down when you see the flare
Of Very pistol searching the air.
Now, over you get; look out for the wire
In the borrow pit, and the empty tins,
They are meant for the Hun to bark his shins.
So keep well down and reserve your fire -
All over? Right : there's a gap just here
In the corkscrew wire, so just follow me;
If you keep well down there's nothing to fear.

. . . .

Then out we creep thro' the gathering gloom
Of NO MAN'S LAND, while the big guns boom
Right over our heads, and the rapid crack
Of the Lewis guns is answered back
By the German barking the same refrain
Of crack, crack, crack, all over again.

To the wistful eye from the parapet,
In the smiling sun of a summer's day,
'Twere a sin to believe that a bloody death
In those waving grasses lurking lay.
But now, 'neath the Very's fitful flares
"Keep still, my lads, and freeze like hares; -
All right, carry on, for we're out to enquire
If our friend the Hun's got a gap in his wire;
And he hasn't invited us out, you see,
So lift up your feet and follow me."

. . . .

Then, silent, we press with a noiseless tread
Thro' no man's land, but the sightless dead;
Aye, muffle your footsteps, well ye may,
For the mouldering corpses here decay
Whom no man owns but the King abhorred,
Grim Pluto, Stygia's over-lord.

Oh breathe a prayer for the sightless Dead
Who have bitten the dust 'neath the biting lead
Of the pitiless hail of the Maxim's fire,
'Neath the wash of shell in the well trod mire.
Ah well! But we've, too, got a job to be done,
For we've come to the wire of our friend, the Hun.
"Now, keep well down, lads; can you see any gap?

    . . . .

Not much, well the reference is wrong in the map"
So homeward we go thro' the friendly night.
That covers the NO MAN'S LAND from sight,
As muttering a noiseless prayer of praise,
We drop from the parapet into the bays.

On 14th August 1916 Robert Beckh wrote 'Billets'; next
evening at 10.30 p.m., Beckh and four soldiers were on patrol in the
Robecq area. They came to a strongly held position, were fired
upon, and retired. As they again approached the German lines, a
machine-gun opened fire and Beckh and one of his men were
killed.

BILLETS

Green fields that are scented and sweet,
God's sunshine, the air, and the trees;
Thy beauties we knew not before,
They were there, and who doubts them that sees?

But we, who bereft for a space
Of the joys that God meant us to share,
Have been living 'mid sandbags, and scorched
Without shade from the sun's ceaseless glare.

Great God! How to welcome the day
When the Trenches are left, and the trees
Promise hopes of a respite from heat,
And from breath-stifling odours release.

For how long? Just four days is the span:
And how fleeting yet heav'n born it seems -
Then again to the Trenches, our goal
And to plan for the Peace of our dreams.

CAPTAIN HUGH STEWART SMITH

'D' Company, 2nd Battalion Argyll and Sutherland Highlanders.

Born: 1889. Whitchurch, Oxfordshire.
Educated: Shrewsbury School.
          Corpus Christi College, Oxford.
Killed: 18th August 1916. Aged 27 years.
Caterpillar Valley Cemetery, Longueval, France.

Hugh Smith joined the Colonial Civil Service in 1912 and went to Northern Nigeria. He resigned his appointment as a District Officer early in 1915. He was commissioned in the Argyll and Sutherland Highlanders in April 1915 and joined the Battalion at the beginning of October in billets at Béthune.

In November 1915 Smith wrote 'Zita':

ZITA

Zita lives in a stricken farm,
And the soldiers see that she takes no harm.
Zita is fat and much alive
And her eyes are grey and her age is five.

Maman was killed by a German shell;
But memory treats all Zitas well;
And nobody squeals a squeal more gay
Than Zita when tickled by "Les Anglais."

And a cure for the whole sad war is mine,
Two short miles from the firing line;
For laughter's real and the war pretence,
In the scheme of Zita's common sense.

Cherie! Your health in Madame's red wine!
Give all tired eyes what you gave to mine!

THE INCORRIGIBLES
(Written from the Front to a Friend)

Keen through the shell-hole in my billet walls
The sad, dirge-laden wind of Flanders calls
(Hark! Ere the words are written, have replied

118

The rumblings of my supperless inside!)
Keen (as I think I said) the north wind bellows,
And makes me envy all you lucky fellows
Who quaff at ease your bitters and your gin
Before you put your grill-room dinners in. -
Spake one to me and prated how that all
In war was Glory, Triumph and Trumpet-call;
And said that Death, who stalked across the field,
But sowed, that Life a nobler crop might yield!
Poor Vapourer! for now I know that he
Was on the Staff or in the A.S.C.,
And in a well-manured hot-bed grew -
The ginger-bread is gilded but for few!
For us, foot-slogging sadly, it is clear
That War is fleas, short rations, watered beer,
Noise and mismanagement, bluster and foreboding,
Triumph but the sequel to enough exploding.
Yet like a ray across a storm-torn sea
Shines through it all the glint of Comedy,
And pompous Death, whose table they have messed at,
Has given the Men another butt to jest at!

The Battalion attacked the German trenches in High Wood at
2.45 p.m. on 18th August 1916 and was met by heavy machine-gun
fire and bombing. Hugh Smith was killed during this attack. Only
a few men managed to get into the German trenches and these were
eventually forced to come back to their own front line; in the end
the position was exactly the same as before the attack.

A piece of light verse was found in Hugh Smith's pocket book
after his death.

On the Plains of Picardy
Lay a soldier, dying
Gallantly, with soul still free
Spite the rough worlds' trying.
Came the Angel who keeps guard
When the fight has drifted,
"What would you for your reward
When the Clouds have lifted?"
Then the soldier through the mist
Heard the voice and rested
As a man who sees his home
When the hill is breasted -

This his answer and I vow
Nothing could be fitter -
Give me Peace, a dog, a friend
And a glass of bitter!

SECOND LIEUTENANT WILLIAM ERIC BERRIDGE

'C' Company, 6th Battalion Somerset Light Infantry.
Born: 3rd August 1894. Redhill, Surrey.
Educated: Eton College.
          New College, Oxford.
Died of Wounds: 20th August 1916. Aged 22 years.
Heilly Station Cemetery, Méricourt L'Abbé, France.

Eric Berridge joined the Oxford O.T.C. in October 1914, was commissioned in the Somerset Light Infantry two months later, and joined the Battalion at the front line trenches at Achicourt-Agny just south of Arras in March 1916.

MARCH 1916

As we wallow in mud-stricken trenches,
  And hark to the sound of the rain,
    Our thoughts fly away
    To localities gay;
We wish we were back there again;
  And we sigh for the frolicsome wenches,
    Who soothed our afflictions of old,
    As we sit in the mire
  And we long for a fire,
For our feet are infernally cold.

We've watched through the summer and winter
  That most inconsiderate Bosch;
    And again in the spring
    It's the very same thing -
And I'd give a blank cheque for a wash:
But, Chloe and fair Araminta,
  And Lalage, don't be afraid;
    Very shortly the Hun
    Will be seen on the run,
And the end will not be long delayed.

For I think very shortly the Kaiser
  Will know what we mean by a strafe:
    And he'll notice with pain
    That he cannot explain

His indisposition to laugh:
Then at last he'll be sadder and wiser,
When dawns the all-glorious day;
And the work will be done
When we know that we've won,
And we'll go back to England - to play.

TO A RAT
(Caught on a piece of wire in a communication
trench 4.45 a.m. April 1916).

Was it for this you came into the light?
Have you fulfilled Life's mission? You are free
For evermore from toil and misery,
Yet those who snared you, to their great delight,
Thought doubtless they were only doing right
In scheming to encompass your decease,
Forgetting they were bringing you to peace
And perfect joy and everlasting night.
Your course is ended here - I know not why
You seemed a loathsome, a pernicious creature;
You couldn't clothe us and we couldn't eat yer,
And so we mocked your humble destiny -
Yet life was merry, was it not, oh rat?
It must have been to one so sleek and fat.

On 4th June 1916, the Battalion diaries recorded that part of the trenches were "completely flattened out." The next day Berridge wrote in a letter:

As I wandered round the kitchen this morning about 7 a.m., I was presented by the Cook with a large cup of tea and the information that it was his forty-eighth birthday - hence the enclosed. They call him 'Primus' because he uses a Primus stove.

A LA SANTE DU CHEF

As through the maze of trenches
We, war-worn, weary, trudge,
With appetite expectant we
Remember Private Rudge.

To see him at his labours,
No one would ever judge
That eight and forty summers have
Been seen by Private Rudge.

Last night they strafed the kitchen, but
He didn't care a fudge;
Until the cheese was toasted well,
He simply wouldn't budge.

His labours are unceasing, and
He never bears a grudge;
So one and all unite in praise
Of Private Primus Rudge.

On the first day of the Battle of the Somme the 6th Battalion held front line trenches in the Blangy area east of Arras, which was a quiet sector. At the beginning of August the Battalion moved to the Somme area and camped on a hill overlooking Albert about five or six miles from the firing line.

On 12th August 1916 the 6th Battalion was sent to relieve the Lancashire Fusiliers in the front line trenches in Delville Wood which was then held partly by the British and partly by the Germans. 'The Devil's Wood' before it was attacked four weeks previously had been thick with leafy trees and dense under growth. "As the Battle progressed the wood was totally ravaged and the ground became littered with broken branches and tangled masses of bushes. The whole area was pock-marked with shell-holes, which both sides had turned as far as possible into posts and machine-gun nests, intersected here and there by trenches and what had been roads through the Wood. It was a terrible place over which to fight."

The History of the Somerset Light Infantry recorded:

...The stench from the decaying dead was awful, gas fumes hung about the shell holes and clung to the undergrowth, weird and ghostly in the semi-darkness were the gaunt long arms of the torn and blasted trees or all that remained of them. The uncertainty of the whereabouts of the German trenches kept the nerves of both officers and men at high tension...

During the night of the 12th/13th August the Battalion sent patrols out in the wood to discover the enemy's position. The Somersets had the best of two encounters with German patrols. The Battalion was relieved on the evening of the 14th and returned to the support trenches in front of Montauban Alley. However, on the nights of the 15th and 16th August the Battalion still had to provide working parties of 250 men to dig in the wood all night.

On 18th August all four companies of the 6th Battalion moved from Montauban to assembly positions in the south east corner of Delville Wood with orders to attack the German line along the north east edge, and German trenches to the east of Delville Wood.

At 6 a.m. on 19th the preliminary bombardment opened on Beer Trench and Hop Alley and continued all morning. At 2.45 p.m. the attacking troops advanced across No Man's Land following the creeping barrage and into the German trenches bayonetting or shooting down all those who refused to surrender.

Eric Berridge was commanding 'C' Company, and their objective to capture Hop Alley was the most difficult of all that day. The bombers established a post at the junction of the Alley with Beer Trench, but at the western end of the Alley where it joined with Delville Wood, there were two German machine-guns in a sap. 'C' Company eventually broke through the heavy trench mortar barrage and Berridge was the first to reach the enemy trench, where he was mortally wounded by a sniper; he died the following day. Ninety Germans were killed and a few prisoners taken.

In the evening the Germans opened their counter attack and all along the line snipers were very active. By night fall the German artillery had the newly won British trenches in range and heavily bombarded the 6th Battalion working to consolidate their position. After repulsing two determined German counter-attacks, the Battalion was relieved and sent to billets at Fricourt. The Regiment's casualties during the week were five officers killed and seven wounded; forty-eight other ranks had been killed and 220 wounded.

During the bombardment before the attack on 18th August Berridge wrote in a letter home:

I am writing this in the midst of a din which you can and probably do hear on the Leas... I enclose my most recent spasm, only half an hour old, which you had better revise and set to music! I fear the whole idea of it is very hackneyed and wants more careful working out...

1916

HYMN

God, wheresoe'er Thou may'st be found
   And Whosoe'er Thou art,
Grant in the Scheme of Things that we
   May play a worthy part;
And give, to help us on the way,
   An all-enduring heart.

We know Thou watchest from above
   This fantasy of woe;
And, whatsoever pain or loss
   We here may undergo,
Let us in this be comforted -
   None from Thy sight can go.

Sometimes in folly we upon
   Thy Name profanely call,
And grumble at our destiny
   Because our minds are small,
And so we cannot understand
   The Mind that ruleth all.

Grant us to see and learn and know
   The Greatness of Thy Will,
That each one his allotted task
   May grapple with, until
We hear at last Thy Perfect Voice
   Bidding us "Peace, be still."

LIEUTENANT CYRIL WILLIAM WINTERBOTHAM

'C' Company, 1st/5th Battalion Gloucestershire Regiment.
Born: 27th February 1887.
Educated: Cheltenham College.
           Lincoln College, Oxford.
Killed: 27th August 1916. Aged 29 years.
Thiepval Memorial to the Missing, near Albert, France.

    Cyril Winterbotham was called to the Bar in 1911 and adopted as prospective Liberal Candidate for East Gloucestershire in September 1913.

    In October 1914 Winterbotham was commissioned in the 1st/5th Battalion Gloucestershire Regiment. He served in France between March 1915 and August 1916. The Battalion was in trenches at Hébuterne, north of Albert, over Christmas 1915. Winterbotham wrote:

A CHRISTMAS PRAYER FROM THE TRENCHES

Not yet for us may Christmas bring
    Good-will to men, and peace;
In our dark sky no angels sing,
    Nor yet the great release
    For men, when war shall cease.

So must the guns our carols make,
    Our gifts must bullets be,
For us no Christmas bells shall see
    These ruined homes shall see
    No Christmas revelry.

In hardened hearts we fain would greet
    The Babe at Christmas born,
But lo, He comes with piercèd feet,
    Wearing a crown of thorn, -
    His side a spear has torn.

For tired eyes are all too dim,
    Our hearts too full of pain,

Our ears too deaf to hear the hymn
  Which angels sing in vain,
"The Christ is born again."

  O Jesus, pitiful, draw near,
    That even we may see
  The Little Child who knew not fear;
    Thus would we picture Thee
    Unmarred by agony.

  O'er death and pain triumphant yet
    Bid Thou Thy harpers play,
  That we may hear them, and forget
    Sorrow and all dismay,
    And welcome thee to stay
    With us on Christmas Day.

Some of Winterbotham's poems were published in the Battalion magazine, *5th Gloucester Gazette*, which was produced in the trenches.

O.C. PLATOON ENQUIRIES

I once had a lovely platoon, Sir,
The finest platoon ever seen,
They could drill 'neath the sun, or the moon, Sir,
They were fit, and their rifles were clean.

They could march, and they knew how to shoot, Sir,
And to bayonet sacks upon sticks,
Equipped from the cap to the boot, Sir,
- Their number was fifty and six.

They were infantry right to the core, Sir,
They trusted in bullets and steel
To finish the terrible war, Sir,
- It bucked them all up a good deal.

But as soon as we landed in France, Sir,
Such terrible changes began
That hardly a man had a chance, Sir,
Of being an Infantry man.

For some for the transport have left, Sir
And one cuts up beef for the Staff,
And others, of whom I'm bereft, Sir,
Mend trousers that suffer from "STRAFE."

There are some who are Sanit'ry men, Sir,
- (We tread upon dubious paths) -
And some became sappers, and then, Sir,
They lived among boilers and baths.

The M.G.0. pinched a few more, Sir,
- And blood-thirsty beggars they be -
They're especially out for the gore, Sir,
Of Huns that are carrying Tea.

One's running a photograph show, Sir,
Another is making a map,
There are servants and grooms, one or two, Sir,
They all leave a bit of a gap.

There are some who are Officers now, Sir,
While others wield clippers and shave,
There are bandsmen all under a vow, Sir,
To hearten the steps of the brave.

The few that remain use the bomb, Sir,
Proficient in anarchist lore
They handle H.E. with aplomb, Sir,
I look on with obvious awe.

If my men are all details am I, Sir,
A detail myself! and if so,
Am I O.C. Platoon still, and why, Sir,
Is what I should just like to know.

In the middle of July 1916 the Battalion moved south from Hébuterne to Bouzincourt and took part in the Battle for Bazentin Ridge. On 14th August it was at Ovillers - La Boiselle and on the 16th Winterbotham assumed command of 'C' Company. The Battalion was ordered to attack a trench near Ovillers on 27th August. A three minute intensive barrage was directed on the German position, and Cyril Winterbotham led his men into the trench during the bombardment. During the attack several dugouts were bombed and in spite of considerable opposition the enemy were eventually forced to retire over open ground and the trench was taken. 200 Germans were killed or wounded, 50 taken prisoner and one machine-gun captured. Cyril Winterbotham was one of 4 officers and 14 other ranks who were killed. A month before, during July 1916, he wrote:

THE CROSS OF WOOD

God be with you and us who go our way
And leave you dead upon the ground you won;
For you at last the long fatigue is done,
The hard march ended, you have rest to-day.

You were our friends, with you we watched the dawn
Gleam through the rain of the long winter night,
With you we laboured till the morning light
Broke on the village, shell-destroyed and torn.

Not now for you the glorious return
To steep Strand valleys, to the Severn leas
By Tewkesbury and Gloucester, or the trees
Of Cheltenham under high Cotswold stern.

For you no medals such as others wear -
A cross of bronze for those approved brave -
To you is given, above a shallow grave,
The Wooden Cross that marks you resting there.

Rest you content, more honourable far
Than all the Orders is the Cross of Wood,
The symbol of self-sacrifice that stood
Bearing the God whose brethren you are.

LIEUTENANT THOMAS MICHAEL KETTLE

9th Battalion Royal Dublin Fusiliers.

Born: 9th February 1880. Artane, County Dublin.

Educated: Clongowes Wood College.

University College, Dublin.

Killed: 9th September 1916. Aged 36 years.

Thiepval Memorial to the Missing, near Albert, France.

Tom Kettle was the third son of Andrew J. Kettle, a prosperous farmer and eminent land reformer. Andrew Kettle, a friend and supporter of Charles Stewart Parnell, was a founder member of the Land League.

Kettle entered University College in 1897; among his contemporaries were Oliver St. John Gogarty, James Joyce, Richard Sheehy and Francis Skeffington. Kettle became a gifted and forceful orator at the University's Literary and Historical Society, but in 1900 he left University College because of ill health. After travelling abroad he returned and gained his degree in 1902 and was admitted into the Honourable Society of King's Inns to read Law in January 1903. Later that year he became a founder member and first President of the Young Ireland Branch of the United Irish League. The following year he turned down a suggestion by John Redmond that he should stand for Parliament, but in 1905 he became joint editor with Francis Skeffington of *The Nationist,* 'a weekly review of Irish thought and affairs'. In his editorial column Kettle stated that his vision was for national independence and not just for Home Rule.

Kettle's friendliness and charm embraced a wide circle of Irishmen from all walks of life. In 1906 he was called to the Bar and adopted by East Tyrone as their parliamentary candidate. In his acceptance speech he outlined the programme of the Irish Party which he said took account of every social injustice and stood for 'nationality and democracy'. "It makes appeal not to the class interest of a few selfish reactionaries but to the mass of the people of all Ireland, whatever their religion..." His own objectives were the mastery and management of Irish affairs; the complete emancipation of tenants from landlords; adequate accommodation and acceptable standards of living for the labourers; a fair educational system for every child, and the abolition of any religious dominance. At the election in July 1906 Kettle won by eighteen votes.

After he returned from a five month visit to America on behalf
of the United Irish League he made his maiden speech in the House
of Commons in May 1907. A born orator, using only a few notes,
he was compared to the other great speakers of the day - Asquith,
Balfour and John Redmond. A contemporary said of him: "Wit and
humour, denunciation and appeal, paradox and epigram, gave point
and effect to his fluent speeches. Tall and straight, with his soft
handsome boyish face and bright eyes, he first startled and then
compelled the attention of the House by his irresistible charm and
luminous argument." He continued to speak for the oppressed and
under privileged and strongly criticised British imperial
administration. When he was not at Westminster, Kettle travelled
and spoke all over Ireland and took the occasional legal brief.

In 1909 Kettle married Mary Sheehy; one of her sisters, Hanna,
was married to Francis Skeffington and the other, Kathleen,
married Francis Cruise O'Brien in 1911. A few weeks after his
marriage, Kettle was appointed Professor of National Economics at
Dublin University.   After the General Election in 1910, when
Kettle increased his majority by 140 votes, the Liberals were
returned to Westminster with a reduced majority and needed the
support of the Irish Nationalist Party. Kettle delivered a number of
powerful major speeches. He supported the suffragette movement
and spoke again on the subject of Home Rule:

> For our part, whatever flag goes down in this constitutional struggle, it
> will not be the flag of Ireland. Governments come and governments
> go, majorities crumble away, parliaments and ministers pass into
> oblivion. We in Ireland stand where we have stood. We are willing
> as regards this country to offer and accept friendship founded upon
> international justice, but so long as you maintain the present system
> which sacrifices Irish interests to English ignorance, so far as you
> deprive Ireland of a voice in the shaping of her own economic destiny,
> so long you will have the undying hostility of the great part of the
> people of Ireland.

In November 1910 Kettle resigned his seat at Westminster as he
found it impossible to combine the duties of Professor and
Parliamentarian, but he continued to be politically active making
speeches and writing articles. In April 1912 the Home Rule Bill
was introduced in the House of Commons.   Supporting the Bill,
Kettle said:

It will attract about itself the sanction and the prestige of success. It will grow by its own inherent vitality; and, looking to the future, I see this from the first as a great bill; I see it accepted heartily and worked intelligently for the benefit of all. I see minorities respected, I see every subordinate class coming to its own after the national freedom has been attained. At the end of it I see an Ireland completely controlling her political life taking her place, as she shall be able to take it, in the human tradition of Europe, and be welcomed amongst the nations of the earth.

The Irish Volunteers were formed in November 1913, and Kettle was one of the first prominent men to be identified with the group. In an article written for *The Daily News* he said:

... In no country is the red barbarism of war as a solvent of differences more fully recognised than in Ireland. In no other is the wastage of the public substance on vast armaments more strongly condemned on grounds alike of conscience and intelligence. If Ireland has a distingushed military tradition, she has another tradition to which she holds more proudly, that of peace and culture... She never oppressed or sought to destroy another nation. What she proposes to herself now is not to browbeat or dragoon or diminish by violence the civil or religious liberty of any man - but simply to safeguard her own.

Kettle suffered increasingly from ill health brought on by depression and bouts of heavy drinking. He went for treatment and returned to the University early in 1914. When war was declared he was in Belgium buying arms for the Volunteers; he stayed on there as war correspondent for *The Daily News*.

... The élan of Belgium takes possession of you. The courage and anguish of this glorious little nation, fighting now for its very life, stir one to something like the clear mood of its own heroism. In every direction there opens a vista of waste and suffering. Already the long trail of wounded has begun to wind its sorrowful way back to the capital. Prisoners arrive, too simple of aspect, one would think, to be the instruments by which Europe is to be tortured to the pattern of a new devilry...

The great outstanding pinnacle of a fact is, perhaps the definitive entrance of England into the comity of Europe. Regret it or not, there can be no more isolation. And the other fact, noted here also as of main importance, is the attitude of Ireland. Mr. Redmond's proffer of friendship, in return for justice, had been made often before, but never in such dramatic circumstances. I am appalled to hear rumours to the effect that Sir Edward Carson proposes at this moment to force Mr. Bonar Law to bedevil the whole situation by a political trick. He actually proposes, one hears, that a course should be followed depriving Ireland of the Home Rule Bill, which is coming to her automatically by the mere efflux of a few weeks. Can such madness still be possible? Is there any imagination left in England?

Here, at the opening of this vast and bloody epic, Great Britain is right with the conscience of Europe. It is assumed that she has reconciled Ireland. A reconciled Ireland is ready to march side by side with her to any desperate trial...

On his return to Ireland in November 1914, Kettle volunteered for active service but with his oratorical gifts and position as a Nationalist he was commissioned in the Dublin Fusiliers and sent all over the country as a recruiting spokesman. There were many opponents to Ireland's support of the Allies and Francis Skeffington, Kettle's pacifist brother-in-law, was prominent in the anti-recruiting campaign. Even though the Home Rule Bill had received Royal Assent in September 1914, a Suspensory Act was passed halting its implementation until after the war; inevitably, unrest in Ireland continued.

On Easter Monday 1916, a group of Irish Volunteers rose in rebellion on the streets of Dublin. Francis Skeffington was arrested, held without charge, and shot in the back in the prison yard. His murder deeply affected Kettle who wrote of him:

... He, who turned away from soldiers, left to all soldiers an example of courage in death to which there are not many parallels...

Three months later Kettle left Dublin and sailed for France.

ON LEAVING IRELAND (JULY 14th 1916)

As the sun died in blood, and hill and sea
Grew to an altar, red with mystery,
One came who knew me (it may be over-much)
Seeking the cynical and staining touch,
But I, against the great sun's burial
Thought only of bayonet-flash and bugle-call
And saw him as God's eye upon the deep,
Closed in the dream in which no women weep,
And knew that even I shall fall on sleep.

After he arrived in France, Tom Kettle was in trenches in the Posen Crater area and wrote to his wife on 24th July 1916:

... This is the afternoon of my second day in the fire trench. My ears are becoming a little more accustomed to the diabolism of sound, but it remains terrible beyond belief. This morning as I was shaving, the enemy began to find us and dropped aerial torpedoes, shells and a mine right on top of our dug-out. Nobody was hurt, thank God. The strain is terrible. It continues from hour to hour and minute to minute. It is indeed an ordeal to which human nature itself is hardly equal. What impresses and moves me above all is the amazing faith, patience and courage of the men. To me it is not a sort of looking-down-on but rather a looking-up-to appreciation of them. I pray and pray and am afraid! - they go quietly and heroically on. God bless them and make me less inferior to them...

Later, from billets at Mazingarbe near Loos, he wrote an essay, 'Silhouettes from the Front':

In the trenches it is the day-by-dayness that tells and tries. It is always the same tone of duty: certain days in billets, certain days in reserve, certain days in the front trench... But this nibbling process works both ways. We nibble; they nibble. They are nibbled; we are nibbled. A few casualties every turn, another grating of the saw-teeth of death and disease, and before very long a strong unit is weak. And, of course, the nerve-strain is not slight. Everybody going up to the trenches from the C.O. down to the last arrival in the last draft knows it to be moral certainty that there are two or three that will not march back. Everybody knows that it may be anybody. In the trenches death is random, illogical, devoid of principle. One is shot not on sight, but on blindness, out of sight ... There is much to nibble the nerves...

... Over there in front across No Man's Land there are shell-holes and unburied men. Strange things happen there. Patrols and counter-patrols come and go. There are two sinister fences of barbed wire, on the barbs of which blood-stained strips of uniform and fragments more sinister have been known to hang uncollected for a long time. The air is shaken with diabolical reverberations; it is stabbed with malign illumination as the Very lights shoot up, broaden to a blaze, and go out. This contrast of night and light and gloom is trying to the eyes. The rifle-grenades and trench-mortars, flung at short range, that scream through the air are trying to the ears...

... Ratavia, as one may designate it, resembles China in that there has never been a census of its population, but that it approximates to the mathematical infinite. They are everywhere - large rats, small rats, bushy rats, shy rats and impudent, with their malign whiskers, their obscene eyes, loathsome all the way from over-lapping teeth to kangaroo tail. You see them on the parados and the shelter-roofs at night, slinking along on their pestiferous errands. You lie in your dug-out, famished, not for food (that goes without saying), but for sleep, and hear them scurrying up and down their shafts, nibbling at what they find, dragging scraps of old newspapers along, with intolerable cracklings, to bed themselves. They scurry across your blankets and your very face. Nothing suppresses their numbers. Not dogs smuggled in in breach of regulations. Not poison, which most certainly ought not to be used. Not the revolver-practice in which irritated subalterns have been known to indulge. Men die and rats increase...

At the beginning of August the Battalion was in the Hulluch sector; Kettle wrote to his wife on the 10th August:

... If God spares me I shall accept it as a special mission to preach love and peace for the rest of my life. If He does not, I know now in my heart that for anyone who is dead but who has loved enough, there is provided some way of piercing the veils of death and abiding close to those whom he has loved till that end which is the beginning.

I want to live, too, to use all my powers of thinking, writing and working to drive out of civilization this foul thing called War and to put in its place understanding and comradeship...

At the end of August 1916 the Irish Brigade was sent to the Somme. On 3rd September, from bivouacs at Billon Farm, Kettle wrote his political testament with instructions that it should be published if he was killed:

Had I lived I had meant to call my next book on the relations of Ireland and England: *The Two Fools: A Tragedy of Errors*. It has needed all the folly of England and all the folly of Ireland to produce the situation in which our unhappy country is now involved.

I have mixed much with Englishmen and with Protestant Ulstermen, and I know that there is no real or abiding reason for the gulfs, salter than the sea, that now dismember the natural alliance of both of them with us Irish Nationalists. It needs only a Fiat Lux, of a kind very easily compassed, to replace the unnatural by the natural.

In the name, and by the seal of the blood given in the last two years, I ask for Colonial Home Rule for Ireland - a thing essential in itself and essential as a prologue to the reconstruction of the Empire. Ulster will agree.

And I ask for the immediate withdrawal of martial law in Ireland, and an amnesty for all Sinn Fein prisoners. If this war has taught us anything it is that great things can be done only in a great way.

The next day, the 4th September, the Battalion was at Carnoy and Kettle wrote the following poem:

TO MY DAUGHTER BETTY, THE GIFT OF GOD

> In wiser days, my darling rosebud, blown
> To beauty proud as was your mother's prime,
> In that desired, delayed, incredible time,
> You'll ask why I abandoned you, my own,
> And the dear heart that was your baby throne,
> To dice with death. And oh! they'll give you rhyme
> And reason: some will call the thing sublime,
> And some decry it in a knowing tone.
> So here, while the mad guns curse overhead,
> And tired men sigh with mud for couch and floor,
> Know that we fools, now with the foolish dead,
> Died not for flag, nor King, nor Emperor,
> But for a dream, born in a herdsman's shed,
> And for the secret Scripture of the poor.

On the night of 5th September Kettle, and Lieutenant James Emmet Dalton marched in pouring rain with their troops to a new position at Trones Wood, near Guillemont. Dalton wrote:

... I was with Tom when we advanced to the position that night, and the stench of the dead that covered our road was so awful that we both used some foot-powder on our faces. When we reached our objective we dug ourselves in...

Seven officers and two hundred men from the 9th Battalion were killed on 7th September. Kettle took over command of 'B' Company and during the night the Battalion dug assembly trenches for the attack on Ginchy which was to take place on the 9th September. In a last letter to his wife, Kettle wrote:

... The long-expected is now close to hand. I was at Mass and Communion this morning at 6 o.c., the camp is broken up, and the column is about to move. It is no longer indiscreet to say that we are to take part in one of the biggest attacks of the war. Many will not come back.

Should that be God's design for me you will not receive this letter until afterwards. I want to thank you for the love and kindness you spent and all but wasted on me. There was never in all the world a dearer woman or a more perfect wife and adorable mother. My heart cries for you and Betty whom I may never see again. I think even that it is perhaps better that I should not see you again.

God bless and keep you! If the last sacrifice is ordained think that in the end I wiped out all the old stains. Tell Betty her daddy was a soldier and died as one. My love, now at last clean will find a way to you...

At the same time, Kettle wrote to a friend and to his brother:

... So you see, even I have no particular certainty of coming back. I passed through, as everybody of sense does, a sharp agony of separation... Now it is almost over and I feel calm. I hope to come back. If not, I believe that to sleep here in the France I have loved is no harsh fate, and that so passing out into the silence, I shall help towards the Irish settlement...

... If I live I mean to spend the rest of my life working for perpetual peace. I have seen war and faced modern artillery, and know what an outrage it is against simple men...

We are moving up to-night into the battle of the Somme. The bombardment, destruction and bloodshed are beyond all imagination, nor did I ever think the valour of simple men could be quite as beautiful as that of my Dublin Fusiliers... I have had two chances of leaving them - one on sick leave and one to take a staff job. I have chosen to stay with my comrades... I am calm and happy, but desperately anxious to live...

PADDY
(After Mr. Kipling)

I went into the talkin' shop to see about the Bill;
The Premier 'e ups and says: "We're waitin'... waitin' still!"
The Tories grinned, and Balfour strung our gamble Haman-high,
I outs into the street again, and to meself sez I:
O, it's Paddy this, and Paddy that, an'
"A cattle-driven crew!"
But 'twas "Murphy o' the Munsters!"
When the trump of battle blew.

When the wind of battle blew, my boys,
When the blast of battle blew,
It was Burke, and Shea and Kelly when
We marched to Waterloo.

I looked into a newspaper to see about the land
That bred the man who broke the sin that Bonaparte planned;
They'd room for cricket scores, and tips, and trash of every kind,
But when I asked of Ireland's cause, it seemed to be behind.
For it's Paddy this, and Paddy that, and
"Don't annoy us, please!"
But it's "Irish Rifles forward - Fast!"
When the bullets talk like bees,
When the bullets yawn like bees, my boys,
When the bullets yawn like bees,
It's "Connaught blood is good enough"
When they're chanting R.I.P's.

Yes! Sneerin' round at Irishmen, and Irish speech and ways,
Is cheaper - much - than snatchin' guns from battle's red amaze:
And when the damned Death's-Head-Dragoons roll up the ruddy
     tide
The Times won't spare a Smith to tell how Dan O'Connell died.
For it's Paddy this, and Paddy that, and
"The Fifth'll prate and prance!"
But it's "Corks and Inniskillings -
Front!" when Hell is loose in France,
When Clare and Kerry take the call that
Crowns the shrapnel dance,
O, it's "Find the Dublin Fusiliers!"
When Hell is loose in France.

We ain't no saints or scholars much, but
Fightin' men and clean,
We've paid the price, and three times
Thrice for Wearin' o' the Green.
We held our hand out frank and fair, and
Half forgot Parnell,
For Ireland's hope and England's too -
And it's yours to save or sell.
For it's Paddy this, and Paddy that,
"Who'll stop the Uhlan blade?"

But Tommy Fitz from Malahide, and
Monaghan's McGlade,
When the ranks are set for judgment,
Lads, and the roses droop and fade,
It's "Ireland in the firin' line!" when the
Price of God is paid.

At 4.45 p.m. on 9th September the attack began with a heavy artillery barrage; a few minutes later the first Irish soldiers reached the village of Ginchy. James Dalton wrote:

... I was just behind Tom when we went over the top. He was in a bent position and a bullet got over a steel waistcoat that he wore and entered his heart. Well, he only lasted about one minute, and he had my crucifix in his hands. Then Boyd took all the papers and things out of Tom's pockets in order to keep them for Mrs. Kettle, but poor Boyd was blown to atoms in a few minutes. The Welsh Guards buried Mr. Kettle's remains...

LIEUTENANT RAYMOND ASQUITH

3rd Battalion Grenadier Guards.

Born: 6th November 1878. Hampstead, London.
Educated: Winchester College.
  Balliol College, Oxford.
Killed: 15th September 1916. Aged 37 years.
Guillemont Road Cemetery, France.

Raymond Asquith was the eldest son of Herbert Henry Asquith and Helen Melland. Four more children were born between 1881 and 1890; during these years H.H. Asquith gained a considerable reputation as a Barrister, became a Member of Parliament, and Prime Minister in 1908.

When Raymond Asquith was thirteen his mother died suddenly of typhoid; three years later his father married Margot Tennant. After Winchester Asquith went up to Balliol in October 1897, successively won all the major University prizes, and "was beyond doubt the most remarkable figure of his Oxford generation."

In 1902 Asquith gained a First in Classical Moderations, Greats and Law. The same year he was elected a Fellow of All Souls College. After he left Balliol he became a barrister and in the summer of 1907 married Katherine Horner, the daughter of Sir John and Lady Horner of Mells Park, Frome, in Somerset. The Asquith's first child was born in 1908; their second daughter in 1910, and their son in April 1916, five months before his father was killed.

Between June and September 1910 Raymond Asquith was at the International Court at The Hague, involved in an arbitration case between England and the United States concerning Newfoundland fisheries; in 1913 he was adopted as prospective Liberal candidate for Derby, and the following year was appointed a Junior Counsel to the Inland Revenue.

At the end of December 1914 Raymond, his younger brother Cyril (Cis) and Harold Macmillan joined the Queen's Westminster Rifles. His two youngest brothers also joined up; Herbert (Beb) was commissioned in the Royal Marine Artillery, later transferring to the Royal Field Artillery, and served in France. Arthur (Oc) joined the Royal Naval Division on its formation and served with the Anson and then the Hood Battalions with Rupert Brooke and Patrick Shaw Stewart (qv).

In July 1915 Asquith transferred to the 3rd Battalion Grenadier

Guards and on 25th October he joined the Battalion in billets at Norrent Fontes, south east of St. Omer about twenty miles behind the line. Two days later he wrote to Lady Diana Manners:

... This war is a pure convention, like debates in the House of Commons, the birthday honours, and all other public (and most private) events. Usually there is a hell of a din here of big guns, today absolute calm. Why? because the King is at the front and they don't want a damned noise when he is there. Why have a damned noise at all, whether he is here or not? Pure convention. In the old days when we had no shells everyone wanted a noise but now we all know there are masses of shells, so why let them off?...

I think you would love being in billets here; there is a sort of strangeness about it that would appeal to you. Two or three rather muddy officers in the parlour of a French cottage and a few faithful servants, very like soldier servants in books, playing with the women in broken French in the kitchen next door, being sweet to children and making terrible smells with onions: out-side big guns booming at a safe distance, dispatch riders, ambulances, etc., rattling over the pavé, in fact all the minor nonsense of war...

On 8th November the Battalion arrived at new billets at La Gorgue, about five miles behind the line, and on the 11th Asquith wrote: "We continue our lap-dog experience here, eating far too much cake and taking far too little exercise."

In cold weather on 14th November the Battalion went into "disgustingly wet and muddy and rather ruinous" trenches just north of Neuve Chapelle. Asquith wrote to his wife on the 16th:

... We marched into the trenches on Sunday evening by a rather circuitous route - about 7 miles I should think, and it took us over 4 hours as the last part was very slow going. About 6 p.m. we reached a ruined village on the road where we halted and put on our trench boots - long rubber things which go almost up to one's waist, but none too long. It was a fine frosty night with a moon and stars. There we picked up our guides and made our way by platoons across open country to our various positions. The point where we left the road was about 1 1/2 miles from the trenches and the communication trenches by which we were supposed to go up were so full of water and mud that we had to go across the top of the open country instead - a wide flat expanse of dead grass elaborately intersected by the flooded communication trenches...

I got in about 8 p.m., but it was nearly 10 before the whole company was in. We set to work digging and draining at once and worked all night. I constantly got lost in the labyrinth both below ground and above. I had a tot of hot rum about 3 a.m, which made the whole difference. We worked away all yesterday and are at it again; tonight the trench will be a very tolerable one. I have a small but dry dug-out in which I got 3 hours sleep last night. It freezes hard in the night and early morning but luckily we have had no rain, and every now and then at irregular intervals Needham [Asquith's soldier servant] brings me a bowl of turtle soup which he seems to think a diet appropriate to the situation in which we find ourselves.

The support trenches are usually more shelled than the fire trenches because there is less risk of the gunners hitting their own men, but we have fared very well in this respect, as the Boches are directing most of their fire at roads in our rear. One shell lighted a short way behind us and spattered me with mud but as I was already thickly coated with it I bore no malice. Shelling, rifle and machine gun fire go on spasmodically all day and all night, but we have had only 2 men killed and about a dozen wounded in the whole battalion: these were shot by snipers while digging in front of the line at night...

From these trenches Asquith wrote to Lady Diana Manners on 19th November:

... An unpleasant feature is the vast number of rats which gnaw the dead bodies and then run about on one's face making obscene noises and gestures. Lately a certain number of cats have taken to nesting in the corpses but I think the rats will get them under in the end; though like all wars it will doubtless be a war of attrition.

The trenches are so filthy that there is a temptation, hard to resist, even by the most lily-livered, to walk about on the top of them instead of the bottom. One has to remind oneself that Mr. Don't-Care was eaten by lions. Rifle bullets, as long as they don't come in great numbers, are rather exciting than alarming; shells, I believe, can be terrifying but so far only rather ill-aimed ones have come my way and no one pays much attention to them. The noise is rather irritating and pointless...

On 26th November the Battalion marched from billets at Laventie to about a mile behind the firing line. On 1st December Asquith, who was in command of a platoon, wrote to his wife:

... I had my first experience of aimed shell-fire yesterday: previously anything which happened to burst near one had simply been a bad shot at something else, but yesterday morning the Boches made a dead set at my little fortress and the road immediately in front of it and fired shrapnel at us for an hour between 9.30 - 10.30 a.m. My redoubt was built of sandbags, not cut deep into the earth as a trench would be in dry country and only too often is in wet, and if they had fired high explosives they would have made us look very silly; but with good narrow breastwork shrapnel is not frightening. The net result of about 100 shells was one of my men wounded not seriously. I had a guard of a corporal and 6 men in a ruined building on the far side of a road about 30 yards from my redoubt and they burst one shell right over the roof of the building throwing up a great cloud of dust and mortar and broken tiles. I made sure that the guard must have suffered severely but when I went over to see found that none of them had been touched. We shelled the enemy heavily yesterday and again today, I hope with more effect...

Just before he went on leave for ten days Asquith wrote to Lady Diana Manners on 26th December 1915:

... I cannot help talking a little trench shop to you now and then, just as you could not help talking hospital shop to all of us. Every now and then the purely scenic effects are so good, not really good, but operatic and sentimental, that I feel sure you would enjoy them if you were here. Shelling and counter-shelling - especially in the dark - quite comes up to Christmas number standards. The odd thing is that as a method of killing people, it somehow just fails to come off - aims at a million and misses a unit almost every time, but misses it, as far as one can judge, by inches only. Red and yellow flame and tall columns of dirt and smoke and sand-bags fly into the air all round you; clods of earth fall upon your neck, the nose-cap of the shell whizzes over your head with a noise of a thousand bad harmoniums played at once by a maniac, and the most respectable soldiers look too idiotically serious for words, while the most disreputable ones shout with laughter and pour out a stream of obscene jokes. You think at first that everybody in the trench must be dead except yourself and after the thing is over you find that 2 men are slightly wounded. Every now and then you pop your head over the parapet to see whether your shells are doing any damage to the Boches, and you see a line of terrific volcanoes bursting out at intervals of 5 yards all along the German line, but if you keep your head up for half a minute a 100 bullets whistle past it at once, showing that the Germans are suffering even less than you are...

Raymond Asquith returned to his Battalion on the 10th January 1916 and immediately found himself designated 'Prisoner's Friend', counsel for the defence, at the Court-Martial of two Scots Guards officers accused of allowing their men to fraternise with the enemy on Christmas Day. Asquith described one of the officers,

Captain Sir Iain Colquhoun of Luss, as a man of "exceptional dash and courage... A perfect man of his type - insolent, languid, fearless..."

Through his father's influence, but against his own wishes, Asquith was sent as an Intelligence Officer to General Headquarters at Montreuil, at the end of January. After four weeks "among the bottle-washers and boot-boys of the staff" he wrote to Katherine on 28th February 1916:

> ... the days here seem as long as the nights used to seem in the trenches - more comfortable but if possible more dull. How I loathe the war. I can't think of anything to do now except write an epic poem bringing in the names of all the railway stations in Belgium...

> Liquid fire and poison gas
> Leave the German where he was.
> Obviously, if we can,
> We must find a bolder plan.
> Why not then invoke the Muse?
> Surely conscience bids us use
> (Since we're fighting for the Right)
> *Every* form of Schrecklichkeit.
> Then, I ask you, why not try
> The magic power of poesy?
> After all the thing's been done;
> Goethe was a bloody Hun.
> Why not in the last resort
> Versify the Train Report?
> I know it's going rather far,
> But - anything to win the war.
> Only insignificant
> Traffic passed from Bruges to Ghent;
> But the line from Ghent to Bruges
> Is quite another pair of shoes.
> Masses of marines (with guns)
> Suspiciously resembling Huns
> (So an agent we employ
> Says - a 'personne digne de foi')
> 40 trains of infantry
> Clothed in grey (surprisingly),
> 90 wagons, men or horses;
> -(So we learn from other sources)-
> How I wonder which they are,

1916

Men or horses, Wallinger?
"Non-éclairés" probably;
But, Oh the difference to me!
Kitchens and pontoons galore -
Looks uncommon like a corps -
Bless me, what can this portend?
Are they going to Ostend?
No, they merely use this line
To conceal their real design.
They are moving troops from Ghent
To the Ypres Salient,
And I haven't any doubt
We shall trace them to Thourout
And (when the returns come in)
Very likely to Menin.
The reports from Gemmenich
Are fit to make a fellow sick
"Fantassins, Artillerie
Graviers, Pierrerie"
By this line they seem to bring
Every kind of bloody thing.
Welkenraedt is just as bad:
Details always drive me mad.
Luckily for all our sakes
Nothing ever comes through Aix.
What is this I find at Diest?
Quite an intellectual feast!
Hour after hour, day after day,
Train after train runs every way,
Young recruits and old 'uns too,
In and out of Beverloo.
It would be a very fair shot
To suspect Louvain or Gerschot
(Or some intermediate station)
As their final destination.
Or will they dare, O *can* they mean
To venture onward to Malines
One asks oneself. I even feel
They may push on to Londerzeel
Along the road to far Courtrai
Where the flying fishes play -
(Youth, you know, will have its way)

Turning East my eyes are dazzled
By the spectacle of Hasselt:
Hanoverian and Saxon,
Some with picks and some with packs on.
Wurtemberger and Berliner,
Brunswickers from Bukovina,
Jagers, Uhlans, Ungedienste,
Landsturm crawling through Pepinster.
Dirty buggers from Belgrade
Pouring in by Welkenraedt.
Yet it really seems an age
Since a movement passed Liège!
How I miss the old effréné
Rough and tumble work at Chênée!
No one cares a row of pins
Any more for Guillemins,
And the latest German plans
Entirely boycott poor old Ans.
They have seen some awful tussles
Nowadays to get to Brussels;
Possibly they pass Namur,
(This is only conjecture)
Turn North West to Ottignies
And so to Schaerbeek - little geese!
As I feared there's not a sign
Of traffic on the southern line.
We pay an intellectual person
God knows what to spy at Hirson
And yet in spite of all his brain
He never spots a bloody train;
He merely gossips with the porters
And then reports a dozen mortars.
Vervins, Mézières, Sedan
Montmédy and Carignan
Might as well be in the sea
For all he does to earn his fee.
Well I think that ends my song;
If you find it overlong
You will pardon me, I trust,
I do but sing because I must.

Asquith rejoined his Battalion at Vlamertinghe in May 1916. On the 23rd he wrote to Katherine:

... I am already more bored with this tiresome camp than ever I was with G.H.Q. We were allowed an easy time today but for the next week we live a terribly strenuous and wearisome life - a certain amount of drill and a great many 'fatigues' - i.e. digging trenches, laying cables, fetching and carrying, hewing wood and drawing water for other people. Personally I prefer anything to drill. But it does seem rather queer that with masses of men in France who have never come within sight of a trench, they should yet find it necessary to take a battalion which has just finished 2 months in the worst and most dangerous part of the line and is supposed to be coming out for a rest and use it to do odd jobs every day (including Sunday) from 6 a.m. onwards, as if it consisted entirely of conscientious objectors.

I knew I should begin grousing as soon as I got away from G.H.Q., but I suppose I should have groused more if I had stayed there. There is no avoiding the boredom of this War, turn which way you may. There is more novelty and excitement about the trenches themselves than any other part of the show, but I should still be discontented if I were made to stay in them for a month on end instead of coming out and doing these bloody fatigues and things...

From Vlamertinghe on 22nd June 1916, Asquith wrote to Katherine and a day later to Lady Diana Manners:

... We came out of the trenches last night and marched into camp about 3 this morning. Now we are out, I suppose there is no harm in saying what I daresay you have already guessed that we were pushed in to relieve the Canadians opposite Hooge. The Canadians had almost all been killed in the recent fighting there (which was unlucky for them) and hardly any of them had been buried (which was unlucky for us). The confusion and mess were indescribable and the stinks hardly to be borne. No one quite knew where the line was and the men were spotted about in little holes in the ground or in the cellars of ruined cottages and the crypts of crumbling churches...

23rd June ... Another night I was in a much worse place than this - the most accursed unholy and abominable place I have ever seen, the ugliest filthiest most putrid and most desolate - a wood where all the trees had been cut off by the shells the week before, and nothing remained but black stumps of really the most obscene heights and thickness, craters swimming in blood and dirt, rotting and smelling bodies and rats like shadows, fattened for the market moving cunnningly and liquorishly among them, limbs and bowels nestling in the hedges, and over all the most supernaturally shocking scent of death and corruption that ever breathed o'er Eden. The place simply stank of sin and all Floris could not have made it sweet... The only dug-out turned out to be a 'dirt trap' if not a death trap, awash with sewage, stale eyeballs, and other debris, so I spent 2 days on a stretcher in a shell hole in the gutter certainly, but looking all the while at the stars with which you have so richly studded my memory.

There is a great deal after all to be said for the existence of evil; it might almost be held to prove the existence of God. Who else could have thought of it?...

At the end of July the Battalion moved in stages by train from the Ypres Salient to the Somme front. En route the men stayed in billets at Le Souich and at the Bois du Parc and arrived in the front line at Hébuterne during the first few days of August where billets were at Bertrancourt and at the Bois du Warnimont.

On the 4th & 8th August Raymond Asquith wrote to Katherine describing his time supervising the reconstruction of a damaged trench:

... I was up at the forward end of this trench, rather engrossed in directing the men's work, when suddenly I found myself surrounded by a mob of terrified figures from the battalion which was holding that part of the line (we were only working on it) who gibbered and crouched and held their hands over their eyes and generally conducted themselves as if the end of the world was at hand. It was very alarming; they had seen one of these damned rum jars [trench mortar bombs] coming and I hadn't. Sure enough in about 5 seconds the thing went off - luckily just the other side of our parapet. The sky was black with smoke and dirt, and the people butted into one in the fog screaming, but much more frightened than hurt.

The explosion was as painful as a sound can be. In the moment immediately preceding it I made up my mind I was dead, and in the moment immediately following I said to myself "I suppose this is shell shock at last, now I shall get home." But it wasn't. The cracking of one's ear drums is painful and the extra-ordinary tension in the air and pressure on one's head and a smell which I can only describe as the smell of infinite force. And then one found after all that one was not much the worse. I felt a piece of the thing hit me on the leg, but alas it only made a small blood blister. I picked another fragment out of the shoulder of my jacket - it had cut through the khaki but not through my shirt, and there was quite a big dent in my steel helmet. A most disappointing result. I don't know why I tell you all this. These new sensations are interesting to oneself at the time, but very boring I fear in narrative...

But really there are patches in this War which are a higher test even than talking to Lady Queensberry at dinner. We shall probably be doing this spade work for another 4 or 5 days and then I hope we shall have a little rest...

8th August. After the first night's rest for 10 days or so I feel more capable of writing a letter than of late, though there is very little to report. We went on night after night marching 5 or 6 miles up to some rather bad trenches which we had to improve. We used to start about 7.30 p.m. after an early dinner and march over flat open country under the setting sun for about 4 miles to a point where we entered the hindmost of the vast maze of communication trenches which heads up to and around the front line. Usually as we approached this point we were spotted by a German balloon or aeroplane which dropped lights to signal to the guns which began loosing off in a desultory kind of way about 5 minutes afterwards, usually just after we had reached cover when it was pleasant enough to hear the shells whistling overhead on to the road behind us. Then we wandered for ages through the widening trenches constantly losing our temper and our way till we got to a dump where we picked up tools and sandbags etc., and then advanced to the scene of operations. We would get there usually about 10.30 p.m., sometimes an hour or so later, and work for 4 hours under rather adverse circumstances, bodies of engineers constantly forcing their way past us carrying long boards, pit props, dug-out frames, and swearing horribly. The trenches we dug in ran out to what had been our front line but it is now (since the crumping it has had during the last month) only a series of isolated posts held or not held as the case may be by nervous and incompetent groups of the new Army.

The first night I found I had nothing at all between me and the Germans except a few dead men whom I found while reconnoitering, so I had to send out a covering party of my own as well as digging. I had to borrow some bombs from the battalion which ought to be there and they got into serious trouble for not covering us and for the remaining nights they took measures to do so. Luckily we were not molested by the enemy except for a few trench mortar shells and rifle grenades. But it was disagreeable, tiring and rather nervous work, as we couldn't possibly have held the line we were in if we had been attacked, and should have had some difficulty in falling back upon any other...

The Battalion was in the Beaumont Hamel Sector in the middle of August with billets at Mailly-Maillet and Sailly-au-Bois, and on 22nd August Asquith commented to Katherine that his father had not written to him once during his ten months 'exile' in France.

Two weeks later the Battalion was at Morlancourt and Asquith received a telegram "Lieutenant Asquith will meet his father at cross roads K.6d at 10.45 a.m." On 7th September he described the meeting to Katherine:

... So I vaulted into the saddle and bumped off to Fricourt where I arrived exactly at the appointed time. I waited for an hour on a very muddy road congested with troops and lorries and surrounded by barking guns. Then 2 handsome motors from G.H.Q. arrived, the P.M. in one of them with 2 staff officers, and in the other Bongie, Hankey, and one or two of those moth-eaten nondescripts who hang about the corridors of Downing Street in the twilight region between the civil and domestic service. We went up to see some of the captured German dug-outs and just as we were arriving at our first objective the Boches began putting over a few 4.2 shells from their field howitzer. The P.M. was not discomposed by this, but the G.H.Q. chauffeur to whom I had handed over my horse to hold, flung the reins into the air and himself flat on his belly in the mud. It was funny enough. The shells fell about 200 yards behind us I should think. Luckily the dug-out we were approaching was one of the best and deepest I have ever seen - as safe as the bottom of the sea, wood-lined, 3 storeys and electric light, and perfect ventilation. We were shown round by several generals who kept us there for half an hour or so to let the shelling die down, and then the P.M. drove off to luncheon with the G.O.C. 4th Army and I rode back to my billets...

On 12th September Asquith wrote to Katherine "I am getting terribly tired of not being at home, and not seeing my sweetest Fawnia. But I must see out the fighting season. Tomorrow we shall move forward again, probably into the line..."

On 15th September the Guards Division advanced on Lesboeufs from their position at Ginchy. The ground around Ginchy was a battered mass of irregular ridges and shell holes. The 3rd Battalion was formed up in four waves, and at 4.00 a.m. was in position. Sandwiches and an issue of rum were served to the men, who then tried to sleep. At 6.00 a.m. the heavy guns started and fired about forty shells apiece in quick succession. This immediately brought down the enemy barrage; twenty minutes later the attack started. Almost at the outset Raymond Asquith was shot through the chest as he led the first half of No. 4 Company. An eye witness reported that in order to prevent his men from knowing of his wound, Asquith lit a cigarette after he fell. He was given morphia by the Regimental Medical Officer but died on the stretcher before reaching the dressing station.

Needham, his soldier servant wrote to Katherine that 'such coolness under shell fire as Mr. Asquith displayed would be difficult to equal'. The Battalion Diary recorded that Asquith 'had endeared himself to both officers and men in an extraordinary degree since he joined the regiment at the beginning of the war, and his preference of service with his Battalion to the good staff appointment which he had just given up had won the admiration of all ranks'. Amongst the many letters Katherine Asquith received from private soldiers, fellow officers, senior generals and friends, was one from Winston Churchill almost three months after Asquith was killed. Churchill wrote that he could not bring himself to write to her before, so great was his grief at the loss of his "brilliant hero friend." Churchill continued:

> ... I always had an intense admiration for Raymond, and also a warm affection for him; and both were old established ties... I remember so vividly the last time I saw him - at Montreuil in early May. We sat or strolled for two hours on the old ramparts in bright sunshine, and talked about the war, about the coming offensive, about his son, about all sorts of things. I like to dwell on these war-time memories. These gallant charming figures that flash and gleam amid the carnage - always so superior to it, masters of their souls, disdainful of death and suffering - are an inspiration and an example to all. And he was one of the very best. He did everything easily - I never remember anyone who seemed so independent of worldly or physical things: and yet he enjoyed everything and had an appreciation of life and letters and men and women, and manners and customs refined and subtle to the last degree...

LIEUTENANT THE HONOURABLE EDWARD WYNDHAM TENNANT

4th Battalion Grenadier Guards.

Born: 1st July 1897. Wiltshire.
Educated: Winchester College.
Killed: 22nd September 1916. Aged 19 years.
Guillemont Road Cemetery, France.

Edward 'Bim' Tennant was the second child and eldest son of Edward and Pamela Tennant. His father became Liberal Member of Parliament for Salisbury in 1906 and was created Baron Glenconner of Glen in 1911.

In 1911 Tennant went to Winchester where he found the monotonous routine of public school life too restrictive and felt he was wasting valuable time confined in such an insular world. His mother wrote in her Memoir:

> ...He had sufficient tact to keep a constant guard over his exuberant individuality, but character is in-born and needs unfolding as much as direction, and I question whether the Public School system provides this...

When Tennant left Winchester he had ideas of becoming a diplomat after he had spent a year in Germany learning the language, but the outbreak of the war changed all his plans to stay with a German family. Just seventeen years of age, he was the youngest Wykehamist to enlist and was commissioned in the 4th Battalion Grenadier Guards in August 1914. A year later he went to France with his Battalion despite a Brigade order that no-one under the age of nineteen should be sent to the trenches. The Battalion left Blendecques on 23rd September and marched towards Vermelles. En route Tennant wrote to his mother:

> ... We only came eight miles last night, the sky was continually lit up by the big guns in the distance and the men, who thought, I believe, they were going into action last night, were somewhat subdued; but brightened on being shown into barns knee-deep in straw and having hot tea served out within a few minutes of arriving... I am in high-explosive good spirits and there is not much I fail to raise a laugh about! The great 'biff' seems to have gone forward quicker than expected, as we are being shoved forward thus... I have the feeling of Immortality very strongly. I think of Death with a light heart and as a friend whom there is no need to fear.

The Battalion arrived behind the front lines at Vermelles on 26th September, the day after the Battle of Loos had started and Lieutenants C.L. Blundell-Hollinshead-Blundell, C.R. Britten, R.D. Leigh-Pemberton and Bim Tennant were left with the transport. The next day Brigadier-General Heyworth received orders to attack Hill 70 near the village of Loos. Hill 70 was taken but the Battalion suffered heavy losses and Tennant became a Company Commander. On 28th September he wrote from his cellar billets:

> ... I saw my first glimpse of the horror of war yesterday, when walking along one of the cobbled streets full of orderlies, cyclists, and military police, some 500 yards behind my cellar. I happened to come along a few minutes after a shell had burst right in the centre of the road, killing six men and two horses. It was terrible. One dead man was a bright greeny-yellow as the result of the lyddite fumes, but the rest were killed equally instantly by pieces of shell. The medical officer who arrived as I came along borrowed my pistol and finished off one of the wounded horses with it. I thought it seemed a shame as the horse had only one or two small cuts and could easily have been seen to. But I suppose they must care for the men first...

Between 3rd and 25th October the Battalion occupied positions to the south of the Hulluch to Vermelles road, two miles north of Loos; the men spent forty-eight hours in the trenches followed by a two day rest period. During this time Tennant wrote 'Light after Darkness':

LIGHT AFTER DARKNESS

Once more the Night like some great dark drop scene
Eclipsing horrors for a brief entr'acte
Descends, lead-weighty. Now the space between,
Fringed with the eager eyes of men, is racked
By spark-tailed lights, curvetting far and high,
Swift smoke-flecked coursers, raking the dark sky.

But as each sinks in ashes grey, one more
Rises to fall, and so through all the hours
They strive like petty empires by the score,
Each confident of his success and powers
And hovering at its zenith each will show
Pale rigid faces lying dead, below.

And so these lie, tainting the innocent air,
Until the Dawn, deep veiled in mournful grey,

Sadly and quietly shall lay them bare,
The broken heralds of a doleful day.

Sunday, 10th October 1915. I write to you from the dug-out which
Osbert Sitwell and I share in the support trench immediately behind
our front line. He is with half our company in the front line, which I
was most of last night and this morning. It is rather exciting being in
the front line, and I always wear my steel cap, night and day. We are
between 150 and 200 yards from the Boche trenches, and the ground
between our wire entanglements and theirs presents an appearance
such as one hopes only to read of. In one place especially where our
men charged in the teeth of a machine-gun a week ago, it is an
absolute shambles, and, of course, is out of the question, as it is
absolutely exposed...

Friday 15th October 1915... I am now in old and rather dilapidated
trenches behind our lines at Hohenzollern Redoubt. We are in the
fifth line support-trenches which sounds very safe but isn't. I have
had a terribly tiring three days. First we were relieved in our other
front trenches on Wednesday at 1 o'clock and then started to walk six
miles to our billets, after taking nearly two hours to thread the endless
communication trenches miles long which lead out near Vermelles. I
have never walked all night and seen the day dawn as I marched,
before; you see after four days in trenches the men can only march
very slowly and as the Brigade Staff failed to send us any guides we
couldn't find the way for ages. Added to this, a motor-cyclist ran into
us in the dark, stunned one man and hurt another's leg...

    After the Battalion moved to billets at Sailly-la-Bourse and to
trenches at Vermelles, Tennant continued the letter:

... I buried four men to-day under shell-fire, and read bits out of
'Revelation' over their grave. I had only a New Testament. It was
rather moving: just the four men of the grave-digging party and I, but
I am very glad to have been able to do it...

18th October 1915... I have not had four hours sleep on end since
Thursday, but I manage to seize 20 minutes or sometimes one hour at
odd times in even odder places... I am in the front line trench again,
but our lines are advanced on each side of me so it is like a broad
avenue of our men with the Boche at one end and us at the other. A
great bombing attack took place yesterday by several battalions of
different Guards Brigades. It was fairly successful, but we lost fairly
heavily, even my battalion which sent its bombers up had over 40
casualties.

Yesterday between 10 and 1 we were subjected to a terrific shell-fire, and as our artillery weren't replying we heard only the awful sound of the approaching high explosive shells: and as they burst, belching black smoke, the earth shook and a shower of small stones and earth descended on us with an occasional piece of shell that whirs like a muffled factory engine and finishes with a thud as it strikes the top of the trench. I used to think I was fairly impervious to noise, but the crash upon crash, and their accompanying pillar of black smoke simply upset me, as they pitched repeatedly within 30 or 40 yards, and some even nearer. I don't think I showed I was any more frightened than anyone else. Perhaps I wasn't. What made it so racking was that there was nothing to do all the time but sit still waiting for the next, and the next. The strain was awful...

On 23rd October Tennant wrote from an Officers' Dressing Station at Béthune, 2 miles from Vermelles. He enclosed a poem, 'A Bas La Gloire', with his letter.

... I feel perfectly well, I am thankful to say, and I shall go back in a day or two (d.v.) as it was mainly that I was 'run down' and these few days' rest have made me feel another person, and capable of going into a ditch for an indefinite period. The nurses here are quite charming, though mostly old...

A BAS LA GLOIRE!

The powers that be in solemn conclave sat
And dealt out honour from a large tureen,
And those unhonour'd said 'twas rather flat,
Not half so sparkling as it should have been.
Those honour'd silently pass'd round the hat,
Then let themselves be freely heard and seen.

And all this time there were a lot of men
Who were in France and couldn't get away
To be awarded honours. Now and then
They died, so others came and had to stay
Till they died too, and every field and fen
Was heavy with the dead from day to day.

But there were other men who didn't die
Although they were in France - these sat in cars,
And whizzed about with red-band caps, awry,
Exuding brandy and the best cigars,

With bands and tabs of red, they could defy
The many missiles of explosive Mars.

But one there was who used to serve in bars
And for his pretty wit much fame had got;
Though really not so fit to serve in wars,
They made him a staff-colonel on the spot,
And threw a knighthood in as well, because
He really had done such an awful lot.

Up fluttered eyebrows (incomes fluttered down),
His erstwhile yeomanry stood all aghast,
This Juggernaut, devourer of renown,
Was he their fellow-mug in days long past?
In France he went by train from town to town,
Men thought his zenith had been reached at last.

To this the Powers That Be replied, "Oh No!",
And they discovered (else my mem'ry fails)
That he had gone by train some months ago
From Paris with despatches to Marseilles!
"See here", they cried, "a well-earned D.S.O.
Because you did not drop them 'neath the rails."

So now from spur to plume he is a star,
Of all an Englishman should strive to be,
His one-time patrons hail him from afar
As "Peerless warrior," "battle-scarred K.G."
And murmur as he passes in his car,
"For this and all thy mercies, glory be!"

But all this time the war goes on the same,
And good men go, we lose our friends and kith,
The men who sink knee-deep in boosted fame
Prove that "rewarded courage" is a myth:
I could sum up by mentioning a name:
A pseudonym will do, we'll call him Smith.

After two weeks' leave at the end of November 1915, Bim
Tennant rejoined his Battalion in billets in the small town of
Laventie. For the next few weeks he was in the trenches between
Chapigny and Winchester Road returning every six days to
Laventie to rest from the fighting.

HOME THOUGHTS IN LAVENTIE

Green gardens in Laventie!
Soldiers only know the street,
Where the mud is churned and splashed about
By battle-wending feet;
And yet beside one stricken house there is a
    glimpse of grass,
Look for it when you pass.

Beyond the Church whose pitted spire
Seems balanced on a strand
Of swaying stone and tottering brick
Two roofless ruins stand,
And here behind the wreckage where the back wall
    should have been
We found a garden green.

The grass was never trodden on,
The little path of gravel
Was overgrown with celandine,
No other folk did travel
Along its weedy surface, but the nimble-footed
    mouse
Running from house to house.

So all among the vivid blades
Of soft and tender grass
We lay, nor heard the limber wheels
That pass and ever pass,
In noisy continuity, until their stony rattle
Seems in itself a battle.

At length we rose up from this ease
Of tranquil happy mind,
And searched the garden's little length
A fresh pleasaunce to find;
And there, some yellow daffodils and jasmine
    hanging high
Did rest the tired eye.

The fairest and most fragrant
Of the many sweets we found
Was a little bush of Daphne flower,
Upon a grassy mound,
And so thick were the blossoms set, and so divine
    the scent
That we were well content.

Hungry for Spring I bent my head,
The perfume fanned my face,
And all my soul was dancing
In that little lovely place,
Dancing with a measured step from wrecked and
    shattered towns
Away... upon the Downs.

I saw green banks of daffodil,
Slim poplars in the breeze,
Great tan-brown hares in gusty March,
A-courting on the leas;
And meadows with their glittering streams, and
    silver scurrying dace,
Home - what a perfect place.

During February 1916 the Battalion was billeted in scattered farmhouses around Herzeele; by the 6th March it had moved to a camp of huts and tents near Poperinghe, where snow and rain made "the whole camp a sea of mud, and one walks from hut to hut on trench boards covered with wire-netting..."

On 15th March the Battalion was sent by train to Ypres and went into dug-outs on the bank of the canal and in the ramparts. The following day it took over a line of trenches.

16th March 1916... There has been a lot of shelling, and we had a man badly hit this morning. As I stood in the door of our dug-out, about 25 feet from the water's edge, it was as though greedy fish were continually rising, as the bits of shell plopped into the canal. Most of the shells burst behind us or in front of us, thank God; but the noise was tremendous, and I feel grateful for the steel roof and walls of our dug-out. It is like a barrel in shape inside, and has a very thick roof of sandbags and loose bricks. The circular part cannot be seen from outside, but it is made of pressed steel, and will stop anything below a

6 inch shell, I believe. There is plenty of room inside, and we all slept in camp beds in it last night, and were quite comfortable... After lunch Osbert and I went for a walk through the town. I have never seen such an abomination of desolation - not a single whole roof in the town. Shell holes 30 feet in diameter and 15 feet deep full of green water; twisted iron staircases standing alone in the ruins of a house - everything knocked down except the tottering top storey bath-room which stands on a pyramid of debris...

Then a lot of shrapnel started coming over, and we both sought our dug-outs (about half a mile away) with dignified haste. A small piece of shrapnel hit the ground between his left foot and my right foot as we went along. Thus in a reserved and stately, but none the less acute panic we reached our dug-out in safety, for which thank God...

Tennant was home on leave at the end of March. When he returned to France he was sent as A.D.C. to General Feilding on Sir John Ponsonby's staff. He rejoined the Battalion at the beginning of June at Poperinghe and went to No. 4 Company with Osbert Sitwell in command. On the 9th June the Battalion went into billets at Tatinghem and four days later Tennant wrote 'The Mad Soldier':

THE MAD SOLDIER

I Dropp'd here three weeks ago, yes - I know,
And it's bitter cold at night, since the fight -
I could tell you if I chose - no one knows
Excep' me and four or five, what ain't alive.
I can see them all asleep, three men deep,
And they're nowhere near a fire - but our wire
Has 'em fast as fast can be. Can't you see
When the flare goes up? Ssh! boys; what's that noise?
Do you know what these rats eat? Body-meat!
After you've been down a week, an' your cheek
Gets as pale as life, and night seems as white
As the day, only the rats and their brats
Seem more hungry when the day's gone away -
An' they look as big as bulls, an' they pulls
Till you almost sort o' shout - but the drought
What you hadn't felt before makes you sore.
And at times you even think of a drink...
There's a leg acrost my thighs - if my eyes
Weren't too sore, I'd like to see who it be,
Wonder if I'd know the bloke if I woke? -

Woke? By damn, I'm not asleep - there's a heap
Of us wond'ring why the hell we're not well...
Leastways I am - since I came it's the same
With the others - they don't know what I do,
Or they wouldn't gape and grin. - It's a sin
To say that Hell is hot - 'cause it's not:
Mind you, I know very well we're in hell.
 -In a twisted hump we lie - heaping high
Yes! an' higher every day. - Oh, I say,
This chap's heavy on my thighs - damn his eyes.

From the middle of June and through much of July the Battalion
was either in the Canal Bank trenches at Ypres or at a rest camp at
Poperinghe. Bim Tennant celebrated his nineteenth birthday on the
first day of the Battle of the Somme.   From the ramparts at Ypres
he wrote 'Re-incarnation' sometime during July:

RE-INCARNATION

I too remember distant golden days
When even my soul was young; I see the sand
Whirl in a blinding pillar towards the band
Of orange sky-line 'neath a turquoise blaze -
(Some burnt-out sky spread o'er a glistening land)
- And slim brown jargoning men in blue and gold,
I know it all so well, I understand
The ecstacy of worship ages-old.

Hear the first truth: The great far-seeing soul
Is ever in the humblest husk; I see
How each succeeding section takes its toll
In fading cycles of old memory.
And each new life the next life shall control
Until perfection reach Eternity.

At the beginning of August the 4th Battalion started its march to
the Somme area.   The men were in trenches at Beaumont Hamel
between 15th - 19th August and then were redeployed to Ville-sur-
Ancre near Albert at the end of the month.
On 8th September Tennant wrote from Carnoy, near the front
line, where the Somme battle was still fiercely raging:

... We left our billets yesterday morning at 8 a.m. in motor lorries, and came up here about seven miles. We are bivouacked here on a slope, with old trenches all round, and our old original trench is 500 yards in front of us. I walked right across all the old trenches last night, and again this morning. Last night Mitchell and I were on a five hour fatigue, repairing a road about three miles away to our front. We worked till dark, being rather hampered by a constant stream of men, waggons, and horses which cut up the road as fast as we mended it. However, we did good work. The whole place up there is littered with rifles, ammunition, clothing, wire, shells, and every sort of stuff. At one point the road had been previously repaired, and instead of rows of staples put across and covered with mud, they had used rifles. Just think of the waste. We were shelled a bit as we prepared to move off about 8.30 p.m., and though only about three shells came, all were uncomfortably close. I am thankful to say that only one man was slightly wounded and we got back here with no further trouble...

There are big guns all round us as I write, but none near enough to be unpleasant, as they were at Vermelles last year. We have nothing to do here, and it is quite fine, though windswept. I now hear that we shall probably take over the most newly won line tomorrow night, which will probably not be a very quiet locality. However, I trust implicitly in God, and am in very high spirits...

September 11th 1916... Up to now I am safe and well; but we have had a fairly uncomfortable time, though we have been lucky on the whole. Poor Thompson (in my Company) was killed yesterday. I shall miss him so, he was such a charming fellow. We have been heavily shelled every where of the line.

September 12th 1916... We were safely relieved last night and are now going back for a day or two. We have had all the kicks and none of the ha'pence in this show, as other batts. had the fun of repulsing attacks and killing hundreds, while we had to just sit and be shelled. No doubt we shall have a better chance soon. The C.O. is very envious of what he calls the 'other chaps hellish good shoot'.

We are delighted to be out, and should be in comfortable quarters by midnight tonight. I have not changed my clothes yet, so shall be glad.

I forgot to tell you that I was developing an absess in a back molar on the morning of the day we went into action. So I forthwith mounted a prehistoric bicycle, rode eight miles in sweltering heat, had gas and tooth out in a brace of shakes, and rode back, getting one or two lifts in lorries...

On September 13th the Battalion moved from bivouacs near Carnoy to a camp in Happy Valley near Fricourt. No. 4 Company and Battalion Headquarters were established in an old German trench 500 yards to the east of Guillemont. On 14th September Tennant wrote to his mother:

> I am longing to see you. God grant it may be soon. I will write to you whenever I get the chance, but no one knows what may happen in the next day or two. I pray I may be alright, but in any case 'Where is Death's Sting?'

The Battalion moved to trenches at Trones Wood on the 18th September, three days after Raymond Asquith had been killed. Tennant wrote to his mother again:

> ... Thank Heaven I have come safely out of this battle after two days and two nights of it. It started properly at 5 a.m. on the 15th and the artillery fire was terrific. We were in support and went up about 7.45 and sat down again further up just the right side of the German barrage. Then I was sent across to another Guards Regiment to go with them, find out where they proposed going, and lead the Battalion up beside it. Off I went, and joined them, and went forward with them... When we were going through a little dip in the ground, we were shot at by Boches on the high ground with rifles, there must have been about twenty shooting at us. I was walking in front with their C.O. and Adjutant, and felt sufficiently uncomfortable, but didn't show it. Bullets scuffed up dust all around with a wicked little 'zump', but they were nearly all short and none of us, at least who were in front, were hit. Thus we went on, and they took up their position between two of these huge steel tanks on the near side of the ridge. Then they lent me an orderly, and I started back to bring the Battalion along; it was an unpleasant journey of about half a mile over nothing but shell-holes full of dead and dying, with any amount of shells flying about. Several whizz-bangs landed very close to me, but I got back to the Battalion and explained the position to them, and then we all went down there and took up a position... The C.O., the Adjutant, the Doctor, and I spent that afternoon, evening and night in a large rocky shell-hole. We were severely shelled on and off the whole time, and about four men were done in in the very next shell-hole a couple of yards away. That night was one of the coldest and most uncomfortable it has ever been my fortune to spend - 'with the stars to see'. Meanwhile most of the Battalion had gone up to support the Brigades who had done the attack at five that morning and lost heavily. At seven or eight next morning we moved our Battalion Headquarters to the line of trenches in front which had been dug the night before. This was safer than our shell-hole, and as we had the worst shelling I have ever experienced during that afternoon and evening, it was probably a very wise move.

An attack took place at 1.15 p.m. that day, and I will tell you more about it when I see you, d.v. My worst job was that of taking messages down the line of trenches to different captains. The trenches were full of men, so I had to go over the open. Several people who were in the trench say they expected every shell to blow me to bits. That night we were again shelled till about 8 p.m. and were relieved about midnight. We got in about 2.30. I was dog-tired and Churchill [Captain Spencer-Churchill], who now commands No. 4 Company, was even more tired. Soup, meat, champagne, and cake, and I went to bed till about 2 p.m. That is the time one really does want champagne, when one comes in at 3 a.m. after no sleep for fifty hours. It gives one the strength to undress... I suppose you have heard who are dead? Guy Baring, Raymond Asquith, Sloper Mackenzie and many others. It is a terrible list... Death and decomposition strew the ground...

On 20th September, the attack opened on the village of Lesboeufs. Tennant wrote what was to be his last letter home:

... Tonight we go up to the last trenches we were in, and tomorrow we go over the top. Our Brigade has suffered less than either of the other two Brigades in Friday's biff (15th), so we shall be in the forefront of the battle. I am full of hope and trust, and pray that I may be worthy of my fighting ancestors. The one I know best is Sir Henry Wyndham, whose bust is in the hall at 44 Belgrave Square, and there is a picture of him on the stairs at 34 Queen Anne's Gate. We shall probably attack over about 1200 yards, but we shall have such artillery support as will properly smash the Boche line we are going for, and even (which is unlikely) if the artillery doesn't come up to our hopes, the spirit of the Brigade of Guards will carry all resistance before it. The pride of being in such a great regiment! The thought that all the old men 'late Grenadier Guards', who sit in the London Clubs, are thinking and hoping about what we are doing here! I have never been prouder of anything, except your love for me, than I am of being a Grenadier. Today is a great day for me. That line of Harry's rings through my mind, 'High heart, high speech, high deeds, 'mid honouring eyes'. I went to a service on the side of a hill this morning, and took the Holy Communion afterwards, which always seems to help one along, doesn't it? I slept like a top last night, and dreamed that someone I know very well (but I can't remember who it was), came to me and told me how much I had grown. Three or four of my brother officers read my poems yesterday, and they all liked them very much which pleased me enormously. I feel rather like saying 'If it be possible let this cup pass from me', but the triumphant finish 'nevertheless not what I will but what Thou Willest', steels my heart and sends me into this battle with a heart of triple bronze.

I always carry four photies of you when we go into action, one is in my pocket-book, two in that little leather book, and one round my neck, and I have kept my little medal of the Blessed Virgin.   Your love for me and my love for you, have made my whole life one of the happiest there has ever been;   Brutus' farewell to Cassius sounds in my heart: 'If not farewell;   and if we meet again, we shall smile.'   Now all my blessings go with you, and with all we love.   God Bless you, and give you peace.   Eternal Love from Bim.

Two days later Bim Tennant was killed by a sniper.   His Commanding Officer, Lieutenant-Colonel Henry Seymour later wrote:

... We all loved him, and his loss is terrible... His Company was holding a sap occupied by Germans and ourselves, a block separated the two.   Bim was sniping when he was killed absolutely instantaneously by a German sniper.   His body is buried in a cemetery near Guillemont.   The grave is close to that of Raymond Asquith, and we are placing a Cross upon it and railing it round today.   Forgive this scribble, we are still in action and attack again tomorrow morning..."

RIFLEMAN NICHOLAS HERBERT TODD

1/12th Battalion London Regiment (The Rangers). Formerly The Queen's Westminster Rifles.

Born: 21st September, 1878. Occold, Suffolk.
Educated: Felsted School.
Keble College, Oxford.
Killed: 7th October 1916. Aged 38 years.
Thiepval Memorial to the Missing, near Albert, France.

Nicholas Todd became a schoolmaster after he left University. He taught at Sedbergh Preparatory School from 1906; he was a popular and talented master for ten years. During Todd's time at Sedbergh, Robert Sterling (qv) was a pupil at the senior school.

In January 1916 Todd wrote:

SWEET ALDBOURNE

There lies a village, far from roar of towns,
Embosomed by the everlasting downs,
Where a grey church beneath the heavens starred
Gleams in the evening like a Christmas Card.
And thither, 'mid the music of the Chimes,
Lantern in hand - like the old Georgian times -
Down the dark streets where shadows come and go,
Lit for a while by the cracked lantern's glow,
We pass, with greetings, as we walk along,
To the bright church, lit up for evensong.

There lies a wood, where the big Roman snail
Sleeps 'neath the moss secure from sleet and gale,
Where the red squirrel shyly leaps and climbs
In search of nuts as in the Roman times,
And the wild winter wind plays pitch and toss
With withered leaves that dance among the moss,
And bright agarics make a wondrous show -
They are agarics, for you call them so.

There lies a village in the Yorkshire Fells
Where Beauty's Fairy wove her subtlest spells,

And many a mountain ghyll runs foaming down
To join the Rawthey tossing clear and brown:
There in the summer after winter's cold
The globe flower spreads its sheet of living gold,
And fairy ferns beneath the dark rocks grow,
Beneath the sunlight's angel-given glow.

There lies a trench in Flanders far away,
Where booming terror thunders night and day;
And duty calls that ever gallant band
To fight for freedom and the Motherland.
So if the call to go across the sea
To join those heroes fighting comes to me,
And if I too shall act the greater part
With faith unwavering and a steadfast heart,
Surely the hours we spent on fell and down
In Wiltshire Wood, by loch and streamlet brown
Surely the times that we together passed
Shall bring a happy vision to the last,
A vision of a Church lit up by prayer,
A vision of Ben Lawers when we were there,
A vision of the silver of the falls,
A vision of sweet summer, and the calls
Of startled grouse across the Perthshire heather,
When you and I went tin in hand together.

In April 1916, at the age of 38, Todd enlisted as a Rifleman in the Queen's Westminsters. He wrote 'A Letter' from Hazeley Down Camp, Winchester on Easter Eve 1916.

A LETTER

Dear Meg, now I'm a simple Tommy
I thought you'd like a letter from me,
Living a silent celibut
With twenty others in a hut.
My bed of wooden boards and tressels
And blankets thick with which one wrestles,
While the cold night wind through the door
Keeps time to rats that scour the floor.
A sergeant stern with language rude
Who tells me that my drilling's crude,

And boots two inches thick, which they
Make me to clean three times a day.
But even here where bugles ring
The Southern lark goes up to sing;
And nobly stretch the long white downs
O'erlooking Hampshire's famous towns,
Where years ago through woods of fir
King Alfred rode to Winchester;
And here is haunted, holy ground
Where Arthur held his Table Round,
And Ethelbert and Athelstane
Drove back the foray of the Dane.

Life full of change, of fear, or hope,
Is like a weird kaleidescope;
Fate turns the handle, and we spin
Like bits of coloured glass within.
Who would have thought that I should go
To fight against a foreign foe?
If I return with half a leg
You'll run much faster than me, Meg,
And in a race around the yard
You'll beat me hollow, which is hard!
I shall forget in forming fours,
And other motions used by Corps,
That ever I took interest
In "dulce et decorum est."

And so farewell - If when May comes,
And snow-white gleam the garden plums,
You run across the yard to school
Hair-braided, with your reticule,
Then think of me, my little maid,
Forming for nine o'clock parade,
And making an egregious hash
Of drill, and growing a moustache!

This thought, that the same evening star
Shines on us both, tho' severed far,
And guides us on our unknown way,
Should cheer us all from day to day.

Nicholas Todd arrived on the Somme in September 1916, and was in the same battalion as Leslie Coulson (qv).

On the evening of the 3rd October the Rangers arrived in the reserve trenches near the ruined village of Guillemont; on the 5th October they went into the front line east of Lesboeufs. On the following afternoon orders were received to attack the German Dewdrop Trench the next day. The leading companies of the first wave moved forward from Rainy Trench at 1.45 p.m. on 7th October and immediately came under very heavy and accurate machine-gun fire from Dewdrop Trench on their left front. Before they had gone 50 yards only about 15 men remained; the second, third and fourth attacking waves suffered a similar fate and the assault petered out. The remnants of the battalion lay out in shell-holes until dusk when they returned to the front line and re-occupied Rainy Trench. Nicholas Todd was killed during the day.

SERGEANT FREDERICK LESLIE A. COULSON

2nd Battalion London Regiment (Royal Fusiliers).
Attached 12th Battalion London Regiment (The Rangers).
Born: July 1889. Hendon.
Died of Wounds: 8th October 1916. Aged 27 years.
Grove Town Cemetery, Méaulte, France.

Leslie Coulson was the younger son of a Fleet Street journalist, known as 'Democritus' and 'Vexatus', of the *Sunday Chronicle*.

A lover of the countryside and open air, Coulson spent many weekends and holidays walking with his brother Raymond, and they 'tramped most of the southern and western counties from end to end.'

Coulson followed in his father's footsteps and was a Reuters' correspondent in London when war broke out. He refused to try for a commission because he preferred to "do the thing fairly. I will take my place in the ranks." He enlisted in September 1914 as a Private in the 2nd Battalion the London Regiment of the Royal Fusiliers.

Slight in build, Coulson suffered from ill-health even before he went into the Army. In December 1914 the Battalion sailed for Malta, and Coulson spent some time in hospital while they were there.

A SOLDIER IN HOSPITAL (VALETTA)

Here, as I lie in this white cot,
The world seems as a dream remote -
The echo of a strident note,
Once heard, now half forgot.

In this dim room sequestered, high
Time does not beat with anvil ring;
The sand runs slow, untroubling
The hours as they go by.

I lie and watch the sunlit wall,
A little space of empty sky,
I watch the shadows creeping by,
Slowly, till evenfall.

And from the crooked street below,
In fits and starts melodious rise
The sounds of bells, and children's cries,
And traffic to and fro.

A caged thrush in his simple rhyme,
Flutes fitfully from hour to hour;
A faint chime from a city tower
Murmurs of fleeting time.

While *there* the vulture beats his wings,
The pulse of war throbs fever high,
Here for a little space I lie
And dream of little things.

The Battalion served in Gallípoli where Coulson was slightly wounded, and then in Egypt where he had another spell in hospital suffering from fever.

In April 1916 the 2nd Battalion was sent to France and when it was disbanded, Coulson, promoted to Sergeant, was attached to the 12th Battalion. He was in trenches at Hébuterne and Fonquevillers during June and July, billetted just behind the line in the villages of Sailly and Bayencourt. In a letter home from one of these devastated villages, Coulson wrote in July 1916:

I have seen men shattered, dying, dead - all the sad tragedy of war. And this murder of old stone, and lichened thatches, this shattering of little old churches and homesteads brings the tragedy home to me more acutely. I think to find an English village like this would almost break my heart.

FROM AN OUTPOST

I've tramped South England up and down
    Down Dorset way, down Devon way,
Through every little ancient town
    Down Dorset way, down Devon way.
I mind the old stone churches there,
The taverns round the market square,
The cobbled streets, the garden flowers,
The sundials telling peaceful hours
    Down Dorset way, down Devon way.

The Meadowlands are green and fair
    Down Somerset and Sussex way.
The clover scent is in the air
    Down Somerset and Sussex way.
I mind the deep-thatched homesteads there
The noble downlands, clean and bare.
The sheepfolds and the cattle byres,
The blue wood-smoke from shepherd's fires
    Down Dorset way, down Devon way.

Mayhap I shall not walk again
    Down Dorset way, down Devon way.
Nor pick a posy in a lane
    Down Somerset and Sussex way.
But though my bones, unshriven, rot
In some far distant alien spot,
What soul I have shall rest from care
To know that meadows still are fair
    Down Dorset way, down Devon way.

On 8th August 1916, Coulson wrote 'The Rainbow':

THE RAINBOW

I watch the white dawn gleam,
    To the thunder of hidden guns.
I hear the hot shells scream
Through skies as sweet as a dream
    Where the silver dawnbreak runs.
And stabbing of light
Scorches the virginal white.
But I feel in my being the old, high, sanctified thrill,
And I thank the gods that the dawn is beautiful still.

From death that hurtles by
    I crouch in the trench day-long
But up to a cloudless sky
From the ground where our dead men lie
    A brown lark soars in song.
Through the tortured air,
Rent by the shrapnel's flare,
Over the troubleless dead he carols his fill,
And I thank the gods that the birds are beautiful still.

Where the parapet is low
　And level with the eye
Poppies and cornflowers glow
And the corn sways to and fro
　In a pattern against the sky.
The gold stalks hide
Bodies of men who died
Charging at dawn through the dew to be killed or to kill.
I thank the gods that the flowers are beautiful still.

When night falls dark we creep
　In silence to our dead.
We dig a few feet deep
And leave them there to sleep -
　But blood at night is red,
Yea, even at night,
And a dead man's face is white.
And I dry my hands, that are also trained to kill,
And I look at the stars - for the stars are beautiful still.

The first two days of October 1916 were spent at Bray Citadel. *The Ranger's War History* recorded:

... October 7th 1916 was a disastrous day for the Rangers and for many others. The attack of the Brigade on our left failed as also did that of the troops on our right. The weather was appalling - the ground was greasy and slippery with recent rain and there was more than one subsequent abortive attack after we were relieved before the position was finally won.

During one of the charges Coulson was shot in the chest. He lived until he reached the Casualty Clearing Station, thanked the stretcher bearers and sent a last message home to his family. He died a few hours later.

WAR

Where war has left its wake of whitened bone,
Soft stems of summer grass shall wave again,
And all the blood that war has ever strewn
　　　　Is but a passing stain.

A few weeks before his death Coulson wrote to his father: "If I should fall do not grieve for me. I shall be one with the wind and the sun and the flowers." After his death the following poem was found among his possessions and returned to his family:

WHO MADE THE LAW?

Who made the Law that men should die in meadows?
Who spake the word that blood should splash in lanes?
Who gave it forth that gardens should be bone-yards?
Who spread the hills with flesh, and blood, and brains?
Who made the Law?

Who made the Law that Death should stalk the village?
Who spake the word to kill among the sheaves,
Who gave it forth that death should lurk in hedgerows,
Who flung the dead among the fallen leaves?
Who made the Law?

Those who return shall find that peace endures,
Find old things old, and know the things they knew,
Walk in the garden, slumber by the fireside,
Share the peace of dawn, and dream amid the dew -
Those who return.

Those who return shall till the ancient pastures,
Clean-hearted men shall guide the plough-horse reins,
Some shall grow apples and flowers in the valleys,
Some shall go courting in summer down the lanes -
THOSE WHO RETURN.

But who made the Law? the Trees shall whisper to him:
"See, see the blood - the splashes on our bark!"
Walking the meadows, he shall hear bones crackle,
And fleshless mouths shall gibber in silent lanes at dark.
Who made the Law?

Who made the Law? At noon upon the hillside
His ears shall hear a moan, his cheeks shall feel a breath,
And all along the valleys, past gardens, croft, and homesteads,
HE who made the Law,
    He who made the Law,
He who made the Law shall walk along with Death.
    WHO made the Law?

LIEUTENANT GEOFFREY BACHE SMITH

19th Battalion Lancashire Fusiliers.

Born: 18th October 1894.
Educated: King Edward's High School, Birmingham.
              Corpus Christi College, Oxford.
Died of Wounds: 3rd December 1916. Aged 22 years.
Warlincourt Halte British Cemetery, Saulty, France.

Geoffrey Smith received a commission in the Oxfordshire and Buckinghamshire Regiment in January 1915, but was transferred to the 19th Battalion Lancashire Fusiliers and went to France in November 1915. On the 30th the Battalion arrived at Albert and the Battalion Diary recorded:

"Marched to new fighting area - Billets situated in town - Town being shelled intermittently".

The Battalion was in trenches in the Senlis area during the first two months of 1916, and returned to trenches near Albert in April. Geoffrey Smith wrote the following poem:

APRIL 1916

Now spring is come upon the hills in France,
And all the trees are delicately fair,
As heeding not the great guns' voice, by chance
Brought down the valley on a wandering air:
Now day by day upon the uplands bare
Do gentle, toiling horses draw the plough,
And birds sing often in the orchards where
Spring wantons it with blossoms on her brow -
Aye! but there is no peace in England now.

O little isle amid unquiet seas,
Though grisly messengers knock on many doors,
Though there be many storms among your trees
And all your banners rent with ancient wars;
Yet such a grace and majesty are yours
There be still some, whose glad heart suffereth
All hate can bring from her misgotten stores,
Telling themselves, so England's self draw breath,
That's all the happiness on this side of death.

The Battalion took part in the battle of the Somme in July 1916; Geoffrey Smith became Intelligence Officer and then Adjutant of the Battalion.

FOR R.Q.G. JULY 1916

O God whose great inscrutable purposes
(Seen only of the one all-seeing eye)
Are as unchangeable as the azure sky,
And as fulfilled of infinite mysteries:
Are like a fast-locked castle without keys
Whereof the gates are very strong and high,
Impenetrable, and we poor fools die
Nor even know what thing beyond them is:
O God, by whom men's lives are multiplied,
Are scattered broadcast in the world like grain,
And after long time reaped again and stored,
O Thou who only canst be glorified
By man's own passion and the supreme pain,
Accept this sacrifice of blood outpoured.

At the end of November the Battalion was at Souastre near Arras working on trenches and roads. On 29th November Souastre was shelled from the direction of Essarts. At 3.30 a.m. Geoffrey Smith was struck by a fragment of a stray shell as he walked down a village street. Although the wound at first seemed slight, it became septic and he died four days later.

Before the war Geoffrey Smith started a poem 'The Burial of Sophocles'. He sent the final version to his friend, J.R.R. Tolkein, from the trenches:

... O seven times happy he that dies
After the splendid harvest-tide,
When strong barns shield from winter skies
The grain that's rightly stored inside:
There death shall scatter no more tears
Than o'er the falling of the years:
Aye, happy seven times is he
Who enters not the silent doors
Before his time, but tenderly
Death beckons unto him, because
There's rest within for weary feet
Now all the journey is complete...

1917

SECOND LIEUTENANT JOHN ARTHUR GRAY, D.C.M.

2nd Battalion Royal Berkshire Regiment.

Born: 1886. High Wycombe, Buckinghamshire.
Killed: 4th March 1917. Aged 31 years.
Sailly-Saillisel British Cemetery, France.

John Gray enlisted as a regular soldier in the Royal Berkshire Regiment in 1905. He went to India with his Regiment, became a sergeant, and was serving in the Indian Commissariat when war was declared. He arrived in France with one of the first Indian contingents in November 1914.

In an effort to dislodge the Germans from the strategically important Aubers Ridge overlooking Lille, the Battle of Neuve Chapelle (10 -13 March 1915) was the first significant land offensive of the War. After methodical preparation, and a hurricane bombardment lasting 35 minutes, Haig's First Army carried out a surprise attack on a 9,000 yard front. 45 minutes later they had captured the town of Neuve Chapelle itself. However after such a promising start the assault was held up, every attempt at exploitation failed at the cost of mounting losses, and with ammunition running low, the battle was brought to an end on 13th March.

The 2nd Royal Berkshires was one of the leading assault battalions in the battle and Gray was badly wounded in the head two days later while consolidating the position won after the third line of German trenches had been taken.

NEUVE CHAPELLE

I

Six months of misery, six months of hell,
Drenched an' 'arf frozen, but sticking it well;
Sniped in the darkness, an' shelled in the light,
Gawd! 'ow we longed fer the chance of a fight.
Diggin' all night wi' the mud to our knees,
Workin' like demons in case we should freeze.
Would the sun never shine? We were stuck in our trench
Wi' the mud, an' the rain! one continual drench
Was wot we 'ad to stick. An' we dreamed every day
Of our pals who 'ad gone, an' the debts we'd to pay.

Till at last came the order - "Go back fer a rest!"
We 'ad seven days o' that, an' I likes work the best,
If that's wot they calls restin' - a drilling all day,
An' diggin' all night - but 'twas making the way
For a glorious attack, so we done the work well.
Then the order came - "Boys, you've to take Neuve Chapelle."

II

Royal Berkshires an' Lincolns to lead the attack,
Irish Rifles an' Rifle Brigade at their back.
An' the Iron Dook 'imself never led troops more fine
Than the old 25th Brigade - "Pride o' the Line!"
Well, we marched out o' billets all singin' an' gay,
At the thoughts of a beautiful scrap the next day.
Till the order came down - "No more singin', no noise,
We are near the position; no more talkin', boys!"
Then in silence we marched to the trench, just an old
Bit o' ditch, full o' water, an' perishing cold.
An' that long weary wait fer the dawn to appear
Will stick in my memory fer many a year.
At last came the mornin', an' with it a strange
Sort o' silence -then boom! as the guns get the range.
"Fix bay'nets, stand steady, an' keep in line well;
An' get ready, boys, fer to take Neuve Chapelle."

III

Then hell was let loose, as a wild, awful sound,
Which deafened our ear-drums an' shook the whole ground,
Grew louder, more fearful, as four hundred guns
Sent their message of death to the lines o' the Huns.
The fierce bark of quick-firers, the howitzers' roar,
An' the dull boom of siege guns, an' field guns galore.
'Twas an earthquake, a cyclone, a landslip in one,
When that 'orrible, awful, bombardment begun.
The stink o' the lyddite, an' thick, yellow smoke,
As 'ouses went down, an' the barbed wire was broke,
An' brave men turned pale an' were trembling wi' dread,
An' the screams o' that shrapnel still rings in my head.
Then we looked to our rifles to see they were right,
Shook 'ands with old pals, case we fell in the fight;
Wished each other good luck, an' old "Smithy" - my pal -
Ses, "I'll meet yer to-night, Jack, when we've took Neuve
    Chapelle."

IV

Now the old foot-sloggers - infantry bold -
Charge! as yer fathers did in the days of old,
Charge! fer yer wimmen, for Gawd an' the right,
What though ye' fall in so glorious a fight.
Over the parapet. 'Tis but a dash
Of a few hundred yards, wi' the roar an' the crash
O' the guns in our ears, an' a deep sobbing breath,
As our pals fall around us, all awful in death.
Fallin' like leaves, but still onward the line
Of the Berkshires and Lincolns swept; Gawd, it was fine!
Grimy and blood-stained, an' plastered in mud,
We broke through their first line, an' then the dull thud
As the bay'nets went 'ome, an' the Huns turned an' ran,
While we follered up closely, fer every man
'Ad a debt to pay back, an' we paid 'em up well,
Wi' some int'rest to spare, 'ere we reached Neuve Chapelle.

V

Onward! still onward! two more lines to take,
"But see - the Bavarians waver - they break!"
These are no Landstrum, no cravens, I'd swear
That the pride o' the whole German army was there.
Tried vet'rans all, an' Gawd, 'ow they fought,
Never was victory more dearly bought.
Shootin' and stabbin', the blood flowing fast,
"One more rush - all together, boys - broke 'em at last!"
Now dig fer yer lives, lads, lay close to the ground.
Same old machine guns, an' same horrid sound,
As the bullets came searchin' us, 'issing like sin,'
Ow we curscd an' we prayed, as we dug ourselves in.
Workin' and seatin' 'midst that 'ail of death,
We got cover at last, an' now - take a breath -
An' a smoke, boys, light up, you've earned one so well,
Three lines o' trenches won, "Now, Neuve Chapelle."

VI

'Ere comes the Irish an' Rifle Brigade,
To show 'em the stuff of which Britons are made.
Faces set grim, not a man lookin' back,
As they pass through our ranks to begin the attack
On the village in front, which is now strongly 'eld

By the curs'd machine guns. But battered and shelled
The old Rifles pressed on, wi' that look on each face
Of a sure, steady purpose, an' pride o' the race.
'Ouse by 'ouse, street by street, they are forcin' 'em back,
Not a pause, or a waver in that fierce attack.
But now the big German guns add to the din,
As the shells whistle over, an' roofs tumble in.
An' 'ouses fly upwards, an' fill us wi' fear
For the brave lads in front there. But 'ark! such a cheer
Rends the air, an' we know they 'ave passed through that hell,
"An' the old 25th Brigade's took Neuve Chapelle!"

VII

Took it, an' 'eld it too, 'gainst fierce attack,
As they came on in thousands we still roll'd 'em back.
Crushed an' defeated, no treacherous Hun
Shall again tread the soil which was so 'ardly won.
Now we look round fer the pals that we've lost.
The Victory is won, but oh, Gawd, wot a cost.
They wern't no saints, but just plain "Reg'lar" boys,
True, rough, and ready, an' fond of a noise.
Still, I'd take their chance on the great Judgment Day
'Gainst some pious gentlefolk, who, I daresay,
Wouldn't a shook 'ands wi them, not in times o' peace.
But the great Master knows, an' when all wars shall cease,
An' the last Roll is call'd, well, I feel sure that then,
Christ won't be too 'ard, cos they died fer men.
An 'E died fer us all, so I'm sure 'twill be well
Wi' the laddies who died when we took Neuve Chapelle.

After a few weeks convalescing Gray was in the front line again
at Fromelles and was promoted to Company Sergeant-Major. He
was awarded the Distinguished Conduct Medal:

For conspicuous gallantry and ability on 9th May 1915 near Rouges
Banes in handling his company after all the officers had been killed or
wounded. He rallied the men under a heavy fire at a critical period of
the engagement moving about from place to place quite regardless of
his own safety and gave a splendid example of coolness and courage.

Gray's head wound continued to cause him great pain and two
pieces of shrapnel and a piece of bone were discovered pressing on
his brain. He was sent home and from the Red Cross Hospital 'The

Glen' at Southend he recuperated and wrote a number of poems. He was commissioned in the Regiment as a Second Lieutenant in November 1916.

In order to reduce the length of their lines of communication the Germans carried out a strategic withdrawal between 25th February and 5th April 1917, to what was known as the Hindenburg Line. This fortified defence system ran from just south of Arras to a point about 2 miles in front of St Quentin, and on south-east to the River Aisne near Soissons. The Germans, with a fiercely resisting rearguard, did not give ground lightly. Gray's battalion was heavily involved in the advance and, in the vicinity of Bapaume, on the morning of the 4th March the Battalion formed the right flank of the assaulting force and attacked 'Pallas' and 'Fritz' trenches. It suffered heavy casualties, and Gray was one of 3 officers and 54 other ranks killed. 6 officers and 173 other ranks were wounded and 20 other ranks were reported missing.

CAPTAIN ARTHUR GRAEME WEST

16th Public Schools Battalion Middlesex Regiment.
6th Battalion Oxfordshire and Buckinghamshire Light Infantry.
Born: 23rd September 1891. Warwickshire.
Educated: Blundells School.
    Balliol College, Oxford.
Killed: 3rd April 1917. Aged 25 years.
HAC Cemetery, Ecoust-St. Mein, France.

At Blundells, where "skill at games was the only passport to popularity", Arthur West, a scholar and naturalist, spent an unhappy five years. In 1910 he won a scholarship to Balliol where he gained a third in Moderations and a second in Greats. His friend and contemporary, C.E.M. Joad, remembered him as being:

> Not pre-eminently witty, generous, genial, or hospitable. He knew few anecdotes, and never told them. Perhaps it was more than anything else by all the things that he was not that he charmed. He was so devoid of push and advertisement, so quiet, tranquil, and unassuming, so eminently companionable, and above all, such a good listener, that, though these things did not constitute his charm, they went some way to explain it...

West returned to Oxford in the autumn of 1914 to start a fifth year at the University, applied for a Commission in December but was rejected because of poor eyesight. In January 1915 he enlisted as a Private in the 16th Public Schools Battalion, Middlesex Regiment. He described the first six weeks as being a time of "irredeemable ugliness".

On 16th November the Battalion left Pepham Down on Salisbury Plain with "4 officers, 122 other ranks, 21 horses, 43 mules, 4 machine-guns, 19 vehicles, also 9 bicycles." It arrived in France on 19th November 1915 and was in billets at Boeseghem and Busnes for ten days and was then in and out of trenches east of Béthune for the next six weeks. From the trenches at Le Hamel, West wrote on Wednesday December 7th:

> ... Paraded at 3.30 in haversacks and water-bottle, groundsheet and leather jerkin for the trenches. Marched along a pretty bad road till dark, past an English Cemetery full of little wooden crosses, until we came to a very ruined village.

It was raining hard by now and we were wet already. We struck off across the open over old trenches for almost a mile. We were meant to go by communication trenches, but they were so full of water that we had to go on top. The mud and water were worse than anything we had ever met, many went in up to their necks, and all of us were soaked up to and over the knees.

We passed the supports and reserve-trenches with fires in braziers and many dugouts draped with groundsheets. In the support trench men were sleeping here and there outside, sitting on the firing platform in groundsheets. The trenches were wet but boarded at the bottom, so one did not walk in more than three or four inches of water. Our platoon was to go to the front-line trenches, which were not trenches at all, but broken bits of trench, the tolerably whole parts of which we held in sections of five. We five were together in post No. G at the extreme left end of that line. It was a very bad place; about ten or fifteen yards of sand-bags were standing, but the tops had been knocked off and the things were low. There was no back to the trench at all, and the water was deep; we had nothing to keep it off us but a few sticks laid across. We had no shelter from the rear or side at all. The general idea was that we were the front line and had to hold it until the supports came up. As there was a wire entanglement between us and the supports they would take a long time to come up and we ourselves should be wiped out; then the supports would be caught in the communication trench like rats in a trap, and killed off, too. Then the reserves would come into play, repulse the enemy and shell them out. The Germans were rather less than 200 yards off, too far to throw bombs, but snipers were active. Though no rifle-bullets ever came near us, the Germans had machine-guns trained along the top of the parapet, and they troubled us a good deal.

At first we were quite amused and laughed at our position but soon the damp and cold and the prospect of twenty-four hours' endurance of it, our isolation and exposure cooled us down and we sat still and dripped and shivered. Flares went up continually, and occasional machine-gun bullets whizzed over us, and snipers shot...

The Battalion was at trenches at Beuvry in February and West wrote to a friend on the 12th:

... We have had rather a bloody - literally - time of it. The tab. I had met early at Woldingham was shot in the head and killed instantly one night standing next to me, and you may have observed that we lost several officers. We had an extraordinarily heavy bombardment. Also I had rather an exciting time myself with two other men on a patrol in the "no man's land" between the lines. A dangerous business, and most repulsive on account of the smells and appearance of the heaps of dead men that lie unburied there as they fell, on some attack or other, about four months ago. I found myself much as I had expected in the face of these happenings: more interested than afraid, but more careful for my own life than anxious to approve any new martial ardour. I become, I assure you, more and more cautious, though more accustomed and easy in face of the Hun...

I have contracted hatred and enmity for nobody out here, save soldiers generally and a few N.C.O.'s in particular. For the Hun I feel nothing but a spirit of amiable fraternity that the poor man has to sit just like us and do all the horrible and useless things that we do, when he might be at home with his wife or his books...

At the end of February the Battalion arrived at Quiéstede, outside St. Omer.

THE NIGHT PATROL
France, March 1916.

Over the top! The wire's thin here, unbarbed
Plain rusty coils, not staked, and low enough:
Full of old tins, though - "When you're through, all three,
Aim quarter left for fifty yards or so,
Then straight for that new piece of German wire;
See if it's thick, and listen for a while
For sounds of working; don't run any risks;
About an hour; now, over!"
                                    And we placed
Our hands on the topmost sand-bags, leapt, and stood
A second with curved backs, then crept to the wire,
Wormed ourselves tinkling through, glanced back, and dropped.
The sodden ground was splashed with shallow pools,
And tufts of crackling cornstalks, two years old,
No man had reaped, and patches of spring grass.
Half-seen, as rose and sank the flares, were strewn
With the wrecks of our attack: the bandoliers,
Packs, rifles, bayonets, belts, and haversacks,
Shell fragments, and the huge whole forms of shells
Shot fruitlessly - and everywhere the dead.
Only the dead were always present - present
As a vile sickly smell of rottenness;
The rustling stubble and the early grass,
The slimy pools - the dead men stank through all,
Pungent and sharp; as bodies loomed before,

And as we passed, they stank: then dulled away
To that vague foetor, all encompassing,
Infecting earth and air. They lay, all clothed,
Each in some new and piteous attitude
That we well marked to guide us back: as he,
Outside our wire, that lay on his back and crossed
His legs Crusader-wise; I smiled at that,
And thought on Elia and his Temple Church.
From him, at quarter-left, lay a small corpse,
Down in a hollow, huddled as in bed,
That one of us put his hand on unawares.
Next was a bunch of half a dozen men
All blown to bits, an archipelago
Of corrupt fragments, vexing to us three,
Who had no light to see by, save the flares.
On such a trail, so lit, for ninety yards

We crawled on belly and elbows, till we saw,
Instead of lumpish dead before our eyes,
The stakes and crosslines of the German wire.
We lay in shelter of the last dead man,
Ourselves as dead, and heard their shovels ring
Turning the earth, then talk and cough at times.
A sentry fired and a machine-gun spat;
They shot a flare above us, when it fell
And spluttered out in the pools of No Man's Land,
We turned and crawled past the remembered dead:
Past him and him, and them and him, until,
For he lay some way apart, we caught the scent
Of the Crusader and slid past his legs,
And through the wire and home, and got our rum.

At the end of March, West was sent to an Officers Training Camp in Scotland; after a few weeks of initial training he wrote:

Friday May 12th 1916 ...A fearful sense of the grimness of things came over me last night, which it would have been hard to express in words even then, and of which it is hard now to recapture even the details...

I knew how many of us did not feel fit here: this, combined with the stupidity of parading us for platoon drill or even physical drill in the wind and wet (we were sometimes kept an hour drilling in the pouring rain), and the ever-increasing viciousness and malice of the Adjutant and C.S.M. towards us, seemed to keep an almost personal fiend of terror hovering above our heads. The war and the Army had never looked so grim. The Army is really the most anti-social body imaginable. It maintains itself on the selfishness and hostility of nations, and in its own ranks holds together by a bond of fear and suspicion, all anti-social feeling. Men are taught to fear their superiors, and they suspect the men. Hatred must be often present, and only fear prevents it flaming out...

I do really care less than I used to do for the fools and bullies in command of me. They certainly do not frighten me at all as they used to. I don't care a jot for the Adjutant or the C.O. when they come and yap or make heavy speeches at me. I do not mind if I am ticked off on parade, and I don't think I should be at all shamed if I were finally turned down altogether... I am approaching more nearly... a state of Nihilism rather than Stoicism... Now I see the great attractiveness and mournful pleasure of the creed that nothing is...

Even the decision of this war is nothing; what does England matter, or whether she wins or not? Any man of sense... must understand that all existence from the earliest Egyptian dynasties and aeons before them, to the present day, and on and on into the future, is without meaning, of no absolute or continuous importance. Mankind is perpetually puffing itself up with strange unearthly loyalties and promised rewards...

There is only one thing real amidst all this decorative garbage, and that is the feeling of pain or pleasure, together with thought. To bring happiness into the world is the only aim of action; action undertaken for any other motive is wasted. We may seek the happiness of ourselves and of others... But all other creations that are supposed to have a claim on my time and life I spurn. I spurn the idea that I am naturally enthusiastic for the success of my hut or Platoon or Company or Battalion; that I am necessarily fonder of my own country than any other, and most of all, now, I reject the presumption that I worship a God by Whose never-wronging hand I conceive all the present woe to have been brought upon the now-living generation of mankind. If there is a God at all responsible for governing the earth, I hate and abominate Him - I rather despise Him. But I do not think there is one...

Arthur West left Scotland in August 1916 and was commissioned in the 6th Battalion, The Oxfordshire and Buckinghamshire Light Infantry. He spent a few weeks leave with his family and friends. On 8th August 1916 he wrote:

I now find myself disbelieving utterly in Christianity as a religion, or even in Christ as an actual figure. I seem to have lost in softness and become harder, more ferocious in nature, and in appearances, certainly, by virtue of my moustache! So violently do I react against the conventional religion that once bound me - or if it did not bind me, at any rate loomed behind me - that I loathe and scorn all emotionalism and religious feeling...

On 19th August, after visiting Joad and his wife, West wrote:

... If the war were to begin to-morrow and were to find me as I am now, I would not join the Army, and if I had the courage I would desert now. I have been reading and thinking fundamentally important things this last few months. What right has anybody to demand of me that I should give up my chance of obtaining happiness - the only chance I have, and the only thing worth obtaining here? Because they are foolish enough - not reasonable enough - to give their own up, that is no reason why I should abandon mine. I asked no one to form societies to help me exist. I certainly asked no one to start this war. To help on happiness as much as possible I do not object, but I believe the best way to do it would be to incite people not to form armies or fight or be absurdly and narrowly patriotic. This feeling must be suppressed, broadened out, not encouraged. My feelings and emotional experiences during these days were so strange and intense that I intend to register them as accurately as possible...

I read a good deal of liberal literature, met some conscientious objectors, moved much among men not at all occupied in the war, and hence suffered a violent revulsion from my old imagined glories and delights of the Army (such as I had had) - its companionship, suffering courageously and of noble necessity undergone - to intense hatred of the war spirit and the country generally...

I so loathed the idea of rejoining the Army that I determined to desert and hide away somewhere. This was so strong with me on Saturday, August 19th, when, rather against my family's wishes, I went down to J [Joad] for the last time. Never was the desire to desert and to commit suicide so overwhelming, and had it not been that I knew I would pain many people, I would certainly have killed myself that night...

On that evening I stayed up late and read B. Russell's *Justice in War Time*, and went to bed so impressed with its force that I determined to stand out openly against re-entering the Army. I was full of a quiet strong belief and almost knowledge that I should not, after all, have to face the trial of entering a new regiment as an officer, and that Waterloo would not see me at 2.10...

In the morning I was still determined. I didn't go to church when asked to do so, but re-read B. Russell, and made up my mind to announce to the family at lunchtime that "I have come to a serious decision, long thought out, and now morally determined on. It will influence me more than you, and yet perhaps you ought to know of it. I am not going to rejoin the Army. There is no object, except the gratification of a senseless rivalry, in prolonging the struggle, it is beastly and degrading. Why do we go on fighting? I will not go on."

I really nearly did say it. Everybody thought me silent and depressed because I was returning to the Army. It was not so. However, I said nothing... After much thought I wrote to the Adjutant of the Battalion telling him I would not rejoin the Army nor accept any form of alternative service, that I would rather be shot than do so, and that I left my name and address with him to act as he pleased.

Shortly after midnight I went down to the post with this letter and two more... I stood opposite the pillar-box for some minutes wondering whether I would post them - then put them in my pocket and returned home to bed.

Next morning my aversion was as great and my determination not to rejoin as strong as ever. This was Monday morning, the day I had telegraphed I would rejoin. I thought I would tell the remainder of the family. I didn't. I got furiously into my new uniform and went off after brekker to cash a cheque and get my hair cut and order a cab. As the barber cut my hair I determined I would go down and telegraph that I could not come to W [Wareham, Dorset], and that explanations were following. I walked to a telegraph-office to do so - and bought two penny stamps and walked out again. I cashed a cheque for £10, saying in excuse that it might help me if I determined to desert. Then I went to order a cab, but thought at the last moment, I would walk on to a telegraph office beyond the cab office. I turned back soon after I had passed the office and ordered the cab. This settled it, I thought.

I returned home, packed, wrote to J [Joad], had lunch... I departed in a state of cynical wrath against myself and the world in general, who would understand so little of what I meant...

As we drew near W [Wareham], horror of rejoining the Army was making me very miserable; moreover, I had been reading B.R. in the train, and was encouraged to believe that - as I put it to myself - I might yet quite succeed in keeping my mind and spirit straight, even if I could not induce myself to acknowledge it among my enemies and those who would be indifferent to me...

Two days later West ended a letter:

... I am almost certain I do wrong to go on - not quite certain, and anyhow, I question if I am of martyr stuff...

Before he left England for France again, West wrote 'God! How I Hate You, You Young Cheerful Men!' He had read the poetry of Rex Freston (qv), his contemporary at Oxford, who had been killed in January 1916. West replied in anger to Rex Freston's poems 'O Fortunati' and 'To the Atheists':

GOD! HOW I HATE YOU, YOU YOUNG CHEERFUL MEN!

God! How I hate you, you young cheerful men,
Whose pious poetry blossoms on your graves
As soon as you are in them, nurtured up
By the salt of your corruption, and the tears
Of mothers, local vicars, college deans,
And flanked by prefaces and photographs
From all your minor poet friends - the fools -
Who paint their sentimental elegies
Where sure, no angel treads; and, living, share
The dead's brief immortality.
                                   Oh Christ!
To think that one could spread the ductile wax
Of his fluid youth to Oxford's glowing fires
And take her seal so ill! Hark how one chants -
"Oh happy to have lived these epic days" -
"These epic days"! And he'd been to France,
And seen the trenches, glimpsed the huddled dead
In the periscope, hung in the rusting wire:
Choked by their sickly foetor, day and night
Blown down his throat: stumbled through ruined hearths,
Proved all that muddy brown monotony,
Where blood's the only coloured thing. Perhaps
Had seen a man killed, a sentry shot at night,
Hunched as he fell, his feet on the firing-step,
His neck against the back slope of the trench,
And the rest doubled up between, his head
Smashed like an egg-shell, and the warm grey brain
Spattered all bloody on the parados:
Had flashed a torch on his face, and known his friend,
Shot, breathing hardly, in ten minutes - gone!
Yet still God's in His heaven, all is right
In the best possible of worlds. The woe,

190

Even His scaled eyes must see, is partial, only
A seeming woe, we cannot understand.
God loves us, God looks down on this our strife
And smiles in pity, blows a pipe at times
And calls some warriors home. We do not die,
God would not let us, He is too "intense",
Too "passionate", a whole day sorrows He
Because a grass-blade dies. How rare life is!
On earth, the love and fellowship of men,
Men sternly banded: banded for what end?
Banded to maim and kill their fellow men -
For even Huns are men. In heaven above
A genial umpire, a good judge of sport,
Won't let us hurt each other! Let's rejoice
God keeps us faithful, pens us still in fold.
Ah, what a faith is ours (almost, it seems,
Large, as a mustard-seed) - we trust and trust,
Nothing can shake us! Ah, how good God is
To suffer us be born just now, when youth
That else would rust, can slake his blade in gore,
Where very God Himself does seem to walk
The bloody fields of Flanders He so loves!

In September 1916 West joined the 6th Battalion Oxfordshire
and Buckinghamshire Light Infantry which was in billets at Corbie
and Méaulte. From Triangle trench he wrote on Sunday 17th
September:

... We got up here about 2.20 a.m. Sunday morning - a terribly long
relief, for we started out for this line from G.... Ridge at 8.30 p.m.
Saturday night. The men were dog-tired when they got here, and
though ordered to dig, complied very unwillingly, and were allowed to
sit about or lean on their spades, or even to stand up and fall asleep
against the side of the trench. It was a smelly trench. A dead German
- a big man - lay on his stomach as if he were crawling over the
parados down into the trench; he had lain there some days, and that
corner of trench reeked even when someone took him by the legs and
pulled him away out of sight, though not out of smell, into a shell-
hole. We sat down and fell into a comatose state, so tired we were.
On our right lay a large man covered with a waterproof, his face
hidden by a sand-bag, whom we took to be a dead Prussian
Guardsman, but the light of dawn showed him to be an Englishman by
his uniform. From where I sit I can see his doubled-up knees...

We try and make out where we are on the map, and find we are at least 1,000 yards away. Then we resolve that as we had practically no sleep last night nor the night before, and I had little even the night before that, we will try and get some. We lie...

Wednesday, September 20th 1916 ...So far I had written when it became evident that our quiet Sunday was to be of the usual kind and we were to be bombarded. H.E. shells, about 6-inch ones, came over with a tremendous black smoke, making an explosion and sending up a column of earth about thirty feet high. The first intimation I had was when I went round the corner to the next bay to see where one had fallen, and found a man with a little ferrety nose and inadequate yellow moustache, in a very long great-coat, sitting muttering away on the firing-step like a nervous rabbit and making vague gestures with his hands and head. He would return no answer to questions, and I was told two men had just been buried in a dug-out near by. I went round and found two more pale men, rather earthy. I talked to them and did my best to comfort them. A few more shells came over, upleasantly near, but it was not yet certain whether they were definitely after us.

Soon this was clear. They worked down a winding trench, and blew in the walls; we lost six men by burying and ten others wounded or suffering from shell-shock. It was horrible. A whistle would be heard, nearer and nearer, ceasing for a mere fraction of a second when the shell was falling and about to explode. Where was it coming?

Men cowered and trembled. It exploded, and a cloud of black reek went up - in the communication trench again. You went down it; two men were buried, perhaps more you were told, certainly two. The trench was a mere undulation of newly-turned earth, under it somewhere lay two men or more. You dug furiously. No sign. Perhaps you were standing on a couple of men now, pressing the life out of them, on their faces or chests. A boot, a steel helmet - and you dig and scratch and uncover a grey, dirty face, pitifully drab and ugly, the eyes closed, the whole thing limp and mean-looking: this is the devil of it, that a man is not only killed, but made to look so vile and filthy in death, so futile and meaningless that you hate the sight of him.

Perhaps the man is alive and kicks feebly or frantically as you unbury him: anyhow, here is the first, and God knows how many are not beneath him. At last you get them out, three dead, grey, muddy masses, and one more jibbering live one.

Then another shell falls and more are buried.

We tried to make them stand up.

It is noticeable that only one man was wounded; six were buried alive.

I shall always remember sitting at the head of this little narrow trench, smoking a cigarette and trying to soothe the men simply by being quiet. Five or six little funk-holes dug into the side of the trench served to take the body of a man in a very huddled and uncomfortable position, with no room to move, simply to cower into the little hole. There they sit like animals for market, like hens in cages, one facing one way, one another. One simply looks at his hands clasped on his knees, dully and lifelessly, shivering a little as a shell draws near; another taps the side of his hole with his finger-nails, rhythmically; another hides himself in his great-coat and passes into a kind of torpor. Of course, when a shell falls on to the parapet and bores down into the earth and explodes, they are covered over like so many potatoes. It is with the greatest difficulty that we can shift the men into another bit of trench and make them stand up. I found myself cool and useful enough, though after we had been shelled for about two and a half hours on end my nerves were shaky and I could have cried for fright as each shell drew near, and longed for nothing so much as to rush down a deep cellar. I did not betray any kind of weak feeling.

It was merely consideration of the simple fact that a shell, if it did hit me, would either wound me or kill me, both of which were good inasmuch as they would put a pause to this existence - that kept me up to my standard of unconcern. And the more I experience it, the more fear seems a thing quite apart from possible consequences, which may occur in a person even when he assents fully to the proposition I have noted above.

I feel afraid at the moment. I write in a trench that was once German, and shells keep dropping near the dug-out. There is a shivery fear that one may fall into it or blow it in.

Yet what do I fear? I mind being killed because I am fond of the other life, but I know I should not miss it in annihilation. It is not that I fear.

I don't definitely feel able to say I fear the infliction of pain or wound. I cannot bind the fear down to anything definite. I think it resolves itself simply into the realisation of the fact that being hit by a shell will produce a new set of circumstances so strange that one does not know how one will find oneself in them. It is the knowledge that something may happen with which one will not be able to cope, or that one's old resolutions of courage, etc., will fail one in this new set of experiences. Something unknown there is. How will one act when it happens? One may be called upon to bear or perform something to which one will find oneself inadequate...

Towards the end of September the Battalion was in billets at Ville-sur-Ancre.

Sunday, 24th September 1916. A Tent... I am unhappier than I ever was last year, and this not only because I have been separated from my friends or because I am simply more tired of the war.

It is because my whole outlook towards the thing has altered. I endured what I did endure last year patiently, believing I was doing a right and reasonable thing. I had not thought out the position of the pacifist and the conscientious objector, I was always sympathetic to these people, but never considered whether my place ought not to have been rather among them than where I actually was. Then I came back to England feeling rather like the noble crusader or explorer who has given up much for his friend but who is not going to be sentimental or overbearing about it, though he regards himself as somehow different from and above those who have not endured as he has done...

"This war is trivial, for all its vastness," says B. Russell, and so I feel. I am being pained, bored, and maddened - and to what end? It is the uselessness of it that annoys me. I had once regarded it as inevitable; now I don't believe it was, and had I been in full possession of my reasoning powers when the war began, I would never have joined the Army. To have taken a stand against the whole thing, against the very conception of force, even when employed against force, would have really been my happier and truer course.

The war so filled up my perspective at first that I could not see anything close because of it: most people are still like that. To find a growing body of men who can really be "au-dessus de la mêlée", who can comprehend and condemn it, who can live in the world beside the war and yet not in it, is extremely encouraging to anyone who can acclaim himself of their brotherhood. Spiritually I am of it, but I am prevented from being among them. I am a creature caught in a net.

Most men fight, if not happily, at any rate patiently, sure of the necessity and usefulness of their work. So did I - once! Now it all looks to me so absurd and brutal that I can only force myself to continue in a kind of dream-state; I hypnotise myself to undergo it. What good, what happiness can be produced by some of the scenes I have had to witness in the last few days?

Even granting it was necessary to resist Germany by arms at the beginning - and this I have yet most carefully to examine - why go on?

Can no peace be concluded?"

Is it not known to both armies that each is utterly weary and heartsick?

Of course it is. Then why, in God's name, go on?

It must be unreasonable to continue. The victorious, or seemingly victorious side, ought to offer peace: no peace can be worse than this bloody stupidity. The maddening thing is the sight of men of fairly goodwill accepting it all as necessary; this angers me, that men *must* go on. Why? Who wants to?

Moreover, I feel quite clearly that I ought to have stood aside. It is these men who stand aside, these philosophers, and the so-called conscientious objectors, who are the living force of the future; they are full of the light that must come sooner or later; they are sneered at now, but their position is firm.

If all mankind were like them there would not have been war. Duty to country and King and civilisation! Nonsense! For none of these is a man to be forced to leave his humanity on one side and make a passionate destroying beast of himself. I am a man before I am anything else, and all that is human in me revolts. I would fain stand beside these men I admire, whose cause is the highest part of human nature, calm reason, and kindliness...

There was but one way for me, and I have seen it only when it was too late to pursue it... To defy the whole system, to refuse to be an instrument of it - this *I* should have done.

Two days later, on 26th September, the Battalion was in the trenches east of Méaulte. Daylight the next day "showed a fearful lot of dead Germans round the trench and an appalling shambles in the dug-outs." On the 29th seven men were killed by a shell as soon as the Battalion reached the trenches by Trones Wood. On 27th December 1916 West wrote to Bertrand Russell:

To-night here on the Somme I have just finished your *Principles of Social Reconstruction* which I found waiting for me when I came out of the line... It is only on account of such thoughts as yours, on account of the existence of men and women like yourself that it seems worth while surviving the war - if one should haply survive. Outside the small circle of that cool light I can discern nothing but a scorching desert. Do not fear though that the life of the spirit is dying in us, nor that hope or energy will be spent; to some few of us at any rate the hope of helping to found some 'city of God' carries us away from these present horrors and beyond the graver intolerance of thought as we see in it our papers. We shall not faint and the energy and endurance we have used here on an odious task we shall be able to redouble in the creative work that peace will bring to do. We are too young to be permanently damaged in body or spirit, even by these sufferings...

The Battalion was in dug-outs in the vicinity of Bouleaux Wood on the 1st January 1917 and the next day moved up into the line; it remained in the trenches until the 4th when it went back to Bronfay Camp. The Battalion continued in and out of the trenches for three further tours and then went to Méaulte for training. In February the Battalion again had more tours of duty in the trenches in front of Guillemont which continued until the 15th March. The following day the Morval Sector, with three small posts, was taken over, after which the Battalion continued to move gradually forward following the retreating Germans in their withdrawal to the Hindenburg Line, until it reached Barastre on the 28th March. On 1st April the Battalion moved from Barastre up into the outpost line. On the morning of 3rd April, Arthur West was killed by a stray bullet during 'stand to'.

SECOND LIEUTENANT WALTER LIGHTOWLER WILKINSON

1st/8th Battalion Argyll and Sutherland Highlanders.
Born: 1886. Bristol.
Killed: 9th April 1917. Aged 31 years.
Highland Cemetery, Roclincourt, France.

Walter Wilkinson's father was chief manager of goods traffic on the Great Western Railway. After his parent's death Wilkinson was adopted by Mrs. William Sharpe, the widow of an author.

At the outbreak of the War, Wilkinson enlisted as a Private in the University and Public Schools Corps. He was commissioned in the Argyll and Sutherland Highlanders in June 1916, and joined the Battalion in huts at Ovillers, north-east of Albert, in January 1917. On 25th January he wrote 'Night in Wartime':

NIGHT IN WARTIME

Night and night's menace; Death hath forged a dart
Of every moment's pause and stealthy pass:
Blind Terror reigns: darkly, as in a glass,
Man's wondering Soul beholds his fearful Heart,
And questions, and is shaken: and, apart,
Light Chance, the harlot-goddess, holding Mass,
Scatters her favours broadcast on the grass
As might a drunkard spill his wares in mart!

Time and sweet Order have forsaken men,
So near Eternal seems the Night's foul sway:
We ask of Life: "Has Chaos come again,
With Ruin, and Confusion and Decay ?"
Yet slowly, surely darkness dies: and then,
Out of the deep night's menace, dawns the Day!

On 17th March, 13 officers and 382 other ranks from the Battalion raided German trenches near Roclincourt, a village 4 kilometres north of Arras on the road to Vimy. There were many German casualties, 10 prisoners were captured and severe damage was inflicted. Of the raiding party 2 officers were killed and 6 were wounded; 19 other ranks were killed, 82 wounded and 25 reported missing. Probably as a result of this action, Wilkinson wrote the following poem:

THE WAYSIDE BURIAL

They're bringing in their recent dead - their recent dead!
I see the shoulder badge: a "Southern crush."
How small he looks - (O damn that singing thrush!)
Not five foot five from boots to battered head!...
Give him a kindly burial, my friends, -
So much is due, when some such loyal life ends!
"For Country!".... Ay, and so our brave do die:
Comrade unknown, good rest to you! - Good-bye!

They're bringing their recent dead! - No pomp, no show:
A dingy khaki crowd - his friends, his own.
I, too, would like - (God, how that wind does moan!)
To be laid down by friends : it's sweetest so!
A young life, as I take it; just a lad -
(How cold it blows; and that grey sky, how sad!)
And yet: "For Country" - so a man should die:
Comrade unknown, good rest to you! - Good-bye!

They're burying their dead! - I wonder now:
A wife? - or mother? Mother it must be -
In some trim home that fronts the English sea.
(A sea-coast country: that the badges show).
And she? - I sense her grief, I feel her tears!
"This, then, the garnered harvest of my years!"
And he?..."For Country, dear, a man must die!"
Comrade unknown, good rest to you! - Good-bye!

It's reeded: he is buried! Comrade, sleep!
A wooden cross at your brave head will stand.
A cross of wood? A Calvary! - The Land
For whose sake you laid down sweet life, will keep
Watch, lad, and ward that none may bring to shame
That Name for which you died!..."What's in a name"? -
England shall answer! You will hear her Cry:
"Well done, my own! my son - good rest : Good-bye!"

A combined offensive by both British and French forces was planned for the Spring of 1917. General Nivelle was to attack the southern end of the Hindenburg Line on the Aisne in a vain attempt to break through the German defences, while the British 3rd Army under Allenby was to support the French by an assault at Arras.

After eight days of heavy bombardment from Givenchy-en-Gohelle to Croisilles, the Battle of Arras started with an attack on a twelve mile front on Easter Monday, 9th April, 1917. At the same time four Canadian Divisions, backed by a British artillery bombardment, advanced on Vimy Ridge, north of the town of Arras.

The initial results at Arras were highly successful, in particular for the Canadians, who took Vimy Ridge. However, after the first day the attacking forces became bogged down, failed to follow up their hard won ground, and allowed the Germans to regroup and hold out.

The French attack was delayed, and when on 16th April it did take place, it was repulsed with heavy losses and with no ground gained. General Nivelle was replaced.

At 5.30 am on the 9th April the 8th Battalion Argyll and Sutherland Highlanders, with 22 officers and 622 other ranks, attacked German trenches east of Roclincourt, near Arras. Although the Battalion succeeded in achieving its objective, they suffered heavily and Walter Wilkinson was killed.

AT LAST POST

Come home ! - Come home!
The winds are at rest in the restful trees;
At rest are the waves of the sundown seas;
And home - they're home -
The wearied hearts and the broken lives -
At home! At ease!

SECOND LIEUTENANT PHILIP EDWARD THOMAS

244th Siege Battery, Royal Garrison Artillery.
Born: 3rd March 1878. London.
Educated: St Paul's School, London.
Lincoln College, Oxford.
Killed: 9th April 1917. Aged 39 years.
Agny Military Cemetery, France.

Edward Thomas was the eldest of six sons. His parents were of Welsh ancestry and his father, Philip Henry Thomas, was a civil servant with the Board of Trade. Edward's childhood was spent in London except for the school holidays when he was sent to stay with relations in South Wales and Swindon. He later wrote of his childhood and recalled an early holiday in Wales which he and his mother spent in Swansea with great-aunt Mary:

> ... I saw the sea and the Gower cliffs and rocks. I collected shells and pebbles that took my fancy, especially one rounded like a Bath bun which we took back to the garden at Swansea, where it remained for twenty years and more. I have loved flat or round seaworn pebbles ever since, and can never carry away as many as I wish from a new coast or hill-side where I am walking...

During a school holiday in Swindon in 1895 Thomas met an old Wiltshire man, known as 'Dad' Uzzell who encouraged his love of the open air and the countryside; Uzzell remained a firm friend, father figure and influence throughout Thomas' life.

Thomas' expert knowledge of natural history developed during his childhood; on his long walks he collected birds' eggs and butterflies and kept notes of the birds, flowers and trees he had seen. From these early notes he had published articles by the time he was seventeen.

"When I think of school I smell carbolic soap", Edward Thomas wrote. He attended several schools until he finally went to St. Paul's in January 1894. He was unhappy at first but later appreciated the opportunities the school offered.

In 1897, Thomas' first book *The Woodland Life* was published. In the Autumn he went up to Oxford and won a history scholarship to Lincoln College. In June 1899 he married Helen Noble and their first child was born six months before he took his finals. Although he now had a family and was financially dependent on his father, who wanted him to enter the Civil Service, Edward Thomas never wavered from his ambition to write.

Over the next years he earned a precarious living as a writer. In addition to biographies, topographical books and essays, he wrote reviews, introductions and edited anthologies. However, he became increasingly bitter, trapped by poverty and family responsibilities into the sort of writing he found unfulfilling and stultifying. To escape the frustration, bouts of depression and sheer hard work, he would stay with friends or go off on his own on walking and bicycling tours of England and Wales. Helen remained patient and loving throughout all his moods and absences.

In 1914 a small group of Georgian poets, Lascelles Abercrombie, Wilfrid Gibson and John Drinkwater were living in and around the Gloucestershire village of Dymock. Rupert Brooke stayed occasionally and the four poets wrote poems for the quarterly, *New Numbers*, which they published from Gibson's house, 'The Gallows'. In the Spring of 1914, at Wilfrid Gibson's suggestion, the American poet, Robert Frost rented the cottage 'Little Iddens' near the village; the Thomas family followed in the late summer, a few days after war had been declared, to live in a cottage next door to the Frosts. During the few weeks they were there Eleanor Farjeon also stayed in rooms near them.

The friendship between Edward Thomas and Robert Frost blossomed; they walked the countryside together and in the evenings the group of friends gathered to enjoy country food and local cider, play word games, cards and charades, sing well-loved folk songs and read poetry and prose. It was during this time that Robert Frost who admired Thomas' prose, encouraged him to write poetry. Thomas later recalled his friendship with Frost in the poem 'The Sun Used to Shine':

THE SUN USED TO SHINE

> The sun used to shine while we two walked
> Slowly together, paused and started
> Again, and sometimes mused, sometimes talked
> As either pleased, and cheerfully parted
>
> Each night. We never disagreed
> Which gate to rest on. The to be
> And the late past we gave small heed.
> We turned from men or poetry

To rumours of the war remote
Only till both stood disinclined
For aught but the yellow flavorous coat
Of an apple wasps had undermined;

Or a sentry of dark betonies,
The stateliest of small flowers on earth,
At the forest verge; or crocuses
Pale purple as if they had their birth

In sunless Hades fields. The war
Came back to mind with the moonrise
Which soldiers in the east afar
Beheld then. Nevertheless, our eyes

Could as well imagine the Crusades
or Caesar's battles. Everything
To faintness like those rumours fades -
Like the brook's water glittering

Under the moonlight - like those walks
Now - like us two that took them, and
The fallen apples, all the talks
And silences - like memory's sand

When the tide covers it late or soon,
And other men through other flowers
In those fields under the same moon
Go talking and have easy hours.

All the poems published during Thomas' lifetime were under his pseudonym, 'Edward Eastaway'. He wrote all his poetry between December 1914 and January 1917 when he went to France, and only a few poems referred directly to the War. One of the earliest written in his first creative burst was 'Old Man':

OLD MAN

Old Man, or Lad's-love, - in the name there's nothing
To one that knows not Lad's-love, or Old Man,
The hoar-green feathery herb, almost a tree,
Growing with rosemary and lavender.

1917

Even to one that knows it well, the names
Half decorate, half perplex, the thing it is:
At least, what that is clings not to the names
In spite of time. And yet I like the names.

The herb itself I like not, but for certain
I love it, as some day the child will love it
Who plucks a feather from the door-side bush
Whenever she goes in or out of the house.
Often she waits there, snipping the tips and shrivelling
The shreds at last on to the path, perhaps
Thinking, perhaps of nothing, till she sniffs
Her fingers and runs off. The bush is still
But half as tall as she, though it is as old;
So well she clips it. Not a word she says;
And I can only wonder how much hereafter
She will remember, with that bitter scent,
Of garden rows, and ancient damson trees
Topping a hedge, a bent path to a door,
A low thick bush beside the door, and me
Forbidding her to pick.

As for myself,
Where first I met the bitter scent is lost.
I, too, often shrivel the grey shreds,
Sniff them and think and sniff again and try
Once more to think what it is I am remembering,
Always in vain. I cannot like the scent,
Yet I would rather give up others more sweet,
With no meaning, than this bitter one.

I have mislaid the key. I sniff the spray
And think of nothing; I see and I hear nothing;
Yet seem, too, to be listening, lying in wait
For what I should, yet never can, remember:
No garden appears, no path, no hoar-green bush
Of Lad's-love, or Old Man, no child beside,
Neither father nor mother, nor any playmate;
Only an avenue, dark, nameless, without end.

Edward Thomas spent the eleven months, between August 1914 and July 1915, indecisive as to whether he should take his family to America and live in New England near the Frosts, or whether he

203

should enlist; the decision finally made, he was passed medically fit in July 1915 and joined the Artists' Rifles. Three months later he was a Lance Corporal instructing young officers at Hare Hall Camp, near Romford, Essex, where Wilfred Owen (qv) arrived under training in November. During his ten months at Hare Hall Thomas composed over forty poems:

RAIN

Rain, midnight rain, nothing but the wild rain
On this bleak hut, and solitude, and me
Remembering again that I shall die
And neither hear the rain nor give it thanks
For washing me cleaner than I have been
Since I was born into this solitude.
Blessed are the dead that the rain rains upon:
But here I pray that none whom once I loved
Is dying to-night or lying still awake
Solitary, listening to the rain,
Either in pain or thus in sympathy
Helpless among the living and the dead,
Like a cold water among broken reeds,
Myriads of broken reeds all still and stiff,
Like me who have no love which this wild rain
Has not disolved except the love of death,
If love it be towards what is perfect and
Cannot, the tempest tells me, disappoint.

On 28th May 1916, Edward Thomas wrote to Helen from Hare Hall:

... I set out with a meal in my haversack for a long walk, but didn't go more than 6 miles all day. I sat down a good deal both in the fields & at an inn; & passed or was passed by the same pair of lovers 3 or 4 times. It was very pleasant too, warm and cloudy. I wrote some lines too & rewrote them...

AS THE TEAM'S HEAD-BRASS

As the team's head-brass flashed out on the turn
The lovers disappeared into the wood.
I sat among the boughs of the fallen elm

That strewed an angle of the fallow, and
Watched the plough narrowing a yellow square
Of charlock. Every time the horses turned
Instead of treading me down, the ploughman leaned
Upon the handles to say or ask a word,
About the weather, next about the war.
Scraping the share he faced towards the wood,
And screwed along the furrow till the brass flashed
Once more.
        The blizzard felled the elm whose crest
I sat in, by a wood-pecker's round hole,
The ploughman said. "When will they take it away?"
"When the war's over." So the talk began -
One minute and an interval of ten,
A minute more and the same interval.
"Have you been out?" "No". "And don't want to, perhaps?"
"If I could only come back again, I should.
I could spare an arm. I shouldn't want to lose
A leg. If I should lose my head, why, so,
I should want nothing more..... Have many gone
From here?" "Yes". "Many lost?" "Yes; good few.
Only two teams work on the farm this year.
One of my mates is dead. The second day
In France they killed him. It was back in March,
The very night of the blizzard, too. Now if
He had stayed here we should have moved the tree."
"And I should not have sat here. Everything
Would have been different. For it would have been
Another world". "Ay, and a better, though
If we could see all all might seem good." Then
The lovers came out of the wood again;
The horses started and for the last time
I watched the clods crumble and topple over
After the ploughshare and the stumbling team.

Thomas was commissioned in the Royal Garrison Artillery in
August 1916, and on 20th September his unit was sent to the Royal
Artillery Barracks at Trowbridge, Wiltshire. Inspired by a bugle
call during the first weeks of training he wrote:

LIGHTS OUT

I have come to the borders of sleep,
The unfathomable deep
Forest where all must lose
Their way, however straight,
Or winding, soon or late;
They cannot choose.

Many a road and track
That, since the dawn's first crack,
Up to the forest brink,
Deceived the travellers,
Suddenly now blurs,
And in they sink.

Here love ends,
Despair, ambition ends,
All pleasure and all trouble,
Although most sweet or bitter,
Here ends in sleep that is sweeter
Than tasks most noble.

There is not any book
Or face of dearest look
That I would not turn from now
To go into the unknown
I must enter and leave alone,
I know not how.

The tall forest towers;
Its cloudy foliage lowers
Ahead, shelf above shelf;
Its silence I hear and obey
That I may lose my way
And myself.

After a fortnight's leave Thomas was sent to Lydd in Kent for further training. He had unexpected Christmas leave with his family and wrote to his six year old daughter, Myfanwy, on 29th December, 1916, after he returned to Lydd:

... Did Mother tell you I wrote a poem about the dark that evening when you did not want to go into the sitting room because it was dark?... On Monday and Wednesday we are going to shoot with real guns... I should not be surprised if we were in France at the end of this month. I do hope peace won't come just yet. I should not know what to do, especially if it came before I had really been a soldier...

OUT IN THE DARK

Out in the dark over the snow
The fallow fawns invisible go
With the fallow doe;
And the winds blow
Fast as the stars are slow.

Stealthily the dark haunts round
And, when the lamp goes, without sound
At a swifter bound
Than the swiftest hound,
Arrives, and all else is drowned;

And I and star and wind and deer,
Are in the dark together, - near,
Yet far, - and fear
Drums on my ear
In that sage company drear.

How weak and little is the light,
All the universe of sight,
Love and delight,
Before the might,
If you love it not, of night.

Thomas arrived at the mobilization camp at Codford on Salisbury Plain on 15th January 1917 and on 29th January he wrote to Helen from Southampton:

This is just goodbye... This is the last of England & over there I shall say no more goodbyes...

The battery arrived at Le Havre in bitterly cold weather; Thomas' first few days were spent censoring the men's letters and overhauling the guns. For the next three months he kept the diary which he had started on the 1st January 1917 and wrote letters to Helen almost every day.

On the 4th February the battery entrained and two days later they arrived at Mondicourt. Thomas went in a lorry to choose billets "all in half-ruined barns" in frozen farmyards. On the 9th Thomas and one half of the Battery were sent to Dainville where they had billets on the Arras road. From here he wrote to Helen on the 10th February describing his visit "through Achicourt and over the railway towards Beaurains" to the observation posts:

This has been a most interesting day. For I was out six hours in the trenches examining observation posts & seeing how much the German trenches could be seen from them. I was able to get quite a lot of information. Also the two of us were exposed to snipers fire & were within 50 yards of three 'plum puddings' from trench mortars...

I saw my first dead man, stretched stiff with his heels together & toes out at an angle of 45 degrees, covered with sacking, a sniper had caught him.

We are billetted in a farm & it's barns on a main road leading to a Cathedral town which the French took some time ago from the Bosh. It is not the sort of place one would choose to live in, tho warm & comfortable, because it is within easy reach of enemy artillery & there are shell holes round about it & one hears the shells arriving & rattling on windows day & night while some of our own guns fire away from behind us over our heads. But I can tell you I don't really mind it at all so far. The weather is still cold but beautifully fine though the snow makes a slight mist by day. The stars are beautiful every night...

On 13th February the battery was positioned in an orchard by Faubourg d'Amiens at the southern edge of Arras, and on the 18th Thomas wrote to Helen:

... Duty down at the guns with very little to do. It is another misty day... The mud is awful & you can't keep your feet warm in a dug-out with a chalk floor. I am to go tomorrow in to the town to do some office work at H.Qs which is rather a blow as it means perhaps that I am the most easily spared officer...

The following day Thomas went as Orderly Officer to Group 35 Heavy Artillery at the Head Quarters in Arras. For a few days he was billetted in "a cold half ruined house with good furniture surviving in it & a china cupboard sealed up by the owner." A few days later he moved to a new billet in a "fine modern house at corner of Rue de l'Abbé Hallain and Boulevard Vauban." The rest of the month was taken up with office routine and working on plans and maps showing to what extent the artillery would be involved in the British offensive planned for Easter Monday. His letters to Helen continued:

February 24th. Things are not so excessively hopeful. The enemy planes are very good. I believe they are holding their artillery back not out of simple poverty. If they do what they could to retaliate on this town it will be one of the hottest places on this side of Hell, if it is this side. I shouldn't be at all surprised if they do something before we do. They know we are preparing. There are bullet holes in most of the windows in this house & one small shell hole in the roof. But you should see the dirty wet ruined house the men are billeted in...

February 27th. It is a fine sunny morning but so was yesterday & the guns made full use of it. The guns here covered an infantry raid & you could not hear a word for over an hour. Then German prisoners began to arrive. Later on hostile shell began to arrive but they were hardly so alarming as they didn't make anything like the same din. In the afternoon I had to go out [to Achicourt] to see if a certain position was visible to the enemy. This was the first time I was really under fire. About 4 shells burst about 150 yards away, little ones, & then in the street fell a shower of machine gun bullets. I confess I felt shy, but I went on with my field glass & compass as far as possible as if nothing was happening. It makes the heart beat but no more than if I were going to pay a call on a stranger. I try to console myself by reflecting that you cannot escape either by running or by standing still. There is no safe place & consequently why worry? and I don't worry... Still no thrushes singing here, not one; only chaffinches.

It becomes harder for me to think about things at home somehow. Although this life does not absorb me, I think, yet, I can't think of anything else. I don't hanker after anything. I don't miss anything. I am not even conscious of waiting. I am just quietly in exile, a sort of half or quarter man...

March 2nd... This afternoon I went to an O.P. in a ghastly suburb of ruined streets [Faubourg Ranville]. The O.P. is in one ruined house & commands a perfect view of No Mans Land & the Hun. It was a fascinating view except for the burst of a shell in a trench. The O.P. is only 7 or 8 hundred yards from the enemy & stands at the very edge of the desolate brown ground that we fight over.

March 7th. It was a lovely morning & very clear & bright & warm... Larks were singing & so was a yellow hammer. But there were far more aeroplanes than larks, sometimes 8 or 9 at a time & more often than larks singing I heard men blowing the alarm on their whistles against hostile planes... A number of shells have just fallen all round our orchard...

As we passed the cemetery two men came along wheeling a sort of canvas stretcher with a dead body stitched up in canvas. You could see the arms folded over the chest. It was like a mummy or a recumbent stone figure over a tomb & it shook as the cart bumped over the rough ground down from the hospital to the cemetery...

I wish I had a friend here tho I am not sure if it would be good to have one with whom I could say everything as a good deal that is left unsaid is also left unthought & the less thought the better. Isn't it strange. I never hear a thrush?

This is the first windy day. The sound of the wind in the house & trees hides the whistling of the shells that come in & go out. It is bitterly cold & raw though not actually freezing. The only merry things are the dead leaves out on the terrace circling round & round & up a little & down again, only about a dozen of them, sycamore leaves, crumpled and black...

March 8th... How optimistic Frost is... I hope he's right. Nobody here sees any way out just yet. I personally don't see any reason to expect anything decisive for a very long time. They can do as they please till they are exhausted I fear & who knows when they will be exhausted. I suspect this retirement will save them for months to come. And then they can retire again - each time giving us spoilt poisonous ground.

But then of course the unexpected always happens. For example, I began to write verses...

Thomas rejoined his Battery in the orchard on 9th March; over the next four weeks he was at Observation Posts at Ronville and Beaurains. He wrote to Helen on the 11th:

At O.P. [Ronville]. At about 12 they began bombarding the city. The shells came over our heads & splashed 300 or 400 yards behind us for the whole afternoon. Towards 4 the shell began to fall closer & closer just over the street & at the end of the street & I had to go down into a dugout. This lasted an hour & then as the light failed the enemy became less troublesome. At 6 I was sitting looking out on a most peaceful looking desolate scene. What used to be fields & meadows looked like rough moorland, like Dunwich moors & brown & rough, sprinkled over with chalk workings & broken with darker bands of dense barbed wire. I could hear the blackbirds chinking as they do at nightfall. A rifle cracked sometimes. During the day a skylark was singing on No Mans Land... We shall take it in turns to sit up during the night in case anything happens before the raid that comes off just after dawn...

Some rain fell on the corrugated iron but the dawn was the softest, loveliest air & sky & light you can imagine & I looked with nothing but pleasure thro my field glasses till punctually at 7 am 60 of our guns began to ship shells into the enemy front line... Then the smoke was so thick that I didn't see the raid at all. I know we got some prisoners but don't know how many we lost. At 7.45 our suburbs began to suffer from retaliation. 25 or 30 small shell fell round us every minute for 3/4 of an hour or more. We hadn't much shelter...

And now a west wind blows. The air is soft & the sky tender & dark. The rooks are at their nests in the large elms on the high ground on the north side of the city. It is going to rain...

March 16th. I had a job yesterday which I couldn't do. It was to climb up the outside of a tall factory chimney [in Arras] & observe from the top. To start you had to go down a wall & then along & then up by rungs against the brickwork. I knew as soon as I was told that I couldn't do it but I thought well perhaps I shall. So I went. Unluckily the chimney was being shelled & 4 shells came over as I arrived & falling so close that I was unnerved. Now Smith who doesn't mind heights has got the job... This was the first time I had failed & you can imagine that dread of the height & the pitch dark chimney & the look out at top with machine guns & artillery firing (tho that hardly entered with my fear) & then the shell & me lying in the mud to escape the splinters...

They are ploughing now in the field adjoining the orchard with 2 pairs of greys & I hear the ploughman talking to them as they turn at the end of the furrow. It is a misty cold morning... The larks & the great tits are singing...

Tomorrow I go to the O.P again. I go there from 8.30 til 9.30 next day & that day is almost a day of rest. The day after is work in the battery. Then the O.P again. And so on, three of us taking it in turn. It is quite a change going up through the city with my 5 men & over the railway by that deadly chimney & up the street that leads straight into the Hun lines, then off to one side through a trench & so up into our little side street. The O.P is wonderfully strong now & would stand a direct hit from a heavy shell & the dug out underneath is safer still for sleeping or retiring to. The day passes quickly, watching & occasionally talking to the R.F.A. man who shares the O.P with us, & meals down in the cellar - candlelight & the evening chatter of the men & then a chance of a quiet night. Up at 5.30 to look out & see nothing perhaps but quiet - breakfast - entering my notes in the log book - picking up & being relieved by Rubin & then trudging back unwashed with a pot of tea to look forward to & an idle hour or two & perhaps a letter from you...

March 19th or 20th I have lost count. I have to be up at 4 again on a bit of an adventure as it seems to my inexperience. I am lying in my sleeping bag smoking while the men dry themselves after being out 2 hours to look for a break in the telephone wire which they found as usual up Windy Corner (so they call it) where the shells fall thickest... I wish I could paint them and the fire and the coloured picture of an Italian Virgin with frame and glass complete which they have rescued from one of the ruins. The boy who is my orderly spent some time polishing up the glass and looking at the face with thoughts which I know nothing whatever about - he never said a word.

March 21st. Well I have had 24 hours of rain & mud in the very front trench of our new lines in this part of the world so exposed that I thought it wise to be prepared not only for an attack but for being taken prisoner. So I had my revolver & I left my diary behind. However all went well except that I got cold & hungry & weary & had shell flying over continuously all night. Here I am dirty & tired but pleased to have been & seen the infantry doing only what they can do in the way of ingenious foraging & making of dugouts... And the larks sang in the cold wet early morning over No Mans Land & shell holes full of blood stained water with beer bottles floating in it. And the 18 inches of clay mud such as you cannot imagine & dangerous mud that it is painful to draw your legs out of...

March 24th. I was in that ghastly village today [Beaurains]... I never thought it would be so bad. It is nothing but dunes of piled up brick & stone with now & then a jagged piece of wall... No Mans Land below the village was simply churned up dead filthy ground with tangled rusty barbed wire over it.

Our new position - fancy - is an old chalk pit [between Agny and Achicourt] in which a young copse of birch hazel has established itself... It is almost a beautiful spot still & I am now sitting warm in the sun on a lump of chalk with my back to the wall of the pit which is large & shallow. Fancy an old chalk pit with moss & even a rabbit left in spite of paths trodden almost all over it. It is beautiful & sunny & warm - the chalk is dazzling. The sallow catkins are soft dark white...

March 25th. Larks & I even heard a thrush far off as I went along at dawn. I said you could not recognise any of the houses in the village [Beaurains] but one has its walnut tree still standing & then there is the one with the little conical slated summer house under the trees. Just above the O.P that was shelled I found a Hun's grave with a cross formed of inverted black bottles & surrounded with small box plants

& covered with daisy roots & larkspur & at the head a small wooden cross with an illegible name on it.

March 31st... This afternoon I have been digging to prepare for the dugout... Showers came on later & shells too but now at 7 all is beautiful & serene & swept clean & the sky high & the wind has fallen. A robin keeps coming in to beg from us where we sit under a shelter that looks more a shelter than it is...

After one of the last showers a rainbow sprang up in front with one foot on a broad misty white track the Huns have made 4 miles away up to the skyline. Everything was so clear & dark & soft in the landscape that had no visible man in it, only tossing fountains of smoke & chalk where our shells burst on the enemy hill opposite. I wonder if any Huns are enjoying the late afternoon sun as much...

April 6th. I was looking for violets in the copse this morning while the guns were idle... so you see I am enjoying the fine weather now...

You can stand up on the bank just behind the guns & look at the green door... There is a little river in between with its aspen & elms mostly felled & the water very dirty. It winds through the flat trampled fields between the billet & the battery which are on gentle opposite slopes. Still not a thrush but many blackbirds...

I you see must not feel anything I am just as it were tunnelling underground & something sensible in my subconscious directs me not to think of the sun. At the end of the tunnel there is the sun. Honestly this is not the result of thinking; it is just an explanation of my state of mind which is really so entirely preoccupied with getting on through the tunnel that you might say I had forgotten there was a sun at either end before or after the business. This will perhaps induce you to call me inhuman like the newspapers, just because for a time I have had my ears stopped - mind you I have not done it myself - to all but distinct echoes of home, friends & England. If I could respond as you would like me to to your feelings I should be unable to go on with this job in your name whether it is to last weeks or months or years - I never even think will it be weeks or months or years - I don't even wonder if the drawers in the sittingroom are kept locked!

April 7th or 8th. Sat. Here I am in my valise on the floor of my dug out writing before sleeping. The artillery is like a stormy tide breaking on the shores of the full moon that rides high & clear among white cirrus clouds. It has been a day of cold feet in the O.P. I had to go unexpectedly. The pretty village among trees that I first saw 2 weeks ago is now great ruins among violated stark tree trunks. But the sun shone & larks & partridges & magpies & hedge-sparrows made love & the trench was being made passable for the wounded that will be harvested in a day or two... Our billet was shelled. The shells fell all round & you should have seen Horton & me dodging them. Goodnight & I hope you sleep no worse than I do.

Sunday [Easter Day]. I slept jolly well & now it is sunshine & wind & we are in for a long day & I must post this when I can..."

The following morning, Easter Monday, the first day of the Battle of Arras opened with a huge artillery bombardment. At 7.30 a.m. Edward Thomas was standing at the Beaurains Observation Post when he was killed by the blast of a shell which exploded near by.

THE CHERRY TREES

The cherry trees bend over and are shedding,
On the old road where all that passed are dead,
Their petals, strewing the grass as for a wedding
This early May morn when there is none to wed.

SECOND LIEUTENANT ROBERT ERNEST VERNEDE

3rd Battalion The Rifle Brigade.
12th Battalion The Rifle Brigade.
Born: 4th June 1875. London.
Educated: St. Paul's School.
          St. John's College, Oxford.
Died of wounds: 9th April 1917. Aged 41 years.
Lebucquière Communal Cemetery Extension, France.

Robert Vernède was of French Huguenot descent; his branch of the family were driven from their estates in 1685 by the Revocation of the Edict of Nantes and emigrated to Holland and then to England. The Vernède ancestral castle was mentioned by Robert Louis Stevenson in his *Travels with a Donkey in the Cevennes.* At St Paul's School, G.K. Chesterton was Vernède's contemporary and remained a lifelong friend.

After he left Oxford Robert Vernède lived in London and wrote articles and short stories. He married Carol Howard Fry in 1902. In 1905 Vernède's first novel *The Pursuit of Mr. Faviel* was published. This was followed by three more novels written between 1906 and 1911; a collection of short stories was published in 1921.

Vernède had a horror of damp and cold and hated English winters, so he and his wife travelled during the winter months. Two travel books resulted from these holidays, *An Ignorant in India* and *The Fair Dominion: A Record of Canadian Impressions* both published in 1911. When war was declared Vernède, who was 39, was four years over age but because the authorities mistakenly took his age to be 35, he was accepted by the Public Schools Battalion of the 19th Battalion Royal Fusiliers as a Private. He was commissioned in the 5th Battalion in early May 1915, and six months later went to the Ypres Salient attached to the 3rd Battalion the Rifle Brigade.

During the ten months between November 1915 and September 1916 the 3rd Battalion was in and out of the trenches, and Vernède vividly described the conditions in letters home to his wife and his greatest friend, F.G. Salter. On February 11th 1916 the Battalion was in trenches at Hooge. Vernède wrote to Salter:

We had a distinctly hot time a few days ago in the front line - two hours of what every one agreed was about the fiercest shelling they had known. Extraordinarily few casualties considering, but it is a cruel business. Even to see men suffering from shock, flopping about the trenches like grassed fish, is enough to sicken one, and some of the face wounds are terrible. They were splendid - most of them will leave any shelter they have got to go and help one of the wounded and they remain cheerful to the last. Nor is it the sort of heedless gaiety I used to suspect them of, but a gallant effort to make the best of things and not let their morale fall below an ideal. Stretcher-bearers dodging about among shells - some of our older N.C.O.'s cheering up the grenadiers of a service Battalion who had got rattled - a latest draft youth who never took his eye off his loophole during the bombardment (so his corporal told me) - these things are rather good. But anyone who hereafter shows a tendency towards exalting war ought to be drowned straight away by his country...

On 13th February the Battalion still in trenches at Hooge came under intensive bombardment and it suffered heavy casualties. Vernède wrote to his wife:

... Really the men were wonderful, as always. There was 'C' Company - lads of twenty, many of them - planted out in burrows for thirty hours, plastered with shells - no communication - T. [Captain G. Tatham] wouldn't let anybody stir by day. And at the end of it only two posts had broken at all - in one of which one was killed, three buried and unable to stir, and the others suffering from shell shock; and in the other they had all dug one another out two or three times before they gave way - besides having three wounded. Then we had the same scene as the night before - reliefs arriving and the wounded being brought down. M. bandaged and I administered laudanum and kola nut for hours.

Then Tatham went off and I moved the Coy. off in a hurricane of snow and icy rain. I'd been wet to the waist for about twenty-four hours and I imagine the men were wetter, and I had no feeling in my legs for about two hours. They put whizz-bangs over us at one point in the open, but we got back to the support camp in the end, just at daylight. I sat up from 6 a.m. to 12 drying my drawers over a brazier (while the others slept) without any trousers on. Later at night we had to move again here... We had to come across open country. Just as we started a terrific bombardment began on both sides, and in a tearing wind and rain we ran right into the Boche barrage and had to bustle through it... I wish I felt really fit to lead these sort of men. I haven't had enough of it to feel really useful... I don't know if this sort of account is interesting. It could be much more so if I could explain the sort of positions, but I have to avoid anything that could be construed into military information and so I rather mix it up. It's extraordinary how one doesn't feel the worse for this sort of thing. I don't know when I've been colder or wetter for twenty-four hours: my teeth simply chattered with cold in that drain pipe... But I am very well...

Five days later Vernède wrote from a Rest Camp near Vlamertinghe:

February 18th. Yesterday we paraded for the G.O.C. Division, who made quite an eloquent speech, if rather inanimate... It rather amused me to read in the paper next day an account of several little artillery engagements which the men quite welcome as a change from the monotony of the trenches. Blithering idiot. If he had ever seen what remained of a Coy. coming out shattered and wounded and drenched and hungry, to tramp for hours through a snowstorm to some place where they can recuperate. Or if he had ever tried even ten minutes of fierce shell-fire. It's true the men stick it and make little of it, once it's all over; but the stoutest of them would probably give anything to be out of it at the time. Isn't there any imagination in those who stay at home that they can stand that sort of bosh in a leading London paper?... The Brigadier, who followed the G.O.C., merely said, 'R.B.s, I'm not eloquent. I only want to tell you how proud I am of you and how pleased I am with you' - which the men seemed to prefer to the more elaborate oration ...

From the Rest Camp, Vernède wrote on 1st March 1916:

... I rather foresee a time (after Peace) when people will be sick of the name of the War - won't hear a word of it or anything connected with it. There seem to be such people now, and I see numbers of silly books and papers advertised as having nothing to do with the war. It's natural, perhaps, that soldiers should want a diversion, and even civilians; but I rather hope that people won't altogether forget it in our generation. That's what I wanted to say in the verses I began about -

> Not in our time, O Lord, we now beseech Thee
> To grant us peace - the sword has bit too deep -

but never got on with. What I mean is that for us there can be no real forgetting. We have seen too much of it, known too many people's sorrow, felt it too much, to return to an existence in which it has no part. Not that one wants to be morbid about it later; but still less does one want to be as superficial as before...

Vernède used the lines he referred to in this letter in his poem 'Before the Assault' which he completed in December 1916:

BEFORE THE ASSAULT

If thro' this roar o' the guns one prayer may reach Thee,
Lord of all Life, whose mercies never sleep,
Not in our time, not now, Lord, we beseech Thee
To grant us peace. The sword has bit too deep.

We may not rest. We hear the wail of mothers
Mourning the sons who fill some nameless grave:
Past us, in dreams, the ghosts march of our brothers
Who were most valiant... whom we could not save.

We may not rest. What though our eyes be holden,
In sleep we see dear eyes yet wet with tears,
And locks that once were, oh, so fair and golden,
Grown grey in hours more pitiless than years.

We see all fair things fouled - homes love's hands builded
Shattered to dust beside their withered vines,
Shattered the towers that once Thy sunsets gilded,
And Christ struck yet again within His shrines.

Over them hangs the dust of death, beside them
The dead lie countless - and the foe laughs still;
We may not rest, while those cruel mouths deride them,
We, who were proud, yet could not work Thy will.

We have failed - we have been more weak than these betrayers -
In strength or in faith we have failed; our pride was vain.
How can we rest, who have not slain the slayers?
What peace for us, who have seen Thy children slain?

Hark, the roar grows... the thunders reawaken -
We ask one thing, Lord, only one thing now:
Hearts high as theirs, who went to death unshaken,
Courage like theirs to make and keep their vow.

To stay not till these hosts whom mercies harden,
Who know no glory save of sword and fire,
Find in our fire the splendour of Thy pardon,
Meet from our steel the mercy they desire...

Then to our children there shall be no handing
Of fates so vain - of passions so abhorr'd...
But peace... the Peace which passeth understanding...
Not in our time... but in their time, O Lord.

At the end of March 1916, the Battalion moved to reserve trenches in the area around Ploegsteert Wood which Vernède described as very peaceful "a most pleasant change from the part of the line we used to be in..." By August the Battalion had moved from the Ypres Salient to the Somme area, and from behind the front line in craters north of Carnoy, Vernède wrote:

August 16th... Did I tell you of a rather nice boy in my platoon who writes a family letter daily always beginning - 'Dear Mum and Dad, and dear loving sisters Rosie, Letty, and our Gladys, - I am very pleased to write you another welcome letter as this leaves me. Dear Mum and Dad and loving sisters, I hope you keeps the home fires burning. Not arf. The boys are in the pink. Not arf. Dear loving sisters Rosie, Letty, and our Gladys, keep merry and bright. Not arf.'

It goes on like that for three pages - absolutely fixed; and if he has to say anything definite, like acknowledging a parcel, he has to put in a separate letter - not to interfere with the sacred order of things. He is quite young and very nice, quiet, never grouses or gives any trouble - one of those very gentle creatures that the War has caught up and tried to turn into a frightful soldier, I should think in vain. I can't imagine him sticking anybody, but I'm sure he would do anything he felt to be his duty...

August 17th. I got into a nasty bombardment last night with a party I had volunteered for - 80 men and only one hit, which was very lucky, as we had to sprint across the open under shrapnel, besides two hours heavy stuff. All quite unnecessary and somebody's fault, but I don't know quite whose and probably never shall. These things will happen at times. The Regimental Sergeant-Major was with me: a terrific person with a wonderful waxed moustache, and it was very funny to see him peering out of various holes in the ground like a coney. He told me he cracked several jokes with some of the young fellows to keep their spirits up; but I can't say that I heard him, and as Brown remarked, that would have been much more awful to them than the actual bombardment. His idea of a joke would be to say - 'Here! You! Put yer cap on straight!'

THE SERGEANT

The Sergeant 'as 'is uses -
I used to doubt of it -
'E did not like the way I washed,
'Is 'ead seemed bulged a bit.
My arms drill seemed to 'urt 'im,
'E'd swear and close 'is eyes;

An' when I 'ad no time to shave
'E would not sympathise.

At 'ome in good old England
When dealin' with recruits
'E seemed to 'ide his better self -
If they 'ad dirty boots.
But in this trench a-sitting
All crouched upon my joints
I do not mind admitting
The Sergeant 'as 'is points.

'E's just been round explainin'
That jumping up to see
If shells is going to burst your way
Is waste of energy.
Shells, though you can't believe it,
Aren't always aimed at you,
But snipers if they see your 'ead
Will put a bullet through.

His words about the Boches
Is also comforting -
'E says as good a shot as me
Could do a dozen in.
An' if it came to baynits,
I'd easy stick a score
The way I fight - I never knew
'E thought me smart before.

"An' anyway," 'e says, "Lad,
Mind this, we're goin' to win:
It's no use thinkin' gloomy thoughts
Whatever fix you're in.
Suppose we did get outed -
England would not forget.
And where's the man that is a man
That would not die for that?"

August 18th ...I am afraid I am in for a Lewis gun course. I suppose
other people would like it, so, pig-headedly, I don't... I don't like
leaving the platoon in these strenuous times. The course is, I believe a
week, far from the firing line. At present I am at the Transport on my

way... might be recalled, but don't think it's likely. I asked to be left with the platoon and can't do more...

August 23rd... I hoped that, as my last letter told you I was going on a course, you would at all events think I was in some safe spot instead of the very unsafe one where I was.

Directly after I finished that letter to you I was wired for to reinforce the Batt. in an attack... We had a three hour walk to the front line. Shells most of the way, and the wounded streaming down an open road between the downs... The men of all regiments, and wounded in every variety of way. To read in the papers you might suppose the wounded were whisked from the battlefield in a motor ambulance. I get rather tired of all that false and breezy representation of a battle.

I've never been so hot in my life as when we came to Batt. Headquarters, just behind our jumping-off trench... From there we went on to join our Coys. in the various bits of Boche trench they had taken. No guide, a hail of shells and a sort of blind stumble through shell-holes to where we fancied the new line was. I found C Company at last. H.Q. in a 30 ft. deep Boche dug-out, choked with dead Germans and bluebottles, and there we had our meals till we started back at 4 a.m. this morning (five days). In between that time I certainly spent some of the most unpleasant hours of my life. It seems that the Batt. had done extraordinarily well and gained the first of two objectives. The second was to be won that night, and next day we were to be relieved. Unfortunately a Batt. on our right had been held up and we had to wait for them in a trench choked with our dead and Boche wounded and dying for two days and then do another attack. The men had been in high spirits over the first part, but naturally the reaction was great when they found that instead of being relieved they were to dig in, and I had never seen them so glum. Here again the breezy reporter is revolting. The Push itself is done in hot blood: but the rest is horrible, digging in when you are tired to death, short rations, no water to speak of, hardly any sleep, and men being killed by shell-fire most of the time.

I was given the C line in front of H.Q. to hold with two-and-a-half platoons, and luckily the Boches never really found it, and I had fewer casualties than anybody. I slept in the bottom of the trench, sometimes in rain (in shorts), without any cover and really never felt very cold. Also, though I don't suppose I got more than an hour at a time, I never felt done for want of sleep. C. and Buxton were the only officers left.

The second attack was made yesterday, and only our D Coy was sent off at the start. C. was to support it if it needed reinforcement. My dear, you never saw anything more dramatically murderous than the modern attack - a sheet of fire from both sides in which it seems impossible for any one to live. I saw it from my observer's post about 100 yds. away. My observer was shot through the head in the first minute. The O.C. of D Company had been badly wounded, and Butler led them on most gallantly. The last I saw of him was after a huge shell had burst just over him (laying out several men) waving on the rest. None of the D officers came back, and very few of the men.

Again the right Batt. failed, and this time the Rifle Brigade was inevitably involved in it, as far as D Coy. went. We gained a certain amount of France back by digging a trench in front of my bit of line about 100 yds. from the Boches in the dark, lit by terrific flares from the German lines. After that we hunted for our wounded till 4 a.m. I found S.S. about 50 yds. from the Boche trench, shot through the heart. R. got back wounded in several places. Butler was last heard of in a shell-hole about 10 yds. from the Boches. He was an awfully gallant fellow. The whole thing was almost too bloody for words, and this, mind you, was victory of a sort for us. We fancy the Boches lost far more heavily, as our guns got on them when they were reinforcing.

I'm too sleepy to tell you any more. The Batt. did magnificently: captured many prisoners and advanced several hundred yards; but the cost is very great...

From a rest camp near Buire-sur-l'Ancre, south-west of Albert, Vernède wrote five days later:

August 27th... the troops after their push are bivouacked in an open field with no cover but their waterproof sheets - constant showers - not very comfortable for men who have hardly slept and never ceased working under shell-fire for a week. Some old noodle's fault, I suppose.

My dear, some of the men are too quaint. One lad, whose brother was killed the last night in the Boche trench, came to me to ask how to write to his sister-in-law about it. He had got as far as - 'My dear Lil, - I now have great pleasure in telling you that Tom ——' and there he had stuck. I had to draft a more sympathetic letter for him...

August 28th... They have got up tents for the men and there's a concert now going on just outside mine. They do pick up their spirits most wonderfully... 9.30 p.m. The concert is coming to an end. The padre has got them to sing 'Abide with Me'. It is rather fine - a starry night, the tents all lighted and looking like a lamp-lit city in this niche of the downs. Away to the north one of those murderous battles is raging.

On the evening of 1st September the Battalion, in reserve behind the lines, was ordered to counter-attack and retake two trenches, which had been lost the night before, near Delville Wood. The attack was launched without proper preparation and although the Battalion took Orchard Trench, Tea Trench was very strongly held by the Germans and the Battalion was unable to progress further. There were 206 casualties including Vernède who was temporarily in command of his Company.

September 2nd. A pleasing Blighty one at last, and almost before you get this I shall, with luck, be in Angleterre with you a-coming to see me. It's shrapnel through the thigh, and hasn't been pronounced on yet by the medical authorities, who have to extract a bit of iron that didn't go quite through. But as I plunked through the trenches knee-deep in mire for six hours afterwards, more or less, it can't be very bad; and I ought to get back before you can think of coming here. I got it in another show suddenly forced upon us, in which I was in charge of the Coy. with C. only subaltern. A shell plumped neatly between six of us, killed Sgt. Oliver and hit the rest in divers ways. It was rather a funny sensation. I thought I'd been bruised. Handed over to C., who a little later got badly hit in the arm. So C Coy., when I last heard of it, is without officers - three platoon sergeants knocked out - two killed - both awfully nice fellows, and A. rather badly hit...

AT DELVILLE

At Delville I lost three Sergeants -
And never within my ken
Had one of them taken thought for his life
Or cover for aught but his men.

Not for two years of fighting
Through that devilish strain and noise;
Yet one of them called out as he died -
"I've been so ambitious, boys" ...

And I thought to myself, "Ambitious!"
Did he mean that he longed for power?
But I knew that he'd never thought of himself
Save in his dying hour.

And one left a note for his mother,
Saying he gladly died
For England, and wished no better thing...
How she must weep with pride.

And one with never a word fell,
Talking's the one thing he'd shirk,
But I never knew him other than keen
For things like danger and work.

Those Sergeants I lost at Delville
On a night that was cruel and black,
They gave their lives for England's sake,
They will never come back.

What of the hundreds in whose hearts
Thoughts no less splendid burn?...
I wonder what England will do for them
If ever they return?

Vernède convalesced at Somerville Hospital, Oxford and at his home. He rejoined the 12th (Service) Battalion in the line at Maricourt on 7th January 1917. During the first three months of the year the men at the front suffered the "most bitter weather with raging, freezing winds." Vernède wrote on January 24th from billets at Bronfay:

... I have been left behind in the damp hut with my sore throat, which the M.O., refers to as laryngitis. It's getting better all the time now, and I get out of the front line with it, which is not so bad in this awful cold weather. Last night was probably the coldest since the war started - 20 deg. of frost... Very miserable for the men, but I believe when they come out we have a long rest behind somewhere. I slip in and out of my valise for meals! It's much warmer in it than anywhere else - with my two waistcoats (your Jaeger one and the new deerskin one that Lily gave me) on, and my fur lining and my trench coat and my blanket on top, and Aunt Fanny's scarf and Frdk.'s Balaclava helmet on my head...

From huts at Guillemont he wrote on February 19th:

... The whole front is extraordinarily desolate in this weather: pock-marked with frozen shell-holes, every kind of abandoned material lying about, and bodies in ghastly attitudes, just as they fell and were constricted to the ground by the frost immovably until the winter chooses to give up its dead. I think if everybody could see these scenes, the general horror would somehow find the way out, which ordinary morals and intelligence don't seem to. The time the men have while they live is bad enough; it's pathetically absurd to see them plunging about in the mire, laden to the teeth, falling into shell-holes in the dark, getting stuck fast, cursing and patient, and half of them ill enough to be in bed or hospital in peace-time. I pulled one little man ahead of me eight times out of mud holes into which he had fallen in the course of about 200 yards as we came out...

February 26th... About morphia. The M.O.s out here vary according to their experience, and I've heard one imploring officers to carry morphia. In many cases it isn't to save life but to alleviate agony for those who must die. Look at the case of the man Shafto got the M.C. for going to give some to - blown out of the trenches on to the barbed wire, quite immovable and dying in great pain, and in any part you may see twenty such. This ground is strewn with the dead who might have been eased a little earlier. I quite admit that it's probably a very dangerous doing, but it's worth taking risks on some occasions. It would be best if all officers knew as far as possible when to and when not to give it...

February 27th... Who do you think came into my dug-out at dead of night and chatted for an hour? Hilaire Belloc - not the one, but his son, a very taking youth of about 18, most intelligent, in the R.E.s. He'd come up to site a trench and we chatted of G.K.C., and Bentley. He knew Daly - that nice boy who had been killed at Guillemont - and had been trying to find his grave. I was very pleased with him and thought the R.E.s had got hold of somebody good at last!...

There were a few spring days at the beginning of March before the weather became bitterly cold again. Sometime during the first three months of the year Vernède wrote 'A Listening Post':

A LISTENING POST

The sun's a red ball in the oak
And all the grass is grey with dew,
Awhile ago a blackbird spoke -
He didn't know the world's askew.

And yonder rifleman and I
Wait here behind the misty trees
To shoot the first man that goes by,
Our rifles ready on our knees.

How could he know that if we fail
The world may lie in chains for years
And England be a bygone tale
And right be wrong, and laughter tears?

Strange that this bird sits there and sings
While we must only sit and plan -
Who are so much the higher things -
The murder of our fellow man...

But maybe God will cause to be -
Who brought forth sweetness from the strong -
Out of our discords harmony
Sweeter than that bird's song.

At the beginning of April 1917 the 12th Battalion moved into the outpost line between Havrincourt Wood and Ruvaulcourt, south west of Cambrai. On 8th April, Easter Sunday, Vernède wrote to his wife:

...I think it will be summer soon, and perhaps the war will end this year and I shall see my Pretty One again.

Later that night, while on patrol in the Havrincourt Wood area, Vernède came under enemy machine-gun fire; he was seriously wounded in the stomach and died on his way to the Field Ambulance a few hours later.

TO C.H.V.

What shall I bring to you, wife of mine,
When I come back from the war?
A ribbon your dear brown hair to twine?
A shawl from a Berlin store?
Say, shall I choose you some Prussian hack
When the Uhlans we o'erwhelm?
Shall I bring you a Potsdam goblet back
And the crest from a Prince's helm?

Little you'd care what I laid at your feet,
Ribbon or crest or shawl -
What if I bring you nothing, sweet,

Nor maybe come home at all?
Ah, but you'll know, Brave Heart, you'll know
Two things I'll have kept to send:
Mine honour for which you bade me go
And my love - my love to the end.

Amongst Vernède's papers, found after his death, were the opening lines of an unfinished poem.

I seek new suns : I will not die;
Earth hath not shown me half her store.

SECOND LIEUTENANT ARTHUR JAMES ('HAMISH') MANN

8th Battalion The Black Watch.

Born: 5th April 1896. Broughty Ferry, Forfarshire.
Educated: George Watson's College, Edinburgh.
Died of wounds: 10th April 1917. Aged 21 years.
Aubigny Communal Cemetery Extension, Aubigny-en-Artois, France.

Hamish Mann was gazetted in July 1915 and joined the 8th Battalion Black Watch at La Comté, a few miles south west of Béthune at the end of August 1916. On 10th September when the Battalion was in trenches at Berthunville, Mann wrote 'The Shell Hole'; and from the small village of Maisnil-Bouché behind the lines between Lens and Arras, he wrote 'Life' on 27th September.

THE SHELL HOLE

In the Shell Hole he lies, this German soldier of a year ago;
But he is not as then, accoutred, well, and eager for the foe
He hoped so soon, so utterly, to crush. His muddy skull
Lies near the mangled remnants of his corpse - war's furies thus
    annul
The pomp and pageantry that were its own. White rigid bones
Gape through the nauseous chaos of his clothes; the cruel stones
Hold fast the letter he was wont to clasp close to his am'rous breast.
Here 'neath the stark, keen stars, where is no peace, no joy, nor any
    rest,
He lies. There, to the right, his boot, gashed by the great shell's
    fiendish whim,
Retains - O horrid spectacle! - the fleshless stump that was his
    limb!
Vile rats and mice, and flies and lice and ghastly things that carrion
    know
Have made a travesty of Death of him who lived a year ago.

LIFE

At least I live. Emotion's fiercest winds
    Sweep through my soul.
Sometimes my heartstrings play the gayest chimes -
    Sometimes a toll.

I am not stagnant. All my Being thrills;
   A raptured song
Resounds throughout my Self with varied tones
   The whole day long.

At least I live: I am not stagnant. Though
   My joy or pain
O'erwhelms me with the terror of despair -
   'Tis not in vain.
So, when oppress'd with fervour let me say:
"Tomorrow I shall sing a richer lay!"

During the first few days of October, 1916, Mann wrote 'The Soldier' and 'Before' from Drop Alley Trench on the Somme. On 8th October, the Battalion was in billets at Albert, and the following day, en route for trenches east of High Wood, Mann wrote 'The Zenith'.

THE SOLDIER

'Tis strange to look on a man that is dead
As he lies in the shell-swept hell,
And to think that the poor black battered corpse
Once lived like you and was well.

'Tis stranger far when you come to think
That you may be soon like him...
And it's Fear that tugs at your trembling soul,
A Fear that is weird and grim!

BEFORE

At least say this: my mem'ry will be dear
With that sad sweetness which is nobly fine.
I ask no more: the rest cannot be changed;
Let memory and tenderness be mine.
And may I die more nobly than I live
(For I have lived in folly and regret):
Then in the last Great Moment when I pass,
I shall have paid my Life's outstanding Debt!

THE ZENITH

To-day I reach the zenith of my life!
No time more noble in my span of years
Than this, the glorious hour of splendid strife,
Of War, of cataclysmal woe, and tears.
All petty are the greatest things of yore,
All mean and sordid is my dearest lay;
I have done nothing more worth while before...
My hour, my chance, my crisis, are to-day!

At the end of March 1917, the Battalion was laid low with an epidemic of German Measles, but was in action again by the 9th April for the Battle of Arras. Hamish Mann, a Platoon Commander, was wounded during the assault and died the following day. From billets at Arras, three days before the attack, he had written his last poem:

THE GREAT DEAD

Some lie in graves beside the crowded dead
In village churchyards; others shell holes keep,
Their bodies gaping, all their splendour sped.
Peace, O my soul... A Mother's part to weep.

Say: do they watch with keen all-seeing eyes
My own endeavours in the whirling hell?
Ah, God! how great, how grand the sacrifice.
Ah, God! the manhood of yon men who fell!

And this is War... Blood and a woman's tears,
Brave memories adown the quaking years.

COMPANY SERGEANT MAJOR WILLIAM HENRY LITTLEJOHN

1st/7th Battalion Middlesex Regiment.
Born: 1891.
Killed: 10th April 1917. Aged 26 years.
Wancourt British Cemetery, France.

William Littlejohn was a civil servant in the Exchequer and Audit Department; he joined the Territorial branch of the Middlesex Regiment when it was inaugurated and became a Sergeant before the war. He served in Gallipoli with the Battalion.

HOLY COMMUNION SERVICE, SUVLA BAY

Behold a table spread!
A battered corned-beef box, a length of twine,
An altar-rail of twigs and shreds of string.
For the unseen, divine,
Uncomprehended Thing
A hallowed space amid the holy dead.

Behold a table spread!
And on a fair, white cloth the bread and wine,
The symbols of sublime compassioning,
The very outward sign
Of that the nations sing,
The body that He gave, the blood He shed.

Behold a table spread!
And kneeling soldiers in God's battle-line,
A line of homage to a mightier King:
All-knowing All-benign!
Hearing the prayers they bring,
Grant to them strength to follow where He led.

On 9th April 1917, the first day of the battle of Arras, the Battalion worked it's way gradually forward through the thick mud and succeeded in capturing Telegraph Hill Trench, the first of the trenches of the Hindenburg Line. The Battalion was in a very insecure position as many of the German front line trenches had not been taken; it was on the extreme right of the British line with its flank in immediate contact with the enemy who were still in the same trench. The Battalion was ordered to take Ibex Trench but the first two attacks failed.

Throughout the night of 9th/10th April carrying parties were employed to bring up fresh supplies of bombs for a renewed attack on Ibex Trench. At 3.00 a.m. the bombing parties moved simultaneously down all the communication trenches killing or taking prisoner those who refused to surrender. 52 unwounded Germans and 3 trench mortars were captured. Orders were then received for the Battalion and four other Battalions to attack Nepal Trench. They met heavy machine-gun fire and the first attempt was unsuccessful. The second attack a few hours later succeeded, and "with bombs and bayonets the Die-Hard Territorials drove the enemy out - adding a further 198 prisoners to those already taken; the trenches and dug-outs full of German dead a horrible shambles."

The Battalion was relieved on the evening of the 11th April and sent back to Agny. During the three days, 9th - 11th April, the Battalion's casualties were 2 officers killed and 8 wounded; 25 other ranks killed, one of whom was William Littlejohn, and 88 wounded. The Commanding Officer said: "Never did the Battalion fight a finer fight, nor with greater good fortune or more brilliant success..."

A PRAYER

Lord, if it be Thy will
That I enter the great shadowed valley that lies
Silent, just over the hill,
Grant, they may say, "There's a comrade that dies
Waving his hand to us still!"

Lord, if there come the end,
Let me find space and breath all the dearest I prize
Into Thy hands to commend:
Then let me go, with my boy's laughing eyes
Smiling a word to a friend.

DRIVER CLIFFORD FLOWER

'B' Battery 242nd Brigade, Royal Field Artillery.
Born: 17th November, 1891.   Leeds.
Educated: Local Board School.
Killed: 20th April 1917. Aged 25 years.
Arras Memorial to the Missing, Faubourg-D'Amiens
Cemetery, Arras, France

Clifford Flower left school at the age of thirteen and a half and was employed as an office boy with a local firm of iron and steel tube manufacturers. At eighteen he transferred to the head-quarters of the firm at Birmingham where he worked in the drawing office.

At the outbreak of the War he was rejected several times for military service as he was half an inch short of the 5 feet 3 inches regulation height. He then wrote a personal letter to Lord Kitchener concluding, "My Lord, I have answered your appeal, will you answer mine?" He received a reply from the War Office by return of post enclosing a sealed document which he was told to take to the local recruiting office. As a result of this order, "Enlist the bearer, Clifford Flower, at once", he joined up as a Private in the 2nd Battalion Warwickshire Regiment. He was transferred to the Royal Field Artillery and three weeks later he was offered a stripe on the condition that he joined the clerical staff. This he declined "preferring to rough it with the ordinary tommies."

Flower arrived in France as a driver with the Battery at the end of March 1915 and was in trenches at Ploegsteert during April. He was wounded in the left arm in August 1915, but remained on duty. Two months later he became a signaller.

A CALM NIGHT AT THE FRONT

The rough Profanity is lost in sleep,
        The body rests, the mind is dreaming:
The men on guard their watch do keep,
        The moon's rays gently beaming.

The rifle fire has died away,
        All silent now; the moon on high
Would set a truce until the day,
        God staying the hand of destiny.

I think that when those dark'ning clouds
    Have gathered up the tempest's lust,
The blackness of the night in shrouds
    Will show how mean the human trust.

The fiend of war that hides in wait
    Will venture forth in boom of guns
And rattling lead, a "Hymn of Hate",
    Wild dirge of men - just women's sons.

I do not doubt there is an end
    To all this slaughter of the brave
By monster forms, who tear and rend
    The innocent before the grave.

O, womenfolk of British lands,
    Who toil and sweat in holiest cause,
O, raise in prayer your clasped hands
    That men may see the curse of wars.

A single star-light held in space
    Has filled the trench with radiance white,
A cautious soldier hides his face,
    Somebody's calling, so, "Good Night".

In April 1917 the 242nd Brigade were at Neuville-St-Vaast between Vimy and Arras. Bombardier Henry Neeld gave an account of those weeks in a letter written to Clifford Flower's mother:

... About the beginning of April we started from the Péronne district on a long march to Vimy Ridge, and were on the road for about eight days. When the battery was on the march Clifford always went a day in front of us to arrange for the billeting, for he was the only man in the battery who could converse fluently with the French villagers. The battery went into action in Souchez village. On Easter Sunday three signallers were asked to volunteer to go over with the Infantry, and Cliff was the first to volunteer. Thomas and Groom were the other two. (I mention these names because I expect you have heard of them from Cliff). They were fully aware of the grave risk they were running, and the weather was absolutely vile at the time, but they had a confidence and sense of duty which one would hardly credit anyone with. They went over with the Infantry on Easter Monday morning about 6 o'clock in a snowstorm, and spent 24 hours in as bad a state as is possible. A couple of days after the advance, the battery moved forward south of Lens somewhere between Avion and Petit Vimy. The place was in a horrible state, everything having been wrecked by our bombardments, and there was only one possible way of getting the guns up, and that was along the Arras-Lens road. The road was under direct observation, and was strewn with hundreds of transport horses, wagons and drivers that had been hit, and was by far the worst place I have ever seen. We made about five attempts to get our guns up, and when I came away had only one in position and about six out of a brigade of 24 guns. There were seven signallers at the battery position, Cliff, Thomas, Groom, Knight, Edgington, Sanders and myself. We had laid all our lines and were the only battery in communication with brigade for two days. On the 19th I wrote home enclosing three of Cliff's pieces of poetry which you had had printed, and he also posted it, as he had to go to Brigade. On the morning of the 20th we were all sitting down in the telephone dug-out having lunch (bread and cheese) and were trying to decide what to do with some rice that we had been given, for we had neither sugar nor milk. After that I knew nothing of what happened until about ten days ago, when I came across Sanders and Edgington, who had both been discharged from hospital. We were in an old German dug-out, therefore the entrance was facing the German lines, and a "Little Willie" shell came in through the doorway causing a terrific explosion owing to its bursting in such a confined space. Cliff and Groom were killed instantly, Thomas died on the way to the dressing-station and Dennis Knight seven days after. Sanders had his lip blown off, and Edgington was wounded internally. I had seven pieces of shrapnel in my head and neck but am quite all right now...

RED'S TRIBUTE TO KHAKI

(Red, the chief of colours, to whom all other
colours pay homage, itself must now pay tribute
to Khaki, the colour of the glorious dead).

Colour magnificent, flaming splendid,
    Monarch potential, crowned in a flame;
Spirit of life before life is ended,
    Symbol of power, dominion and fame.

Blooming fair on the apple's ripe skin,
    Roses voluptuous and poppies allure,
Luscious and warm on the lips of women,
    Cheer to the heart when the heart is pure.

To you bow the spirits of every hue,
   Majestic, torrential, transcendent RED,
But pay you the tribute to virtue due,
   KHAKI - the shade of the glorious dead.

CAPTAIN JOHN EUGENE CROMBIE

4th Battalion Gordon Highlanders.

Born: 30th April, 1896. Aberdeen.
Educated: Winchester College.
Died of Wounds: 23rd April 1917. Aged 20 years.
Duisans British Cemetery, Etrun, France.

Eugene Crombie was the son of J.W. Crombie, Member of Parliament for Kincardineshire; his grandfather and great grandfather had also been Members of Parliament and Crombie hoped to follow in their path. "He showed every promise of becoming an eloquent speaker, possessing a fine voice, a good presence and considerable dramatic talent..."

Crombie was commissioned in the 4th Battalion Gordon Highlanders at the outbreak of the War. The Battalion arrived in France at the end of February 1915 and was in and out of trenches at La Clythe during the next three months. Crombie was wounded in April 1915 and subsequently underwent major operations in England. After convalescing he rejoined his Battalion at Ovillers in November 1916. The following month Crombie wrote two poems, 'Desolation' from the trenches and 'The Mist', from huts.

DESOLATION

Over the bare, blank line of the ridge,
Over the stump of Sentinel Tree,
The moon slowly crosses the unseen bridge
That is set in the sky from the hills to the sea.

The sun's pale sister, moving yet dead,
The scars show dark on her weary face:
Is it strife of a million years that have bled
Her heart's life, and set Death's frosty sheen in her place?

Is she watching our strife, the tired moon? Can she see
How the earth's face is scarred, her life ebbing fast?
And only the shorn stump of Sentinel Tree
Prays in silence, "How long will her agony last?"

THE MIST

Always the rolling mist,
Wrapping the scene in wet and fleecy fold,
Moved as a curtain by the sluggish wind,
Lifting and swaying, falling damp and cold,
It sweeps, yet passes never, soft and blind.
Have sunbeams never kissed
These dreary hills and life-forsaken slopes -
Hidden like women's shoulders in a gown
That mars their beauty? Only shattered hopes
And ghostly fears people the shadowed down.
These sunless wreaths are curling round my heart:
The deadening fingers of the passing years
Are closing, and I cannot thrust apart
Their tightening grip... No ray of sun appears,
Only the rolling mist.

The Battalion was in billets in the Bois de Maroeuil, west of
Arras, in March 1917; Crombie wrote to his mother:

It has turned dreadfully cold here again and of course we can't get
fires in the tents. It will be much more comfortable in the line, and I
am quite looking forward to going there. It is beautifully sunny to-
day, so Sinclair and I are going to Arras to have a look at it. From a
distance there seems quite a lot of it left, and I believe there is a square
of cloisters built by the Moors, which is almost untouched and very
pretty...

... I have just returned from Arras. Oh, Lord! what a spot! For sheer
desolation I have not seen anything to equal it, and I can't describe the
feeling it gives to go into it...It's far the biggest town I have seen, in
fact I suppose it is the biggest on our front, and it is just in the state
that makes the horror of it most impressive, like seeing a strong
healthy man dying of some disgusting wasting disease, and his limbs
dropping off with scurvy. We went through a sort of Arc de Triomphe
straight into one of the main streets. The street was narrow, and all
the houses on either side very tall. There are no inhabitants except for
men living in the cellars, and every house shows hopeless
dilapidation, but almost the worst part is that the outer walls are for
the most part still standing and through the unglazed windows and the
holes from the shells, you saw the broken rafters, torn bits of
wallpaper, and debris of bricks and furniture at the bottom. And there
was the long narrow ribbon of street utterly silent, and the walls, with
nothing but ruin behind them, aslant and tottering, till it seemed a push

238

with your hand would overset them: and indeed they do collapse frequently, for we saw many heaps of bricks, and there are large notices everywhere warning you to walk close into the walls and not in the middle of the streets. You can't conceive the effect of a really big town in that state, however you try; it is far worse than seeing the place totally ruined, and in heaps of bricks and nothing more. It is those ghastly, sightless, purposeless walls that catch you, and the silence. For the life of me I could not have talked loud; I think the echo would have sent me mad. We went down to the Cathedral, an enormous high building, and once I suppose rather fine, in the usual Romanesque style. Its outer walls are standing too, but it has no roof, and it's no place to stay in and admire, for chunks of masonry were falling down at the rate of about one a minute. That sort of ruin I have seen before - but those streets!...

The following day, 3rd March, Crombie wrote to a friend and a few days later composed a poem, 'The Shrine' from his billets.

... As for the morals of the war, they are horrible. Perhaps they are a little worse than we are, but the point is that by fighting we have hopelessly degenerated our own morals. For instance, listen to this. Without going into details, for "mopping up" a captured trench i.e. bombing out the remaining inhabitants, you have parties of nine men specially equipped. When you come to a dug-out, you throw some smoke bombs down, and then smoke the rest out with a smoke bomb, so that they must either choke or come out. Now when they come out they are half blinded and choked with poisonous smoke, and you station a man at the entrance to receive them, but as you have only got a party of nine, it would be difficult to spare men if you took them prisoners, so the instructions are that these poor half-blinded devils should be bayoneted as they come up. It may be expedient from a military point of view, but if it had been suggested before the war, who would not have held up their hands in horror? The fact is, that if we decide to beat the German at his own game, we can only do it by being more Prussian than the Prussian; if we hate all that is Prussian, we shall become all that we hate. If we do win, it is only an argument for the Prussian, that if he had been a little more Prussian he would have won, and he will probably strive to be more so the next time, which is the very thing we wanted to avoid, and it can only be prevented by our keeping our top-dog attitude to him. It's absolutely Gilbertian, but I don't think we will make the German a pacifist except by example, and we have given him back his own example only rather more efficiently. But, the question is, what else could we do? If we did not fight, we admitted the superiority of his example, as it showed us that he could conquer us, and that by conquest he could force on us his principles. It is an extraordinary tangle when you think of it. And I am sorry to be pessimistic, but I doubt if it will have helped us to find God. Among the millions actually fighting it seems only to have increased the drunkenness and vice - perhaps some among those at home, anxious for dear ones fighting, may have learnt to rely on Him.   It is wonderful to think of Peace, and all this ghastliness ended..."

THE SHRINE

The first bright spears have pierced the armoured brown,
Broadened and drooped, and snowdrops speck the field:
The lengthening gaze of daylight looking down
Is shocked to see the hedge-row winter sealed
Sleeping in nakedness, and stirs her frame
And with the hawthorn bids her hide her shame.

Returning through the fields at evening hour
I lay before Thy shrine my offering,
My candle-flame a yellow crocus flower,
Its life but newly lit to Thee I bring
In thanks that I can see Thy guiding hand
In every flower that decorates the land.

On 8th April 1917, the eve of the Battle of Arras, Eugene Crombie wrote his last poem, from billets in the village of Bray.

EASTER DAY, 1917 - THE EVE OF THE BATTLE

I rose and watched the eternal giant of fire
Renew his struggle with the grey monk Dawn,
Slowly supreme, though broadening streaks of blood
Besmirch the threadbare cloak, and pour his flood
Of life and strength on our yet sleeping choir,
As I went out to church on Easter morn.

Returning with the song of birds and men
Acclaiming victory of throbbing life,
I saw the fairies of the morning shower
Giving to drink each waking blade and flower,
I saw the new world take Communion then -
And now 'tis night and we return to strife.

Two weeks later the Battalion was fighting at Bullecourt. On 23rd April, a week before his 21st Birthday, Eugene Crombie died of wounds he received that day in an action to capture the Chemical Works at Roeux, near Arras.

An entry in the Regimental History stated:

Some officers with long experience thought April 23rd witnessed the hardest fighting of any British offensive since the beginning of the War. Despite the heavy losses and the numerous failures to reach objectives, the majority of the troops were convinced that they had won a victory. They had by no means given up hope of winning another.

SECOND LIEUTENANT FRANCIS ST VINCENT MORRIS

3rd Battalion Sherwood Foresters.

No 3 Squadron RFC.

Born: 21st February 1896. Blackwell Vicarage, Ashbourne, Derbyshire.
Educated: Brighton College.
Died of wounds: 29th April 1917. Aged 21 years.
St Sever Cemetery, Rouen.

Vincent Morris, the youngest son of Canon and Mrs Morris, was still at school when the War started and was not able to leave until the end of the summer term 1915. He wrote of his frustration in 'The Eleventh Hour'.

THE ELEVENTH HOUR
A Sonnet

Is this to live? - to cower and stand aside
    While others fight and perish day by day?
    To see my loved ones slaughtered, and to say:-
'Bravo! bravo! how nobly you have died!'
Is this to love? - to heed my friends no more,
    But watch them perish in a foreign land
    Unheeded, and to give no helping hand,
But smile, and say:- 'How terrible is War!'

Nay: this is not to love nor this to live!
I will go forth; I hold no more aloof;
And I will give all that I have to give
And leave the refuge of my father's roof:

Then, if I live, no man will say, think I,
'He lives: because he did not dare to die!'

In the same month as he wrote this poem Morris was gazetted 2nd Lieutenant in the 3rd Battalion Sherwood Foresters, the regiment in which his father had served as a Chaplain. When he realised that his chances of going to France were remote he was transferred to the Royal Flying Corps.

In April 1917, a few weeks after he arrived in France, Morris' aeroplane came down in a blizzard at Vimy Ridge. He had several cuts to his head; his left thigh and right leg were fractured. The latter had to be amputated and after making some progress he underwent another operation. He died whilst under the anaesthetic just three weeks after his crash. After his death an untitled poem written a few days before his accident was found on two separate pieces of paper in his pocket book:

> Through vast
>   Realms of air
>   we passed
> On wings all-whitely fair.
>
>   Sublime
> On speeding wing
>   we climb
> Like an unfettered Thing.
>
>   Away
> Height upon height;
>   and play
> In God's great Lawns of Light.
>
>   And He
> Guides us safe home
>   to see
> The Fields He bade us roam.

SECOND LIEUTENANT HAROLD PARRY

17th Battalion King's Royal Rifle Corps.
Born: 13th December 1896. Bloxwich.
Educated: Queen Mary's Grammar School, Walsall.
       Exeter College, Oxford.
Killed: 6th May 1917. Aged 20 years.
Vlamertinghe Military Cemetery, Belgium.

Harold Parry was educated at Queen Mary's Grammar School, Walsall where he became Captain of School, Captain of Football and Captain of Cricket. He won an Open History Scholarship to Exeter College Oxford, and went up in October 1915. A month later he wrote "I am going to try and get into the Army at the end of this term, I think. I have no wish to remain a civilian any longer..."

In February 1915 he wrote from Devon to his father and mentioned the death in action of a fellow Exonian, Hugh Freston (qv) "a poet of no mean ability... ...brilliant and intellectual..."

Harold Parry was commissioned in the King's Royal Rifle Corps and although many of his poems were written on active service "on backs of envelopes, untidy and half undecipherable scrap-books, neat and orderly manuscript, prim typewritten portfolios", there was no mention of the war in any of them.

Parry joined the 17th Battalion in the front line at Hébuterne on 25th September 1916; on 14th October he wrote to a friend:

> ... once you get into the fighting line, and see everywhere the promise of youth being ruined and shattered for ever, when you see clear minds and healthy bodies sacrificed daily for the sins that are not theirs, and then read of the petty factions and narrowness of outworn sects at home - sects controlled, encouraged and upheld by the very people who ought to be paying the price out here - it makes one feel awfully sad and awfully angry that things should ever have turned out in this wise. I pray God to end this slaughter quickly, though as yet, the end seems far, far off, and it is my firm belief that were the peoples in the trenches allowed the rule which is rightly theirs the matter could and would be settled with satisfaction at once...

> The average Fritz is as sick at heart over all this destruction as we are. We are preached a doctrine of frightfulness, and yet is it not sufficiently sad to think, when you come across an unburied dead German, perhaps this day his wife and children mourn for him, and in

the future can know neither peace nor comfort? I must confess it distresses me beyond measure, for I am not a soldier at heart. The real evil in this conflict is not of the individual so much as of the powers that be. They, in their pride, and safety say "We will fight the matter to a finish," or, "We must crush Germany utterly and for ever."

If these dignitaries could only be set in the trenches for a wee short space, and made to carry heavy coils of wire for long distances up long communication trenches - blasted by the incessant force of the guns - I could guarantee that the war would not last longer than time to fix up provisional peace terms made it necessary. This is the hope of every Tommy who has come out of this hell once - and of every Fritz as well - but it can't be done, and I suppose the war will drag on its bloody length, intensifying each day its already untold misery, until at last peace comes through sheer exhaustion...

The Battalion was fighting at the Schwaben Redoubt in the middle of October 1916; in four days it lost 300 men and nearly all the officers. One of his Company later wrote of Parry at this time:

... He shared his toffee and cakes from home amongst the boys, and during a heavy shelling in Schwaben we got on a dead Bosche in a dug-out, not noticing in the darkness, thinking it was a heap of old bags and tunics. He handed his chocolates round and cigarettes; we sang and forgot the shells. The warning came, "They are coming over." Out he jumped in a breath, pulled his revolver and climbed on top 'on his own'. He told us all off to different posts and threw bombs like rain...

Towards the end of October the Battalion went into Divisional Reserve at Martinsart and Parry wrote:

...Fritz... knows every inch of the ground about here perfectly, and gives us little rest. Every dug-out he has marked, and knows the exact position because it is all captured ground that we are holding now. Fields ploughed up with innumerable shell-holes and trenches blown to atoms. A few battered and dead tree stumps with here and there a pile of broken bricks complete the panorama of what was once a wonderfully pretty place, quiet with the deepest quietude of rustic life, and beautiful with the beauty of woods and vales and flowers.

Two hundred years will not suffice to efface the traces of this tragedy from the land. Things can never be as they were, and the greatest indictment that war can have, is the forlorn and shell-shattered land about here with its rude and pathetic crosses to mark the last resting-place of those who in the fullness of their youth - at the beginning of love and hope and ambition - were cut off from life, and utterly destroyed as far as things temporal are concerned...

Amongst our last batch of prisoners were many boys - who could not be more than sixteen or seventeen years old - and a few old men who were long since past the time when they were physically fit for such a strife as this. These people have no Prussian militarism in them. They do not fight for lust of fighting nor hate because they are told to. Naturally they are not in the best frame of mind towards us because we have been doing our best (or rather worst) to try and kill them, and yet they are glad to be captured - they know we treat them well. Many of them told us that they had merely been waiting the opportunity to surrender, since they were tired of war, and could no longer endure its strain. Of course, all the Bosches are not like this, but I think that outside the Prussians there are not many who would not be glad to see things settled - no matter on what basis...

On 1st November 1916 Parry wrote to his mother:

...I have been through a road in a beautiful wood to-day. The leaves were gold and brown and all kinds of rich colours, and the birds were still singing in the trees. Everything seemed peaceful, and yet man was striving with man for life blood only a few short miles away. How unreal and horrible it all seems. It is a nightmare intensified, and these occasional glimpses of the things that are beautiful and right are, after all, only like flashes in a thunder cloud, flashes which serve to show up the destructive storm cloud in all its wildness and terror.

How long will it be before I can walk about the fields of home again in peace, and escape from this inferno in which all good things seem to be swallowed up and lost?...

How long will it be before I can look round and see the old familiar lawns and trees and pools, instead of the desolate and shell-shattered villages, the torn-up earth and the forlorn crosses on the broken heights...?

> O smiling fields,
> O valleys happy with summer,
> Where wild flowers blow upon the sunlit air,
> And streams in silence take their tranquil course;
> Where all day long the birds sing in the brake,
> And the grass falls before the mower's scythe
> In straight, sweet swathes:
> I long for you, and hope days hence
> That I shall come again

And share your peace.
O deep, deep peace,
Wherein Love grows
And blossoms to its flower of loveliness...
Only to kiss my Love upon the brow,
As twilight deepens into night along the vales...
My Lord,
Lead me again into those fields of home,
And make me glad.

7th November 1916... I have just sat down on an extremely hard seat in a newly captured Bosche dug-out to indite these few lines, or perchance more, to you. We have had a terrific combat with the water, and even now I can hear (when the guns are quiet for a while) its sweet and gentle murmur as it flops down into the dug-out step by step. Eventually we managed to stop it coming down our stairway too quickly, by an ingenious arrangement of two mess tins and a petrol can with the one end knocked out. The trench is a sea of muddy water, with an underlying layer of watery mud, and if one ventured out without going along the much battered remnant of a parapet one would be literally up to the waist in mud before a hundred yards had been covered.

What it'll be like if the rain keeps on till morning I don't know (someone had upset the tin, and water is rising rapidly), for it's simply pouring in now. Why did Tennyson write 'The Brook'? And why should't I write a lyric to the 'River that runs into everyone's dug-out'?

I come from trenches deep in slime,
Soft slime so sweet and yellow,
And rumble down the steps in time
To souse "some shivering fellow".

I trickle in and trickle out
Of every nook and corner,
And, rushing like some waterspout,
Make many a rat a mourner.

I gather in from near and far
A thousand brooklets swelling,
And laugh aloud a great "Ha, ha!"
To flood poor Tommy's dwelling.

And so on and so on until I can't write more, because the water is up to my neck or eyes or some equally vulnerable part of my anatomy...

On the 1st May 1917 the Battalion was in billets at Ypres and working on railway construction; five days later Harold Parry was killed by shellfire in Ypres.

A SONNET

Deep in the slumbering night hide me away,
Where I may gaze upon unmoving stars,
And feel the scented airs around me play,
Blown from between the golden turned bars
That lie far, far beyond the land of sight,
But not too far beyond the land of sense;
That in the silent starry vaulted night,
The inward soul, across a space immense,
May glimpse the journey's end, and courage take
From vision. So in the searching light of day
Memory may bring a vintage that will slake
My thirst and strengthen me upon the way;
That, though in utter dark, I may not sleep
Whene'er God calls to me across Time's deep.

SECOND LIEUTENANT BERNARD FREEMAN TROTTER

11th Battalion Leicestershire Regiment.

Born: 16th June 1890. Toronto, Canada.
Educated: Woodstock College, Ontario.
            McMaster University.
Killed: 7th May 1917. Aged 26 years.
Mazingarbe Communal Cemetery Extension, France.

    Bernard Trotter was the son of a Canadian University Professor. His delicate health prevented him from enlisting with the Canadian Forces at the outbreak of the War, but he was at the University of Toronto reading English Literature at the end of 1915 when Canadian University men were asked to apply for commissions in the British Army. He sailed for England in March 1916 and wrote the following poem on the eve of his departure.

DREAMS

Not as we dream them,
    Rose-sweet and wonderful,
Laughter-thrilled, magical,
    Our dreams come true.

Always some hidden,
    Unforeseen circumstance,
Seeming malevolence,
    Darkens the view.

Something we want not,
    Ugly and masterful,
Sprouts through the beautiful,
    Wars with our joy.

Someone is missing:
    Gone the sweet comradeship,
Commerce of eye and lip -
    Barren is Troy.

Yet go we ever,
    Though earthly experience

Mocks at their radiance,
   Dreaming our dreams.

Dreams without reason,
   Rose-sweet and wonderful,
Laughter-thrilled, magical, -
   Fools? - So it seems.

Or is there a feeble
   Spark of the infinite
Burning in Hell's despite,
   In me and you,

Lighting us onward
   Through the inscrutable
To a land wonderful
Where, as we dream them,
   Our dreams will come true?

Trotter spent some months training at Oxford, and was then particularly pleased to be commissioned in the Leicestershire Regiment, as his father was born in the County and members of his family still lived there.

He joined the Battalion at Béthune in December 1916 and in April 1917 he became Assistant Transport Officer. The Battalion was in the front line in the Mazingarbe area, west of Loos.

...I have been up the line every night this week except last. It is a weird life in many ways, but it is surprising how soon one becomes accustomed to it. The sudden kettle-drum staccato of the machine-guns searching for working parties, the vivid flares of the Very lights and the dense darkness which succeeds, the whistle of the salvo of shells overhead, hardly make you raise your head, unless something is a bit close. Then, of course, you hug the bank, or the bottom of the trench, and wait till the row stops or the light goes out, and carry on... Yesterday was Sunday and for the first time since leaving the Base I was able to attend service. It gave one a new thrill at their majesty and beauty to repeat the Te Deum and the Nunc Dimittis in a room scarred, walls and ceiling, with shrapnel; and with the roll of the guns for accompaniment instead of the organ... My present surroundings are hardly conducive to the study or production of poetry, though they frequently produce momentary poetical impulses which, if more reflective opportunities come, may not be wholly lost...

AN APRIL INTERLUDE - 1917

April snow agleam in the stubble,
   Melting to brown on the new-ploughed fields,
April sunshine, and swift cloud-shadows
   Racing to spy what the season yields
Over the hills and far away:
Heigh! and ho! for an April day!
   Hoofs on the highroad: Ride - tr-r—ot!
   Spring's in the wind, and war's forgot,
As we go riding through Picardy.

Up by a wood where a brown hawk hovers,
   Down through a village with white-washed walls,
A wooden bridge and a mill-wheel turning,
   And a little stream that sports and brawls
Into the valley and far away:
Heigh! and ho! for an April day!
   Children and old men stop to stare
   At the clattering horsemen from Angleterre,
As we go riding through Picardy.

On by the unkempt hedges, budding,
   On by the Château gates flung wide.
Where is the man who should trim the garden?
   Where are the youths of this country-side?
Over the hills and far away
Is war, red war, this April day.
   So for the moment we pay our debt
   To the cause on which our faith is set,
As we go riding through Picardy.

Then the hiss of the spurting gravel,
   Then the tang of the wind on the face,
Then the splash of the hoof-deep puddle,
   Spirit of April setting the pace
Over the hills and far away:
Heigh! and ho! for an April day!
   Heigh! for a ringing: Ride - tr-r—ot!
   Ho! - of war we've never a thought
As we go riding through Picardy.

On Sunday 6th May, 1917, Bernard Trotter wrote home:

... Had a fairly quiet trip last night, though there were a few bits of excitement. At times the Bosch is a most methodical man. He picks out a certain spot on the road and drops a shell on it for luck at regular intervals of time. We ran across him in one of these moods. We could see ahead a nice black crump go up as regularly as clock-work about once a minute. It's easy then. You go up as close as you dare, wait for one to go off, and then make a dash for it, hell-for-leather, sparks flying from the pavé, wheels rattling, din most glorious. It's really rather fun once in a while, and not particularly dangerous... This morning we had a romp with some little French kiddies who came around our stores shed. It seems strange to think of these kiddies here, some of them not old enough to remember life without the sound of the guns...

The following night Bernard Trotter was in charge of transport carting slag for repairing roads at Loos. His company of men was under heavy fire and had just unloaded their sixth and final consignment of slag. A high explosive shell burst close to Trotter, who fell from his horse and was killed instantly. His parents received the manuscript of his last poem, the day after he was killed.

ICI REPOSE

A little cross of weather-silvered wood,
Hung with a garish wreath of tinselled wire,
And on it carved a legend - thus it runs:

"Ici repose - " Add what name you will,
And multiply by thousands: in the fields,
Along the roads, beneath the trees - one here,
A dozen there, to each its simple tale
Of one more jewel threaded star-like on
The sacrificial rosary of France.

And as I read and read again those words,
Those simple words, they took a mystic sense;
And from the glamour of an alien tongue
They wove insistent music in my brain,
Which, in a twilight hour, when all the guns
Were silent, shaped itself to song.

O happy dead! who sleep embalmed in glory,
Safe from corruption, purified by fire, -
Ask you our pity? - ours, mud-grimed and gory,
Who still must grimly strive, grimly desire?

You have outrun the reach of our endeavour,
Have flown beyond our most exalted quest, -
Who prate of Faith and Freedom knowing ever
That all we really fight for's just - a rest,

The rest that only Victory can bring us -
Or Death, which throws us brother-like by you -
The civil commonplace in which 'twill fling us
To neutralize our then too martial hue.

But you have rest from every tribulation
Even in the midst of war; you sleep serene,
Pinnacled on the sorrow of a nation,
In cerements of sacrificial sheen.

Oblivion cannot claim you: our heroic
War-lustred moment, as our youth, will pass
To swell the dusty hoard of Time the Stoic,
That gathers cobwebs in the nether glass.

We shall grow old, and tainted with the rotten
Effluvia of the peace we fought to win,
The bright deeds of our youth will be forgotten,
Effaced by later failure, sloth, or sin;

But you have conquered Time, and sleep forever,
Like gods, with a white halo on your brows -
Your souls our lode-stars, your death-crowned endeavour
The spur that holds the nations to their vows.

CAPTAIN WILLIAM OLIPHANT DOWN M.C.

4th Battalion Royal Berkshire Regiment.
Born: 1886. Gillingham, Dorset.
Died of Wounds: 22nd May 1917. Aged 31 years.
Hermies Hill British Cemetery, France.

Oliphant Down enlisted in the 15th Royal Hussars at the outbreak of the war. He was commissioned in the 4th Battalion Royal Berkshire Regiment in January 1916 and joined the Battalion in the front line near Hébuterne the same month. On 8th April Down led a patrol on a raid against the German trenches; the following day he wrote 'F.T. Blank Blank':

F.T. BLANK BLANK

A whisper wandered around
Of a plan of the G.O.C.'s,
And figures surveyed the ground
In stealthy groups of threes;
But the whole Brigade was there
Or pretty well all the lot,
When we dug a trench at Never-mind-where
On April the Never-mind-what.

The Whats-a-names dug the trench,
The Who-is-its found the screen,
And we mustn't forget to mench
The Thingummies in between;
The Tothermies built the fence
And the R.E.'s also ran;
For we didn't spare any expense
With labour a shilling a man.

There isn't much else to tell,
Though the enemy made a song
And tried to blow it to Hell,
But got the address all wrong,
For you'll find it is still out there
In the bally old selfsame spot!
That trench which we dug at Never-mind-where
On April the Never-mind-what.

On 2nd July 1916 the Battalion was in bivouacs at Mailly-Maillet waiting to move up to the attack; when the orders were cancelled there was great disappointment and the Battalion returned to trenches at Hébuterne. By 27th August it had moved a little further south to trenches at Ovillers; Down was one of four men who were given immediate awards after an attack when one hundred Germans were killed or wounded and ten prisoners were taken. Down and two other officers were given the M.C., and a Private awarded the D.C.M. Down's citation read:

> For conspicuous gallantry in action. He made an excellent reconnaissance of an enemy strong point, and brought back most useful information. Two nights later he commanded the right platoon in an attack, and after entering the enemy's trench led a bombing party which killed ll of the enemy.

On 15th May 1917 the Battalion was in the front line at Hermies. Oliphant Down was one of fifteen casualties the Battalion suffered during the six weeks it was in this sector of the Front. The Battalion diary recorded on 22nd May:

> Captain W.O. Down's death was a great loss to the Battalion. He proved himself a most excellent officer, always thinking of his command. He knew his work thoroughly and his many qualities had endeared him to all ranks.

PICARDY PARODIES No. 2 (W.B. Y..ts)

I will arise and go now, and go to Picardy,
And a new trench-line hold there, of clay and shell-holes made,
No dug-outs shall I have there, nor a hive for the Lewis G.,
But live on top in the b. loud glade.

And I may cease to be there, for peace comes dropping slow,
Dropping from the mouth of the Minnie to where the sentry sings;
There noon is high explosive, and night a gunfire glow,
And evening full of torpedoes' wings.

I will arise and go now, though always night and day
I'll feel dark waters lapping with low sounds by the store,
Where all our bombs grow rusty and countless S.A.A.;
I'll feel it in my trench-feet sore.

PICARDY PARODIES   No. 3.

(To the tune of 'They wouldn't Believe me')

Got the 'cutest little trench
With the acutest little stench,
Where yer've gotter stand and freeze,
Up in the water to your knees,
And there's rats beyond belief
Growing fat on bully beef;
Oh, it certainly seems fine
Just to think you're in the line.

But, when I tell them how sick of it I am,
They'll never relieve me, they'll never relieve me:
My clothes, my boots, my face, my hair
Are in a state beyond repair,
I'm the dirtiest thing that one could see.
But, when I tell them, and I'm certainly going to tell them,
That is not what I came out to do:
They'll never relieve me, they'll never relieve me,
But leave me here until the moon turns blue.

Got the 'cutest little trench,
Which we undertook to wrench
From the Alleyman one day,
When the dawn was turning grey;
And we gave those Bosches hell,
So that they turned grey as well;
We were rather rough, I fear,
From Ovillers to Poseer.

For, when they told us they wanted to give in,
They couldn't deceive us, they couldn't deceive us,
And so with bombs and bayonits
We made an end of poor old Fritz.
'Twas the bloodiest day that one could see,
For, when they told us, and they certainly tried to tell us,
That they'd surrender if we would desist,
We wouldn't believe them, we wouldn't believe them,
But wiped them off the German Army List.

LIEUTENANT GERALD GEORGE SAMUEL

10th Battalion Royal West Kent Regiment.
Born: 6th May 1886. London.
Educated: Eton College.
Killed: 7th June 1917. Aged 31 years.
Menin Gate Memorial to the Missing, Ypres, Belgium.

After he left Eton, Gerald Samuel devoted his time to the working men and boys of London's East End; he later built and endowed a Home for Orphans where he planned to live himself.

At the outbreak of the War he was twice rejected for the Army because of poor eyesight but eventually gained a commission in the 10th Battalion Royal West Kent Regiment in October 1915. Shortly before he left for the Front in April 1916 he wrote a 'Farewell Message to the Members of the Stepney Jewish Lads' Club' with whom he was closely involved:

> ... Anyhow, I have done my best to help you, to make life easier for you, and to enable you to grow up honourable and honest Jews and Englishmen. There is nothing of which we can be more proud than our race and religion. It is a great heritage, and it is a duty for every one of us to keep it pure and unaltered, and to hand it down to our descendants, as our ancestors have preserved it for us.

Samuel was twice wounded and wrote most of his poetry over the fourteen months he was in Belgium and France; the Battalion was in front line trenches at Le Bizet from the end of May 1916 and had moved south to the Somme area by September when it was at Delville Wood.

LIFE AND DEATH

Life and Death were playing,
   And Life had seemed to win,
Until, her progress staying,
Death mocked her tears and praying,
And gaily went on slaying,
   With triumph in his grin.

Yet Life still went on gaining,
   And Death seemed in despair,

Until, no longer feigning
To feel his luck was waning,
A loathsome plague unchaining,
    He poisoned all the air.

But Life was not defeated,
    And ceaseless efforts made.
But Death would not be cheated,
And all his wiles repeated,
And made men's passions heated,
    Till War gave him its aid.

And so through all the ages
    Shall Life and Death contend,
And while the battle rages,
In vain we turn the pages,
For not the wisest sages
    Shall ever learn the end.

By the end of November 1916 the Battalion had returned to
Flanders and was at Voormezeele in May 1917. On 5th June it was
in position on the left wing of an impending attack on the Messines
Ridge. At 3.10 a.m. on 7th June nineteen mines were exploded
simultaneously under the German front line with devastating effect.
The shock from the explosions was felt in London and other parts
of England. A massive bombardment then opened, and 80,000 men
of Plumer's Second Army pressed forward to take the Ridge and
consolidate the capture of their limited objectives.

The initial explosions and attack were so effective that the 41st
Division met little opposition from the enemy until they reached the
ridge of the Dammstrasse, the old drive to the White Château
occupied by the Germans. The 10th Battalion Royal West Kent
Regiment, commanded by Colonel Wood-Martyn stormed the
position, captured forty prisoners and, after a further push under
heavy shell-fire, consolidated a defensive line. They held this
position under increasing German shellfire and their casualties
totalled nine officers and 228 other ranks by the time they were
relieved four days later.

As he led his Company, Gerald Samuel was one of five officers
and 30 men in the Battalion killed.

1917

CONSOLATION

Oh! I sigh when I think of the men
  In the trenches of Flanders and France;
  And I dream of the days of romance,
  Of the bow and the shield and the lance,
And the chivalrous tales that the pen
Of a poet could celebrate then.

For the brutal inventions of crime
  Are the weapons of battle to-day;
  And the guns that remorselessly slay
  Blow the ramparts and shelters away.
And there in the mud and the slime
Are the heroes who fall in their prime.

There is much that a poet could tell
  That was valiant and noble and brave
  In the gallant young lives that they gave;
  But the stories are lost in the grave,
For all who could speak of them fell
In the pitiless welter of shell.

And I grieve for the widows who weep,
  And the parents and orphans forlorn,
  And the hearts that in anquish are torn;
  And yet it is idle to mourn
For the dead are serenely asleep,
And our faith in the Lord we must keep.

For the faith that is steadfast and clear,
  Brings to sorrowing hearts the reward
  That belief in our God can afford.
  They are happy who trust in the Lord:
They find comfort to whom He is dear
And who know that His spirit is near.

LIEUTENANT COLONEL WILLIAM AMBROSE SHORT C.M.G.

14th Brigade, Royal Field Artillery.

286th Brigade, Royal Field Artillery.

Born: 11th April 1871. Oswestry, Shropshire.
Educated: Winchester College.
Killed: 21st June 1917. Aged 45 years.
Cité Bonjean Military Cemetery, Armentières, France.

William Short was commissioned in the Royal Field Artillery in February 1891 and served in India for ten years.

He was commanding 68 Battery in 14 Brigade when war broke out and arrived in France in August 1914. On the 13th September the Battery crossed the Aisne by a partially destroyed bridge at Venizel, a small village east of Soissons. They arrived at Bucy-le-Long, a village a little to the north, under heavy shellfire. After they had been relieved and sent back, Short wrote the following poem:

VENIZEL

Let me go back to Venizel,
    And farther still across the plain;
    A garden grows beside the Aisne
With sweet, black plums, that like me well.

Beyond the bridge at Venizel
    The sunny, level plain is laid.
    Last week we crossed, and had for shade
The yellow bursts of German shell.

And once again at Venizel
    My boys the Prussian fire withstood.
    Stout hearts still sleep within the wood
Beside the bridge, for which they fell.

Let us go back to Venizel;
    To Bucy highlands let us win.
    The road is northward to Berlin
And our advance the Prussians' knell.

During December 1914 and January 1915 the Battery was in action near Le Bizet, north of Armentières. At Christmas Short wrote 'To Madame Josephine Six: Who Kept the Estaminet at...', and early in the New Year of 1915 he wrote 'To the Headmaster of Winchester: on Receipt of his Present':

TO MADAME JOSEPHINE SIX

Above the din of fierce and bloody war
   Sometimes the gentle voice of kindness speaks,
And that's why I'm attracted more and more
   By the society of Madame Six,
Who laughs at shells and mocks a German gun,
But knows so well how bacon should be done.

Four hundred paces from the German lines
   In her it is my privilege to meet
Th'essential feminine, whose soul combines
   That curious passion to watch menfolk eat
With anxious doubts whether they're warm and dry -
A Pet in fact, not merely an Ally.

She cooks our meals; she warms our frozen feet;
   She takes the sentry coffee in the snow
(Across a not too wholesome bit of street);
   Her roof is riddled, but she will not go.
What can I do for her? At any rate
It's Christmas, and I'll wish her 'la bonne fete'.

TO THE HEADMASTER OF WINCHESTER

When failing light marks afternoon's decay,
I may desert the trench, and take the way,
   Muddy but pleasant, to my cheerful farm,
And Teuton fireworks close down for the day.

Before the stove our frozen limbs we roast;
An atmosphere of talk and tea and toast
   Surrounds us, while a faithful Bombardier
Brings in the mighty sack, that holds our post.

At such an hour there fell into my hand
A little present from my native land -
   Your chocolate and greeting - both to me
Were sweeter than the juice of Samarcand.

Latin has faded, as grey hairs have sprung
(Your slave was never deemed a jig, when young).
   I grasp your classic phrase and kindly wish,
But let me thank you in my native tongue.

On 10th April 1915 Short wrote 'Farewell: To the Fourth Division': and in August 1915 from Mailly-Beaucourt he wrote 'Ploegsteert Wood'.

FAREWELL: TO THE FOURTH DIVISION

When I, old comrades, in more peaceful climes
Would learn of that stern field, whence I have gone,
And study page eleven of the Times
Or terse communications of Sir John
For deeds heroic, moving, sad, or strange,
North of the L——s, I'm told, there is no change.

Except the change of Spring, perhaps. The sun
Has dried that trench, where waist-deep water lay.
The cooing Taube cannot see the gun
For poplar buds; and now in open day
Adventurous men may reach the Sniper's Farm;
The willows keep the Mons fatigue from harm.

But spring nor summer, cold nor tropic heat,
Nor time nor place, removed however far -
Whether we drift apart, or if we meet -
Shall alter Friendship disciplined by War.
Ah! doubt me not, my friends, where'er I range
In our affection there shall be no change.

PLOEGSTEERT WOOD

For once there needs no effort to persuade
The choice of duty - secrecy and shade
Are in the Wood; the treeless, glaring road
No certain conduct to the Barricade.

The hazel undergrowth on either side
Gives covert, where the tuneful thrush may hide,
And still make music; high above the oaks
Tower like queens, modest but dignified.

But, since man's virtue cannot here command
Good fortune, how shall these escape the brand
Of foreign hate, these quiet, patient trees,
Graceful and strong, types of their fatherland?

For ragged scar and cicatrice unclean
Disfigure even here each sylvan queen,
And further on more wounds, till sparse bare trunks
Rise naked, shamed, stripped of their kirtle green.

There, since the autumn leaves began to fade,
Th' uncertain battle back and forth has swayed.
Anon flowed good West Count y blood, anon
Grey-coated Saxons in the earth were laid.

And now at last, diminished though they be,
Maimed, outraged, friends to all adversity,
The oaks stand once again in Belgian ground;
Captives of winter, summer sets them free.

In April 1917 Short assumed command of 286th Brigade of the
Royal Field Artillery in the Houplines - L'Epinette Sector, near
Armentières and was killed in action two months later.

CAPTAIN CHARLES JOHN BEECH MASEFIELD M.C.

'C' Company, 1st/5th Battalion North Staffordshire Regiment.
Born: 15th April 1882. Cheadle, Staffordshire.
Educated: Repton School.
Died of Wounds: 2nd July 1917. Aged 35 years.
Cabaret-Rouge British Cemetery, Souchez, France.

A first cousin of John Masefield, Charles Masefield was articled to his father's firm of Solicitors when he left school. He qualified in 1905 and practised in Derby, Wolverhampton and Cheadle. In 1910 he married Muriel Bussell. An active member of the North Staffordshire Field Club, he led several excursions and read some noteable papers on the history and archaeology of Staffordshire. His novel, *Gilbert Hermer,* was published in 1908; a book of poetry came out in 1911 followed by a collection of satires in 1914.

Masefield did not enlist immediately at the outbreak of the War because the head of the family firm had recently died. He was commissioned in January 1915 in a Territorial Battalion, the 5th Battalion, North Staffordshire Regiment. As part of 46th Division, the first Territorials to join the Expeditionary Force as a Division, they went to France in March 1915.

In July 1915 the Battalion was in trenches near Sanctuary Wood; Masefield wrote a sonnet 'Two Julys':

'TWO JULYS' : SONNET

I was so vague in 1914; tossed
Upon too many purposes, and worthless;
Moody; to this world or the other lost,
Essential nowhere; without calm and mirthless,
And now I have gained one for many ends,
See my straight road stretch out so white, so slender,
That happy road, the road of all my friends,
Made glad with peace, and holy with surrender.

Proud, proud we fling to the winds of Time our token,
And in our need there wells in us the power
Given England's swords to keep her honour clean.
Which they shall be which pierce, and which be broken,
We know not, but we know that every hour
We must shine brighter, take an edge more keen.

Although the Battalion was involved in the diversionary attack on Gommecourt on 1st July 1916, Masefield did not rejoin from Base until the following day. For the next two months the Battalion was in trenches at Ransart and in billets at Bailleulmont. In letters home Masefield wrote of the conditions he was living under.

3rd - 5th July 1916. The misery of the trenches was indescribable. Water generally up to our middle, sometimes for a mile of track as deep as that. All look less like men than like some monstrous creatures born of mud, so coated and covered with it they were. We are in the Front Line; but just here in the peculiar position of being unable to see the Boche's Front Line, as we are on the crest of a rise, and Fritz down in the hollow below us. So what you see when you look over the parapet is merely a luxuriant growth of thistles and barbed wire for 10, 20 or 40 yards, and then nothing until, on the other side of the hollow 400 yards away, you see Fritz's second and third lines, barbed wire, etc. All we do at the moment is to hold our line secure...

... There is a sea of yellow mud everywhere, all over your clothes and hands, in the water you wash in (when you do wash), and standing water all over the floor of the dug-out I'm writing in. The men are wonderful. Their lives are several degrees wretcheder than ours when it rains, yet I have not heard one grouse yet...

17th August 1916. Courses and trenches pretty well comprise an officers life here... I shot a partridge with my revolver in the trenches the other day - a sitting shot needless to say! We had him for dinner tonight, a very welcome change from the eternal ration beef... There are a lot about No Mans Land, where of course they have a very peaceful existence among the rank grass and thistles...

8th October 1916... We raided the Boche trenches one night, and reckon about eight Boches were killed without any losses to ourselves. Two of our officers have got the Military Cross for this. In reply the Boches paid us two return visits. The first was a complete failure, and they left a dead man behind them; but the second time, by dint of rushing at top speed into and out of the trench, they managed to take a prisoner back with them, but we think we hit some of them. As a result of all this, trophies are quite common in the Company - Boche rifles, caps, and cigars (carried by Fritz in his cap), etc...

From the Brigade Reserve at Berles-au-Bois Masefield wrote on 17th October 1916:

... We have been having a pretty quiet time lately, but while we were in the trenches Fritz took it into his head to shell this village, and, as it is possible he may do so again at any moment, the men all have to sleep in caves cut out of the chalk, and we in cellars. Our cellar isn't at all a bad bedchamber - pretty dry, and we have moved our wire-netting mattresses down into it..."

CANDLE-LIGHT

Candle-light is so mellow and warm
When a man comes in all hungry and cold,
Clotted with mud, or wet from the storm -
Only of candle-light you shall be told.

Of Madame's brave, sad eagerness,
And French serenity of dress,
Her quiet, quick ways as she goes
To dry our heavy, sodden clothes
And bring all hot the great ragout
That makes once more a man of you,
Her pains to help us put away
The sights that we have seen all day,
Her talk of kine and oats and rye
And Francois' feats when but so high -
You'd never guess, did you not know,
He died for France three months ago.
And then there's Marthe, whom he has left
(So proud, and yet so all bereft),
And Marie, with her hair in ties,
Looking at you with great round eyes
That make you wish to Heaven you were
The hero that you seem to her.
And last and least
There's Francois' little Jean Baptiste,
For whom, deep slumbering in his cot,
All wounds and wars and deaths are not.
Such is the household every night
Illumined by the candle-light.

Search-lights are so blinding and white
The things they show you shall not hear,
Enough to see them; it is not right
We should tell of them too, my love, my dear.

At the end of October 1916 Masefield was granted three months special leave after the death of his uncle, his only partner in the firm. He returned to France in May 1917, and on the 14th June he was awarded the Military Cross for gallantry during a raid on enemy trenches near Lens. The citation read:

> During a raid upon enemy trenches he led his company with great dash and skill under heavy trench-mortar barrage, attacking a party of the enemy single-handed. After inflicting heavy casualties and taking three prisoners he successfully withdrew his Company, having shown conspicuous gallantry and good leadership throughout.

Charles Masefield was never to know of this award. He was taken prisoner by the Germans after being wounded in an attack on Lens on 1st July, 1917 and died of his wounds the following day. The History of the 5th North Staffordshire Regiment gives an account of the action.

> ... Lens was a very formidable position, as the numerous houses made excellent defences, and a few troops would be able to hold back an attack. If, however, the defenders were sufficiently demoralised, a sudden blow might prove successful. It was evident that the Germans had begun to realise the danger, and would strengthen the defences. The attack then must be made at once, before the worn-out German Division was relieved.

> It was decided to make this attempt on the morning of the 1st of July (a disastrous anniversary for the 46th Division). The attack was to be made on a three Brigade front, the objective being from the Souchez River in the South, through 'Aconite' and 'Aloof' Trenches, to the junction point of the Sixth Division North-West of Lens. The Higher Command admitted that the attack was a gamble, its success depending on whether the worn-out German Division had been relieved or not.

> The front of attack was about 400 yards. The two waves assembled in two rows of trenches at 2 a.m. on the morning of Sunday July 1st. The assault was fixed for 2.43 a.m., just before dawn.

> The attack at first progressed favourably, and the men passed through the wire into the streets. On the left the Germans had some machine-guns which they had rushed through the barrage, and these held up 'A' and 'B' Companies, so that they could not reach their objective. 'C' and 'D' Companies on the right had much less opposition, and, pushing down the streets, reached their objective, the 'Aconite' Trench, leaving the 6th South Staffs to mop up the Germans in the

houses. On reaching their objective they worked along to their left, hoping to meet 'A' Company.

Meanwhile on the extreme left the Sherwood Brigade, with a 2nd Battalion of their own Regiment, advanced upon the Lens-Lievin Road. It was an ideal ground for defence, with houses, slag-heaps, and other obstacles, and, in spite of their efforts, they could not reach their objective. On the right the Lincolns and Leicester Brigade had been more successful but had not been able to gain their full objective. The result of all this fighting was that 'C' and 'D' Companies, who had reached their objectives, and sent a last message to say they were consolidated, were being cut off. The remainder of the 5th North Staffs made most desperate but unavailing attempts to get through, and the fighting was most severe, being hand to hand in streets and houses. Finally, at 7 p.m., the attempt to relieve the two Companies was abandoned, and the relics of the Battalion were withdrawn. The attack had been a failure, and, as the enemy had fought skilfully and with courage, it was assessed that they were probably a fresh Division. The total casualties of the 46th Division were 50 officers and 1,000 men.

One of the men, who was made a prisoner of war, gave further details on his return to England:

'C' and 'D' Companies obtained their objectives, and held some of the houses. We were hopelessly cut off by the enemy, who was fully prepared for a big counter-attack, and a box barrage was thrown round us. Men were falling fast from shot and shell, and from bombs thrown into the houses... Captain Masefield fought heroically, and was severely wounded, and died at Leforest, after being taken prisoner...

"IN HONOREM FORTIUM"

I sometimes think that I have lived too long,
Who have heard so many a gay brave singer's song
Fail him for ever, - seen so many sails
Lean out resplendent to the evil gales,
Then Death, the wrecker, get his harvest in.
Oh, ill it is, when men lose all, to win;
Grief though it be to die, 'tis grief yet more
To live and count the dear dead comrades o'er.

Peace. After all, you died not. We've no fear
But that, long ages hence, you will be near -
A thought by night - on the warm wind a breath,

Making for courage, putting by old Death,
Living wherever men are not afraid
Of aught but making bravery a parade. -
Yes, parleying with fear, they'll pause and say
"At Gommecourt boys suffered worse that day;"
Or, hesitating on some anxious brink
They will become heroic when they think
"Did they not rise mortality above
Who staked a lifetime all made sweet with love?"

LIEUTENANT JOHN COLLINSON HOBSON
116th Company, Machine Gun Corps (Inf.) (Formerly 12th Battalion Royal Scots).
Born: 27th August 1893. Hampstead.
Educated: Westminster School.
           Christ Church College, Oxford.
Killed: 31st July 1917. Aged 23 years.
Menin Gate Memorial to the Missing, Ypres, Belgium.

John Hobson had a distinguished record at Westminster. He shot at Bisley in the School Eight in 1911 and boxed for the School in the same year. He was awarded his 1st Eleven Cricket Colours and played in the annual match against Charterhouse in 1912. He was head of his House between 1911 - 1912 and edited the House Magazine. He obtained a History Scholarship to Christ Church and played an active part in College and University life in the two years before the War.

In September 1914 he was gazetted to the 12th Service Battalion of the Royal Scots, and went to France in May 1915. He was promoted, commanded his Company, and was then sent to train at the Machine Gun School at Grantham in June 1916. Three months later he returned to the Front in command of a section of the 116th Machine Gun Company.

THE MACHINE GUN

Here do I lie,
   Couched in the grass
With my machine-gun
Loaded, lurking, ready.
Fast must he fly
   Who fain would pass.
Sure is my eye,
My hand is steady.

The sky is blue,
   The planes are humming,
But my machine gun
Waits and watches ever.

Fair is the view,
Though guns be drumming,
   Though yonder hill from this
King Death doth sever.

All around me
   Blows the dogrose;
But my machine gun
Hidden is in daisies,
   Lurking is he
   Where the grass grows,
Peering ever forth
Through summer hazes.

Come ye who may,
   Foeman in air, or earth!
For my machine gun
Sings for you alone,
And in his lay
   To silvery death gives birth.
Now lifts now lowers he
His deadly tone.

Speak him not fair!
   He peers, but does not see
My black machine gun
Who waits from night to morn.
Silent in his low lair,
   Mighty, unseen and free,
Dealer of death and wounds
To those who scorn.

Here do I lie,
   Hidden by grass and flowers,
With my machine gun,
Ghost of modern war.
The sun floats high,
   The moon through deep blue hours,
I watch with my machine gun
At Death's grim door.

The Third Battle of Ypres started on 31st July 1917 with an

allied attack early in the morning. Heavy bombardment and torrential rain in the days immediately before the offensive produced a quagmire of thick mud and slime round the village of St. Julien, which had been in enemy hands since April 1915. The battle for the village was fought as a series of actions on the only firm ground in the area, the concrete blockhouses built by the Germans.

Hobson's Company took part in the attack on St. Julien and under a fierce enemy barrage he went out in advance of the line to select positions for his guns. He was some 200 yards to the west of a spot on the Ypres-St. Julien Road, known as Corner Cot, when he was struck by a shell and killed instantly.

A fellow officer later wrote:

> We were heavily shelled long before the push-off, and were smothered with dirt thrown up by shells bursting a few yards away. Owing to the darkness, the barrage put up by the Hun and the fact that our landmark was completely obliterated, we lost direction and struck a road which took us along under the enemy barrage the whole way. Then we had to push on through the barrage again until we reached our destination. All this time he [Hobson] had been strolling about quite unconcernedly, as if he were out on a pleasure jaunt, cheering his men up, and setting a splendid example.

The village was eventually captured three days later, on 3rd August, with the cost in British casualties of 145 officers and 3,716 other ranks.

WAR

Silver days are passing,
   Golden days have gone,
When war was all a pastime
   Of battles lost and won.

My heart is sad and weary
   For the months have grown to years,
War is no more a pastime,
   But a thing of bitter tears.

Romance it was in old days,
   Trenches were green in June,
Flanders was gold in the sunshine
   Or silvered by the moon.

1917

Grand days of summer marching
   With hedgerows specked with dust!
Dear comrades at my shoulder
   To laugh with and to trust!

Red wine at every tavern!
   Omelettes of gold and brown!
Green fields and hay at bedtime,
   As soft as thistledown!

The music of the bullet!
   The drowsy boom of guns!
The drone of Scottish pipers!
   The songs of Scotland's sons!

Oh! Comrades of the old time
   Who will not fight again,
I shall remember always
   Those days of sun and rain!

The orchard at Givenchy
   When soft May winds did blow,
Loos in that great September,
   And Ypres in days of snow.

Oh! Comrades of the old time,
   The weary months go by,
New faces are about me
   New friends with me to die!

Soon will the long white causeways
   Be canopied with green,
Red poppies soon be blowing
   Where battlefields have been.

But I shall still be dreaming
   Of Scottish boys I knew,
Marching in dreams to Ploegstreet
   And drinking wine with you.

And where you too lie dreaming
   Beneath the turf so wet,

Remember me, remember,
 For I shall not forget!

Ay, silver days are passing,
 And golden days have gone
When war was all a pastime
 Of battles lost and won.

AS I CAME UP FROM WIPERS

As I came up from Wipers
 Before the break of day,
When silver rain was falling
 And the light was silver grey,
I heard a cock start crowing,
 And I heard a bugle call,
And I heard a throstle singing,
 On a ruined ivied wall.
But my heart was sad and weary
 And a tear was in my eye,
For thinking of a lassie
 In a country far away.
Sweet lassie can ye hear me?
 There's a picture in my head,
A land of purple mountains
 And heather hills so red.
Oh! till we meet in Scotland
 As once before we met,
Remember me! my dearest,
 For I shall not forget!

As I came up from Vlamertinghe
 The dawn was in the sky,
And the little larks were soaring
 And twittering in the sky.
The mists were on the meadows,
 The dew was on the flowers,
The early sun had touched with gold
 The graceful ruined towers.
But my heart was sad and heavy,
 My mind was full of care,

For thinking of a laddie
   Who was lying buried there.
Oh! laddie, can ye hear me?
   Do you mind that winter's day
When you and I together
   Marched up the self-same way?
Our hearts were strong and cheery,
   Our faces hard and set
Ay, laddie, you remember!
   And I shall not forget!

PRIVATE ELLIS HUMPHREY EVANS

15th Battalion Royal Welch Fusiliers.
Born: 13th January 1887. Near Trawsfynydd, North Wales.
Educated: Trawsfynydd Elementary School.
Killed: 31st July 1917. Aged 30 years.
Artillery Wood Cemetery, Boesinghe, Belgium.

Ellis Evans was the eldest son of Evan and Mary Evans. His aptitude for poetry became evident at an early age and he was given every encouragement at home. His father, who owned a remote hill farm a few miles from the village, was a 'home spun' poet and so too was his maternal grandfather.

After leaving the local school Ellis Evans helped his father on the family farm. He won the first of his six bardic chairs at Bala in 1907; and was given his bardic name 'Hedd Wyn' at a concert held on the banks of Llyn y Morynion (The Lake of the Maidens) in Merionethshire in August 1910. He just failed to win the Chair at the National Eisteddfod at Aberystwyth in 1916.

During the early months of the War Hedd Wyn wrote four lines mourning the death in battle of a young man in a neighbouring village:

> His sacrifice will not pass, and his
> Dear name will not be forgotten
> Though Germany has stained
> Its iron fist in his blood.

In October 1916 Hedd Wyn started work on 'Yr Arwr' ('The Hero') his awdl (a long eisteddfodic poem using several of the traditional 24 strict metres) for the Eisteddfod to be held at Birkenhead in 1917. Before he had completed his awdl he was called up in January 1917; he enlisted in the Royal Welch Fusiliers and was sent to Litherland camp near Liverpool for training. Although he read the English poets, wrote a few poems and spoke English, Welsh was his native language; he found that at the military camp "there is little poetry but plenty of poets for most of the men and officers are Welshmen..."

In the Spring of 1917 Hedd Wyn was granted seven weeks leave to return home and work as a ploughman on the farm. During these weeks he composed more lines of 'The Hero' which he completed in the middle of July after he arrived in the village of Fléchin on the frontier between France and Belgium with the 15th Battalion Royal Welch Fusiliers, part of the 38th (Welsh) Division. His father wrote:

... What surprises me most of all is that he produced such a good awdl, with the Army and its claws on his back all the time, he had some respite in the end before he went over to France, for four days and he wrote 250 of it (sic) and what grieves me is that he was trying to finish it on the roadside in France - he was determined to finish it...

Hedd Wyn wrote from France to a friend:

Heavy weather, heavy soul, heavy heart. That is an uncomfortable trinity, isn't it?... I never saw a land more beautiful in spite of the curse that has landed upon it. The trees are as beautiful as the dreams of old Kings...

The 15th Battalion left Fléchin on 15th July and marched through the villages of Steenbecque, St. Sylvestre-Cappel, Proven, and St. Sixte until it reached Dublin Camp and Canal Camp on the banks of the Comines-Ypres canal in fine weather five days later. The eastern side of the canal was in German hands. The 15th Battalion was one of five Battalions with orders to capture Pilckem Ridge and the villages of Pilckem and Langemarck.

On 30th July, the eve of the Third Battle of Ypres, Major-General C.G. Blackader sent a message to his troops:

Tomorrow the 38th (Welsh) Division will have the honour of being in the front line of what will be the big battle of the war. On the deeds of each individual of the Division depends whether it shall be said that the 38th (Welsh) Division took Pilckem and Langemarck and upheld gloriously the honour of Wales and the British Empire. The honour can be obtained by hard fighting and self-sacrifice on the part of each one of us. Gwell angau na chywilydd.

The 15th Battalion crossed the canal in the early hours of 31st July. It reached the village of Pilckem, a little over a mile away from the canal, in a short time. It progressed to a spot later named Battery Copse where it was fiercely attacked by the enemy. Every officer in the Battalion was either killed or wounded and for three days Regimental Sergeant Major Jones, was in charge of the Battalion. He was ordered to hold on to a ridge of land, later named Iron Cross Ridge, 200 yards from the Green Line about a mile from the village of Langemarck. During the fighting on Iron

Cross Ridge, Hedd Wyn was wounded in the chest by a piece of trench mortar shell. He was taken to an aid post where he asked, in English, with a cheerful smile 'Do you think I will live?' His last words 'I am very happy' were also spoken in English; he died a few hours later.

WAR

Woe that I live in this dire age,
When God on far horizon flees,
Yonder men high and lowly wage
Their little vile authorities;

And seeing God had turned away,
A sword they raised to slay their own;
We hear the tumult of the fray,
On humble homes its shadows frown;

And there, the weeping willow trees
Bear the old harps that sang amain,
The lads' wild anguish fills the breeze,
Their blood is mingled with the rain.

A few weeks after Hedd Wyn was killed the National Eisteddfod was held in Birkenhead. The Chair was placed in the centre of the stage with the eisteddfodic sword resting across its arms. When the Archdruid, Dyfed, called out three times for the winning poet to stand up, there was no response.

'In a trembling voice and broken sentences, Dyfed announced that the chief bard had fallen on the field of battle in France on the last day of July. He explained who he was, that he was a shepherd from Trawsfynydd and announced his name... Then, as there was no-one to be chaired, the sword was removed and the Chair draped with a black cover.'

from THE HERO

...I sang to the long hope of my life
And the magic of the aspiration of youth;
The passion of the wind and the scent
Of the lightning of the path
Ahead were in my poem.

1917

My muse was a deep cry
And all the ages to come will hear it,
And my rewards were grievous violence;
And a world that is
One long bare winter without respite...

LANCE CORPORAL FRANCIS LEDWIDGE

5th Battalion Royal Inniskilling Fusiliers.
'B' Company, 1st Battalion Royal Inniskilling Fusiliers.
Born: 19th August 1887. Slane, Co. Meath.
Educated: Slane Board School.
Killed: 31st July 1917. Aged 29 years.
Artillery Wood Cemetery, Boesinghe, Belgium.

Francis Ledwidge was the eighth child of Patrick and Anne Ledwidge of Slane in County Meath. After Patrick Ledwidge died when Francis was five years old the family suffered hardship and poverty. Francis left school at the age of fourteen and was employed by a local farmer. The Bishop of Kerry described farm labourers at this time as "the worst-housed, the worst-paid, and the worst-fed class of their kind in any civilised country in the world." In the summer of 1907 Ledwidge went to work on the roads and his wages increased from 12/6d to 17/6d a week. His first poem was published in *The Drogheda Independent* in 1910 and from 1911 he contributed a weekly article, partly written in Irish, to *The Independent*; he also had poems printed in various local magazines and newspapers.

In 1912 Ledwidge sent his copybook of poems to Lord Dunsany who arranged for one of the poems to be published in *The Saturday Review*. Dunsany helped Ledwidge select poems for his first book and his encouragement and patronage introduced Ledwidge to Ireland's literary coterie. Almost all the poems Ledwidge wrote before he enlisted praised the fields and hills of Meath which he loved, and he wove old folk-lore and the haunting presence of the fairy world into much of his poetry.

Francis Ledwidge was one of the founder members of the Slane branch of the Meath Labour Union; in 1908 he left his job on the roads to work in a local copper mine. He appealed to the management on behalf of his fellow workers for better working conditions and when the request was ignored he organised a strike and was instantly dismissed. He returned to work on the roads until November 1913 when he was offered a year's post as Secretary to the County Labour Union. In the Spring of 1914 he joined the newly formed Irish Volunteers and was subsequently elected Secretary of the Slane branch. With the bitter question of Home Rule for Ireland in the balance, the aim of the Volunteers was 'to secure and maintain the rights and liberties common to the whole people of Ireland'.   In October 1914 Ledwidge enlisted in the 5th Royal Inniskilling Fusiliers, the Regiment in which Lord Dunsany was serving as a Captain.

Some of the people who know me least imagine that I joined the Army because I knew men were struggling for higher ideals and great emprises, and I could not sit idle to watch them make for me a more beautiful world.   They are mistaken.   I joined the British Army because she stood between Ireland and an enemy common to our civilisation and I would not have her say that she defended us while we did nothing at home but pass resolutions.

In November Ledwidge wrote to a friend in Slane:

... This life is a great change to me, and one which somehow I cannot become accustomed to. I have lived too much amongst the fields and the rivers to forget that I am anything else other than 'the Poet of the Blackbird'... We have plenty of time to ourselves and are well looked after. I am glad I joined tho' sometimes homesick, but fame and poetry will come again (D.V)...

Ledwidge was promoted to Lance-Corporal a few weeks after he joined the Army and in July 1915 he sailed with his Battalion as part of the 10th Division for the Dardanelles, where British and Anzac troops, who had survived the first three terrible months of slaughter, were desperate for reinforcements of men and ammunition.

On 6th August the Battalion landed at Suvla Bay. Ledwidge and his companions were faced with unburied bodies, dysentery and appalling heat as they dug their trenches. On 15th August the 5th Battalion attacked the Turkish strongholds on the hills which dominated the beaches. Eight hours later the survivors of the Battalion retreated into the trench from where they had left to make the attack.   Six officers had been killed; over 300 officers and men were wounded or missing. In the first nine days the Battalion was reduced to half its original complement. Ledwidge wrote to Lord Dunsany:

It is surprising what silly things one thinks of in a big fight. I was lying one side of a low bush on August 15th, pouring lead across a little ridge into the Turks and for four hours my mind was on the silliest things of home. Once I found myself wondering if a cow that I knew to have a disease called 'timber-tongue' had really died. Again a man on my right who was mortally hit said: 'It can't be far off now', and I began to wonder what it was could not be far off. Then I knew it was death and I kept repeating the dying man's words: 'It can't be far off now'.

But when the Turks began to retreat I realized my position and, standing up, I shouted out the range to the men near me and they fell like grass before a scythe, the enemy. It was Hell! Hell! No man thought he would ever return. Just fancy out of 'D' Company, 250 strong, only 76 returned. By Heavens, you should know the bravery of these men: Cassidy standing on a hill with his cap on top of his rifle shouting at the Turks to come out; stretcher-bearers taking in friend and enemy alike. It was a horrible and a great day. I would not have missed it for worlds.

By the end of September when the devastated 10th Division had lost more that 10,000 men they were evacuated. The 5th Battalion Royal Inniskilling Fusiliers was sent to fight in Salonika and encamped on the Greco-Serbian border. The Battalion historian described the conditions:

Our site was very rough, with rock and stunted undergrowth, and it was thus very difficult to erect our bivouacs. There were two men in each bivouac, these being formed by two ground sheets with a great-coat to close the weather end. It can be imagined what it was like on a mountain ridge under the conditions described, the temperature on the 23rd November being 30 degrees below freezing point. We suffered untold hardships... from the severe frost and bitterly cold winds. There were hundreds of cases of severe frost bite amongst the troops. The nearest field ambulance was a long distance back and the position of our Battalion was about two miles from the nearest place to which a limbered wagon could get...

At the end of November a violent blizzard swept across Gallipoli and Serbia. Suffering from the intense cold Ledwidge wrote two poems in his mountain bivouac and then sent them in a letter to Lord Dunsany.

Remember in reading the enclosed the circumstances under which they were written. 'When Love and Beauty Wander Away' was written by Lake Doiran one awful night of thunder and rain. I was thinking of the end of the world as the Bible predicts it and tried to imagine Love and Beauty leaving the world hand in hand, and we who could not yet die, standing on the edge of a great precipice with no song, no love, no memory...

WHEN LOVE AND BEAUTY WANDER AWAY

When Love and Beauty wander away,
And there's no more hearts to be sought and won,
When the old earth limps thro' the dreary day,
And the work of the Seasons cry undone:
Ah! what shall we do for a song to sing,
Who have known Beauty, and Love, and Spring?

When Love and Beauty wander away,
And a pale fear lies on the cheeks of youth,
When there's no more goal to strive for and pray,
And we live at the end of the world's untruth:
Ah! what shall we do for a heart to prove,
Who have known Beauty, and Spring, and Love?

During December 1915 the British were forced to retreat under severe attacks from the Bulgarians. Ledwidge marched for six days and lost his manuscripts apart from a few rain soaked pieces of paper he managed to keep in his haversack. He collapsed from the pain caused by the inflammation in his back and was taken to a hospital in Cairo where he remained for four months. In February 1916 he wrote to Dunsany.

... I'm afraid I'm not getting better. My back is very painful and weak and I have a terrific headache. There are Navvy imps in my head. I am going somewhere for sulphur baths, perhaps these will do me good. My dreams are awful things and I hate going asleep because of them... A 'C. of E' chaplain who lives here called to see me one day because he had heard of my book. He seemed to be taking a great interest in me and promised me a book of poetry, but suddenly he saw on my chart that I was an R.C. and hurried from me as if I were possessed. He never came over to me since although he has been in the ward many times. I wonder if God asked our poor chaps were they R.C.'s or C.of E.'s when they went to Him on August 15th...

Ledwidge was sent home to a hospital in Manchester in April 1916 where he remained for a few weeks. The news of the Easter Rising, particularly the execution of his friend and fellow poet, Thomas MacDonagh, upset him deeply. In May he was court-martialled and stripped of his lance-corporal's stripe for overstaying his leave and insubordination.

For the next seven months Ledwidge was at Ebrington Barracks,

Derry.   He rejoined his Battalion in the village of Picquigny, north east of Amiens in bitterly cold weather at the end of December 1916. Two days before the year ended he wrote 'Ceol Sidhe' (Fairy Music):

CEOL SIDHE

When May is here, and every morn
Is dappled with pied bells,
And dewdrops glance along the thorn
And wings flash in the dells,
I take my pipe and play a tune
Of dreams, a whispered melody,
For feet that dance beneath the moon
In fairy jollity.

And when the pastoral hills are grey
And the dim stars are spread,
A scamper fills the grass like play
Of feet where fairies tread.
And many a little whispering thing
Is calling to the Shee.
The dewy bells of evening ring,
And all is melody.

Ledwidge was drafted to 'B' Company, 1st Battalion Royal Inniskilling Fusiliers, part of the 29th Division and sent first to Carnoy and then to a camp in the village of Le Neuville, near Corbie. While he was here he started a correspondence with the Irish poetess, Katherine Tynan, who first wrote to him in January 1917. He replied to her letter:

If I survive the war, I have great hopes of writing something that will live. If not, I trust to be remembered in my own land for one or two things which its long sorrow inspired. My book has had a greater reception in England, Ireland and America than I had ever dreamt of, but I never feel that my name should be mentioned in the same breath with my contemporaries.

You ask me what I am doing. I am a unit in the Great War, doing and suffering, admiring great endeavour and condemning great dishonour. I may be dead before this reaches you, but I will have done my part. Death is as interesting to me as life. I have seen so much of it from Suvla to Serbia and now in France. I am always homesick. I hear the roads calling, and the hills, and the rivers wondering where I am. It is terrible to be always homesick.

The Battalion was in billets at Le Neuville at the beginning of
March. On 8th March Ledwidge hailed what was to be his last
Spring:

SPRING

Once more the lark with song and speed
Cleaves through the dawn, his hurried bars
Fall, like the flute of Ganymede
Twirling and whistling from the stars.

The primrose and the daffodil
Surprise the valleys, and wild thyme
Is sweet on every little hill,
When lambs come down at folding time.

In every wild place now is heard
The magpie's noisy house, and through
The mingled tunes of many a bird
The ruffled wood-dove's gentle coo.

Sweet by the river's noisy brink
The water-lily bursts her crown,
The kingfisher comes down to drink
Like rainbow jewels falling down.

And when the blue and grey entwine
The daisy shuts her golden eye,
The peace wraps all those hills of mine
Safe in my dearest memory.

At the beginning of April the 1st Battalion arrived in Arras; the
city was in ruins and the huge network of ancient underground
cellars and caves were packed with refugee civilians and soldiers
waiting for the battle of Arras to begin. On the 16th April the
Battalion was in the firing line south east of the village of Monchy-
le-Preux. Three days later it was relieved and returned to billets in
the caves. This pattern continued throughout May and towards the
end of the month Ledwidge wrote to Katherine Tynan enclosing a
poem:

I would have written to thank you for the sweets, only that lately we
were unsettled, wandering to and fro between the firing-line and

resting billets immediately behind. This letter is ante-dated by two hours, but before midnight we may be wandering in single and slow file, with the reserve line two or three hundred yards behind the fire trench. We are under an hour's notice. Entering and leaving the line is most exciting, as we are usually but about thirty yards from the enemy, and you can scarcely understand how bright the nights are made by his rockets. These are in continual ascent and descent from dusk to dawn, making a beautiful crescent from Switzerland to the sea. There are white lights, green, and red, and whiter, bursting into red and changing again, and blue bursting into purple drops and reds fading into green. It is all like the end of a beautiful world. It is only horrible when you remember that every colour is a signal to waiting reinforcements of artillery and God help us if we are caught in the open, for then up go a thousand reds, and hundreds of rifles and machine-guns are emptied against us, and all amongst us shells of every calibre are thrown, shouting destruction and death. We can do nothing but fling ourselves into the first shell-hole and wonder as we wait where we will be hit ...

ASCENSION THURSDAY, 1917

Lord, Thou has left Thy footprints in the rocks,
That we may know the way to follow Thee,
But there are wide lands opened out between
Thy Olivet and my Gethsemane.

And often times I make the night afraid,
Crying for lost hands when the dark is deep
And strive to reach the sheltering of Thy love
Where Thou are herd among Thy folded sheep.

Thou wilt not ever thus, O Lord, allow
My feet to wander when the sun is set,
But through the darkness, let me still behold
The stony bye-ways up to Olivet.

The Battalion was ordered north to the Ypres area and arrived at Proven on 27th June; it was in trenches intermittently and the canal bank was under heavy shell-fire. On 1st July 1917 Ledwidge wrote to Edward Marsh:

Just now a big strafe is worrying our dug-outs and putting out our candles, but my soul is by the Boyne cutting new meadows under a thousand wings and listening to the cuckoos at Crocknaharna ...

On 15th July, during a lull in the bombardment leading up to the Third Battle of Ypres, Ledwidge wrote:

HOME

A burst of sudden wings at dawn,
Faint voices in a dreamy noon,
Evenings of mist and murmurings,
And nights with rainbows of the moon.

And through these things a wood-way dim,
And waters dim, and slow sheep seen
On uphill paths that wind away
Through summer sounds and harvest green.

This is a song a robin sang
This morning on a broken tree
It was about the little fields
That call across the world to me.

Ledwidge had spent seven months at the front without leave and on 20th July from billets at Proven he wrote of his weariness and longing for home to Katherine Tynan; two days later, on the same day as the Battalion went to Arras to the front line in front of Monchy-le-Preux, Ledwidge wrote the poem 'To One Who Comes Now and Then', recalling visits from one of his closest friends, Matty McGoona:

We have just returned from the line after an unusually long time. It was very exciting this time, as we had to contend with gas, lachrymatory shells, and other devices new and horrible. It will be worse soon. The camp we are in at present might be in Tir-na-n'Og, it is pitched amid such splendours. There is barley and rye just entering harvest days of gold, and meadow-sweet rippling, and where a little inn named 'In Den Neerloop' holds its gable up to the swallows, bluebells and goldilocks swing their splendid censers. There is a wood hard by where hips glisten like little sparks and just at the edge of it mealey leaves sway like green fire... I would give £100 for two days in Ireland with nothing to do but ramble on from one delight to another. I am entitled to a leave now, but I'm afraid there are many before my name in the list. Special leaves are granted, and I have to finish a book for the autumn. But, more particularly, I want to see again my wonderful mother, and to walk by the Boyne to Crewbawn and up through the brown and grey rocks of Crocknaharna. You have no idea of how I suffer with this longing for the swish of the reeds at Slane and the voices I used to hear coming over the low hills of Currabwee. Say a prayer that I may get this leave, and give as a condition my punctual return and sojourn till the war is over. It is midnight now and the glow-worms are out. It is quiet in camp, but the far night is loud with our guns bombarding the positions we must soon fight for...

TO ONE WHO COMES NOW AND THEN

When you come in, it seems a brighter fire
Crackles upon the hearth invitingly,
The household routine which was wont to tire
Grows full of novelty.

You sit upon our home-upholstered chair
And talk of matters wonderful and strange,
Of books, and travel, customs old which dare
The gods of Time and Change

Till we with inner word our care refute
Laughing that this our bosoms yet assails,
While there are maidens dancing to a flute
In Andalusian vales.

And sometimes from my shelf of poems you take
And secret meanings to our hearts disclose,
As when the winds of June the mid bush shake
We see the hidden rose.

And when the shadows muster, and each tree
A moment flutters, full of shutting wings,
You take the fiddle and mysteriously
Wake wonders on the strings.

And in my garden, grey with misty flowers,
Low echoes fainter than a beetle's horn
Fill all the corners with it, like sweet showers
Of bells, in the owl's morn.

Come often, friend; with welcome and surprise
We'll greet you from the sea or from the town;
Come when you like and from whatever skies
Above you smile or frown.

Ledwidge never saw his beloved Ireland again as all leave was cancelled until after the battle.   Nine days later, on 31st July, the opening day of the third Battle of Ypres, 'B' Company was behind the front lines in the vicinity of Pilckem Ridge, west of the village of Boesinghe.   It was the feast day of St. Ignatius of Loyola and in the morning Francis Ledwidge assisted Father Devas, Chaplain to the Irish Division, at Mass held in a wood.   That evening, during a violent rainstorm, Ledwidge was laying wooden planks over the muddy quagmire of the battlefield to enable guns and equipment to move forward.   Drenched to the skin he paused for a mug of tea and a shell from the continuous heavy enemy bombardment exploded nearby killing him instantly.

A SOLDIER'S GRAVE

Then in the lull of midnight, gentle arms
Lifted him slowly down the slopes of death,
Lest he should hear again the mad alarms
Of battle, dying moans, and painful breath.

And where the earth was soft for flowers we made
A grave for him that he might better rest.
So, Spring shall come and leave it sweet arrayed,
And there the lark shall turn her dewy nest.

LIEUTENANT THOMAS ERNEST HULME

'B' Company, 1st Battalion Honourable Artillery Company.
Naval Siege Battery, Royal Marine Artillery.
Born: 16th September 1883. Staffordshire.
Educated: High School, Newcastle-under-Lyme.
      St. John's College, Cambridge.
Killed: 28th September 1917. Aged 34 years.
Coxyde (Koksijde) Military Cemetery, Belgium.

T.E. Hulme was born at Gratton Hall, the family home between the villages of Hulme and Upper Hulme in Staffordshire. The Hulmes were landowners who became ceramic manufacturers and Hulme grew up in the atmosphere of traditional country squirarchy with its rigid Victorian attitudes and values - a way of life from which he later rebelled. He won a Mathematics Exhibition to St. John's College, Cambridge but was sent down in 1904; the reasons are unclear but he seems to have been involved in numerous brawls and disturbances and he was given 'the largest mock funeral ever seen in the town'. His father disowned him but later agreed that his son could go to University College, London to read biology and physics. Hulme's wish to study philosophy had been disregarded and in 1906 he gave up his studies and left for Canada to avoid the consequences of his father's decision that he should sit the Civil Service Examination. He spent two years in Canada followed by seven months in Brussels learning French and German.

When Hulme returned to London in 1908 he was given a small allowance by an aunt which enabled him to become independent of his father. A large, forceful and often aggressive man, Hulme's brilliance as a conversationalist soon placed him at the centre of various literary groups and he was recognised as one of the dominant figures in London's intellectual life. Almost immediately he started to write for *New Age*, a journal edited by the Fabian arts group. He also formed the Poets' Club and was elected honorary secretary. Hulme believed that romanticism in poetry must give way to classicism - 'absolutely accurate presentation and verbiage.' He wrote only a few poems, six of which were published in his lifetime; his interests lay more in the theory of poetry and in philosophy. He passionately believed that 'man is by nature bad or limited' and based his thinking in philosophy, history, politics, art and poetry on this idea. The first experimental imagist poems were read and discussed at the Poets' Club's meetings and from this the Imagist Movement was born.

AUTUMN

A touch of cold in the Autumn night
I walked abroad,
And saw the ruddy moon lean over a hedge
Like a red-faced farmer.
I did not stop to speak, but nodded;
And round about were the wistful stars
With white faces like town children.

ABOVE THE DOCK

Above the quiet dock in midnight
Tangled in the tall mast's corded height,
Hangs the moon. What seemed so far away
Is but a child's balloon, forgotten after play.

Hulme gradually drew away from the Poets' Club and formed a more elite group who met weekly at the Eiffel Tower, a Soho Restaurant. In 1912 he was reinstated at St. John's College, Cambridge, but his time there was shortlived and he went to Berlin to study German philosophy and psychology. Before and after his time in Berlin, Hulme hosted weekly gatherings at 67 Frith Street. These were attended by influential figures in the world of literature, art and politics.

At the outbreak of the War Hulme enlisted as a Private in the Honourable Artillery Company; after training he joined the Battalion in Flanders on 13th January 1915, alternating between trenches at Kemmel and billets at Locre and Lindenhoek. Between 30th December 1914 and 19th April 1915, he kept a diary which he wrote in the form of letters to his aunt.

Friday Jan 15th... I wanted to see what the trenches were like, so I volunteered to go as one of a party which was going up the trenches at night, to take up large bundles of wood to put at the bottom of them for the men to stand on... There were about 100 of us. We wore our overcoats & carried rifles. We were formed up about 5 o'clock when it was dark, told to load our rifles & then we filed past a barn where each man drew a long bundle of faggots about 8 ft. long. We then went off in single file down a long road lined with poplars, nearly all the way. The Germans kept firing off rockets & star shells. These latter hang in the air for a few minutes & light up the whole road. We were told that whenever one of these went off we were to stand still & bend our heads down so that the white of our faces could not be seen. After a time we began to hear bullets whizzing over our heads all fairly high. All that worries anyone is the uncomfortableness of the faggots. Also I had not put the sling of my rifle on properly & was wondering all the while whether it would not slip off my shoulder on to the ground & draw attention to me personally & to my clumsiness. After about a mile along the road, we turned off along the fields & made for the trenches. Here the uncomfortable part started. It seemed to be absolutely all mud. It's bad enough walking over uneven ground in the dark at any time when you don't know whether your foot is landing on earth or nothing the next step. Every now & then you fell over & got up to your knees in the mud... What makes it infinitely worse is that, every now & then you lose sight of the man in front of you. The line ahead of you runs over a rather more dangerous part & you must keep up at all costs, though it's all in the dark & you are floundering about all the time. You simply must keep up, because if you once lost the man in front, you wouldn't know what on earth to do, you might even walk up to the German lines. We finally had to cross a series of great ditches of mud & deposit the faggots under the shelter of some rising ground about 40 yards behind the trenches...

From billets at Locre Hulme wrote on 27th January:

I have had a very uncomfortable time this week. As I told you last week after 4 days rest we go down to a place near the trenches. We marched off there last Wednesday, late in the day so as to get there after dark, or we might be shelled on our arrival. We never know whether we shall get a good or a bad billet when we arrive there, it's always different. We were led into the chapel attached to a school and our section managed to get a corner by the altar. It looks very curious to see a lot of troops billeted in a place like this, rifles resting on the altar & hanging over statues of the saints, men sleeping on the altar steps... It was rather cold as all the windows were smashed & we have no blankets now. We lit a brazier, ie., an old bucket with holes knocked in it, burning charcoal and coke. We had nothing to do the first night... The next night we went up to a kind of circular reserve trench... We were challenged at the entrance & then entered a narrow passage going down to the level of the trenches. I don't think I've been so exasperated for years as I was in taking up my position in this trench. It wasn't an ordinary one but was roofed over most of the way leaving passage about 4 ft: absolutely impossible for me to walk through. I had to crawl along on my hands & knees, through the mud in pitch darkness & every now & then seemed to get stuck altogether. You feel shut in and hopeless. I wished I was about 4 ft. This war isn't for tall men. I got in a part too narrow and too low to stand or sit & had to sit sideways on a sack of coke to keep out of the water. We had to stay there from about 7 p.m. till just before dawn next morning, a most miserable experience. You can't sleep & you sit as it were at the bottom of a drain with nothing to look at but the top of the ditch slowly freezing. It's unutterably boring. The next night was better, because I carried up a box to sit on & a sack of coke to burn in a brazier. But one brazier in a narrow trench among 12 men only warms about 3. All through this night, we had to dig a new passage in shifts. That in a way did look picturesque at midnight - a very clear starry night. This mound all full of passages like a mole hill & 3 or 4 figures silhouetted on top of it using pick or shovel. The bullets kept whistling over it all the time, but as it's just over the crest of a hill most of them are high, though every now & then one comes on your level & it is rather uncomfortable when you are taking your turn at sentry. The second night it froze hard, & it was much easier walking back over the mud.

In reality there is nothing picturesque about it. It's the most miserable existence you can conceive of. I feel utterly depressed at the idea of having to do this for 48 hours every 4 days. It's simply hopeless. The boredom & discomfort of it, exasperate you to the breaking point...

From 5th February the men were billetted in farms round Lindenhoek. They were back in trenches at Kemmel on the 9th February:

Feb. 10th. The last day of the last 4 days rest here was like summer. We had breakfast outside the cobbler's cottage and in the afternoon went up to the Inn on the hill and they all drank wine outside. A regular who was up there said "Who says there's a war now" & it certainly did seem absolutely remote from it... The same evening we marched straight from here up to the trenches. We went to the firing line again... We had to spend the night in the open air as there were very few dugouts. There was a German rifle trained on a fixed part of the trench just where we were. It's very irritating to hear a bullet time after time hit the same spot on the parapet. About lunch time this rifle continually hitting the same place, spattered dirt from the parapet over my bread and butter... It showed, however, that it was a dangerous corner and the next day another company of our regiment took our place in this trench, a man in exactly the place where our section was, getting curious at the repetition of a shot in the same spot, got up to look with his field glasses. He stayed up a second too long and got shot through the head dead... Towards the end of the same day, the

Germans started to shell our trench. It was a dangerous trench for shelling because it was very wide so gave no protection to the back. Our N.C.O. told us to shift to a narrower part of the trench. I got separated from the others in a narrow communication trench behind with one other man. We had seen shells bursting fairly near us before and at first did not take it very seriously. But it soon turned out to be very different. The shells started dropping right on the trench itself. As soon as you had seen someone hurt, you began to look at shelling in a very different way. We shared this trench with the X regiment. About 10 yards away from where I was, a man of this regiment had his arm and three quarters of his head blown off a frightful mess, his brains all over the place... The worst of shelling is, the regulars say, that you don't get used to it, but get more & more alarmed at it every time. At any rate the regulars in our trenches behaved in rather a strange way. One man threw himself down on the bottom of the trench, shaking all over & crying. Another started to weep. It lasted for nearly 1 1/2 hrs and at the end of it parts of the trenches were all blown to pieces. It's not the idea of being killed that's alarming, but the idea of being hit by a jagged piece of steel. You hear the whistle of the shell coming, you crouch down as low as you can and just wait. It doesn't burst merely with a bang, it has a kind of crash with a snap in it, like the crack of a very large whip. They seemed to burst just over your head, you seem to anticipate it killing you in the back, it hits just near you and you get hit on the back with clods of earth & (in my case) spent bits of shell & shrapnel bullets fall all round you. I picked up one bullet almost sizzling in the mud just by my toe. What irrates you is the continuation of the shelling. You seem to feel that 20 min. is normal, is enough - but when it goes on for over an hour, you get more & more exasperated, feel as if it were "unfair". Our men were as it happened very lucky, only three were hurt slightly & none killed. They all said it was the worst experience they have had since they were out here. I'm not in the least anxious myself to repeat it, nor is anyone else I think. It was very curious from where I was; looking out and over the back of the trench, it looked absolutely peaceful. Just over the edge of the trench was a field of turnips or something of that kind with their leaves waving about in a busy kind of way, exactly as they might do in a back garden. About 12 miles away over the plain you could see the towers & church spires of an old town very famous in this war. By a kind of accident or trick, everything was rather gloomy, except this town which appeared absolutely white in the sun and immobile as if it would always be like that, and was out of time and space altogether. You've got to amuse yourself in the intervals of shelling, and romanticising the situation is as good a way as any other. Looking at the scene the waving vegetables, the white town & all the rest of it, it looks quite timeless in a Buddhistic kind of way and you feel quite resigned if you are going to be killed to leave it just like that. When it ceased and we all got back to our places everybody was full of it. We went back that night to a new billet in a barn, so near the line that we weren't allowed to have light at all, but spread our bread & butter in the dark, or by the intermittent light of electric torches pointed down. The next night we went up to new trenches altogether... This time we weren't in the firing line, but in a line of dug-outs, or supports.

These dug-outs were about 2 ft. deep, so you can imagine how comfortable I was. They put me in one by myself. It felt just like being in your grave, lying flat just beneath the surface of the ground & covered up. And there I had to be for 24 hours unable to get out until it was dark next night for we could be seen from the German lines. We were relieved very late and altogether were out 30 hours instead of 24. We had a couple of men wounded on the road up, so we went back by a safer way across the fields. A man I know quite well had a bullet entered one side of his nose & came out near his ear. They have sent him back to England & say he will remain.

I'm getting more used to this kind of life and as long as I don't get hurt or it doesn't rain too much, don't mind it at all.

From billets at Locre Hulme wrote on February 20th:

We went down to the trenches on a Saturday. We form up at dark in the one street of the town here. There is generally a lot to be done on the last day as we have to clean up all our billets ready for the other brigade marching up after their 4 days at the trenches. While we are formed up there in the street waiting, some of the other regiments of our brigade who go to the trenches at the same time as we do are sure to march past. A regiment on the march here is a very curious sight. In spite of the fact that they have to clean themselves and their clothes in their 4 days of rest, they all look a general pale, washed out, dusty muddy colour. The officers march on foot generally at the head of their platoons, looking very little different to their men, except that they generally carry a roughly trimmed piece of wood, about as long as a shepherds crook, as a walking stick. They find these useful in the muddy paths up to the actual trenches. Very few are in any kind of step and they slouch along generally two deep, for only the centre of the road is really passable. The exception to the slouching is an occasional section when the two front men play a mouth organ or bones, when they march well to-gether. Their packs look a good deal lighter than ours, they don't get so many parcels. At intervals come the officers' horses, generally unmounted (they ride them however at the end of 4 days when they are coming back from the trenches & are more tired). At the end come the mules carrying extra ammunition, the transport & finally the field kitchens, usually boiling something &

stuffed up with odd bits of wood ready for fuel & the cooks leaning on them as they walk behind. This time we did not go straight up to the trenches but into "close billet" for the night. This is a large barn. It's comfortable except that it's well within range & if only the Germans one day find out we are here, they will drop a shell on us, and then we should most of us be done for. On the morning of the next day we had all suddenly to get ready & come downstairs, because shells were falling uncomfortably near. We always have a guard outside to report aeroplanes & the nearness of shells for this purpose. None of us are ever allowed out in the daytime. How near it is to the trenches may be judged from the fact that this time one of our sentries was shot dead by a stray bullet. The next night we went up to the trenches. I think I told you in my last letter that we are now holding a different part of the line, a mile or so N of our old trenches, worse trenches and a worse path up to them. Last time we went up to them by a road but we had one man wounded (there are too many stray bullets passing over it) so we went up by a new way over the fields. Suddenly when we were going up a fearfully muddy field by the side of a wood in a long line & single file, a shell whizzed over us & burst a few yards behind the last man. I happened to be looking backward when it burst. Being night it was very bright & looked more like a firework than anything else. We at once got the order to lie flat in the mud on our faces and although it isn't pleasant to be flat on your face in pure mud, yet the presence of the shells makes us do it without any reluctance. I didn't see much after that, for I had my head down flat, but they put about 20 shells over us, rather smallish shells they must have been which seemed to go whizz-bang - very quickly. They fell all along the line of the 50 men, but all a little wide. We got bits of earth flung over us but nothing more. They all thought their last hour had come for to be caught & shelled in the open like that is the most dangerous thing that can happen to you. You have no protection like you have in a trench. It was soon over however & then we got up and continued our walk to the trenches, most of us expecting suddenly to hear the same explosion again. We had to cross several shell & Jack Johnson holes full of water bridged by a single plank & in the dark most of us fell in once before we got there. We got to miserable trenches where we were not allowed to have a brazier and we sat there absolutely wet through up to the pips for 24 hours. That's the worst of getting wet here, it isn't like after a day's shooting when you can get home & change. The next night when we got back, an attack from the Germans was expected. We had to sleep in our boots etc all night & couldn't take anything off. That made 48 hours thoroughly wet through. The extraordinary thing is that it doesn't hurt you. It hasn't hurt us at any rate, though when the regiment last spent 3 days in the trenches before Xmas they lost 250 men & 11 officers through sickness. It makes you very depressed however & weakens you - it gave me diarrhoea. This last 6 days have been unusual for all kinds of things have been happening to the north of us of which we hear rumours. We are told over night that further up the line certain trenches are to be retaken & the next day we hear they have been taken. I expect you have read all about it in the papers & of course as it is only a few miles from us, it affects us. We have to be ready for a counter attack...

In the trench that day (it couldn't properly be called a trench, just a ditch with sandbags on the top) we sat all day and watched shells burst in the field behind us. Fortunately never nearer than 20 yards. In the next trench, a different company of our regiment in, they killed one man & wounded 15 that afternoon. The most annoying part of being in the trenches is the waiting for the "relief". You get ready long before it comes. Sometimes it comes hours after you expect it. You listen & think you hear voices & feet. At last it's coming. Then it turns out that you were mistaken. Finally a German star shell reveals them to you half-way across the field. They are all standing immobile in the middle of the field bent down. It is curious how this continuous shelling and the apprehension of it has altered some men. They keep very quiet all day long & hardly say anything. This day in the trenches I should think 50 or 60 dropped in the one field, making holes all over it like a sort of smallpox. It is these holes filled with water which make walking up the roads at night so annoying. The 4 days when we came back we were told we shouldn't be relieved for some days. However we were relieved after 6 days and marched back very late to our rest town, everyone fearfully exhausted. I have written much too long a letter. I want to post it at once so that it won't be delayed like the others were. I can't tell you much, but as a result of the recent fighting there are all kinds of changes...

At the end of this letter there was a note by the censor. 'Please inform sender next letter of this length will not be passed.'

March 2nd. The first time up we went back again into the trenches where we were shelled. This is a bad trench in which you just have to sit out in the open all night. It froze hard and all the rifles were white in the morning. The next time it was our turn to have a rest, but they gave us (the platoon about 40 men) a fatigue up to the trenches, carrying up hurdles and barbed wire. Except for the danger from stray bullets, this is compared to going into the trenches, a pleasure trip. You are very light carrying only a rifle. It was a bright moonlight night, and the way up to the trenches is a straight narrow road. There were far too many men to carry the stuff and 4 of us carried one hurdle ragging each other all the way up, suggesting that the fat man should sit on top of it and we would carry him up. Half way up we met the stretcher bearers, carrying down one of our men who had been killed during the day. They hurry along quite in a different way when they are carrying a dead and not a wounded man. I think they break step and hurry along like lamplighters to avoid getting caught by a stray bullet themselves. It's curious how the mere fact that in a certain direction there really are the German lines, seems to alter the feeling of a landscape. You unconsciously orient things in reference to it. In peacetime, each direction on the road is as it were indifferent, it all goes on ad infinitum. But now you know that certain roads lead as it were, up to an abyss.

When we came back from this fatigue it so happened it was very quiet, no bullets about at all, and we strolled back exactly as though we were walking home late from a party on a moonlight night. These fatigues are not always so lucky. Last week the tennis player Kenneth Powell was killed carrying up corrugated iron. (It seems curious the way people realize things. I heard a man say "It does seem a waste. Kenneth Powell carrying up corrugated iron". You see he was interested in games). This is a curious life - in that there is nothing certain or fixed. You never come back to the same billets. You can never leave anything. You have no place that belongs to you. You really are as nomadic as an animal...

The Battalion had its longest stretch in the Kemmel trenches between the 5th and 16th March and eight men were killed and thirty wounded during those days. On 21st March Hulme wrote from billets at Westoutre:

I think I told you that for the first nine days we were continually in a kind of reserve trench. The second morning there we saw what so far I think has been the most complete war scene yet. I mean the most conventional, shut off, the most like war in a theatre as it were. Just below us about 300 yards away was a large farm with its buildings on a hill... It is the business of the artillery on both sides to shell likely "close billets", sometimes getting the information as to which farms & villages are close billets from spies. Most of the farms round about have been destroyed only the walls standing & another man said early in the morning that it was curious that this farm was entirely untouched looking very peaceful... In the middle of the morning we suddenly heard a shell whistling over which burst just over the roof. Then a second, whose smoke was all red showing that it had hit the roof, the red tiles broken up into dust mixing with the smoke. Three or four more shells & then we saw two pigs rushing out of the courtyard. We thought the place was empty & that the Germans were wasting their shells. Then we saw one figure going across a field on the other side of the farm but we couldn't tell whether a soldier or

perhaps a Belgian civilian. The shelling went on droppng all over the
roof till one caught fire. Then we caught sight of about 30 bent
figures creeping along the road along the ridge from the farm. To
make you realize the actual scene, there was a hedge on this side of
the road and an avenue of trees. There were more shells & finally the
whole of one roof burning. More & more groups of men creeping
along the road (at this distance we could only see a kind of bent
silhouette). This went on till I should think several hundreds more
had left (they were probably all asleep resting after the trenches).
Then there was a fearful row of ammunition popping off sounding
exactly like continuous rifle fire in the trenches. Then another
building caught fire (in which I suppose those wounded by the shells
had been put). One man came out of an open door & ran across a
field & behind a haystack after a minute another followed, then there
were about ten there, when the Germans dropped a few shells over it.
Then along the road men began to come back & fetch out the
wounded from the burning barn. As they came back along the road
very slowly helping the men along they were spotted & got German
rifle fire at them. The place went on burning for nearly two days. The
whole scene being extremely depressing. Enormous red flames,
exactly like a poster of war & destruction & then miserable looking
black figures & probably very tired people crawling out... I was on
sentry one night & saw a whole regiment passing up in single file to
take up their position for an attack. One man was shot about 20 yards
from me. I saw in the dark, the line stop & people cluster round him,
the line pass on & then finally stretcher bearers carry him off... I had
myself too one night up there the unpleasant job of carrying down one
of our men who had been shot dead through the heart. This is a very
unpleasant job when you have to go in pitch darkness a way you don't
know very well over mud & ditches. I'm glad it wasn't a man I knew
but it's very queer as you carry him down shoulder high, his face is
very near your own. One day after an attack I saw a man come
staggering across a field as if he were drunk, holding his head, finally
falling down just outside our barbed wire entanglement. It turned out
to be a Tommy who had been blown right out of our trenches by our
own artillery...

The Battalion was in trenches at St. Eloi and billets at
Dickebusch from 23rd March until the end of April.

April 9th 1915. We left the filthy barn we are billeted in about seven
o'clock marched down a side road over a hill about three miles to a
smashed up village just behind the new trenches we were going to.
We were marched up to a chateau all blown to pieces. When we got
there we had to wait about 2 hours outside while they tried to find
places for us inside. That's how they do things in the army. They

never seem to think 5 minutes before they do a thing. Eventually some of us were stowed in a dug-out just deep enough for us to crawl through, just like a rabbit hole and told we were to stay there for 48 hours a perfect nightmare for people of my size. Eventually they came and after looking round had found us a room in a house in a village that had a roof on it. The room had no windows and was filled with layers of straw which we daren't move for fear of what might be underneath. However it was very comfortable after the dug-out. Here we stayed for 48 hours, the second night being out from 10 till 2 carrying barbed wire up to the trenches. This was a hideous affair. When we got there nobody knew where they were to go and so we stopped there for 30 minutes behind the firing trench while they found out, a very uncomfortable time. One bullet hit the trestles the fat man was carrying and a piece of the wood flew up his arm. It's the kind of fooling unnecessary business which makes one so fed up. After 48 hours we went up to the trenches... We got into an open trench about 1.30 having started at 10, so you may tell what sort of a job it was, to go along 2 miles.   There were no shelters and it poured continually for several hours. Fortunately the next 36 hours it was finer and then we marched back about 10 p.m. to a rest barn... Every night we have had to march back to the trenches about 4 miles and dig. The night before last we were out from 8 p.m. till 4 in the morning. We have only had a proper night's rest in the last three weeks. This isn't a proper diary I have just told you in a hurry what we have been doing... We are back again to the trenches to-night for four days continuously. We shall be glad when we do get our rest... This is a curious thing, we move as you know always at night and troops going always in the same direction make definite paths. One of our snipers walking about in the daylight discovered that one of these paths that we walk over led right over the chest of a dead peasant (Belgian).

TRENCHES: ST ELOI

Over the flat slope of St. Eloi
A wide wall of sandbags.
Night,
In the silence desultory men
Pottering over small fires, cleaning their mess-tins:
To and fro, from the lines,
Men walk as on Piccadilly,
Making paths in the dark,
Through scattered dead horses,
Over a dead Belgian's belly.

The Germans have rockets. The English have no rockets.
Behind the line, cannon, hidden, lying back miles.
Before the line, chaos:

My mind is a corridor. The minds about me are corridors.
Nothing suggests itself. There is nothing to do but keep on.

On the 14th April 1915, Hulme was wounded at St. Eloi; a bullet went through his elbow and killed the soldier with him. He was invalided back to England and after he was discharged from hospital he was 'lost' by the War Office. Although he told his friends that he saw no reason to go back until he was asked, he tried to obtain a commission in the Royal Marine Artillery.

> It would be extremely depressing to me to start again as a private at this stage of the war. It was very different in the first months of the war, when one was excited about the thing. Besides, even impersonally, I do think I am suited to have a commission of this kind. Mathematics was always my subject and I should pick up the theoretical part, the calculations, etc., of which there is quite a lot in connection with the very big guns of the RMA, more easily than most people, and should enjoy the work. I am also about the build for heavy gun work...

During the year Hulme was in London before he received his commission he wrote a series of War Essays under the pseudonym 'North Staffs'. These were published in the *New Age* between November 1915 and March 1916 and in the *Cambridge Magazine* between January and March 1916. In these Essays he defended the necessity of the war and attempted to refute the arguments given by Bertrand Russell and other pacifists. On 5th February Hulme wrote 'The Kind of Rubbish we Oppose', which brought a letter to the *Cambridge Magazine* from Russell; Hulme followed with 'North Staffs Resents Mr. Russell's Rejoinder' to which Russell again replied. In 'Why we are in Favour of this War', printed in the *Cambridge Magazine* on 12th February 1916, Hulme wrote:

> ... Reasons which are sufficient to make us reject 'pacifist philosophy' are *not* sufficient to make us accept this *particular* war. The fact, for example, that a high value should be attached to military heroism, has nothing to do with the justification of a particular event in which such heroism may be displayed. This is an absolutely different question.

There are, moreover, at this moment, a class of pacifists who do not accept 'a pacifist philosophy' and whose reasons for objecting to the war are based on the nature and causes of *this* war itself...

So it comes about that we are unable to name any great positive 'good' for which we can be said to be fighting. But it is not necessary that we should; there is no harmony in the nature of things, so that from time to time great and useless sacrifices become necessary, merely that whatever precarious 'good' the world has achieved may just be preserved. These sacrifices are as negative, barren, and as *necessary* as the work of those who repair sea-walls. In this war, then, we are fighting for no great *liberation* of mankind, for no great jump upward, but are merely accomplishing a work, which, if the nature of things was ultimately 'good', would be useless, but which in this actual 'vale of tears' becomes from time to time necessary, merely in order that bad may not get worse...

Hulme was commissioned in the Royal Marine Artillery on 20th March 1916 and after training in Portsmouth he went into action at Oost-Duinkerke Bains on the coast behind Nieuport in Belgium. He was on leave in London at the end of August 1917; he was killed less than a fortnight later by an unexpected burst of shell fire.

When the news of Hulme's death reached London it caused widespread pain and sorrow. A friend wrote that he "was a deeply religious man... I believe that in essentials he was already a Catholic, although not in a ritualistic sense, but in the spiritual. And anyhow, he was the nearest thing to a genius that I have met in my life. As big inside as outside." Another friend, who knew of Hulme's numerous love affairs, said that when he was killed "half the women in London went into mourning."

IN THE CITY SQUARE

In the city square at night, the meeting of the torches.
The start of the great march,
The cries, the cheers, the parting.
Marching in an order
Through the familiar streets,
Through friends for the last time seen
Marching with torches.
Over the hill summit,
The moon and the moor,
And we marching alone.

1917

The torches are out.
On the cold hill,
The cheers of the warrior dead.
(For the first time re-seen)
Marching in an order,
To where?

CAPTAIN ERIC FITZWATER WILKINSON M.C.

'A' Company, 8th Battalion West Yorkshire Regiment (Leeds Rifles).

Born: January 1891. Portesham, near Weymouth, Dorset.
Educated: Dorchester Grammar School.
            Ilkley Grammar School.
            Leeds University.
Killed: 9th October 1917. Aged 26 years.
Tyne Cot Memorial to the Missing, Passchendaele, Belgium.

Eric Wilkinson read for an Engineering degree at University; he failed his Finals and returned to Ilkley Grammar School as a master in 1911. He was gazetted Second Lieutenant in the 8th Battalion West Yorkshire Regiment in October 1914; six months later the Battalion arrived in France and went to trenches in the vicinity of Laventie in May.

Near St. Julien on the night of 15th July 1915, Wilkinson and Riflemen Clough and Mudd went on patrol in front of the trenches. The latter was shot through the chest and his cries brought heavy fire from the Germans. Wilkinson and Clough carried him back a distance of 120 yards, but before they were able to pass through the barbed wire to reach their trench Rifleman Clough had to fetch wirecutters. Wilkinson and Clough were awarded the M.C. and D.C.M., respectively.

At the end of the year Wilkinson looked back in a poem 'Ghosts at the Old Château':

GHOSTS AT THE OLD CHATEAU
1914

Swish of silk and satin
    In the hall and stairs;
Murmured words and laughter,
    Little plaintive airs;
Stately ladies passing,
    Curtseying as they go;
Fine and courtly gallants
    Gravely bowing low.
Silent feet are treading
    Ghostly minuets;
Air with longings laden,

1917

Longings and regrets;
Dreams and hopes long vanished,
Love and smiles and tears,
Bearing old-time fragrance
Down the vale of years.

1915

Wailful winds are whistling
Through the ruined halls;
Roofless stands the chateau,
Tottering the walls.
Incense of the ages
Gleaned from old desires,
Swept away and perished
In the German fires.
Gauntly stand the ruins,
Peaks of jagged stone;
Black beneath the sunlight,
Mournfully alone.
Only in the moonbeams,
Sadly sobbing low,
Wistful spectres hover -
Ghosts of long ago.

From February until July 1916 Wilkinson was Intelligence Officer for the Battalion. On 30th June 1916, the eve of the Battle of the Somme, he wrote:

TO MY PEOPLE, BEFORE THE GREAT OFFENSIVE

Dark with uncertainty of doubtful doom
The future looms across the path we tread;
Yet, undismayed we gaze athwart the gloom,
Prophetically tinged with hectic red.
The mutterings of conflict, sullen, deep,
Surge over homes where hopeless tears are shed,
And ravens their ill-omened vigils keep
O'er legions dead.

But louder, deeper, fiercer, still shall be
The turmoil and the rush of furious feet,

The roar of war shall roll from sea to sea,
And on the sea, where fleet engages fleet.
Then fortunate who can unharmed depart
From that last field where Right and Wrong shall meet.
If then, amidst some millions more, this heart
      Should cease to beat,

Mourn not for me too sadly; I have been,
For months of an exalted life, a King;
Peer for these months of those whose graves grow green
Where'er the borders of our empire fling
Their mighty arms. And if the crown is death,
Death while I'm fighting for my home and King
Thank God the son who drew from you his breath
      To death could bring

A not entirely worthless sacrifice,
Because of those brief months when life meant more
Than selfish pleasures. Grudge not then the price,
But say, "Our country in the storm of war
Has found him fit to fight and die for her,"
And lift your heads in pride for evermore.
But when the leaves the evening breezes stir,
      Close not the door.

For if there's any consciousness to follow
The deep, deep slumber that we know as Death,
If Death and Life are not all vain and hollow,
If Life is more than so much indrawn breath,
Then in the hush of twilight I shall come -
One with immortal Life, that knows not Death
But ever changes form - I shall come home;
      Although beneath

A wooden cross the clay that once was I
Has ta'en its ancient earthy form anew.
But listen to the wind that hurries by,
To all the Song of Life for tones you knew.
For in the voice of birds, the scent of flowers,
The evening silence and the falling dew,
Through every throbbing pulse of nature's powers
      I'll speak to you.

On the first day of the Battle, Wilkinson took part in the attack on Thiepval and was wounded. In a letter from hospital he wrote:

... During the night I went up to support some men of another division in a trench we had taken and found it had been recaptured. I went in with twelve men and said 'Hello', to the first person I met, who promptly lobbed a bomb at me. Greatly scandalised I said, 'English, you thundering fool', whereat he and divers unruly companions did pelt us with bombs. Five of us got away, three wounded...

One of his sergeants later said that Wilkinson "had so many hairbreadth escapes that we had got to think he had a charmed life; he didn't know what fear was..."

Wilkinson was promoted to Captain in February 1917. On 7th May he led a raid on enemy trenches in the Aubers Ridge vicinity and was later mentioned in despatches.

During the night of 21st/22nd July 1917 the Battalion, which was in the line at Nieuport, suffered heavily from a German gas attack. All but 44 men were sent to hospital with severe symptoms including temporary blindness and the Battalion was withdrawn. Wilkinson spent two months in hospital and then at Lady Michelham's Convalescent Home in Dieppe, where he wrote one of his last poems.

FRANCE
(August 1917)

Her head unbowed, her knee unbent,
   Her sad, proud eyes unfaltering,
Her white robe soiled and stained and rent,
   Her red sword-point unwavering.

Her banner in her strong left hand,
   Unconquered, free as Freedom, waves;
She stands amidst her ruined land,
   Her broken homes, her children's graves.

Her mighty heart beats firm, although
   Her breast with patriot blood is wet,
And victory shall find her so,
   Heroic and undaunted yet.

When Wilkinson rejoined his Battalion near Ypres in the middle of September 1917, the Battalion was preparing for the attack on

Passchendaele Ridge. The Regimental War Diaries described the events of the 8th and 9th October.

> 8th. The morning was taken up by moving to St. Jean where dinners were taken and sandbags, bombs and other stores drawn. At 5 p.m. in heavy rain the Battalion being the third in the Brigade moved off to the assembly position. This entailed a 12 mile march in single file along trench grids. Owing to the darkness, gaps in the grids and halts, the rear company only arrived in the assembly position for the attack west of Passchendaele five minutes before zero.

> 9th. In spite of almost insuperable difficulties of weather conditions and ground, the Battalion advanced under the barrage towards its objectives. 'B' and 'C' Companies were detailed for the first, 'A' and 'D' for the second objective. Owing to high casualties amongst the officers and N.C.O's the position became obscure. Much hostile machine gun fire and sniping was encountered, and eventually the Battalion dug itself in short of its first objective after an advance of about 300 yards. Headquarters were established at Kronprinz Farm. The Commanding Officer, Lt. Colonel R.A. Hudson, D.S.O., was killed early in the attack and the command devolved upon Major Brooke, M.C., the Adjutant who at one time had only two officers beside himself available...

Twenty three officers went into the attack; eight, including Eric Wilkinson, were killed; ten were wounded and there were 301 casualties amongst the other ranks. The Ridge was taken on 30th October but lost almost immediately. The following week the Canadians retook it and held it against repeated counter-attacks.

TWENTIETH-CENTURY CIVILISATION

> There's a roar like a thousand hells set free,
> And the riven, tortured ground
> Sways like a tempest-smitten tree;
> And the earth shoots up in jets all around
> And blows like spray at sea
> When the wild white horses chafe and fret
> Till the boulders back on the beach are wet
> With the far-flung foam. But the hollow sound
> Of the waves that roar on the shifting shore
> Would be lost and drowned in the furious din,
> When these fruits of man's great brain begin
> To pound the ditch that we are in.

The trench is soon a hideous mess
Of yawning holes and scattered mud
And tangled wire and splintered wood,
And some poor shapeless things you'd guess
Were once made up of nerves and blood,
But now are no more good
Than the tattered sandbags - nay, far less,
For these can still be used again.
(Heed not the dark-red stain,
For that will quickly disappear
In the sun and wind and rain).
Above our heads - not very high,
As they fall on the German trenches near -
Our own shells hurtle wailing by,
But the noise cannot deaden the dreadful cry
Of a soul torn out of the shattered form;
While those who are still survivors try
(Like a ship - any port in a storm)
To hide in the holes the shells have made
And blindly, grimly, wait
Till the storm of shot and shell abate,
And it's "Bayonets up!" and blade to blade,
We can strike for ourselves and the brave dead boys,
Who, hiding in holes, have met their fate
Like rats in a trap;
But we perhaps shall have better hap,
For already there's less of the awful noise,
We can hear the machine guns stuttering death.
They're coming at last! And we draw our breath
Through hard-clenched teeth, as our bullets fly
Towards the serried ranks that are drawing nigh;
They stagger and fall, but still press on
To the goal they think they have nearly won.
And we wait and wait till they're almost here,
Then it's "Up, lads! Up! Let 'em have the steel!"
With a wild hoarse yell that is half a cheer,
We are out and their torn ranks backwards reel.
Then back to the trench to bury and build,
And count our wounded and count our killed;
But out in the front there are many who lie,
Their dead eyes turned to the quiet sky -
We have given our own lads company.

SECOND LIEUTENANT WILLIAM ROBERT HAMILTON

Coldstream Guards (Attached 4th Battalion Guards Machine Gun Regiment).
Born: 1891. Capetown, South Africa.
Killed: 12th October 1917.   Aged 26 years.
Tyne Cot Memorial to the Missing, Passchendaele, Belgium.

William Hamilton was a Lecturer in Philosophy at University College, Cape Town when War broke out. He came to England and joined the Coldstream Guards in August 1916. He collected his poems together while training for the Machine Gun Regiment and wrote in the Preface of his book that "most of the poems in this book were written in barracks in the intervals between parades. Some of their imperfections may be due to this..."

His book was published after he went to the Front and a copy of it reached him only a few days before he was killed during the Battle of Passchendaele.

WAR SONNETS
I

The spoils of youth are shaken from the net:
The golden promise spilt, and in despite
Of nature's well-laid plan, a nation's might
Of intellect becomes a dull regret.
And ye, who lightly talk of England's debt;
Who muddle into government and war,
Spilling the garnered ointment from the jar
The Past upon the Future's altar set -
How shall ye meet this greater debt incurred
Of reasonable hope outraged, and how
Restore the sweetness to the People's song:
Revive its pristine trust in those whose word
May yet precipitate a greater wrong
Than that whose bitterness we harvest now!

III

If it be true that tragedy is waste,
And that the Spirit of Denial stalks
Throughout the sphere of evil, then He walks
Unchecked among the fields and homes defaced,

310

Unhindered in the human soul debased,
By blood and rapine and the lust to kill,
To the low level of the brutish will,
The Satyr in Divinity encased!
How narrow is the margin that divides
Man who is highest, from the bestial kind;
The day of culture from primeval night!
How slender is the God-head that resides
In peoples who confuse their Might with Right,
And put their armed force before the Mind!

VI

The voice of Wisdom in the market-place:
The cry of Charity within the walls:
The song of Faith and Hope that filled our halls,
Are silenced, one and all, before the face
Of grimmest-visioned War. The name of Grace,
The milk of human kindliness, the trust
In governments and peoples, and the just
And reasonable councils of the race,
Passed out as weeping exiles from our gates,
While lordly trumpetings announced the reign
Of Blood and Iron and insatiate Mars!
For it is written, ye of low estates,
That Kings shall drive the Juggernaut of wars,
Although their own best counsel cries, Refrain.

VII

Yea, it is rumoured that the very Gods
Who held the scales of equity, were foes,
And on the mount Olympus, dealt such blows,
That, likened to them, guns are hazel rods!
Is it not written, too, that at their nods,
The Greeks and Trojans valiantly strove,
And Helen, weeping, her fair mantle wove
While Hector with Achilles vainly plods!
The Greece of Pericles was smitten down:
Proud Rome in all her glory victim fell
To the barbarian with the greater brawn,
Who, conquering, assumed the victor's crown
He wore but for a day, until the dawn
Of those more spirited he could not quell.

LIEUTENANT EWART ALAN MACKINTOSH M.C.
5th Battalion Seaforth Highlanders.
4th Battalion Seaforth Highlanders.
Born: 4th March 1893. Brighton, Sussex.
Educated: Brighton College.
St. Paul's School.
Christ Church College, Oxford.
Killed: 21st November 1917. Aged 24 years.
Orival Wood Cemetery, Flesquières, France.

At the age of sixteen, Alan Mackintosh won a scholarship from Brighton College to St Paul's. He became editor of *The Pauline* during his last year.

In December 1914 Mackintosh was commissioned in the 5th Battalion Seaforth Highlanders; he played the pipes and spoke Gaelic which particularly endeared him to the men in his Regiment by whom he was known as 'Tosh'. Mackintosh joined the Battalion at Laventie in July 1915. From the front line opposite Thiepval in October 1915 he wrote:

IN NO MAN'S LAND
(Hammerhead Wood, Thiepval, 1915)

The hedge on the left, and the trench on the right,
And the whispering, rustling wood between,
And who knows where in the wood to-night
Death or capture may lurk unseen,
The open field and the figures lying
Under the shade of the apple trees -
Is it the wind in the branches sighing,
Or a German trying to stop a sneeze?

Louder the voices of night come thronging,
But over them all the sound is clear,
Taking me back to the place of my longing
And the cultured sneezes I used to hear,
Lecture-time and my tutor's 'handker'
Stopping his period's rounded close,
Like the frozen hand of the German ranker
Down in a ditch with a cold in his nose.
I'm cold, too, and a stealthy snuffle

From the man with a pistol covering me,
And the Bosche moving off with a snap and a shuffle
Break the windows of memory -
I can't make sure till the moon gets lighter -
Anyway shooting is over bold.
Oh, damn you, get back to your trench, you blighter,
I really can't shoot a man with a cold.

On 15th May 1916 the Battalion was just west of Arras in the Maroeuil area. Mackintosh and one other officer made a raid on German trenches and Mackintosh wrote a poem 'To my Sister':

TO MY SISTER

If I die to-morrow
I shall go happily.
With the flush of battle on my face
I shall walk with an eager pace
The road I cannot see.

My life burnt fiercely always,
And fiercely will go out
With glad wild fighting ringed around,
But you will be above the ground
And darkness all about.

You will not hear the shouting,
You will not see the pride,
Only with tortured memory
Remember what I used to be,
And dream of how I died.

You will see gloom and horror
But never the joy of fight.
You'll dream of me in pain and fear,
And in your dreaming never hear
My voice across the night.

My voice that sounds so gaily
Will be too far away
For you to see across your dream
The charging and the bayonet's gleam,
Or hear the words I say.

And parted by the warders
That hold the gates of sleep,
I shall be dead and happy
And you will live and weep.

The following day Mackintosh won the Military Cross 'for conspicuous gallantry' in another raid on a German trench. He carried Private David Sutherland, one of his wounded men, for over 100 yards through the German trenches with the enemy following close behind; Private Sutherland died of his wounds as he was hoisted out of the trench and had to be left at the enemy front line. Mackintosh wrote a poem in memory of this incident:

IN MEMORIAM
Private D. Sutherland Killed in Action in the German Trench, May 16th 1916, and the Others who Died.

So you were David's father,
And he was your only son,
And the new-cut peats are rotting
And the work is left undone,
Because of an old man weeping,
Just an old man in pain,
For David, his son David,
That will not come again.

Oh, the letters he wrote you,
And I can see them still,
Not a word of the fighting
But just the sheep on the hill
And how you should get the crops in
Ere the year got stormier,
And the Bosches have got his body,
And I was his officer.

You were only David's father,
But I had fifty sons
When we went up in the evening
Under the arch of the guns,
And we came back at twilight -
O God! I heard them call
To me for help and pity
That could not help at all.

Oh, never will I forget you,
My men that trusted me,
More my sons than your fathers',
For they could only see
The little helpless babies
And the young men in their pride.
They could not see you dying,
And hold you while you died.

Happy and young and gallant,
They saw their first-born go,
But not the strong limbs broken
And the beautiful men brought low,
The piteous writhing bodies,
They screamed, "Don't leave me, Sir,"
For they were only your fathers
But I was your officer.

Mackintosh was wounded and gassed at High Wood at the beginning of August 1916.

TO THE 51st DIVISION: HIGH WOOD, JULY - AUGUST 1916

Oh gay were we in spirit
In the hours of the night
When we lay in rest by Albert
And waited for the fight;
Gay and gallant were we
On the day that we set forth,
But broken, broken, broken
Is the valour of the North.

The wild warpipes were calling,
Our hearts were blithe and free
When we went up the valley
To the death we could not see.
Clear lay the wood before us
In the clear summer weather,
But broken, broken, broken
Are the sons of the heather.

In the cold of the morning,
In the burning of the day,
The thin lines stumbled forward,
The dead and dying lay.
By the unseen death that caught us
By the bullets' raging hail
Broken, broken, broken
Is the pride of the Gael.

Mackintosh was sent home to recuperate; he then spent eight months as a bombing instructor with the Cadet Corps at Cambridge, where he became engaged to Sylvia Marsh, a Quaker girl. They planned to live in New Zealand after their marriage. Mackintosh wrote poetry and a few parodies and songs during his time at Cambridge. Included in these were poems and a parody mourning those in his Battalion who were killed at Beaumont-Hamel while he was still recovering in hospital.

BEAUMONT-HAMEL
(Captured, November 16th 1916)

Dead men at Beaumont
In the mud and rain,
You that were so warm once,
Flesh and blood and brain,
You've made an end of dying,
Hurts and cold and crying,
And all but quiet lying
Easeful after pain.

Dead men at Beaumont,
Do you dream at all
When the leaves of summer
Ripen to their fall?
Will you walk the heather,
Feel the Northern weather,
Wind and sun together,
Hear the grouse-cock call?

Maybe in the night-time
A shepherd boy will see
Dead men, and ghastly,

Kilted to the knee,
Fresh from new blood-shedding,
With airy footsteps treading,
Hill and field and steading,
Where they used to be.

Nay, not so I see you,
Dead friends of mine;
But like a dying pibroch
From the battle-line
I hear your laughter ringing,
And the sweet songs you're singing,
And the keen words winging
Across the smoke and wine.

So we still shall see you,
Be it peace or war,
Still in all adventures
You shall go before,
And our children dreaming,
Shall see your bayonets gleaming,
Scotland's warriors streaming
Forward evermore.

SNIPER SANDY
(Sergeant Alexander Macdonald, Killed in Action at Beaumont-
Hamel, November 18th 1916)
Tune: Sister Susie's sewing shirts for soldiers.

Sandy Mac the sniper is a-sniping from his loop-hole,
With a telescopic rifle he is looking for a Hun.
If he sees a sniper lurking, or a working-party working,
At once he opens fire on them, and bags them every one.
And when you come into our trench, by night-time or by day,
We take you to his loop-hole, and we point to him and say -

Chorus -
"Sniper Sandy's slaying Saxon soldiers,
And Saxon soldiers seldom show but Sandy slays a few,
And every day the Bosches put up little wooden crosses
In the cemetery for Saxon soldiers Sniper Sandy slew."

Now in the German trenches there's a sniper they call Hermann,
A stout and stolid Saxon with a healthy growth of beard,
And Hermann with his rifle is the pride of every German,
Until our Sandy gets on him, and Hermann gets afeared,
For when he hears the bullets come he slides down to the ground,
And trembling he gasps out to his comrades all around -

Chorus -
"Sniper Sandy's slaying Saxon soldiers,
And Saxon soldiers seldom show but Sandy slays a few,
And every day the Bosches put up little wooden crosses
In the cemetery for Saxon soldiers Sniper Sandy slew."

The Seaforths got so proud of Sandy's prowess with his rifle,
They drew up a report on him and sent it to the Corps,
And ninety-seven was his bag - it doen't seem a trifle -
But Sandy isn't cetain that it wasn't rather more,
And when Sir John French heard of it, he broke into a laugh,
And rubbed his hands and chuckled to the Chief of General Staff -

Chorus.... "Sniper Sandy, etc."

In October 1917 Mackintosh returned to France and joined the 4th Battalion Seaforth Highlanders in huts at Courcelles-le-Comte, near Bapaume. He wrote a farewell poem to his fiancée, on 20th October:

TO SYLVIA

Two months ago the skies were blue,
The fields were fresh and green,
And green the willow tree stood up,
With the lazy stream between.

Two months ago we sat and watched
The river drifting by -
And now - you're back at your work again
And here in a ditch I lie.

God knows - my dear - I did not want
To rise and leave you so,
But the dead men's hands were beckoning
And I knew that I must go.

The dead men's eyes were watching, lass,
Their lips were asking too,
We faced it out and payed the price -
Are we betrayed by you?

The days are long between, dear lass,
Before we meet again,
Long days of mud and work for me,
For you long care and pain.

But you'll forgive me yet, my dear,
Because of what you know,
I can look my dead friends in the face
As I couldn't two months ago.

One of the last poems Mackintosh sent home, 'War, the Liberator', was scribbled on a mud smeared piece of paper. It was written in response to a poem 'Non-Combatants' by Evelyn Underhill, on women's uncomplaining courage letting their men go to war.

WAR, THE LIBERATOR

Surely War is vile to you, you who can but know of it,
Broken men and broken hearts, and boys too young to die,
You that never knew its joy, never felt the glow of it,
Valour and the pride of men, soaring to the sky.
Death's a fearful thing to you, terrible in suddenness,
Lips that will not laugh again, tongues that will not sing,
You that have not ever seen their sudden life of happiness,
The moment they looked down on death, a cowed and beaten
    thing.

Say what life would theirs have been, that it should make you
    weep for them,
A small grey world imprisoning the wings of their desire?
Happier than they could tell who knew not life would keep for
    them
Fragments of the high Romance, the old Heroic fire.
All they dreamed of childishly, bravery and fame for them,
Charges at the cannon's mouth, enemies they slew,
Bright across the waking world their romances came for them,
Is not life a little price when our dreams come true?

All the terrors of the night, doubts and thoughts tormenting us,
Boy-minds painting quiveringly the awful face of fear,
These are gone for ever now, truth is come contenting us,
Night with all its tricks is gone and our eyes are clear.
Now in all the time to come, memory will cover us,
Trenches that we did not lose, charges that we made,
Since a voice, when first we heard shells go shrilling over us,
Said within us, "This is Death - and I am not afraid!"

Since we felt our spirits tower, smiling and contemptuous,
O'er the little frightened things, running to and fro,
Looked on Death and saw a slave blustering and presumptuous,
Daring vainly still to bring Man his master low.
Though we knew that at the last, he would have his lust of us,
Carelessly we braved his might, felt and knew not why
Something stronger than ourselves, moving in the dust of us,
Something in the Soul of Man still too great to die.

On 20th November 1917, the Battle of Cambrai opened with the British using tanks in sufficient numbers for the first time. In spite of an initial success in which the great mass of tanks on a six-mile front cleared two lines of the Hindenburg positions in four hours, the dominant Bourlon Ridge was never taken, and the Germans were allowed to regroup and counter-attack. By the first few days of December, General Byng's Third Army had withdrawn from most of its gains and the stalemate of 1917 was resumed.

During the fighting on the second day, the 4th Battalion Seaforths was involved in a heavy German counter-attack while holding a salient in the village of Fontaine Notre-Dame near Cambrai. The Battalion suffered heavy losses. Alan Mackintosh was killed by a bullet in his head.

GHOSTS OF WAR
(Sent from France in October 1917)

When you and I are buried
With grasses over head,
The memory of our fights will stand
Above this bare and tortured land,
We knew ere we were dead.

1917

Though grasses grow on Vimy,
And poppies at Messines,
And in High Wood the children play,
The craters and the graves will stay
To show what things have been.

Though all be quiet in day-time,
The night shall bring a change,
And peasants walking home shall see
Shell-torn meadow and riven tree,
And their own fields grown strange.

They shall hear live men crying,
They shall see dead men lie,
Shall hear the rattling Maxims fire,
And see by broken twists of wire
Gold flares light up the sky.

And in their new-built houses
The frightened folk will see
Pale bombers coming down the street,
And hear the flurry of charging feet,
And the crash of Victory.

This is our Earth baptizèd
With the red wine of War.
Horror and courage hand in hand
Shall brood upon the stricken land
In silence evermore.

LIEUTENANT-COMMANDER PATRICK HOUSTON SHAW-STEWART, R.N.V.R.,

CHEVALIER OF THE LEGION OF HONOUR, CROIX DE GUERRE.

Hood Battalion Royal Naval Division.

Born: 17th August 1888.
Educated: Eton College.
           Balliol College, Oxford.
Killed: 30th December 1917. Aged 29 years.
Metz-en-Couture Communal Cemetery British Extension,
France.

Patrick Shaw-Stewart was the son of a retired Major-General. His parents were middle-aged when he was born and died when he was in his early twenties. He was fond of them and they were proud of his achievements but it was difficult to have a close relationship. His early affections were given to his nanny, known as 'Dear' and they remained devoted friends until his death. He was a King's Scholar at Eton and one of seven editors of a College magazine, *The Outsider*. (The other editors included Julian Grenfell (qv), Charles Lister, Edward Horner, whose sister later married Raymond Asquith (qv), and Ronald Knox). He won the covetted Newcastle Scholarship in 1905 and a classical scholarship to Balliol later in the same year but he did not go up to the University until January 1907. His academic achievements were outstanding and he was considered 'possibly the most brilliant of all the Balliol men killed in the war.'

He was determined and ambitious both intellectually and socially and was attracted to the glamorous world of his Eton and Balliol friends, especially Julian Grenfell's family at Taplow Court, near Maidenhead in Berkshire. In 1910 he left Balliol with a First in Greats, was awarded a Law Scholarship and elected to a Fellowship at All Souls. The following year, through his close relationship with Julian Grenfell's mother, Lady Desborough, he was offered a position on the staff of Barings Bank. He was a Managing Director of the Bank before he reached the age of twenty-five.

In August 1914 Shaw-Stewart wrote to Lady Diana Manners:

I am the most unmilitary of men. I hated field days at Eton. I hate the very thought of taking the field now. I do not particularly dislike the Germans - my chief European preoccupation is the ultimate hegemony of the Russians, which it seems to me we are fighting to achieve and I know full well that though I may be a bad banker I should be a 100 times worse soldier. Again, I frankly recoil from wounds and death and I think (with the minimum of arrogance) that others are fitter food for powder than me. These things being so, ought I to go?...

By the following month he had made his decision and having volunteered for Winston Churchill's newly formed Royal Naval Division he was first sent to Dunkirk as interpreter and then as Embarkation Officer, "which, as far as I can make out, means standing on the quay and saying "mind the gangway", and "all landing tickets, please." After a fortnight he felt he was doing work "any ex-Colonel of seventy could do." At the end of four weeks he was recalled and in December 1914, after two months of initial training, he was sent to Blandford Camp in Dorset to join the Hood Battalion, commanded by a New Zealander, Bernard Freyburg. His fellow officers included Raymond Asquith's brother, Arthur (Oc); Rupert Brooke; two talented musicians, F.S. 'Cleg' Kelly, an Australian and fellow Etonian and Balliol man; and Denis Browne, a Rugby friend of Brooke's; and an American, Johnny Dodge.

By January 1915 there was deadlock on the Western Front and the British Government looked for a fresh opening where an offensive could be launched. With the entrance of Turkey into the War on the side of the Central Powers, Russia calling for help from the Allies, Italy wavering, the uncertainty of Greece and Roumania, and unrest in Turkey itself, the War Cabinet decided on a Military enterprise against Turkey in the Eastern Mediterranean. The aim was to force the narrow Straits of the Dardanelles to open up the southern route to Russia.

At the end of February the Hood Battalion sailed on board the Grantully Castle. Shaw-Stewart wrote before he left England:

It is the Dardanelles, the real plum of this war: all the glory of a European campaign... without the wet, mud, misery, and certain death of Flanders...

The Battalion reached Port Said at the end of March and went to a camp in the desert nearby. Patrick Shaw-Stewart, Rupert Brooke and 'Oc' Asquith had two days leave which they spent in Cairo, but after they returned to camp Shaw-Stewart became ill with dysentery and was sent to the Casino Hotel in Port Said. He wrote to Ronald Knox:

... Two days later I was joined by Rupert, who had the same complaint but worse, with high fever; he was put in my room because the hotel was full, and because I thought I was well, but I relapsed slightly and in the end we shared that room for a week, completely starved (with one or two adventures in eggs and the little sham soles of the Mediterranean, which brought about relapse and repentance), and weak as kittens, disabilities which did not prevent me from enjoying it greatly. This enjoyment was perhaps not diminished by the thought of the wind-swept camp, where one of our stokers remarked that the continual absorption of particles of sand was rapidly forming in his interior a tomb-stone, the removal of which would, he felt, present a problem...

Rupert and I were trundled on board the Grantully Castle when the battalion pushed off rather hastily about April 11th, this time meaning business. Our protestations of fitness were true in my case but not in Rupert's, although after two or three days in his cabin he began to get up and go about, officially well but really pulled down. On this voyage the Hood had the Grantully to themselves, which vastly improved every one's temper and enjoyment. It further enabled a rearrangement of tables in the dining-saloon, and a table was formed consisting of Charles [Lister], Rupert, Arthur Asquith, Denis Browne, Cleg Kelly, Johnny Dodge, and myself, under the presidency of one of the ship's officers, who was occasionally, I think, a little surprised at our conversation. I subsequently happened to hear that this table was known to the others as "the Latin Club"; I do not know what piece of pedantry on whose part was responsible for the title. Certainly some noteworthy conversations were held there; it seemed always somehow to happen that we were left there at dinner among the patient stewards, long after everyone else had gone, experimenting on the rather limited repertory of the ship's vintages, and amusing one another none too silently. I wish I could recapture something of the subject-matter... we were very wise indeed. But always, whatever the matter in hand, Charles and Rupert delighted each other and the rest of us; they also walked on deck together, and I suspect talked of less hilarious and more permanently significant things... and about April 17 we anchored in the southern bay of Scyros, that smelt to heaven of thyme.

Here, next day, Charles and I wandered all over the south half of the island in brilliant sunshine and sweet smelling air: we were fed on milk and goat's cheese by a magnificent islander - whom we identified with Eumaeus - in his completely Homeric steading, were rowed back to our ship by another sturdy Greek fisherman and his still sturdier wife, and were greeted over the ship's side with slight sarcasm by Rupert, who had taken our watches and suffered endless boredom to enable us to overstay our scheduled time without dire consequences. Here we floundered about on precipitous perfumed hill-sides packed with spring flowers and sharp stones, in the throes of Battalion and Divisional Field Days more bewildering, unexpected, and exhausting than any we had previously dreed on the Dorsetshire downs, till Rupert, who would not be left behind, felt tired and went to bed early while we still sat and smoked and talked after dinner. Here, one day after, we knew that the germ of pneumonia had attacked him, weak as he was, in the lip, and I was frightened to see him so motionless and fevered just before he was shifted - lowered over the side in a couch from the Grantully to a French hospital ship - and here, after one day more, Charles commanded the burial-party and I the firing-party, when we buried him among the olives of Scyros the night before we sailed for the Peninsula...

The Hood Battalion landed at Cape Helles on 29th April, four days after the first landings and Shaw-Stewart wrote to his sister:

The last two days we've been on the spot, listening to the most prodigious bombardment that ever was. It seems amazing that any Turks can have lived through it, but they have, the devils, and given our first landing-party a poorish time, I'm afraid. But from what we have just heard they have done magnificently. Both the Australians (and N.Z.) and the 29th accomplished a miraculous landing; I'm glad it wasn't us who had to do it, because, though our men will probably be very steady, I doubt if they are quite the raging fiends the Australians seem to be when they're roused - which made that landing possible. I think the heaviest work has been done already, and the remainder will be very exciting, but not anything like so difficult and dangerous.

Just over a week later, on 8th May, Shaw-Stewart wrote:

I suppose every one feels much as I do after a week or so of war, it is very exciting, and a thing a man should not have missed; but now I've seen it and been there and done the dashing, I begin to wonder whether this is any place for a civilised man, and to remember about hot baths and strawberries and my morning *Times*. We have been a good bit in the trenches (I am lying in a reserve one now, just in case the enemy's shrapnel should be wider of the mark than usual), and twice in action. The second day was exciting enough for any one: my next-door neighbour hit four times, and me finding myself to my great surprise in a position so much in front of the army that I had to pretend to be a daisy and crawl away with a few men at dusk. Since then I have been hit at three yards range with an accidental shot plumb on the right heart, where the bullet lodged in my trusty Asprey steel mirror - almost as good an advertisement for that firm as Oc's wound for the Government.

When he heard that Julian Grenfell (qv) and Edward Horner had been wounded, Shaw-Stewart wrote to Lady Desborough on the 9th June:

> You can imagine what I have felt about the two of them... and thinking of you out there. In ordinary times I could have thought of nothing else, but two days after I was forced to think very hard about my own battalion, who suffered cruelly in a charge on a Turkish trench on the Fourth of June, in which out of fifteen officers left six were killed, including Denis Browne, and five wounded, leaving only me and three others now. I was filled with disgust and rage at the crushing folly of it for a time, but my native stolidity asserted itself - with the result that two others out of the four of us left have been sent to Alexandria for a rest, and two of us are carrying on!

Later that month on the island of Imbros, where the remnants of the Division were sent to rest, Shaw-Stewart wrote 'I saw a Man this Morning' on a blank page in his copy of *A Shropshire Lad*:

I SAW A MAN THIS MORNING

I saw a man this morning
Who did not wish to die:
I ask, and cannot answer,
If otherwise wish I.

Fair broke the day this morning
Against the Dardanelles;
The breeze blew soft, the morn's cheeks
Were cold as cold sea-shells.

But other shells are waiting
Across the Aegean sea,
Shrapnel and high explosive,
Shells and hells for me.

O hell of ships and cities,
Hell of men like me,
Fatal second Helen,
Why must I follow thee?

Achilles came to Troyland
And I to Chersonese:
He turned from wrath to battle,
And I from three days' peace.

> Was it so hard, Achilles,
> So very hard to die?
> Thou knowest and I know not -
> So much the happier I.
>
> I will go back this morning
> From Imbros over the sea;
> Stand in the trench, Achilles,
> Flame-capped, and shout for me.

At the end of July the junior British liaison officer at the French General Headquarters was badly wounded and Shaw-Stewart was sent to replace him. "So for the moment here I am in inglorious safety on the gilded Staff and speaking French for dear life"; by October he was senior liaison officer and wrote to 'Dear' on All Souls Day, 1915:

> I never told you properly the noble history of your last cake, one of the glorified currant loaf kind with a crust... General Birdwood was doing temporary Commander-in-Chief... and invited himself to tea with the French General. The latter was in despair at not having anything sufficiently 'serious' to offer an English General for tea - knowing that we tend to make a meal of it - and I stepped into the breach with the offer of my 'plum cake' (an adopted French word pronounced 'ploom kak') which had then just arrived. It made a noble show in the middle of the table and had the greatest success. "Is this from France?" asked General Birdwood, between two mouthfuls. "No it is the gift of Capitaine Stuart", said General Brulard. "From Scotland, sir," said I, amid loud cheers. So the cake had really a worthy fate...

After over eight months of fighting since the Allied invasion of Gallipoli, 25,000 men had died, 75,000 were wounded and 12,000 were missing. During December 1915 the evacuation of the remaining troops took place, and on 8th January 1916 the last men of the Royal Naval Division were taken off. For his services with the French Shaw-Stewart was awarded the Legion of Honour.

> January 8th 1916... Well, I have certainly seen the campaign of the Dardanelles - the beginning, the end, and all the middle... On the whole, it's nothing to be proud of for the British Army or the French either - nine months here, and pretty heavy losses, and now nothing for it but to clear out. I wonder what next?

The next step for Patrick Shaw-Stewart after a few weeks leave was as liaison officer, with the French again, in Salonika. He felt isolated from his old Battalion which was sent to France. On 18th April 1916 he wrote to Lady Desborough:

> Nothing can conceal from me the fact that I am superfluous here: they have enough liaison already, and even when (or if) this front becomes active, I shall not be what Lord Kitchener (I think) calls 'pulling my weight'. Therefore (don't tell any one), I am seriously considering applying to 'return to duty', either in the R.N.D., or (if they are quite effete) in the Army.

In July he wrote to Raymond Asquith (qv) from Karamudli:

> I'm just back from three days' continuous riding to do the liaison with the nearest British. Rather a lovely journey, the first day all winding among mountain passes, getting up half-way to the col, whence you can look down over the flat plain between us and the Bulgars, and up across at the really very handsome heights on which the Bulgars habitually sit: the second day in the plain along a lake with cranes and egrets and little diving ducks all over it. I was tempted to bathe, but a military policeman whom I came across told me there were five feet of mud, and, anyhow, it was forbidden.

Patrick Shaw-Stewart was awarded the Croix de Guerre for his work with the French during their advance in August 1916 but he became increasingly frustrated that he was unable to join his Battalion in France.

On 22nd September 1916, mourning Raymond Asquith, he wrote to his sister:

> ...I am very miserable about Raymond. I was most awfully fond of him, and admired him, his brain, and his wit, and all his delightful qualities, more than any one else whatever. It makes me more inclined than anything that has happened yet, to 'take off my boots and go to bed.' Decidedly it's queer - when people like Julian died, you felt at least they had enjoyed war, and were gloriously at home in it: but Raymond! that graceful, elegant cynic, who spent his time before the war pulling Guardsmen's legs, to be killed in action in the Grenadiers, it is so utterly incongruous, and he so completely devoid of any shred of support from glamour...

Shaw-Stewart returned to England in January 1917 for leave. He had suffered from dysentery and jaundice while in the Middle

East and was certain he must, "do everything to avoid going back to that absurd Salonika". He was still determined to get to France and wrote on 3rd March 1917:

I have had my Board yesterday morning, and they passed me for General Service with the recommendation that I should not be sent back to the East. That was my own suggestion: they would quite certainly have passed me for anything I jolly well liked. That being so, I shall in a day or two probably be informed of it officially by the W.O., whereupon I will communicate with Freyburg, who will apply for me. It will all take some time probably: nothing is done in a hurry in the British Army... I feel more and more that I have been right to play my last card to get out of Salonika and back to France...

Six weeks later he was in France and rejoined the Hood Battalion, which had been diminished and battered during the attack on Gavrelle. A few days before he arrived Bernard Freyburg, who had won the Victoria Cross at Beaumont Hamel in November 1916, was promoted and 'Oc' Asquith took over command of the Battalion; Shaw-Stewart became his second-in-command. He was sent for a Lewis-gun training course at Etaples at the beginning of July, and when he returned to Roclincourt he found Asquith had gone on leave and he was temporarily in command of the Battalion.

I am not a very good regimental officer, and... don't enjoy it overmuch. You don't get as much leisure when out of the line as you did in Gallipoli: too much damned training, which (next to fighting) I dislike more than anything... Every time I remember that nearly all my friends are dead, I take some form of imaginary morphia, and promise myself work or love or letters, or fall back on the comforting reflection that I may soon be dead myself (wonderfully cheering that).

After a Company Commander's Course in September 1917, Shaw-Stewart returned to the Battalion to find he was once again in temporary command. He was in England on leave during December and visited many of the families of his friends who had been killed. Over two years before he had written from the Dardanelles:

... The fact is that this generation of mine is suffering in their twenties what most men get in their seventies, the gradual thinning out of their contemporaries... Nowadays we who are alive have the sense of being old, old survivors."

He rejoined the Battalion in bitterly cold weather to find himself a Lieutenant-Commander and again in temporary command of Hood Battalion as 'Oc' Asquith had been promoted to Brigadier. The Naval Division was in position on the crest of Welsh ridge, north of Cambrai. There were many successive days of severe frost during the last fortnight of December but work on the construction of a continuous front support line on the Ridge was pressed forward. From Christmas Day onwards the enemy shelling markedly increased and at dawn on December 30th the Germans launched an attack against the whole front.

An artillery officer with Shaw-Stewart wrote of the circumstances surrounding his death:

It was in the early morning, about dawn; he was going round his line; The Germans put up a barrage. The gunner pressed him to send up the S.O.S. rocket, but Patrick refused, and maintained that it was only a minor raid on another part of the line, and that if he sent up the S.O.S. signal the people would only think he was "windy". As a matter of fact, they did make a big attack about an hour later, and his battalion was the only one that did not give ground.

He was hit by shrapnel, the lobe of his ear was cut off and his face spattered so that the blood ran down from his forehead and blinded him for a bit. The gunner tried to make him go back to Battalion H.Q. to be dressed, but he refused, and insisted on completing his round. Very soon afterwards, a shell burst on the parapet, and a fragment hit him upwards through the mouth and killed him instantaneously...

1918

RIFLEMAN COLIN MITCHELL

8th (later 3rd) Battalion The Rifle Brigade.
Born: Mere, Wiltshire.
Killed: 22nd March 1918.
Pozières Memorial, Ovillers-la-Boiselle, France.

Colin Mitchell served as a Rifleman in the 8th Battalion the Rifle Brigade in July 1915. As a result of his experiences at Hooge he wrote a poem:

HOOGE: (JULY 31st 1915)

Hooge! More damned than Sodom and more bloody,
'Twas there we faced the flames of liquid fire.
Hooge! That shambles where the flames swept ruddy:
A spume of heat and hate and omens dire;
A vision of a concrete hell from whence
Emerged satanic forms, or so it seemed
To us who, helpless, saw them hasten hence.
Scarce understood we if we waked or dreamed.
"Stand To! Stand To! The Wurtembergers come!"
Shouting vile English oaths with gutter zest.
And boastful threats to kill they voice, while some,
In uniforms of grey and scarlet dressed,
Wear flame-projectors strapped upon their backs.
How face a wall of flame? Impossible!
"Back, boys! Give way a little; take the tracks
That lead to yonder wood, and there we'll fill
Such trenches as are dug, and face the foe,
And no Hell-fire shall move us once we're there.
We're out to win or die, boys; if we go
Back and yet back, leaving good strongholds bare,
We'll save our lives, perhaps, but not our name.
There's no one in this well-trained company
Who'd save his skin and perjure his good fame."
We hold the wood, but, oh, how can it be?
The shells are raining down amidst the trees,
Snapping the full-girthed trunks that downward crash
In dire proximity to us. The breeze
Bespeaks hot human blood. The scarlet splash
Shows everywhere, and everywhere the maimed

Are crawling, white-lipped, to a dug-out where
The doctor in a drip of sweat seems framed,
So hard he works to hide the horrid stare
Of wounds adrip; while many pass away,
And need no lint to bind their frailty,
For God has ta'en them; 'tis their triumph day,
And all their sins shall expiated be.

Thus are we thrown in Life's great melting-pot,
Humanity much matrixed; but the ore
Looms purer when the crucible is hot:
'Tis on this truth that we should set our store.

The collapse of Russia late in 1917 enabled Germany to concentrate the bulk of her forces against the British and French on the Western Front. On 21st March 1918 the Germans, in an all out attempt to knock out the Allies before the United States forces had a chance to tip the balance of power, launched a massive onslaught in the early hours of the morning. Forced to give ground, the British 5th Army under General Gough fell back in disorder. It was not until the first few days in April that the German advance was stemmed and turned.

By this time Colin Mitchell had transferred to the 3rd Battalion The Rifle Brigade. On the first day of the German Spring Offensive the Battalion was in the outpost line facing north east between Bellenglise and Levergies, five miles north of St. Quentin. The Battalion was heavily attacked and severely bombarded but held the line. The next day, when there was a danger of being outflanked it was ordered to withdraw. The Battalion disengaged from the enemy with some difficulty and withdrew ten miles to the west spending the night in huts at Montecourt. There were casualties and Colin Mitchell was among those killed.

Colin Mitchell wrote all his poetry in camp, train, trench and hospital during his years serving in France.

TRAMPLED CLAY

We crept into the gas-polluted night,
A little band allotted for fatigue;
And yard by yard we searched a quarter league
Of ground new won by blood and strife and might;
Of ground dear lost, dear gained, and dearer held,
Where shell on shell still burst among the felled.

We went to seek the dead; with rough respect
To roll their mangled bodies down the shade
Of crater-lips that shrieking shells had made.
O, Mary, Mother, in white samite decked!
Beyond the chaos of our earthly strife,
What of the waiting mother, sister, wife?

The dreamer lay with blood-gout on his lips,
The strenuist with virile limbs stretched wide,
His leaded "cosh" still lying at his side,
His bombing-jacket corded to his hips.
(At home the English journals said that we
Had gained another easy victory).

We left them covered with an earthy shroud;
"Dust to the dust", without a single prayer
Save, mayhap, one that Pity murmured there.
But Pity's voice is never very loud,
And we are used to seeing comrades die,
And leaving them, perforce, just where they lie.

Thy Hand doth clothe the lily, warm the day;
Sol's cloth of gold most tenderly is drawn
Across the opalescent robes of Dawn;
Yet see, O, God! this mass of trampled clay,
These gaping wounds, these bodies shrapnel-torn
Vengeance is Thine! Let vengeance now be sworn.

DARKNESS AND DAWN

Paler and paler wanes the afterglow,
From regal red to soft-toned amethyst.
The heron wings, majestically and slow,
His homeward way above the rising mist.
Stilled for a space is Nature's evensong,
And many stars are throbbing in the sky.
The day of waiting has been over-long:
"Thank God for evening!" is our grateful cry.

But when the evening ebbs and dark draws near,
How oft its sable mysteries affright;

How oft the spreading tentacles of fear
Entwine some trembling watcher of the night!
The sleeper moans, uneasy in his rest;
The fire burns low; Death's stealthy step goes by.
No longer are our feeble prayers suppressed:
"God, send the Dawning!" is our fevered cry.

THE RESERVE BILLET

Down, down in a cellar's darkness; down in a clammy gloom,
Lighted by draught-sucked candles and shadowed by silhouettes
Of men in the stretched-out postures that weariness begets.
Down, down in a cellar's darkness: the darkness of a tomb.
And 'tis heigh-ho for the warmth and glow
Of God's refreshing Sun.

Down, down in a cellar's darkness, many a weary day;
Tortured by home-fed longings that never will dormant be;
Prisoned in feudal fashion in the twentieth century;
Thus the juggernaut of Duty rolls on its brutal way
And 'tis heigh-ho for the warmth and glow
Of God's refreshing Sun.

Down, down in a cellar's darkness, hid in a shell-raked town;
Cats screaming on the garbage in a brawl for noisome fare,
And heavy shrapnel shrieking as it rends the outer air.
God! here's a seventeen-inches! Just list to it roaring down!
And 'tis heigh-ho for the warmth and glow
Of God's refreshing Sun.

Down, down in a cellar's darkness, the very walls asway,
Rocking like ships of matchwood when the seas are hungering.
Hark to the clang of the shovels the white-faced sergeants bring.
"If we are buried alive, boys, God help us all to-day!"
And 'tis heigh-ho for the warmth and glow
Of God's refreshing Sun.

Down, down in a cellar's darkness; no dwelling-place for Hope;
She leaves such habitations for a world of cleaner air,
Hard, hard 'twould be for such as she to linger longer there;
But down in a cellar's darkness grim Duty still does grope.
And 'tis heigh-ho for the warmth and glow
Of God's refreshing Sun.

CAPTAIN THEODORE PERCIVAL CAMERON WILSON

10th Battalion Sherwood Foresters.
Born: 1889.
Killed: 23rd March 1918. Aged 29 years.
The Arras Memorial to the Missing, Faubourg-D'Amiens
Cemetery, Arras, France.

The son of a clergyman, from Little Eaton in Derbyshire, Cameron Wilson became a schoolmaster; he wrote two novels and contributed to periodicals before the War. He enlisted as a Private in the Grenadier Guards in August 1914 and was later commissioned in the 10th Battalion Sherwood Foresters. He joined the Battalion in trenches at Armentières at the beginning of February 1916, and was in and out of the trenches for the next two months. He wrote to his mother on the 1st March:

... I saw about 50 German prisoners marched through the village. Three officers were in front - white, broken, muddy, and one of them wounded. Most of the men were very boyish and intelligent looking, but one officer, who looked about 20, was one of the noblest looking men I have ever seen. He held his head up and looked so proud that I could have wept. War is indescribably disgusting. Any man who has seen it and praises it is degenerate.

I had a long time to think, by myself, on that fatigue job - under the stars, and please God I'll live to put some of it in print, one day, but I can't write it in a letter. The rats interrupted me. They are fat and grey and bold. One came and looked at me and squealed at about 3 o'clock in the morning when I could see no prospect of going to bed ever, and so infuriated me that I slashed at him with my stick and splashed my whole face so with mud that I had to spend the next hour or so trying to get a lump of it out of my eye. I missed the rat, and imagined him with a paw to his horrible nose - laughing at me... As to my own feelings under fire, I was horribly afraid - sick with fear - not of being hit, but of seeing other people torn, in the way that high explosive tears. It is simply hellish. But thank God I didn't show any funk. That's all a man dare ask, I think. I don't care a flip whether I'm killed or not - though I don't think I shall be - the chances are about 100 to 1. Out here you must trust yourself to a bigger Power and leave it at that. You can't face death (I've used the phrase myself about this war). There's no facing it. It's everywhere. You have to walk through it, and under it and over it and past it. Without the sense of God taking up the souls out of those poor torn bodies - even though they've died cursing Him - I think one would go mad...

DURING THE BOMBARDMENT

What did we know of birds?
Though the wet woods rang with their blessing,
And the trees were awake and aware with wings,
And the little secrets of mirth, that have no words,
Made even the brambles chuckle, like baby things
Who find their toes too funny for any expressing.

What did we know of flowers?
Though the fields were gay with their flaming
Poppies, like joy itself, burning the young green maize,
And spreading their crinkled petals after the showers -
Cornflower vieing with mustard;   and all the three of
    them shaming
The tired old world with its careful browns and greys.

What did we know of summer,
The larks, and the dusty clover,
And the little furry things that were busy and starry-
    eyed?
Each of us wore his brave disguise, like a mummer,
Hoping that no one saw, when the shells came over,
The little boy who was funking - somewhere inside!

In April 1916 Cameron Wilson wrote to his aunt:

... I'm writing in a trench not very far from the Germans and I've just heard the first cuckoo! It's blazing sunlight. Behind, there is a French town - quivering in the heat - chimneys and roofs apparently intact from here, though the whole place in reality is a mere husk of a town. Nearer, between the town and us, is a village, which is quite a ruin - its church spire a broken stump, its house walls honeycombed with shell fire. Then comes a great blazing belt of yellow flowers - a sort of mustard or sharlock - smelling to heaven like incense, in the sun - and above it all are larks. Then a bare field strewn with barbed wire - rusted to a sort of Titian red - out of which a hare came just now, and sat up with fear in his eyes and the sun shining red through his ears. Then the trench. An indescribable mingling of the artificial with the natural. Piled earth with groundsel and great flaming dandelions and chickweed, and pimpernels, running riot over it. Decayed sandbags, new sandbags, boards, dropped ammunition, empty tins, corrugated iron, a smell of boots and stagnant water and burnt powder and oil and men, the occasional bang of a rifle, and the click of a bolt, the occasional crack of a bullet coming over, or the wailing diminuendo of a ricochet. And over everything the larks and a blessed bee or two. And far more often, very high up in the blue - a little resolute whitish-yellow fly of an aeroplane - watching, watching - speaking, probably, by wireless to the hidden stations behind the lines; dropping, when he thinks fit, a sort of thunderous death on to the green earth under him; moving with a sort of triumphant calm through the tiny snow-white puffs of shrapnel round him. And on the other side, nothing but a mud wall, with a few dandelions against the sky, until you look over the top, or through a periscope, and then you see barbed wire and more barbed wire, and then fields with larks over them, and then barbed wire again - German wire this time - and a long wavy line of mud and sandbags - the German line - which is being watched all day from end to end with eyes which hardly wink. The slightest movement on it - the mere adjusting of sandbag from below - is met with fire. The same goes on of course with our line. Look over the top for longer than two seconds and you are lucky to step down without a bullet through your brain. By day it's very quiet. Some twenty shells or so have come over this morning from the German side. You hear a sound rather like a circular saw cutting through thin wood and moving towards you at the same time with terrific speed - straight for your middle it seems, till you get used to it! It ends in a terrific burst - a shower of earth or bricks or metal, a quiet cloud of smoke - and sometimes a torn man to be put out of sight, or hurried down to the dressing station. Sometimes, but astonishingly seldom with this desultory shelling. Of course a real bombardment where the sky is one screaming sheet of metal, is hell indescribable. This place is very quiet, on the whole. But even the beauty of Spring has something of purgatory in it - the sort of purgatory a madman may know who sees all beautiful things through a veil of obscenity. Whatever war journalists may say, or poets either, blood and entrails and spilled brains are obscene. I read a critique of Le Gallienne's out here, in which he takes Rupert Brooke to task for talking of war as 'cleanness'. Le Gallienne is right. War is about the most unclean thing on earth. There are certain big clean virtues about it - comradeship and a whittling away of non-essentials, and sheer stark triumphs of spirit over shrinking nerves, but it's the calculated death, the deliberate tearing of fine young bodies - if you've once seen a bright-eyed fellow suddenly turned to a goggling idiot, with his own brains trickling down into his eyes from under his cap - as I've done, you're either a peace-maker or a degenerate..."

SONG OF AMIENS

Lord! How we laughed in Amiens!
For here were lights, and good French drink,
And Marie smiled at everyone,
And Madeleine's new blouse was pink,
And Petite Jeanne (who always runs)
Served us so charmingly, I think
That we forgot the unsleeping guns.

Lord! How we laughed in Amiens!
Till through the talk there flashed the name
Of some great man we left behind.
And then a sudden silence came
And even Petite Jeanne (who runs)
Stood still to hear, with eyes aflame,
The distant mutter of the guns.

Ah! How we laughed in Amiens!
For there were useless things to buy,
Simply because Irene, who served,
Had happy laughter in her eye;
And Yvonne, bringing sticky buns,
Cared nothing that the eastern sky
Was lit with flashes from the guns.

And still we laughed in Amiens,
As dead men laughed a week ago.
What cared we if in Delville Wood
The splintered trees saw hell below?
We cared... We cared... But laughter runs
The cleanest stream a man may know
To rinse him from the taint of guns.

On 3rd May 1916 Cameron Wilson wrote to a friend:

... Do teach your dear kids the horror of responsibility which rests on
the war-maker. I want so much to get at children about it. We've
been wrong in the past. We have taught schoolboys "war" as a
romantic subject. We've made them learn the story of Waterloo as a
sort of exciting story in fiction. And everyone has grown up soaked in
the poetry of war - which exists, because there is poetry in everything,
but which is only a tiny part of the great dirty tragedy. All those

picturesque phrases of war writers - such as "he flung the remnants of his Guard against the enemy", "a magnificent charge won the day and the victorious troops, etc. etc.", are dangerous because they show nothing of the individual horror, nothing of the fine personalities smashed suddenly into red beastliness, nothing of the sick fear that is tearing at the hearts of brave boys who ought to be laughing at home - a thing infinitely more terrible than physical agony...

MAGPIES IN PICARDY

The magpies in Picardy
Are more than I can tell.
They flicker down the dusty roads
And cast a magic spell
On the men who march through Picardy,
Through Picardy to hell.

(The blackbird flies with panic,
The swallow goes like light,
The finches move like ladies,
The owl floats by at night;
But the great and flashing magpie
He flies as artists might).

A magpie in Picardy
Told me secret things -
Of the music in white feathers,
And the sunlight that sings
And dances in deep shadows -
He told me with his wings.

(The hawk is cruel and rigid,
He watches from a height;
The rook is slow and sombre,
The robin loves to fight;
But the great and flashing magpie
He flies as lovers might).

He told me that in Picardy,
An age ago or more,
While all his fathers still were eggs,
These dusty highways bore

Brown, singing soldiers marching out
Through Picardy to war.

He said that still through chaos
Works on the ancient plan,
And two things have altered not
Since first the world began -
The beauty of the wild green earth
And the bravery of man.

(For the sparrow flies unthinking
And quarrels in his flight.
The heron trails his legs behind,
The lark goes out of sight;
But the great and flashing magpie
He flies as poets might).

On 1st June the Battalion was undergoing 'intensive training' in the vicinity of Difques and Inglinghem. Cameron Wilson wrote to his friend Harold Monro at the Poetry Bookshop and at about the same time wrote the poem 'A Soldier':

I wish you were here, with your sympathy and your power of laughing at the same things as the man you're with - laughing and weeping, almost, it would be here. Here's a thing that happened. When I first "joined" out here I noticed a man - a boy, really, his age was just 19 - who had those very calm blue eyes one sees in sailors sometimes, and a skin burnt to a sort of golden brown. I said to him, "When did you leave the Navy?" and he regarded this as the most exquisite joke! Every time I met him he used to show his very white teeth in a huge smile of amusement, and we got very pally when it came to real bullets - as men do get pally, the elect, at any rate. Well, the other day there was a wiring party out in front of our parapet - putting up barbed wire (rusted to a sort of Titian red). It is wonderful going out into 'No Man's Land'. I'll tell you about it one day - stars and wet grass, and nothing between you and the enemy, and every now and then a very soft and beautiful blue-white light from a Very pistol - bright as day, yet extraordinarily unreal. You have to keep still as a statue in whatever position you happen to be in, till it dies down, as movement gives you away. Well, that night they turned a machine gun on the wiring party and the 'sailor boy' got seven bullets, and died almost at once. All his poor body was riddled with them and one went through his brown throat.

When I went over his papers I found a post-card addressed to his mother. It was an embroidered affair, on white silk. They buy them out here for 40 centimes each, and it had simply 'Remember me' on it...

A SOLDIER

He laughed. His blue eyes searched the morning,
Found the unceasing song of the lark
In a brown twinkle of wings, far out.
Great clouds, like galleons, sailed the distance.
The young spring day had slipped the cloak of dark
And stood up straight and naked with a shout.
Through the green wheat, like laughing schoolboys,
Tumbled the yellow mustard flowers, uncheck'd.
The wet earth reeked and smoked in the sun...
He thought of the waking farm in England
The deep thatch of the roof - all shadow-fleck'd
The clank of pails at the pump... the day begun.
"After the war..." he thought. His heart beat faster
With a new love for things familiar and plain.
The Spring leaned down and whispered to him low
Of a slim, brown-throated woman he had kissed...
He saw, in sons that were himself again,
The only immortality that man may know.

And then a sound grew out of the morning,
And a shell came, moving a destined way,
Thin and swift and lustful, making its moan.
A moment his brave white body knew the Spring,
The next, it lay
In a red ruin of blood and guts and bone.

       . . . .

Oh! nothing was tortured there! Nothing could know
How death blasphemed all men and their high birth
With his obscenities. Already moved,
Within those shattered tissues, that dim force,
Which is the ancient alchemy of Earth,
Changing him to the very flowers he loved.

       . . . .

"Nothing was tortured there!" Oh, pretty thought!
When God Himself might well bow down His head
And hide His haunted eyes before the dead.

Cameron Wilson served as a Staff Captain with the 51st Brigade from the end of May 1917 and was mentioned in despatches that year. *The Westminster Gazette* published his poem, 'Sportsmen in Paradise' under his pseudonym 'Tipuca', in June 1917.

SPORTSMEN IN PARADISE

They left the fury of the fight,
And they were very tired.
The gates of Heaven were open, quite
Unguarded, and unwired.
There was no sound of any gun;
The land was still and green:
Wide hills lay silent in the sun,
Blue valleys slept between.

They saw far off a little wood
Stand up against the sky.
Knee-deep in grass a great tree stood...
Some lazy cows went by...
There were some rooks sailed overhead -
And once a church-bell pealed.
"God! but it's England," someone said,
"And there's a cricket field!"

Cameron Wilson returned to his Battalion in front line and support trenches at Hermies in January 1918. The Battalion's War History says:

He made a fine Regimental Officer during the short time he was with the battalion... He threw every part of his keenness and energy into the work, and was promoted Captain in February. The man himself was extraordinarily interesting; he contributed several truly witty articles to *Punch* - notably 'David' in 1917, and had published verse in several papers. Altogether he was a gay light-hearted modern of the best type.

As a result of the German break through in their Spring Offensive, the Battalion was ordered to evacuate Hermies at 1.00 p.m. on 23rd March 1918, and to take up a point to the south to cover two other Battalions' withdrawal. Although the evacuation was carried out in good order, "masses of the enemy appeared over the high ground from Havrincourt to Velu Wood and the hostile machine gun fire on the retreating units, as they passed along the Havrincourt-Bertincourt valley, was extremely heavy and caused numerous casualties." Theodore Cameron Wilson was killed in the area of Villers-au-Flos, near Bertincourt at about 4.00 p.m.

The following poem was found in his pocket after his death:

HEAVEN

Suddenly one day
The last ill shall fall away;
The last little beastliness that is in our blood
Shall drop from us as the sheath drops from the bud,
And the great spirit of man shall struggle through,
And spread huge branches underneath the blue.
In any mirror, be it bright or dim,
Man will see God staring back at him.

LIEUTENANT COLONEL CHARLES WALTER BLACKALL

3rd Battalion The Buffs.
4th Battalion South Staffordshire Regiment.
Born: 1876. Folkestone.
Killed: 25th March 1918. Aged 42 years.
Arras Memorial to the Missing, Faubourg D'Amiens Cemetery, Arras, France.

Charles Blackall served in the 3rd Battalion The Buffs between 1900 and 1908 and fought with them during the South African Campaign. He retired from the Army in 1911 and spent the next three years in the theatrical world. In 1914 he returned from America and rejoined his old Regiment at the outbreak of War.

Early in 1915 Blackall was with the 1st Battalion Royal Welch Fusiliers, attached to The Buffs, and his poems in *Songs from the Trenches* describe some of the discomforts and hardships suffered by the troops in the winter of 1914-15. In his preface Blackall said, " I may mention that all the incidents described in this little volume are either facts or founded on fact."

Blackall's poem, 'W.G.C.G.' is dedicated to W.G. Gladstone's grandson, who was killed in action on 13th April 1915, serving with the Royal Welch Fusiliers.

W.G.C.G.

Possessor of an honoured name,
Right nobly he upheld the same.
Now on the Roll of England's fame
    His name is writ.

Among his gifts the magic wand
Of influence he had command,
Yet scorned its use, and served his land
    With British grit.

His stay with us was all too brief,
Too quickly came his "next relief";
Yet One above, Who knows our grief,
    Had thought it best.

Though sadly short his life's brief span,
Of this be truly sure we can:
A very gallant gentleman
    Now takes his rest.

"ATTACK!"

You are standing watch in hand,
All waiting the command,
While your guns have got their trenches fairly set.
When they lengthen up the range,
You feel a trifle strange
As you clamber up the sand-bag parapet.

It's a case of do or die -
Still, you rather wonder why
Your mate drops down beside you with a screech;
But you're very soon aware,
When a bullet parts your hair,
That HE's not the only pebble on the beach.

It's each man for himself,
For your Captain's on the shelf,
And you don't know if he's wounded or he's dead.
So never count the cost,
Of your comrades who are lost,
But keep the line on forging straight ahead.

The high-explosive shell
Has blown their wire to hell,
And their trench is like a muddy, bloody drain.
They are bolting left and right,
And the few that stay to fight -
Well, not many see their Fatherland again!

But there's one cove that you've missed,
And he cops you in the wrist
As you're stooping down to help a wounded chum.
Though you're feeling mighty faint,
As you're not a blooming saint,
You blow his blasted brains to kingdom come!

You've done your little job,
And you drop down with a sob,
For you're feeling half a man and half a wreck.
And you say a little prayer -
Which for you is rather rare -
For you got it in the arm, and not the neck.

When the evening shadows fall,
You do your best to crawl,
Till the stretcher-bearers find you in a creek.
Then you feel as right as rain,
And forget the aching pain,
For you'll see Old England's shores within a week.

A NIGHT OF HORROR

I heard a shell come sailing,
Come sailing o'er to me;
I looked around for cover,
No cover could I see.
I flung myself face downwards
Upon my manly chest,
And in a six-inch puddle
Of slime I came to rest.

Nearer and yet still nearer
That paralysing sound
Came whimpering towards me.
With fear my limbs were bound,
My courage long had left me,
I lay like one accurs't,
And still that awful wailing!
When would the damned thing burst?

My nerves were strained to breaking,
My senses seemed afloat,
The suffocating mud and slime
Were trickling down my throat.
With fingers crooked like talons,
I dug as one distraught.
Never a man fought harder
For life than I then fought.

"Give me a minute longer!"
I prayed, and dug again.
The sky with shells seemed teeming,
To my disordered brain.
Too late! The wail had changed to
A rushing, mighty shriek.
My end was nigh upon me,
I lay with blenchèd cheek.

An icy hand now gripped me,
I knew my hour had come.
I tried to cry for succour,
My parchèd lips were dumb.
A rending crash! Ah, Heavens!
I woke! Upon the floor.
A moke was softly braying
Outside the billet door!

THEIR DUG-OUT

The Company Sergeant-Major
And the Company Q.M.S.
Have the snuggest little dug-out
And a most superior mess.
And if anything your needing,
It's always to be found
In their handy little, sandy little dug-out underground.

If you're visiting your sentries,
And the night is wet and cold;
If you're feeling rather fed up,
And just a trifle old,
You'll find a drop of something hot,
To finish up your round,
In their rummy little, hummy little dug-out underground.

You suddenly get orders
That you're going to be relieved.
Your Sergeant-Major's missing,
And you feel distinctly grieved.
"Hi, you! Where's the Sergeant-Major?"

"Well, sir, judging by the sound,
In his dozy little, cosy little dug-out underground."

All's quiet in the trenches,
And you're standing idly by,
When you see a Minnehaha
Come sailing through the sky.
Valour? Discretion has it:
And you're, with a blithesome bound,
In their funky little, bunky little dug-out underground.

You get an urgent "memo"
"Render a return of tools."
No one seems to know the numbers,
So you curse them all for fools.
But you bet your Q.M.S. is,
For a penny to a pound,
In his snuggy little, fuggy little dug-out underground.

They're a brace of rare good sportsmen,
So give them each their due.
You'd do your damnedest for them,
And they'd do the same for you.
So I wish them back to England,
With a comfy little wound,
From their frowsy little, lousy little dug-out underground.

From October 1917, Blackall served with the 11th Battalion Cheshire Regiment, and took over command of the 4th Battalion South Staffordshire Regiment at Lagnicourt on 11th December, 1917. The German Spring offensive opened on 21st March 1918 and the Battalion marched to Fremicourt, near Bapaume. The Battalion Diary records:

6 pm 24th March. Took up position in trench west of Bapaume-Arras road.

Charles Blackall was killed the following morning.

PRIVATE ISAAC ROSENBERG

12th Battalion Suffolk Regiment.
11th Battalion King's Own Royal Lancaster Regiment.
1st Battalion King's Own Royal Lancaster Regiment.
Born: 25th November 1890. Bristol.
Educated: Baker Street Board School, Stepney.
          Birkbeck College School of Art.
          Slade School of Art.
Killed: 1st April 1918.   Aged 27 years.
Bailleul Road East Cemetery, St. Laurent-Blangy, France.

    Isaac Rosenberg's parents immigrated from Lithuania after the birth of their first child in 1885. His father, Barnett, came from a 'family of landowners, scholars and rabbis' and although Barnett Rosenberg had been a student in Lithuania, after he arrived in England he chose to become a pedlar. He taught himself to read, write and speak English, studied and wrote Hebrew and Yiddish poetry, a love he shared with his poet son and which greatly influenced Isaac's work.

    Isaac Rosenberg was born in a slum area of Bristol; he was one of twins but the other baby died at birth. When Rosenberg was seven the family moved to a one room apartment behind a rag and bone shop in Stepney, in the east end of London. Although he became less orthodox as he grew older, Rosenberg was brought up in the Jewish faith.

    From an early age Rosenberg sketched and wrote poetry. He left school in 1904 at the age of fourteen and was apprenticed to a firm of engravers continuing his poetry writing and drawing in the evenings after a long day at work. Between 1907 and 1909 he attended evening classes in painting at Birkbeck College, London, where his talent was appreciated and he won three prizes during his time there.

    In 1910 Rosenberg met a middle aged school mistress, Miss Winifreda Seaton who encouraged him, criticised his poems and recommended books to read. He continued to correspond with her until his death. In some of his letters to Miss Seaton he refers to his poor background and lack of education:

    ... It is horrible to think that all these hours, when my days are full of vigour and my hands and soul craving for self-expression, I am bound, chained to this fiendish mangling-machine, without hope and almost desire of deliverance, and the days of youth go by... I really would like to take up painting seriously; I think I might do something at that; but poetry - I despair of ever writing excellent poetry. I can't look at things in the simple, large way that great poets do. My mind is so cramped and dulled and fevered, there is no consistency of purpose, no oneness of aim; the very fibres are torn apart, and application deadened by the fiendish persistence of the coil of circumstance.

During 1911 Rosenberg met a group of young, intellectual Jewish men who came from the same poor background and area as himself. Joseph Leftwich, John Rodker, Samuel Winsten, Mark Gertler and David Bomberg shared a passionate love of art and literature, formed a close circle of friendship and became known as the Whitechapel Group. In October 1911, sponsored by wealthy patrons, Rosenberg enrolled at the Slade School of Art and during his two years there he continued writing poetry, although he confided to Laurence Binyon, "I find writing interferes with drawing a good deal and is far more exhausting." He met influential writers and intellectuals, including T.E. Hulme (qv) and Edward Marsh; the latter bought one of his paintings. In 1912 Rosenberg had a pamphlet of his poems *Night and Day* printed at his own expense.

Short in stature and physically frail Rosenberg's health deteriorated during 1913, and the following June, as he was suffering from a lung complaint, the Jewish Education Aid Society paid for his passage by sea for a holiday with his sister in South Africa. The month before he sailed he exhibited at the Whitechapel Art Gallery Exhibition of Twentieth Century Artists.

In Capetown Rosenberg gave a series of lectures on modern art and had a few poems and articles published. On 8th August 1914 when he heard the news that War had been declared he wrote to Marsh "I despise war and hate war." He returned to England in March 1915.

In June 1915 Rosenberg was "thinking of enlisting if they will have me, though it is against all my principles of justice." Three months later he had changed his mind. "I feel about it that more men means more war, - besides the immorality of joining with no patriotic convictions." However, Rosenberg finally enlisted in the Bantam Regiment of the 12th Suffolks. "I wanted to join the RAMC as the idea of killing upsets me a bit, but I was too small. The only regiment my build allowed was the Bantams."

In October he wrote from the Depot at Bury St. Edmonds:

...I have to eat out of a basin together with some horribly smelling scavenger who spits and sneezes into it etc... Besides, my being a Jew makes it bad amongst these wretches...

THE JEW

Moses, from whose loins I sprung,
Lit by a lamp in his blood
Ten immutable rules, a moon
For mutable lampless men.

The blonde, the bronze, the ruddy,
With the same heaving blood,
Keep tide to the moon of Moses,
Then why do they sneer at me?

In December 1915 Rosenberg wrote to Marsh "Nothing can justify war. I suppose we must all fight to get the trouble over." He continued to find life in the Army "unbearable" and he hated everything about it. He felt isolated and vulnerable because of his faith, class, and artistic temperament. He was bullied and victimised and frequently under punishment.

... Every other person is a thief, and in the end you become one yourself, when you see all your most essential belongings go, which you must replace somehow. I also got into trouble here the first day. It's not worth while detailing what happened and exposing how ridiculous, idiotic, and meaningless the Army is, and its dreadful bullyisms, and what puny minds control it...

In the Spring of 1916 Rosenberg was transferred to the 11th Battalion King's Own Royal Lancaster Regiment, part of the 40th Division, and in June he arrived in France and was stationed near Béthune. He wrote to Miss Seaton:

We made straight for the trenches, but we've had vile weather, and I've been wet through for four days and nights. I lost all my socks and things before I left England, and hadn't the chance to make it up again, so I've been in trouble, particularly with bad heels; you can't have the slightest conception of what such an apparently trivial thing means. We've had shells bursting two yards off, bullets whizzing all over the show, but all you are aware of is the agony of your heels...

During the summer Rosenberg wrote to John Rodker's wife, Sonia, and enclosed 'In the Trenches', with the comment, "here's a little poem, a bit commonplace I'm afraid."

IN THE TRENCHES

I snatched two poppies
From the parapet's ledge,
Two bright red poppies
That winked on the ledge.
Behind my ear
I stuck one through,
One blood red poppy
I gave to you.

The sandbags narrowed
And screwed out our jest,
And tore the red poppy
You had on your breast...
Down - a shell - O! Christ,
I am choked... safe... dust blind, I
See trench floor poppies
Strewn. Smashed you lie.

During July and August 1916 Rosenberg worked at a desk in the 40th Division Salvage Office where he had some spare time to think about the future.

My plan is to teach drawing at a school a few days in the week, which leaves plenty of leisure to write, as I am convinced I am more deep and true as a poet than painter...

On 4th August he wrote to Edward Marsh "enclosing a poem I wrote in the trenches, which is surely as simple as ordinary talk. You might object to the second line as vague, but that was the best way I could express the sense of dawn."

BREAK OF DAY IN THE TRENCHES

The darkness crumbles away.
It is the same old druid Time as ever,
Only a live thing leaps my hand,

A queer sardonic rat,
As I pull the parapet's poppy
To stick behind my ear.
Droll rat, they would shoot you if they knew
Your cosmopolitan sympathies.
Now you have touched this English hand
You will do the same to a German
Soon, no doubt, if it be your pleasure
To cross the sleeping green between.
It seems you inwardly grin as you pass
Strong eyes, fine limbs, haughty athletes,
Less chanced than you for life,
Bonds to the whims of murder,
Sprawled in the bowels of the earth,
The torn fields of France.
What do you see in our eyes
At the shrieking iron and flame
Hurled through still heavens?
What quaver - what heart aghast?
Poppies whose roots are in man's veins
Drop, and are ever dropping;
But mine in my ear is safe -
Just a little white with the dust.

Towards the end of August 1916, Rosenberg rejoined his Platoon in the trenches and told Marsh "I have been forbidden to send poems home, as the censor won't be bothered with going through such rubbish..." A few weeks later he wrote to Laurence Binyon:

> ...Winter has found its way into the trenches at last...but is not the least of the horrors of war. I am determined that this war, with all its powers for devastation, shall not master my poeting; that is, if I am lucky enough to come through all right. I will not leave a corner of my consciousness covered up, but saturate myself with the strange and extraordinary new conditions of this life, and it will all refine itself into poetry later on...

With the 40th Division Rosenberg was gradually moving south towards the Somme. In November 1916 his Regiment was in the Hébuterne sector, north of Bapaume. After Christmas they moved again and were stationed between Bouchavesnes and Rancourt, south of Bapaume. The conditions were appalling after six months of fighting and terrible weather. The whole area consisted of "a mass of shellholes; of a general sea of mud; of lesser lakes and lagoons of icy water. Trenches did not exist, except for short lengths on higher ground; of communication trenches there was none..."

Always troubled by weak lungs Rosenberg became ill early in January 1917. He was assigned to a Works Battalion behind the lines and wrote to Marsh on the 18th:

...But though this work does not entail half the hardships of the trenches, the winter and the conditions naturally tells on me, having once suffered from weak lungs, as you know. I have been in the trenches most of the 8 months I've been here, and the continual damp and exposure is whispering to my old friend consumption...

February 8th, 1917 ...I've sketched an amusing little thing called 'the louse hunt', and am trying to write one as well...

LOUSE HUNTING

Nudes - stark and glistening,
Yelling in lurid glee. Grinning faces
And raging limbs
Whirl over the floor one fire.
For a shirt verminously busy
Yon soldier tore from his throat, with oaths
Godhead might shrink at, but not the lice.
And soon the shirt was aflare
Over the candle he'd lit while we lay.

Then we all sprang up and stript
To hunt the verminous brood.
Soon like a demons' pantomime
The place was raging.
See the silhouettes agape,
See the gibbering shadows
Mixed with the battled arms on the wall.
See gargantuan hooked fingers
Pluck in supreme flesh
To smutch supreme littleness.
See the merry limbs in hot Highland fling
Because some wizard vermin
Charmed from the quiet this revel

When our ears were half lulled
By the dark music
Blown from Sleep's trumpet.

Towards the end of February Rosenberg moved from the Works Battalion and was attached to a Trench Mortar Battery for a few weeks. After another medical examination he was passed fit and transferred again to 229 Field Company, Royal Engineers, attached to his Regiment.

The continual transfers, being passed from one unit to another because he did not fit in, were considered 'a symptom of his unsoldierliness' by Captain Frank Waley, the O.C. of the Trench Mortar Battery. The bitter weather continued through the winter months. At the end of March the Division was withdrawn from the front line to join the Pioneers building and repairing railways and roads. The following month the Division was moved forward to Gouzeaucourt north east of Cambrai and on 21st April the 11th King's Own Royal Lancaster Regiment attacked the village of Beaucamp which they gained after heavy fighting and severe losses. On 8th May Rosenberg wrote a happier letter to Marsh:

We are camping in the woods now and living great. My feet are almost healed now and my list of complaints has dwindled down to almost invisibility. I've written some lines suggested by going out wiring, or rather carrying wire up the line on limbers and running over dead bodies lying about...

DEAD MAN'S DUMP

The plunging limbers over the shattered track
Racketed with their rusty freight,
Stuck out like many crowns of thorns,
And the rusty stakes like sceptres old
To stay the flood of brutish men
Upon our brothers dear.

The wheels lurched over sprawled dead
But pained them not, though their bones crunched,
Their shut mouths made no moan,
They lie there huddled, friend and foeman,
Man born of man, and born of woman,
And shells go crying over them
From night till night and now.

Earth has waited for them
All the time of their growth
Fretting for their decay:
Now she has them at last!
In the strength of their strength
Suspended - stopped and held.

What fierce imaginings their dark souls lit
Earth! have they gone into you?
Somewhere they must have gone,
And flung on your hard back
Is their souls' sack,
Emptied of God-ancestralled essences.
Who hurled them out? Who hurled?

None saw their spirits' shadow shake the grass,
Or stood aside for the half used life to pass
Out of those doomed nostrils and the doomed mouth,
When the swift iron burning bee
Drained the wild honey of their youth.

What of us, who flung on the shrieking pyre,
Walk, our usual thoughts untouched,
Our lucky limbs as on ichor fed,
Immortal seeming ever?
Perhaps when the flames beat loud on us,
A fear may choke in our veins
And the startled blood may stop.

The air is loud with death,
The dark air spurts with fire
The explosions ceaseless are.
Timelessly now, some minutes past,
These dead strode time with vigorous life,
Till the shrapnel called 'an end!'
But not to all. In bleeding pangs
Some borne on stretchers dreamed of home,
Dear things, war-blotted from their hearts.

A man's brains splattered on
A stretcher-bearer's face;
His shook shoulders slipped their load,

But when they bent to look again
The drowning soul was sunk too deep
For human tenderness.

They left this dead with the older dead,
Stretched at the cross roads.
Burnt black by strange decay,
Their sinister faces lie
The lid over each eye,
The grass and coloured clay
More motion have than they,
Joined to the great sunk silences.

Here is one not long dead;
His dark hearing caught our far wheels,
And the choked soul stretched weak hands
To reach the living word the far wheels said,
The blood-dazed intelligence beating for light,
Crying through the suspense of the far torturing wheels
Swift for the end to break,
Or the wheels to break,
Cried as the tide of the world broke over his sight.

Will they come? Will they ever come?
Even as the mixed hoofs of the mules,
The quivering-bellied mules,
And the rushing wheels all mixed
With his tortured upturned sight,
So we crashed round the bend,
We heard his weak scream,
We heard his very last sound,
And our wheels grazed his dead face.

At the end of May 1917 the Regiment moved behind the lines into reserve but Rosenberg had been sent back to the R.E. unit. He was again working hard physically loading huge rolls of barbed wire on to wagons which were then taken up to the lines each night.
During the summer Rosenberg wrote the following poem:

RETURNING, WE HEAR THE LARKS

Sombre the night is.
And though we have our lives, we know
What sinister threat lurks there.

Dragging these anguished limbs, we only know
This poison-blasted track opens on our camp -
On a little safe sleep.

But hark! joy - joy - strange joy.
Lo! heights of night ringing with unseen larks.
Music showering our upturned list'ning faces.

Death could drop from the dark
As easily as song -
But song only dropped,
Like a blind man's dreams on the sand
By dangerous tides,
Like a girl's dark hair for she dreams no ruin lies there,
Or her kisses where a serpent hides.

After fourteen months in France Rosenberg was given ten days leave at the end of September 1917, and then rejoined his Regiment in the trenches. The men worked in torrential rain and two weeks after his return Rosenberg collapsed with influenza. He spent the next two months in hospital and by the time he was discharged in mid December and rejoined the Battalion at Achicourt, south west of Arras, he had written all but one of his trench poems. Once back in the trenches in the La Fontaine region, near Bullecourt, he had little time or energy to write and he became increasingly depressed. On 26th January 1918 he wrote to Marsh:

... I am back in the trenches which are terrible now. We spend most of our time pulling each other out of the mud. I am not fit at all now and am more in the way than any use. You see I appear in excellent health and a doctor will make no distinction between health and strength. I am not strong...

At the beginning of February Rosenberg was one of two hundred soldiers transferred to the 1st Battalion at Bernaville where they were training. He wrote to Miss Seaton on the 14th:

We had a rough time in the trenches with the mud, but now we're out for a bit of a rest, and I will try and write longer letters. You must know by now what a rest behind the line means. I can call the evenings - that is, from tea to lights out - my own; but there is no chance whatever for seclusion or any hope of writing poetry now. Sometimes I give way and am appalled at the devastation this life seems to have made in my nature. It seems to have blunted me. I seem to be powerless to compel my will to any direction, and all I do is without energy and interest.

Rosenberg wrote to Gordon Bottomley in February saying that since he left hospital "all the poetry has gone quite out of me." On 7th March 1918, he wrote to Bottomley again:

I believe our interlude is nearly over, and we may go up the line any moment now, so I answer your letter straightaway. If only this war were over our eyes would not be on death so much: it seems to underlie even our underthoughts. Yet when I have been so near to it as anybody could be, the idea has never crossed my mind, certainly not so much as when some lying doctor told me I had consumption. I like to think of myself as a poet; so what you say, though I know it to be extravagant, gives me immense pleasure.

At the beginning of March the Battalion, as part of the 3rd Army, moved to Arras for training; on the 19th they were sent into the front line Greenland Hill/Fampoux section near Arras. On the 21st March the great German Spring offensive was launched. After three days fighting the Battalion was relieved and sent back as Brigade reserve to Blangy. On the 28th the Germans again attacked and broke through the front line. Rosenberg's Battalion, in reserve trenches, found itself holding the new front line and lost seventy men. For a further three days they remained in the trenches under heavy shell fire and constant threat of attack. Patrols were sent out each night over the exposed and cratered ground to repair wire and report on enemy activity. When the attack eased in the early hours of All Fool's Day, the few survivors in Rosenberg's Company were ordered further back for a brief respite. The circumstances surrounding Rosenberg's death are not clear. Perhaps he had been sent out on patrol, or he may have volunteered to stay in the front line as a Jewish soldier in his Battalion told his family. His body was never found and even now there is doubt as to where he was finally buried.

A few days later Edward Marsh received a letter, dated 28th March and postmarked 2nd April. "...I wanted to write a battle song for the Judaens but can think of nothing strong and wonderful enough yet. Here's just a slight thing..."

THROUGH THESE PALE COLD DAYS

Through these pale cold days
What dark faces burn
Out of three thousand years,
And their wild eyes yearn,

While underneath their brows
Like waifs their spirits grope
For the pools of Hebron again -
For Lebanon's summer slope.

They leave these blond still days
In dust behind their tread
They see with living eyes
How long they have been dead.

LIEUTENANT JOHN BROWN M.C.

9th Battalion Royal Scots.

9th Battalion Seaforth Highlanders (Pioneers).

Born: 30th August 1891. Fife, Scotland.

Educated: Merchiston Castle School.

Balliol College, Oxford.

Killed: 11th April 1918. Aged 26 years.

Voormezeele Enclosure No. 3, Belgium.

John Brown enlisted in September 1914 in the 9th Battalion Royal Scots, and went to Ypres at the end of February 1915. He wrote an account in a letter home of the weeks in 'A' Company between February and April 1915:

... At Abeele we entered our first French estaminet, and felt that it wasn't such a bad war. It was a Sunday. Next day we marched a mile to our billets in a farmhouse. We remained there ingloriously about a week, making fascines and listening to the thunder of the guns. There is no sound so depressing as heavy gunfire in the distance. Then we heard to our annoyance, after falling in with all our parcels hastily slung around us, that 'B' Company, not 'A', were to be the first to go up. But our turn came, and after a weary march we arrived at a small wood with huts in it about a mile from Dickebusch, where we were to stay. 'B' Company had been up in the firing line on fatigues, but 'A' Company was the first to go into the trenches. As it was growing dark we fell in, loaded and slung our rifles, and marched off in file. It is not a cheering experience going up to the trenches for the first time. Every stray bullet that whistles harmlessly past seems to be specially meant for you, and every star-shell seems to be revealing you to some machine gun. There are bursts of rifle and machine-gun fire. All round us - for Dickebusch was part of the Ypres Salient - rose the German star-shells. Our progress was like a goods-train shunting. Suddenly the men in front stop, then those behind bump into them, and no sooner has this happened than the head of the column races on again. We got to the brasserie, the dumping station, where guides from the 2nd Camerons, with whom we were to go in, took us off in batches. When the first star-shell went up many of us hastily fell down as we had practised. But noticing that the guides stood still we gave up the practice. We filed along, and, before we realised where we were, found ourselves falling into a pool, which was the door of the trench we were to hold. There we saw mud-caked figures in balmorals and gum boots, the 2nd Camerons. The trench was a breastwork with one dugout for the officer. No one was allowed to sleep at night, so we spent our time on sentry or fatigues. We will always remember our reception by the Camerons - quite little men, to whom war was a trade, not an experience. Orders had come that we were to show more activity, so at four o'clock we had our first experience of putting our heads over the parapet and pumping rapid at the Germans, until our bolts jammed, who replied with two shrapnel, which made some of us bob our heads down. But we summoned up our courage and carried on feeling very brave. I think shrapnel is one of the things in war one can never teach oneself to have a friendly feeling for. Like the horse who was fed on sawdust, one dies before one becomes used to it. We were bucked that the Bosche made no return to our little morning greeting, and settled down to breakfast. A lark rose behind our trench. We spent our day looking at intervals at the Germans' trench through a periscope, and wondering if the Germans would suddenly sally forth. It takes one long to learn that the art of modern war is to avoid fighting at any cost. In front of the trench dead Frenchmen were lying in lines. The German trenches were in front of a wood. In the afternoon we repeated our dose of rapid, and when we had finished our artillery took up the good work, sending their shells whistling over our parapet to land in the German trench. We looked over the parapet and enjoyed our first and for a long time our last sight of the strafing of the Bosches. Then there was heavy gun fire on the left, and then we heard cheering and rifle fire. We were attacking Hill 60. We were only in for 24 hours, and were to be relieved that night. But sleep kept seizing upon us, as we had been too excited to sleep all day, and at night it was forbidden. Then we got back, marched along the road enlivened by stray bullets, and so back to our huts at Dickebusch.

The next evening, when we were thinking of a good night's sleep, the attack on St. Eloi started, and we stood to all night. It was our first experience of a great bombardment - mad that we were being shelled, but we expected at any moment to fall in and march up. There were few of us who were longing to go up like our corporal, who had been in South Africa, but in time we too got the feeling that we mustn't be left out when something was doing. We went up to dig near the brasserie, and our practice on the Braids stood us in such good stead that we astonished the engineer officer. Result, we were sent up night after night to dig trenches in the gap at St. Eloi.

The road up to St. Eloi had one great advantage over that up to the brasserie, that till we were near Voormezeele there were never stray bullets to worry us. But Voormezeele was not a cheering spot. Bullets kept whacking against the walls of the houses. The whole of the middle of the church had been blown away. We went down beside a canal, then on past a deserted bus, and up into the area where bullets cracked amd we had to dig our trench along a hedge. Night after night we went up laden with barbed wire stops and coils of wire, and worked while the quiet moon and stars watched us, and the bullets cracked around. It was a beautiful sight when we were on the morning shift, and saw the young moon blushing red as she retired to rest. One gets a very friendly feeling for the gentle moon. The weather had improved, and by day we lay about and watched the aeroplanes being shelled. At intervals we were organised into parties of scavengers to clean the camp. It was one of the most tiring times we had, but one evening we fell in and trekked wearily but thankfully back to billets in a farm near Poperinghe, Westoutre. There we spent three days doing nothing but rest. We bought pork chops, and had our first taste of tea with cigarette flavouring.

From our quarters in the barn we marched to Ypres. When we first arrived at Ypres it was very gay. The square in front of the Cloth Hall was thronged with British and French troops. All the shops were open, some of them even selling pictures of the first bombardment. One large church - I have forgotten its name - had one enormous shell-hole through the roof. Otherwise it was untouched. We were billeted in a convent. At night we went out across the moat to the south, and dug in comparative comfort and safety. The gate was a beautiful sight, with the towers and moat, when the moon was up, throwing the shadows of the trees on the water. The only incident that cast a shadow over some of us was that we were chosen as bombers. We tried to joke about it, and say that we would get plenty of elbow-room in the trenches, but we were very gloomy for a few days. We drew up a set of hints to young bombers:

1. Always leave the detonators behind - a bomb without a detonator is quite harmless.

2. Never take the safety pin out before you throw the bomb. This ensures that it will not burst if you strike the trench. The Germans will probably throw it back, but it is unlikely it will fall in your part of the trench.

3. Always have a fuse a foot long.

At about this time Brown wrote a poem and another letter home which continued the account of the Battalion's activities during April 1915:

> Ye seeds of sorrow that lie hidden deep
> In darkness 'neath the earth of my sad heart,
> Why does not life within your hard husks leap?
> Why do ye lie so cold and still apart?

Fear not that when ye shoot into the light
I'll tear ye up ere ye have time to flower,
For I will tend and keep ye free from blight,
And warm you with my smiles; til one soft hour

Will see your buds break into flowers of mirth,
Tossing before the dancing April wind,
That blows over my soul's fresh turned earth,
While pleasant Spring encompasseth my mind.

On the 4th April the little girls kept saying 'tranches', and in the evening we marched out through the Menin Gate to the firing line again. We took over dugouts from the French in Sanctuary Wood. They were really more like huts than dugouts, and very comfortable. On the 7th we moved a mile east to Glencorse Wood. Here the dugouts were long pits about 5 feet wide, 4 deep, and 20 long, covered with branches and a little earth. One had the feeling that once one got in one would never get out again. It was not pleasant to come back at night from some fatigue when the rest had gone to bed, and crawl over their bodies to one's place, to be awakened in a few hours to stand to.

On the 10th we relieved 'C' and 'D'. Our route was over the open. The trench we had was in the middle of a wood. Between us and the German trenches the trees had almost all been destroyed. On our right was a cottage, and lying out in front an old cart. The Germans opposite were fairly active. While we were standing to we used to see their fires rising. Then when they had had a good meal they amused themselves by knocking down the top of the parapet on our food. There were few traverses in the trenches, and it was enfiladed to some extent by snipers. In the evening, when the shells were passing over to Ypres, we used to look back and see the towers and spires of Ypres grey against the setting sun... On the 13th the 9th Argylls relieved us... About five o'clock, utterly done, we came to the huts at Vlamertinghe on the other side of Ypres. After four days we moved up again...

On the afternoon of the 22nd April some of us were in Vlamertinghe shopping, buying wine, tins of fruit, and some chops. The Canadian Artillery passed through going up to Ypres. It was a fine sight. We had just come back when suddenly a terrific bombardment began. There is nothing more depressing than the boom of a bombardment when you are waiting to go into it. We stood to. 'D' Company were up on a fatigue. Then at 9.30 we got the word to fall in. We knew we were in for something and abandoned most of our parcels in the dark huts, for all lights were put out. We took the railway. All along it we met old women with bundles flying from Ypres. In front was the glare of the burning city and the thunder of the guns. Then we came on to the main road between Vlamertinghe and Ypres. It was full of troops moving up. There were some cavalry beside us who called out to us: 'Give them hell'. We wondered vaguely how we would do it. Down a side road we went, and lay down in some fields. After an hour or two we moved to Ypres, passing through at a weary double, now and then turning to look at the Cathedral and Cloth Hall. A few weeks ago the shops were open, the square crowded with the bright uniforms of the French; now it was deserted, and sought only by shells, and the quarter where we were billeted was in flames.

Over the Menin Bridge we went, and just as we were getting rather nervous at being in the open when dawn broke, we reached Potijze Wood, where we came across a battery that had moved three times during the night, and lay down. For some time we lay and watched troops filing in and out. The battery was doggedly shelling just beside us. At ten we fell in, moved out, and struck the main road in double file. We had only time to think that now we were in for it when the enemy began to shell us, and a machine gun also turned its attention to us. In front walked the tall figure of the C.O., then came 'A' Company. We hurriedly made the shelter of a small village, Wieltje. In the middle was an open space where there was a road, and the Germans were shelling the gap with shrapnel. We doubled across in small parties, wondering if we would suddenly be smitten down. Then we formed up again, and moved on more carefully, turned to the left, and lay down along a small dip with some houses at the end. We did not know then, but that was St. Julien. Here we listened for the sound of our own shells, but had always to confess they were German. We lay there for some time. We could stretch out our hands, and pick up spent shrapnels. We will always remember two sights. One was a signaller coming crouching along like a shot rabbit, the other the figure of a Lieutenant swanking along as if he were in Princes Street.

After lying some time we got the order to move back. We went in file well spaced out, taking advantage of all cover. We passed dead horses and empty shell-cases where a battery had been in action. In the air were large white clouds formed by the heavy shrapnel. Farms were in flames, and 'coal-boxes' burst, sending their smoke towering up like a huge heavy foliaged tree. We passed through Wieltje, and came close to Potijze, outside which we saw a battalion digging themselves in. We hoped we were going to rest then. We had left 'B' Company at Wieltje, though we did not know it, where they lined a hedge, and advanced soon after. We were on their left. Three small guns were behind supporting us. On our left were the Duke of Cornwall's Light Infantry.

We lined a hedge, and were ordered to dig ourselves in. Some of us managed to get some biscuits from a tin lying behind the hedge.

Others cleaned their rifle bolts. In about five minutes we were ordered to put up our tools, and file round the hedge. As soon as we got round we began to advance at the double in open order. Bullets seemed to cover all the ground by our feet. We advanced by short rushes. For the first part of a rush one feels very brave and happy, for the last, dead tired. We did not fire a shot, but advanced silently and swiftly amid the noise around us, up and on as hard as we could go, then down, a panting rest, and on again. Weariness had left us, the bullets were thick about our feet. After advancing over several fields we lay down behind a hedge. On our right was a hedge, and just over it the Germans dropped six 'coal-boxes'. We could feel the ground shaking beneath us as we lay. This must have been to cover the German retreat, for soon their fire ceased, and we walked forward about 100 yards, and lay down on a road. We had driven the Germans back by sheer determination, without firing a shot and practically unsupported by artillery. We had not even fixed our bayonets. One South African came up to me and said: "A most disappointing finish."

After lying unmolested on the road, when dusk came on we moved along to the left past the position the Duke of Cornwall's Light Infantry had held. There, wounded were lying out calling for stretcher-bearers - a horrible sound. Then we were ordered to dig ourselves in at right angles to our former position. As we would certainly be enfiladed, we put all our energy into it. No sooner had we finished and lain down in our scoops than we again got orders to move, and trudged back again. About two hours before dawn we halted near Shell Trap farm, sent out a covering party in front, and proceeded to work on a most elaborate trench, but after an hour of rather heartless work we were ordered to dig in any way we could, and, just before dawn, got under cover. At dawn rifle fire broke out again, but we were left alone. We had little food, and some no water. All day we worked on. Around us were burning farms, clouds of shrapnel smoke in the air, and 'coal-boxes' sending up towering trees of smoke. At dust, just as we were beginning to get our trench into shape, we were relieved by 'B' Company, and moved to some breast-works behind a hedge. It rained all day. 'Coal-boxes' came gurgling over us, and wounded were passing all day. In front were some cows. Our trench faced west. That night rations came up, the first for three days, and we sent postcards home. In the morning we marched back to Potijze Wood. Here there was bully to be had for the picking up. We saw the Indians advance through the wood, and an English regiment filing back, some of them with German helmets on their bayonets. It was very pleasant lying in the shallow dugouts, with no fatigues and nothing to do but rest.

On 4th May the Battalion was in a new line of trenches at Hooge and on the 8th Lieutenant W.S.S. Lyon (qv) was killed. Towards the end of May the Battalion was in a position on the Ypres - Vlamertinghe Road. John Brown was severely wounded and sent to Leicester Hospital. He wrote a few untitled poems at this time.

> Arise, my heart, and dance,
> And laugh, my soul!
> The sun may look askance,
> And o'er the sky clouds roll.

> If a man's own soul is cold,
> No July sun can warm;
> If joy a man's heart hold
> No winter blast can harm.

> So walk the world with a springing pace,
> Breathe in the whistling wind,
> Till the red blood runs its riot race,
> And warms the ice-bound mind.

John Brown was commissioned in the 6th Battalion Seaforth Highlanders in August 1915 and joined the Battalion in trenches at Vimy Ridge ten months later. On 14th July 1916 from billets near Acq he wrote to Professor Toynbee, who had been his History Tutor at Balliol:

> ... I am out again with the 6th Seaforths and am enjoying myself down to the ground. We are in a most interesting part of the line. War as an officer is a picnic compared to war as a Tommy. I am sure you would have enjoyed yourself in the trenches. Anything may happen at any moment. The Boche is a most excellent entertainer, and always provides some sort of entertainment. We had a great time the other day playing hide-and-seek with Minnie of the fairy feet. She is not the sort of lady one would say to, 'Any time you're passing, drop in'. There seems to be some signs of the end now. I wonder what we will do then...

Between 16th and 26th July the Battalion was at Fricourt Wood and Bécordel-Bécourt and went into reserve in Mametz Wood on the 26th. On 24th July Brown wrote to his aunt:

> ... We are more or less out of it just now... I was in a Boche dugout and the first thing that greeted me was an enormous mirror. The old

Hun believes in being comfortable, though I expect he isn't very just now. I am at present labouring under the weight of a reputation for cheeriness and coolness which I live in daily fear of losing. I was three nights out on patrol lying on the top of a small crater between the lines, quite exciting, especially getting out, as the Boche had two very keen machine gunners. Also we became involved in one of our own schemes of indirect fire...

On 1st August the Battalion went into support trenches at Bazentin-le-Grand, Bazentin-le-Petit and Windmill Trench immediately behind High Wood. Parties went out at night to work on Seaforth Trench which was in advance of the front line. Between the 4th and 7th August the Battalion took over Black Watch Trench. Brown wrote another letter to his aunt on the 5th August:

... The Boche shrapnel makes clouds like great woolly bears and dogs. They bark quite like a live dog. It is a fine bracing place. I shall soon have been out two months... It has been very hot here. I very nearly had a blighty the other day. I was standing up and encouraging the men to come out of their trenches and dump some tools, with great energy, as I had no desire to stand long there, when something large dropped near. I felt its breath hot on me and fell with great speed into a trench, being smitten on the thigh, but the blood would not come. I left my tunic outside the dugout door the other day and it was smitten, so that I looked like a happy combination of officer and tramp, with the tramp predominating...

Towards the end of August, Brown was invalided home suffering from trench fever. Sometime during the year he had written another untitled poem:

> For weeks the rains of sorrow have soaked
> The wood in my heart's cold hearth;
> And the windows and doors of my soul are choked,
> And the sunbeams can find no path.
>
> And half-burnt matches are strewn around,
> That flamed and could not light
> The fire that I laid with care on the ground
> To warm life and make it bright.
>
> The sun of love alone can dry
> The sticks that will not burn:

No patent match that wealth can buy
Will give the light I yearn.

So I sit and shiver and wait for Spring,
While sad-voiced winds still roar,
Till April in her hands shall bring
Love's first beams to my door.

Brown returned to France again in January 1917 and joined the 7th Battalion Seaforth Highlanders in trenches at Blangy, outside Arras. On 9th April the Battalion captured the village of St. Laurent Blangy and nine days later, from billets at Duisans, Brown wrote a letter describing the Battle of Arras:

... When we moved up to the line there was a hell of a row, as we were moving through our guns in full blast. One battery in particular was belching out flame and nearly blew us away. We got up all right. Just before going over I went round with a bottle dishing out the rum, feeling more like a V.A.D. than anything on earth. I had just finished when it was time to go over. Every one, with the exception of a few who could hardly speak, were quite cheery, and we had a bit of a joke. I had the wind well up in case my watch had suddenly gone five minutes fast. I saw the other people going over, so walked out. The barrage was on the front line; we were within about 10 yards of it. A man on my right was hit and I kept shouting to the men to keep back. Wind well up in case I should get hit. My platoon sergeant ran up and asked me how long the barrage was going to be on the front line. I took out my watch and stood looking at it with the shells bursting in a line of foam in front. It was a queer sight - the lines of waiting men standing slightly bent forward, the white of the bursting shells, and the queer light of early morning. Then the barrage lifted, and I shouted and waved my rifle and we went in. To my great joy there was no one there. But a pale flare went up on the left and a machine gun started. But we were well behind. We pushed on. I had a pain in the small of my back. By this time the most of my platoon had disappeared off to the left. I went on, and saw a cellar with a window and door. I looked in, saw two Boche running out at the back. I shot one and missed the other, and was feeling terrifically bucked when one had a shot at me. So, wind well up, I fell flat, and seeing no one pushing on near, retreated rapidly. Then there was an extraordinary scene. The Boche got into a strong point at the top and began bombing. I tried to get some men to work round. My sergeant began sniping them. One of the stretcher-bearers was in a state of fury, flinging mud. It was at this moment that a man came up and asked me for an escort for prisoners. I was extremely peevish with him. I went off to try and get some men. When I got back the Boche were clearing out and a great crowd had collected, so I got on to where I was supposed to go and got into a shell-hole with a few men. That was the end of the excitement. I found my company commander behind me I am glad to say, and retired into a cellar with my sergeant to have some breakfast. A wounded Boche came up to us when we were in the shell-hole, badly wounded. When my sergeant was dressing him, the Boche kept patting him on the shoulder. We were I think the only lot who got our objectives up to time...

Brown was awarded the Military Cross. The citation read:

For conspicuous gallantry and resource when defending, with two platoons, an isolated post. Although wounded, he successfully held his trench for a day and a night with the enemy on both flanks in the same trench and repelled several counter attacks. His fearlessness and resource were most marked.

Brown was sent home to recuperate from the wounds and on 5th April 1918 he joined the 9th Battalion (Pioneers) Seaforth Highlanders at Vierstraat in Belgium. On 10th April the Battalion moved into Brigade Reserve at Piccadilly Farm. The following day, while holding a trench against the German advance near Wytschaete, John Brown was killed by a shot from a sniper.

While at Balliol in 1911 Brown wrote a poem based on the legend of Achilles, which he entered for the Newdigate Prize. It ended with the following verse:

> And thus the music of Achilles' life
> Burst from its prison, singing its sweet song
> Unheard but by the soul. Meanwhile the strife
> Of war rekindled round him; but its sound
> Sung him that love in life was ne'er so strong
> As love that passed, at death, laughing beneath the ground.

LIEUTENANT COLONEL JOHN EBENEZER STEWART M.C.

8th Battalion Border Regiment.

4th Battalion South Staffordshire Regiment.

Born: 1889. Coatbridge, near Glasgow.

Educated: Glasgow University.

Killed: 26th April 1918. Aged 29 years.

Tyne Cot Memorial to the Missing, Passchendaele, Belgium.

After he left University John Stewart became a teacher at Langloan School, Coatbridge. He enlisted as a Private in the Highland Light Infantry at the outbreak of the War; two months later he was commissioned in the 8th Battalion the Border Regiment. The Battalion arrived in France at the end of September 1915 and was in and out of the trenches at Ploegsteert from the beginning of October until January 1916 and behind the lines at Strazeele during February.

BEGINNINGS

The dismal rain was dripping from the peak of
    the Colonel's cap,
The waterproof sheets were streaming, but who
    of us cared a rap?
The dreary dark closed round us, but blithe we
    took the trail
And trudged the pavé highway from
    Hazebrouck to Strazeele.

From Hazebrouck to Strazeele,
Le Bizet through Nieppe,
And on to Ploegsteert Village
Is only just a step;
Where the long battle-line
Curves round the battered wood,
We set our faces to the foe,
And made our promise good.

Short days of wintry weather, long nights of rain
    and cold,

We fought the slithering parapets and stalked the
    foeman bold;
We dug and drained and builded a sector for a
    king -
And there were fewer of us when we marched
    out in the spring.

From Ploegsteert to La Creche
And back into Strazeele
It isn't much I grant you
To spin into a tale.
But now we have a story, -
It's bloody, but it's good -
And most we've done we learned to do
In front of Ploegsteert Wood.

On 2nd July 1916 the Battalion went to front line trenches south of Thiepval.

BEFORE ACTION

Over the down the road goes winding,
A ribbon of white in the corn -
The young, green corn. O, the joy of binding
The sheaves some harvest morn!

But we are called to another reaping,
A harvest that will not wait.
The sheaves will be green. O, the world of weeping
Of those without the gate!

For the road we go they may not travel,
Nor share our harvesting;
But watch and weep. O, to unravel
The riddle of this thing!

Yet over the down the white road leading
Calls; and who lags behind?
Stout are our hearts; but O, the bleeding
Of hearts we may not bind!

In August the Battalion was in front line trenches opposite Beaumont Hamel and at the beginning of October in dugouts in the

old German front-line at Ovillers. On 21st October Stewart
commanded 'D' Company during an attack on Regina Trench, the
longest German trench on the Western Front on Pozières Ridge.

By December 1916 the Battalion had returned to Ploegsteert;
Stewart was awarded the Military Cross in the New Year's Honours
of 1917 'for consistently good work' and was wounded on 14th
June 1917 during the Battle of Messines.

THE MESSINES ROAD
"An highway shall be there, and a way"

I
The road that runs up to Messines
Is double-locked with gates of fire,
Barred with high ramparts, and between
The unbridged river, and the wire.

None ever go up to Messines,
For Death lurks all about the town,
Death holds the vale as his demesne,
And only Death moves up and down.

II
Choked with wild weeds, and overgrown
With a rank grass, all torn and rent
By war's opposing engines, strewn
With debris from each day's event!

And in the dark the broken trees,
Whose arching boughs were once its shade,
Grim and distorted, ghostly ease
In groans their vexed souls and afraid.

Yet here the farmer drove his cart,
Here friendly folk would meet and pass,
Here bore the goodwife eggs to mart
And old and young walked up to Mass.

Here schoolboys lingered in the way,
Here the bent packman laboured by,
And lovers at the end o' the day
Whispered their secret blushingly.

A goodly road for simple needs,
An avenue to praise and paint,
Kept by fair use from wreck and weeds,
Blessed by the shrine of its own saint.

III

The road that runs up to Messines!
Ah! how we guard it day and night!
And how they guard it who o'erwean
A stricken people, with their might!

But we shall go up to Messines
Even thro' that fire-defended gate.
Over and thro' all else between
And give the highway back its state.

In the middle of November 1916, the much fought over
Beaumont Hamel was eventually captured.

ON THE TAKING OF BEAUMONT HAMEL

If you have dug in No Man's Land
From dusk till dawn,
Toiled on a job that's undermann'd,
And carried on
Although your pal fell on his spade,
You know how victories are made.

So 'twas when Beaumont Hamel fell.
We shared the pride
Of those who fought and won so well,
Tho' by the side
Of that brave throng we were not seen
Behind the fiery barrage screen.

Strength that was ours had leaked in toil
That they might fight;
Blood that was ours had drenched the soil
Where they trod light:
Graves of our dead were there to show
The way it was not ours to go!

After Charles Blackall (qv) was killed on 24th March 1918, commanding the 4th Battalion, South Staffordshire Regiment, the battalion suffered such heavy casualties at Ploegsteert Wood between 9th and 15th April that it was reduced to only one hundred men.   During a further fierce attack on the 15th the Germans captured Bailleul and the whole line was forced to retire to previously prepared positions round Kemmel.   On 21st April John Stewart took over command of the battalion;   on the 23rd the German attack on Kemmel Hill failed, but two days later they renewed the bombardment with increased intensity.   Kemmel Hill was deluged with gas shells, and the enemy succeeded in pushing forward about 1,000 yards in front of Kemmel village.   In heavy fog at 3.00 a.m. on the 26th, the 10th Cheshires, 1st Wiltshires and 4th South Staffords counter-attacked.   Two hours later they had gained their objectives and were established east of Kemmel Beck, but John Stewart was killed during the fighting.

PROMISE

(On visiting in Spring a wood where severe
fighting took place last year)

Green grew the woods but yester year,
When, deep embosomed in the mould,
The snowdrop raised a silver spear
In brave defiance of the cold;
When primrose cups of yellow gold
Still held the February snow,
And windy March's entrance bold
Made daffodilly trumpets blow.

But other spears the woods have seen,
Heard other trumpets sounding high;
The budding boughs of tender green
Are broke, and scattered wide they lie:
For men have come to fight and die,
To fill the primrose cups with blood
So freely that the grasses nigh
Are soiled with the o'er-spilling flood.

Another Spring! The broken trees
With bruised arms yearn to the sun;
No daffodils laugh in the breeze;

Of primrose goblets there are none;
There he whose battles all are done
Sleeps in his shallow grave and rough;
But bursting from his heart, lo, one
Pure snowdrop spear. It is enough!

ON REVISITING THE SOMME

If I were but a Journalist,
And had a heading every day
In double-column caps, I wist
I, too, could make it pay;

But still for me the shadow lies
Of tragedy. I cannot write
Of these so many Calvaries
As of a pageant fight;

For dead men look me through and through
With their blind eyes, and mutely cry
My name, as I were one they knew
In that red-rimmed July;

Others on new sensation bent
Will wander here, with some glib guide
Insufferably eloquent
Of secrets we would hide -

Hide in this battered crumbling line
Hide in these promiscuous graves,
Till one shall make our story shine
In the fierce light it craves.

CAPTAIN CLAUDE FRANK LETHBRIDGE TEMPLER

1st Battalion Gloucestershire Regiment.

Born: 5th July 1895. India.
Educated: Wellington College.
Killed: 4th June 1918. Aged 22 years.
The Loos Memorial to the Missing, Dud Corner Cemetery,
Loos, France.

Claude Templer was gazetted Second Lieutenant in the 1st Battalion the Gloucestershire Regiment in August 1914 and went to France with the Regiment three months later.

At La Bassée on 22nd December 1914 he was advancing ahead of his platoon to reconnoitre a German trench when he met a German N.C.O. Templer was on the point of shooting the German when he was knocked senseless to the ground from behind. He was taken prisoner and sent to the prison camp, a converted oil factory, at Hanover-Munden.

Templer was confined to the hospital suffering from concussion and shrapnel wounds in his legs. On 7th April the following year he made his first attempt to escape with seven Russian officers. He was free for a week and came near to the Dutch border but was discovered by villagers asleep in a ditch. He was taken to various military prisons and eventually transferred to Burg Camp. Templer and a fellow officer, Captain B.W. Allistone, started planning another escape in September but this was discovered, and they were sentenced at Burg Civil Gaol to one year and one week's imprisonment "for damage to public property and the theft of a plank."

Templer made four attempts to escape from Burg Gaol, all of which failed; on the first attempt he managed to get through the town but was recaptured soon after; on the fourth, a drug used on the gaolers proved ineffective. He was transferred a further three times and made another two unsuccessful attempts to gain his freedom.

On 1st May 1915, when his civil prison sentence was completed, Templer was sent by train to Magdeburg Camp. During a break at a country station he attacked his guard and escaped on a bicycle which he abandoned after fifteen miles. He hid in a wood for 24 hours but was recaptured and once again court-martialled. He was complimented on his "military method of escape" and sentenced to six weeks "very close arrest" in Magdeburg Civil Gaol. He was detained in a cell one yard wide by four yards long, ventillated by a window one foot square, with the additional penalty of "no exercise, no parcels and no smokes."

At the end of six weeks Templer was returned to Magdeburg Camp and once again became involved with tunnelling and various escape attempts by fellow prisoners. Before he was able to complete his own plans he was moved to Augustabad Camp where again he escaped but after two days freedom he was recaptured and sent to the fortress of Custrin. Another escape attempt followed and in June 1917 he was transferred to the Camp at Strohen from where he made his final and successful escape after serving five weeks in cells under close arrest. Templer described the grim conditions at this camp:

Strohen, without exception, was the worst camp I was in in Germany from every point of view. The sanitary arrangements were very bad and the food impossible to eat. The rooms were very much overcrowded. The treatment reminded one of that in 1914. In the prison those who were under close arrest had small dark cells and were allowed no smokes or parcels. The system of punishment there was summary, there was no question of court-martial or appeal. If one was supposed to have committed a crime one was sent off to the cells by the Commandant on the evidence of the sentries or of an Unter-Offizier... The guards and Unter-Offiziers were encouraged to be as brutal as possible and prisoners had no means of getting redress. There was absolutely no inducement to run straight. They seemed to be doing their best to incite a mutiny and the Commandant had orders to keep the prison full.

There was a waiting list of a hundred. I saw the Senior Officer of the camp do fifteen days imprisonment for having formulated the requests of the other prisoners and handed them in. He was charged with mutiny... There were four cases of distinct provocation to mutiny which took place inside the camp and in three of these cases officers were bayoneted...

After a month of tunnelling from a bathroom to a barn below, Templer and two other officers (Captain Harrison and Lieut Gilbert Insall VC, RFC) escaped into the barn where they remained until nightfall. Their absence was discovered and the Commandant, unaware that he was standing just above the three missing officers, gave orders to the guards for immediate pursuit. That night a violent rainstorm drove a sentry to take shelter just inside the barn and the three men in stockinged feet walked silently past him and, having heard the Commandant's earlier instructions, eluded the search parties.

They travelled for nine days and narrowly escaped being attacked by a bull as they were milking a cow in a field. They eventually reached the river Ems; at midnight they swam across the river and after cutting through a series of barbed fences found themselves in Dutch territory; they reached England on 13th September 1917.

Claude Templer rejoined his Battalion at Gorre, a small village just north of Bethune, on 19th April 1918. The Battalion had suffered losses during a recent attack on Festubert. Templer wrote in a letter:

The guns are playing a tzigane, their wild hearts in leash they beat an even measure at the will of the war wizards. But sometimes they burst their chains and passion rages unrestrained. And then comes the even measure again.

I love the beautiful guns. They are the priests of my faith. All night long they proclaim the truth, for they say: Look Life and Love and Death in the face without flinching and like a flame that springs from a smouldering fire, the world spirit that has power over all things is born in your soul and a sword is placed in your hands by whose magic the whole universe may be subdued.

The Battalion returned to the line at Hohenzollern on 1st May and after six days went into reserve at Annequin:

8th May 1918... Once upon a time, it seems years and years ago, I hadn't got much to do and I could spend all day hunting and running down beautiful thoughts across the green fields of dreamland. Perhaps some day that time will come again. I love this life with its intenseness of feeling, its sudden thrills, its challenges. But I love also my other life... No time for poetry now. But poetry time will come back again... My dream-world has always been a beautiful shadow world. What a fever of joy it is waiting for the day in the shadows. Day must come. I long for it so. But I want it to be a real June day, an all conquering fearless day, that fears not to love, but loves all it's life and dies loving. Then shall my night be sweet.

Annequin, south of the La Bassée Canal, was only a few miles from where Templer had been wounded and captured almost four years before. On the evening of the 4th of "a real June day" he led a raiding party consisting of 2 other officers and 100 other ranks on the enemy's outpost and support lines west of Auchy-les-Mines. Although one soldier was killed, one was reported missing, one officer and six soldiers were wounded, the raid was successful and the company took two prisoners. As he returned across No-Man's Land with his men to their own lines, Captain Templer was struck by a stray shell and killed.

Claude Templer wrote poetry and essays during his two and a half years in captivity. Only a third of his manuscripts were eventually returned from Germany.

TRENCHES OF FLANDERS (Fragment)

Trenches of Flanders
That guard Calais.
Rain sodden, blood sodden,
Shot swept, and shell trodden;
Trenches of Flanders
That bar the way.

THE WHEEL

The reason is a wheel. It's radius:
Infinity. It's midmost point of all:
Heaven. Its utmost rim: Hell. As for us,
We whirl within the vortex. We don't fall
Or rise, but outwards drift or inwards strive,
And though to drift is easy, a weird thrall
Enchants, entices everything alive
Towards that mystic midmost point of all.

The reason is a soul. My soul, your soul.
The soul of Paradise, the soul of Hell,
The soul of all creation. And the whole
Is boundless. 'Tis the cause of things as well
As their effect. And wisdom infinite
And love sublime, and bravery supreme,
At the great midmost point of all unite
To form the supreme power that weaves the dream
And breathes the breath, and spins the magic spell.
Here is Joy's Zenith, here is Heaven. Here love.

And they who on the field of honour fell:
They who with dauntless will for wisdom strove:

They who for love's sake suffered shame and pain
Upon the cross, shall after many turns
Of the great life wheel meet. Here once again
Lovers meet. Here the flame of worship burns.
Here Christ and Buddha and Mahomet reap
An equal harvest. Here the burning breath
Of love goes forth to waken those that sleep
In sin's soft arms, goes forth to conquer death.

And they who on the utmost rim of Hell
Drift o'er the sunless seas of sorrow, even
The farthest drifted feel the magic spell:
This is their agony... to dream of Heaven.

PURISTAN

They who, their cartridges spent, cut up, surrounded and beat
Fight back at fate till the end, scorning both death and defeat;
Who, though they know in their hearts that their resistance is vain,
Stand to the ground that they hold for that their duty is plain.

Who, at the end when the foe bid them surrender or die,
Die in the pride of their hearts, doing their duty thereby:
They have attained the ideal, their souls climb heaven. Their eyes
Pierce thro' the dream to the real; they have attained Paradise.

MAJOR CLAUDE QUALE LEWIS PENROSE M.C. AND BAR

245th Siege Battery Royal Garrison Artillery.

Born: 10th August 1893. Florida.
Educated: United Services College.
Died of wounds: 1st August 1918. Aged 24 years.
Esquelbecq Military Cemetery, France.

Claude Penrose spent his early childhood in Florida. He was educated at the school Rudyard Kipling immortalised in *Stalky & Co*. In his last year at school Penrose wrote poetry and won the painting prize. He continued to design and paint until he went to France, producing bookplates, Christmas cards, decorative panels, coats of arms and 'innumerable small studies made in oils and water colours.' Penrose went to the Royal Military Academy Woolwich in 1911 and two years later he was gazetted to the Royal Garrison Artillery. He went to France in November 1914 and remained there, apart from the occasional home leave, until his death in August 1918.

THE GOAL
(1914)

Let us not think, "What lies beyond the end?"
Lest we should faint and fail and turn aside,
Dizzy and tremulous as men who bend
Over some high rock, cleft agape and wide,
And hear below the lap of rising tide.

My soul all weary with strange wayfaring,
(What I have grasped is far from my desire)
I press along, still straitly following
The cloud of smoke by day, by night of fire.
I know my goal; my seeking shall not tire.

On 20th February 1915 Penrose described events in his diary, and four days later wrote 'Billets at Dawn':

They have christened me observation officer, and given me a pretty free hand. This morning I insisted on taking into use again an old observation station of ours, well forward, the only disadvantage of which is that it is a bit bullety at times - therefore, I think, abandoned. However, I went down there with a sergeant, and we both followed up a wire we found yesterday and suspected of being a 'gallant' one, as it was the sort they use. Quite unexpectedly we found ourselves about a hundred yards in rear of the trenches... and a bullet came past me - not many inches off either - so I moved back along a ditch. They started crumping the next field, so I moved still faster, and, when I reached the observation station, I found that a man by the door of the house at the other side of the road had just been sniped in the hinder part - like another celebrity. He seemed to think it an unsatisfactory way of being laid out. Then, this afternoon, I went to cadge sandbags from the RE to make a splinter-proof round the window, and got drenched to the skin; but as I got twice as many sandbags as I wanted, and had a nice warm billet to return to, all's well.

BILLETS AT DAWN

The grey dawn wakes a wilderness;
No song of birds salutes the morn.
Seeing the land, a man could guess
The pain and sorrow it has borne.

No song of birds salutes the morn;
The rain-drops blur the window-pane.
Long time the bare brown fields have worn
The sullen glint of winter's rain.

Seeing the land, a man could guess
That it was sore oppressed with war,
And one can hear the pitiless
Guns' boom come through the open door.

The pain and sorrow it has borne,
Seeing the land, a man could guess.
No song of birds salutes the morn;
The grey dawn wakes a wilderness.

On 10th March 1915 Sir John French's First Army attacked with four Divisions at Neuve Chapelle on a two mile front. Claude Penrose took part in this battle and was subsequently mentioned in despatches. One of his junior officers wrote:

At 4am on the 11th Lieutenant Penrose gave me a message and told me to take it to 118th advanced section. It was very dark, and I was very inexperienced and nervous; there were lots of German prisoners coming down, many without escorts, and I felt a lightness of heart and superiority over these prisoners. I had to go along a road (rue du Bacquerot) to get to the two advanced guns that, the day before, had been in our front line. The road was being heavily shelled and machine-gunned, and I thought I should never get to the guns. I ran as hard as I could with the message, and eventually reached the guns. The sight that met my eyes sickened me; the guns were almost upside down; several of the gunners were lying around, dead; and the remainder, several of whom were wounded, were crouched behind a haystack, while the enemy was shelling as fast as possible.

When I got back to the Observation Post with the answer to the message, I told Lieutenant Penrose all I had seen, and he was sorry because he had sent me. He went out immediately to assist them, and would let nobody go with him. He was away for sometime, and we began to wonder what had happened; but soon he came back and all was well. I don't know what he did when he went out; but he saw Colonel Phillips, who was the Brigade Commander, and that night the two advanced guns were brought back...

Next year, at the Battle of the Somme, Claude Penrose wrote his impression of the early morning hours on 1st July 1916:

There was something suspended in the atmosphere, besides the great white mist wreath that hung like a halo round the hills I came down from the Bray-Corbie road soon after dawn. The mist was there most mornings, hesitant, half-rising, then falling - a cloud rather, so that we saw clearly above it, and as clearly below, in the bottom of the valley, while in it we had a scope of 50 yards, if as much. But the other thing that could be discerned almost as clearly by all of us who knew what this day was to bring was the potential thunder, waiting to roll out, amid the uncanny stillness of the early morning - a stillness that could be felt, after the previous week's incessant bombardment, more keenly than the chill of the dawn, as we swung along out of the village and up, on to the Bronfay road. As we turned the corner the first gun spoke; then they started all round us, and something seemed to give way. A kind of quiet content took the place, from that moment, of the strained expectancy in the faces that we saw as we passed. One great roar drowned all lesser sounds. The engine's insistent throb sank to a distant purr; and, as we climbed the last bit of hill to the new railway loop, the 12 inch Howitzers behind us, under the east slope of the valley, were firing at their maximum rate, their great low-pitched reports filling the air - stolid, determined beings that seemed to have minds of their own and a sense of direction, as I watched them, over my shoulder, feel up and up for their elevation, stop, fire, recoil, and recuperate majestically, immensely - dignified and relentless...

ON THE SOMME

Who heard the thunder of the great guns firing?
Who watched the line where the great shells roared?
Who drove the foemen back, and followed his retiring
When we threw him out of Pommiers, to the glory of the
    Lord?

Englishmen and Scotsmen, in the grey fog of morning
Watched the dim, black clouds that reeked, and strove to
    break the gloom;
And Irishmen that stood with them, impatient for the
    warning,
When the thundering around them would cease and give
    them room

Room to move forward as the grey mist lifted,
Quietly and swiftly - the white steel bare;
Happy, swift and quiet, as the fog still drifted,
They moved along the tortured slope and met the foeman
    there.

Stalwart men and wonderful, brave beyond believing -
Little time to mourn for friends that dropped without a
    word!
(Wait until the work is done, and then give way to
    grieving) -
So they hummed the latest rag-time to the glory of the
    Lord.

All across the No Man's Land, and through the ruined
    wiring,
Each officer that led them, with a walking-cane for sword,
Cared not a button though the foeman went on firing
While they dribbled over footballs to the glory of the
    Lord.

And when they brought their captives back, hungry and
    downhearted,

They called them "Fritz" and slapped their backs, and, all
    with one accord
They shared with them what food they'd left from when
    the long day started
And gave them smokes and bully to the glory of the Lord.

The Battle of the Somme continued; Claude Penrose was
slightly wounded twice and in September 1916 after the attack on
Combles he was awarded the Military Cross:

> For displaying great gallantry and energy in command of a group of
> Survey Posts throughout the operations. After the attack on September
> 15th he got two posts into action on a hill close behind the front line
> and continued observing under circumstances of great difficulty and
> danger.

In October 1917 Penrose was promoted to Major and given
Command of 245th Siege Battery; he was mentioned in despatches
two months later. He kept a pocket diary between January 1st and
30th July 1918. The space for each day's entry measured 2 1/2
inches by 1 inch and the writing was so small that it could not be
read without a magnifying glass.

On 3rd December 1917 the Armistice between Bolshevik Russia
and Germany was signed and General Ludendorf was then able to
throw his entire military strength against the Allies on the Western
Front. The American arms build up in Europe was taking effect and
any military initiative by Germany had to be grasped without delay.
The offensive came on 21st March 1918 with an attack by 62
German Divisions on a 47 mile front between Arras and Le Feve.

This punched a huge gap in the Allied defences south of the
Somme; the Allies fell back in disarray. Claude Penrose was one of
only two Battery Commanders decorated during the Allied retreat
for his conspicuous gallantry and devotion to duty between 21st and
24th March, which won him a Bar to his Military Cross. His
Brigade Commander wrote later to his father:

> ... He commanded his Battery with his usual coolness, and when he
> was shelled particularly heavily he walked about encouraging both
> officers and men. His example caught on, and the Battery maintained
> itself in action throughout the day until it was ordered to retire about
> 10 pm on the 21st. During the 21st he went out three times on special
> reconnaissances through the Hun barrage to our front line and sent
> back most valuable and accurate information. He also engaged a Hun

battery he saw coming into action so successfully that it was put out of action.

On the night of the 21st we were ordered to withdraw our guns. The Huns had pushed up their guns and were putting a terrific barrage on the battery position. In spite of this your son successfully got away 5 guns, the 6th having been knocked out by a direct hit. Two guns had to be manhandled almost 1 1/2 miles... During the 22nd he again distinguished himself by his personal reconnaissances during a critical period of the day, pushing right through the village of Villers Faucon in spite of the barrage.

On the 24th he got his Battery into action near Mount St. Quentin, outside Péronne, and fought it until the Boches were peppering him with machine guns; then he calmly commenced to retire. Unfortunately he lost two guns at this place owing to a breakdown in the transport from shellfire...

Having written the day before that he was by no means certain whether he would be granted the leave he was due, Claude Penrose wrote home on the 29th July 1918:

Leave - one month - commencing on 3.8.18... you'll see me soon...

Two days later the Command post near St Omer was hit by an 8 inch shell. After freeing himself from the debris Penrose rescued his injured subaltern. He walked unaided to his billet and then collapsed four hours later and was taken to the 2nd Canadian Casualty Clearing Station. He had serious internal injuries, and "was operated upon, but grew rapidly worse, and at 5.30 pm next day, passed away very peacefully, suffering little... Although conscious to the last, he was unconscious of pain, owing to the great shock."

PRIVATE JOHN STEPHEN MARCUS BAKER

2nd/20th Battalion London Regiment.

7th Battalion London Regiment.

Born: 14th November 1896. Stockwell, London.

Killed: 8th August 1918.   Aged 21 years.

Vis-en-Artois Memorial to the Missing, Haucourt, France.

John Baker enlisted in the 2nd/20th Battalion London Regiment in February 1915. The Battalion arrived in France in June 1916 and was in trenches in the vicinity of Acq the following month.

IN THE LINE
(Bully Greney, 1916)

There was Sammy and Len and me
Up at the Cap-du-Pont,
In a sweet little dug-out built for three,
Talking as we were wont.
And we spoke of the days gone by,
Of times before the War.
We talked of such things with a weary sigh
Then suddenly stopped, and each one's eye
Grew wide, as flashes split the sky.
And we heard the big guns roar
Out of the dug-out, and out on the top, we watched the
    midnight strafe
For about an hour, with never a stop, or it might have
    been an hour and a half
And the night breeze blew, as cold as cold, which at
    other times we'd have cursed
And we pitied the Boche a hundredfold as we watched
    the big shells burst.
Then the strafe died down and the breeze blew on
Like a seawind after a storm.
We voted the sight had been tres bon
And went into the warm
And drank our rum with a gusto then
For the gas wind makes you dance.
Oh! the sights of a lifetime you see when
You're a wagger out in France.

TO A DESERTED BATTLEFIELD
(Souchez-Vimy, 1916)

Carency, Souchez, Lorette Heights.
Silent and still 'neath summer nights,
Scene of the fight of a thousand fights,
Grave of a thousand dead.
Ghastly yet peaceful 'neath the skies,
Your broken ruins like sightless eyes,
From your mouldering stones a spirit shall rise,
To march at your Nations head.

The clarion call like the cry of a bird
Has gone to the living - the dead have heard,
In silent graves have souls been stirred,
And France shall live!
This message give,
March on to Victory.

The Battalion served in Salonika and Egypt from the end of June 1916, but Baker probably transferred to the 2nd/7th Battalion sometime after January 1917 when it went to France. The Battalion arrived at Mailly-Maillet in April, and was in trenches at Bullecourt towards the end of May.

ON THE WAY TO THE SOMME
(1917)

There were heads held high and proud,
There were faces bright and gay,
When the Army of the Londoners
Marched on its southward way.

Through fields of ripening corn,
By trees in leaf and flower,
They marched in early morn.
They marched in Even's hour.

Past quiet villages, untouched by War's red hand,
Unheard the Boom of guns - unknown the Hunnish
 band;

The peace of many years hung softly from the sky
In that sweet country where we passed - there
    London's men marched by.

For many marched along
Thro' sunshine and thro' rain,
And many sung the laughing song,
They'll never sing again:

The voices once we heard,
The pals of work and play,
Were left down in the south
Those voices stilled for aye.

But ever in our ears
When oft we march along,
And through the coming years
Shall ring the triumph song,
For those who went to fight
To keep our London free
They conquered in the right,
And so shall deathless ever be!

The Battalion was in the Ypres area during the latter part of 1917 and in February 1918 it became part of the 1st/7th Battalion London Regiment.

By August 1918 Baker had become a signaller. The Battalion was at Bonnay, east of Amiens on 7th August 1918; the following day its objective was the high ground north east of Malard Wood. A deep ravine leading out of the north side of the wood had to be crossed to gain this. At 4.20 a.m. the barrage started and the assault was launched. A thick mist lay upon everything, platoons were soon separated and sense of direction was difficult, particularly by the tanks, which did not really take the full part intended in the action. The 6th, 7th and 8th Battalions became mixed up. Eventually elements of the 7th Battalion were reorganised and sent forward to hold the high ground east of the ravine.

In this assault the 'Shiny Seventh' played a very important role, attacking with great determination, and gaining all its objectives. It was sometime during that day Jack Baker was killed.

SPRING 'OUT HERE'.
(France)

The weeds on the Parapet,
Lift to the sunshine,
Across the sad landscape,
Still, wrecked, and torn.
The bright stars of nature
Disguise the grim shell-holes,
And o'er desolation
A new life is born.

Whispers of Springtime
Stealing so gently,
Tell to a wanderer
Weary, aroam,
Of flowers of the valley,
The birds of the Woodlands,
Of Life, Love, and Beauty,
Awaiting at Home.

Oh!. When shall I know the sweet joy of returning,
Mother and sweetheart to welcome me in,
Forgetful of suff'ring - Death and the fighting,
Happy once more in the midst of my kin.

LIEUTENANT COLONEL JOHN HAY MAITLAND HARDYMAN D.S.O. M.C.

8th Battalion Somerset Light Infantry.

Born: 28th September 1894. Bath.
Educated: Fettes College.
         Edinburgh University.
Killed: 24th August 1918. Aged 23 years.
Bienvillers-au-Bois Military Cemetery, France.

John Hardyman served on the Student Representative Council while he was taking an Arts Course at the University of Edinburgh. He was elected a Fellow of the Zoological Society of Scotland. He enlisted in the 4th Battalion Somerset Light Infantry in August 1914 and was commissioned in the 9th Battalion the following February.

ON LEAVE
(February, 1915)

The mad breeze laughs the clouds along,
The young ash shouts his clean-limbed song,
Nibbling green and chocolate slopes
Silvery brown the old hedge gropes,
I with wakening nature cry,
'Why should I die?' 'Why should I die?'

Out there it's different: we don't fear to die;
We kill, yet hate not, live, yet wonder why,
Till, worn with waiting, spent with ceaseless strain,
With present issues each man drugs his brain:
The daily letter's homely happenings,
Life's three-and-twenty unimportant things,
The third-back dug-out's need of strengthening,
How the deep mine is slowly lengthening,
Poor Freddie's death, the latest hand-grenade -
Of such is life in mud-bound Flanders made.

Is this, then, youth's fulfilment? Mothers all,
It was for this ye bore us: Duty's call,
Poor bleeding Belgium's honour, Austria's Duke!
The Jingo's clap-trap is his own rebuke...

Get thee behind me, Satan. Well I know
That through self-sacrifice the soul must grow.
And that this testing time, this struggle sore,
Shall leave old England stronger than before.

Hardyman became Acting Adjutant of the 7th Somerset Light
Infantry at Wareham and was then attached to the Brigade Staff at
Swanage in 1915; during the first half of 1916 he was attached to
the Divisional Staff at Salisbury where as a junior Second-
Lieutenant he displayed his administrative ability in the
organisation of 60,000 troops. He joined the 8th Battalion at the
front sometime during the Autumn of 1916 and became Adjutant.

1916
Via Crucis

'Lord Jesus of the trenches,
Calm 'midst the bursting shell,
We met with Thee in Flanders,
We walked with Thee in hell;
O'er Duty's blood-soaked tillage
We strewed our glorious youth;
Yes, we indeed have known Thee,
For us the Cross of Truth.

Allow us to return, then,
And teach them, in their pain,
That only through sacrifice
Shall soul meet soul again;
Come victory or failure,
To leave it all to Thee,
For soul was never vanquished
By nailing to a tree'.
Gently the Saviour answered:
'Let not your spirits grieve,
But though from death returned ye
Yet would they not believe.

'Down on your knees, My people,
My people, kneel and pray.
No longer sadden heroes
Who cast their lives away,

Who died that ye might conquer,
Whose sacrifice is vain
Unless a chastened people
Turn to their God again'.

'Lord God, before Thy footstool
A humbled people kneel;
We knew we were true metal,
We thought that we were steel,
And we forgot the furnace,
Forgot the Cross, our plea,
Forgot that we were strengthless
Till tempered, Lord, by Thee;
Forgot that all our virtues
Are but as filthy rags,
Counted our strength in armies,
Our wealth in money-bags...
Lord God, we own our folly,
And Thou wilt hear our prayer;
Lord God, accept our sacrifice,
And in Thy mercy spare.'

1916

See on the wall in fiery letters writ:
'How shows the nation in this hour of stress?'
Our prelates at reprisal meetings sit,
Our prophets pander to the halfpenny press.

Our poets - well, we have none; and our priests
A double income drain from Church and State.
The foe is at the gate; the city feasts -
With fur and feathers at the usual rate.

The 8th Battalion Somerset Light Infantry fought in the Battle of Arras in April 1917; on 28th and 29th April the Battalion took part in the Battle of Arleux over a front stretching between the Arras-Cambrai road and the Souchez River. It met heavy opposition, telephone wires were cut by the intense fire from the enemy's guns, runners became casualties and visual signalling was impossible. Hardyman was awarded the Military Cross:

For conspicuous gallantry and devotion in several dangerous reconnaissances, in one of which he was wounded. He displayed great bravery in organising the clearance of wounded from a medical aid post near an ammunition dump, which had been set on fire by a shell.

FROM A BASE HOSPITAL IN FRANCE

Christ! I am blind! God give me strength to bear
That which I most have dreaded all my days:
The palsied shuffling, grasping air,
The moving prison five foot square,
The haunting step that isn't there -
These pictures dance before my sightless gaze ...

Between April 1917 and May 1918 Hardyman was promoted from Lieutenant to Lieutenant Colonel and he took over command of the 8th Battalion on 6th June 1918 at Picquigny, west of Amiens. Later that month the Battalion moved nearer the front line to Souastre.

On the night of 10th/11th August 1918 the Germans raided the Battalion front line which ran east of the north eastern end of Bucquoy. Immediately the SOS signal was sent up Hardyman went to the scene of action and his presence undoubtedly made all the difference to his men, who were only "boys who had seen little or no previous service." The enemy were driven back suffering many casualties, and a second raid in the early hours of the following morning was repulsed without difficulty. Hardyman was awarded the Distinguished Service Order for his 'conspicuous gallantry and devotion to duty' that night.

The citation stated:

After the enemy had penetrated the line in three places he went forward through a heavy barrage to the forward posts, rallied the garrison, and encouraged them by his coolness and absolute disregard of personal danger to successfully repel repeated enemy attacks extending over two days and three nights. Thanks to his gallant leadership and endurance, the position which was of great tactical importance was maintained.

Six days later, on the 17th August, Hardyman and his Battalion gathered in a barn at Souastre to cheer their Chaplain, the Reverend Theodore Hardy, after he returned from an informal ceremony at 3rd Army Headquarters at Frohen-le-Grande. Here King George V invested Hardy, already the holder of the D.S.O and M.C., with the Victoria Cross which he had won in April. Immediately after the men had welcomed their Chaplain, they marched back to billets in Fonquevillers. The Battalion then moved up into the front line near Bucquoy on the night of 19th/20th ready for the next phase in the final offensive against the German army.

Early on 21st August the Battle of Albert began, with the Third Army making, and maintaining, substantial progress in their assault. The objective of the 8th Battalion Somerset Light Infantry, was the German main line which lay about 300 yards on the reverse slope of the high ground east of Bucquoy. At the start John Hardyman had his Headquarters just west of the village, and later moved to Bucquoy Cemetery after it had been recaptured. The Regimental History records:

> Under an extremely accurate barrage, which greatly assisted the infantry, the attack began at 4.50 a.m. on the 21st. At that hour it was fairly light, but there was a very heavy mist which prevented visibility for more than about forty yards. With great steadiness the 8th Somersets advanced straight on to their objective and captured it with very few casualties, taking sixty prisoners and six machine-guns. About an hour after the objective had been taken the 5th Division passed through and advanced, capturing Achiet-le-Petit and Logeast Wood.
>
> On the 23rd August Achiet-le-Grand and Bihucourt were attacked. In this assault the 8th Somersets provided two companies as mopping-up parties to work with the tanks which were attacking Achiet-le-Grand. These parties captured no less that 200 Germans who were hiding in dug-outs and the cellars of ruined buildings: also 15 machine-guns which the wily enemy no doubt anticipated using on the back of our men as they went forward. At 4 p.m. the Battalion was ordered to take over the line in front of Bihucourt and moved up to do so, but the enemy still held a machine-gun pocket just south of the village. After darkness had fallen one company of the Somersets attacked the pocket and half occupied it, thus practically ensuring the safety of the right flank of the village which previously had been in the air...

On 24th August the 8th Battalion captured the village of Biefvillers-lès-Bapaume. Hardyman then moved his battle Headquarters to high ground immediately west of the village and during a personal reconnaissance he was killed by a shell. He was buried at Bienvillers-au-Bois. During the five days between 21st and 26th August the 8th Battalion lost their Commanding Officer, 5 officers wounded and 164 other ranks killed, wounded or missing.

The Battalion captured 300 Germans, 2 trench mortars, 13 machine-guns and 3 howitzers.

A year before his death John Hardyman, a personal friend of Ramsay Macdonald, was elected to the Council of the Union of Democratic Control. He asked that if he was killed his epitaph should be: "He died as he lived, fighting for abstract principles in a cause which he did not believe in."

SECOND LIEUTENANT HENRY LAMONT SIMPSON

1st Battalion Lancashire Fusiliers.
Born: 5th June 1897. Crosby-on-Eden, Carlisle.
Educated: Carlisle Grammar School.
                Pembroke College, Cambridge.
Killed: 29th August 1918. Aged 21 years.
Vis-en-Artois Memorial to the Missing, Haucourt, France.

Henry Simpson was commissioned in the 1st Battalion Lancashire Fusiliers in June 1917, and was at Ypres two months later. He wrote a letter to his English master at school:

> The more I see of men, the more I love them... A common song (even now and then a dirty song) can make one glad and sad beyond words, because one has heard men singing it times out of number. In all seriousness, the cheap popular songs of the last few years can move me infinitely more than the divinest music, because of the men I have heard sing them. This is not merely a sentimental lingering over dead friendships and individual passions - that element is very small. The main thing is a love for, a passionate faith in, my fellow men... I believe with all my heart that man is, in the main, a loveable, and, at bottom, a good creature. (Curse the word good! but you know what I mean - worthy, sterling, right, true, real). He sings dirty songs and swears, and is altogether a sensual drunken brute at times; but get to know him, start by loving him, believe in him through thick and thin, and you will not go unrewarded.

> I am aware that this is chaotic, illogical, and possibly, to the wordly wise, BOSH. But it is a belief that was struggling in me even at school, that flowered forth in the Army in England, and that bore good fruit in France. It is a part of me, the best part of me, and right or wrong I shall stick to it. (The right or wrong is for your benefit - I know I am right). And because I believe this furiously, I want to write - to let everybody know it; and for the first time in my life I absolutely cannot write a line. I have not yet arrived at 'recollecting in tranquillity'; I am too much sizzling with belief to be coherent...

Simpson was wounded and sent to hospital in Carlisle, and by June he was back with his battalion in the area east of Hazebrouck. On 13th June Simpson wrote 'Last Song' and three days later he wrote 'Last Nocturne':

LAST SONG

All my songs are risen and fled away;
   (Only the brave birds stay);
All my beautiful songs are broken or fled.
   My poor songs could not stay
Among the filth and the weariness and the dead.

There was bloody grime on their light, white feathery wings,
   (Hear how that lark still sings),
And their eyes were the eyes of dead men that I knew.
   Only a madman sings
When half of his friends lie asleep for the rain and the dew.

The flowers will grow over the bones of my friends;
   (The birds' song never ends);
Winter and summer, their fair flesh turns to clay.
   Perhaps before all ends
My songs will come again that have fled away.

LAST NOCTURNE

   The search-light swords
Stab the sky
Miles back,
Light taut cords
Of gold, high
Against the black.

   A star-flare
Of showering red
Surprises night,
And hangs in air,
Painting the dead
With ruddy light.

   The pale wax
Of their faces
Turns to blood
By dim tracks
In dark places
Of the wood

Where I go
Hurrying on.
Suddenly
I stumble low
On some one.
God on high!

His face was cold,
And very white;
There was no blood.
I grew old
That night
In the wood.

He was young,
My enemy -
But lips the same
As lips have sung
Often with me.
I whispered the name

Of the friend whose face
Was so like his;
But never a sound
 In the dim place
Under the trees
Closing round.

Then I cursed
My Nocturnes -
I hated night;
Hated it worst
When the moon turns
Her tired light

On horrible things
Man has done
With life and love.
Only a fool sings
When night's begun
And the moon's above.

I cursed each song
I made for men
Full of moonlight
Lasting night-long;
For I knew then
How evil is night.

I cursed each tune
Of night-dim wood
And Naiad's stream,
By that mad moon
Asearch for blood
And the waxen gleam

Of dead faces
Under the trees
In the trampled grass,
Till the bloody traces
Of the agonies
Of night-time pass.

At the end of August 1918 the Battalion was in the front line at Strazeele, a few miles from Hazebrouck; Harry Simpson was killed by a sniper's bullet on the 29th August.

"If it should chance that I be cleansed and crowned
With sacrifice and agony and blood,
And reach the quiet haven of Death's arms,
Nobly companioned of that brotherhood
Of common men who died and laughed the while,
And so made shine a flame that cannot die,
But flares a glorious beacon down the years -
If it should happen thus, some one may come
And, pouring over dusty lists, may light
Upon my long-forgotten name and, musing,
May say a little sadly - even now
Almost forgetting why he should be sad -
May say, 'And he died young', and then forget..."

LIEUTENANT ALEC CORRY VULLY de CANDOLE

4th Battalion Wiltshire Regiment (Attached 49th Company Machine Gun Corps).

Born: 26th January 1897. Cheltenham.
Educated: Marlborough College.
Killed: 3rd September 1918. Aged 21 years.
Aubigny Communal Cemetery Extension, France.

Alec de Candole was the son of a clergyman. He won an open Classical Exhibition to Trinity College Cambridge in December 1915, and wrote poetry on the War while still at school. He left Marlborough and enlisted in April 1916. The Master of Marlborough wrote of him: "...Like Charles Sorley (qv), his rather older contemporary at school, whom he greatly loved, he was a splendid rebel: a rebel against the institutional, the conventional and the traditionally accepted, when and where, if tried by canons of truth and principle, he found them wanting..."

de Candole was commissioned in the 4th Wiltshire Regiment and sent to Flanders in April 1917. From Palace Camp at Dickebusch in June 1917 he wrote the following poem:

IN THAT ROUGH BARN WE KNELT

In that rough barn we knelt, and took and ate
Simply together there the bread divine,
The body of God made flesh, and drank in wine
His blood who died, to man self-dedicate.
And even while we knelt, a sound of hate
Burst sudden on us, as our shrieking line
Of guns flashed bursting death, a thunderous sign
Of raging evil in our human state.
Strange state! when good must use (nor other can)
The tools of ill, itself from ill to free,
And Christ must fight with Satan's armoury.
What strange and piteous contrast may we scan,
The shell that slays, and Christ upon the tree,
The love that died, and man that murders man!

Alec de Candole was wounded at the end of October 1917. After convalescing at home he was sent to a camp on Salisbury Plain. During this time he wrote 'I saw them laughing once', and on the train after attending a Service in Salisbury Cathedral two days after Christmas 1917 he wrote 'Salisbury Cathedral'.

I SAW THEM LAUGHING ONCE

I saw them laughing once; they held their sides
And laughed till old Olympus shook again, -
The blessed gods, who watch whate'er betides
On earth below, saw man with man in vain
Strive in besotted hate, crawl out at night
And creep about, and hide in fear the day,
Burrowing beneath the earth at dawn's first light,
And sleeping all the golden hours away
Of sun and pleasure; then when night grows chill,
Though bright the full moon shines upon the earth
He calls it dark, comes out, and works his will.
Small wonder surely for Olympus' mirth,
At war, sans right, sans reason, and sans mind,
This wild supremest folly of mankind!

SALISBURY CATHEDRAL

I Prayed here when I faced the future first
Of war and death, that GOD would grant me power
To serve Him truly, and through best and worst
He would protect and guide me every hour.
And He has heard my prayer, and led me still
Through purging war's grim wondrous revelation
Of fear and courage, death and life, until
I kneel again in solemn adoration
Before Him here, and still black clouds before
Threat as did those which now passed through are bright;
Therefore, with hope and prayer and praise, once more
I worship Him, and ask that with His might
He still would lead, and I with utter faith
Follow, through life or sharpest pain or death.

Alec de Candole hoped to become a clergyman after the War and during his nine months at home he wrote *The Faith of a Subaltern: Essays on Religion and Life.* He revised this profession of his faith after he returned to France; the book was published the year after his death.

> ... Without the possibility of evil there could be no good; without free-will there could be no virtue. Man's highest good could not possibly be attained without the strengthening and purifying power of contest; he could not even know what good was had he not seen and known evil. Therefore the love of God which desires our highest good, has decreed that we shall know good and evil and shall have the choice between them, which shall be ours.
>
> This may be thought inconsistent with the notion that in the long run every one shall become perfect. No; for now we are dealing with eternity. If the love of God has decreed that man's good shall be made good in battle, it has also decreed that none shall be finally lost in that battle; yet those who are weak or cowardly or treacherous cannot but pay the penalty. It rests with the man's own soul what he shall suffer before he conquers. We cannot conceive to what extremities the love of God may have to go before a man will see that good is his good and so take sides against evil.
>
> Love, then, is the key of the universe, its heart, its foundation-stone. Love is the source and the end of morality, the supreme truth, and the ideal beauty...

On his return to Belgium in July 1918, de Candole joined the 49th Company Machine Gun Corps at Ypres. In the same month he wrote two poems:

AS ONE WHO WANDERS

As one who wanders on a desert plain,
   An arid waste of dead sterility,
   Then finds a green oasis suddenly,
And slakes his thirst there, and forgets his pain,
Resting awhile from the long journey's strain
   'Neath the cool shade of some o'erarching tree
   In full content, and yearneth longingly
In that sweet place for ever to remain;
So has it been my fortune all this day
   Beneath the cloud-flecked blue of heaven's wide dome
   To rest in quiet ease, my spirit at home,
All weary care and labour put away,
Free now and happy, ere again I roam,
   Once more in void and barren paths to stray.

AND IF A BULLET

And if a bullet in the midst of strife
Should still the pulse of this unquiet life,
'Twere well: be death an everlasting rest,
I oft could yearn for it, by cares opprest;
And be't a night that brings another day,
I still could go rejoicing on my way,
Desiring in no phantom heav'n to dwell,
Nor scared with terror of any phantom hell,
But gazing now I find not death a curse
Better than life perchance, at least not worse;
Only the fierce and rending agony,
The torment of the flesh about to die,
Affrights my soul; but that shall pass anon,
And death's repose or strife be found, that gone;
Only with that last earthly ill to cope
God grant me strength, and I go forth with hope.

At the beginning of September 1918, the Battalion was in Aubigny, west of Arras. On 4th September the Battalion Diary recorded that Alec de Candole was killed in a bombing raid on Bonningues. Two days before he died he wrote his last poem:

WHEN THE LAST LONG TREK IS OVER

When the last long trek is over,
    And the last long trench filled in,
I'll take a boat to Dover,
    Away from all the din;
I'll take a trip to Mendip,
    I'll see the Wiltshire downs,
And all my soul I'll then dip
    In peace no trouble drowns.

Away from noise of battle,
    Away from bombs and shells,
I'll lie where browse the cattle,
    Or pluck the purple bells;
I'll lie among the heather,
    And watch the distant plain,
Through all the summer weather,
    Nor go to fight again.

CAPTAIN VIVIAN TELFER PEMBERTON M.C.
216th Siege Battery Royal Garrison Artillery.
Born: 9th May 1894. Cheltenham.
Educated: Cheltenham College.
　　　　　Sidney Sussex College, Cambridge.
Killed: 7th October 1918. Aged 24 years.
Bellicourt British Cemetery, France.

Vivian Pemberton was commissioned in the Royal Munster Fusiliers in 1914 and later transferred to the Royal Garrison Artillery. He won a Military Cross during the first half of 1918. The Citation read:

> For conspicuous gallantry and devotion to duty. When the enemy had broken through he kept his guns in action until the last possible moment, and when forced to withdraw them organised his men so that they kept up a steady rifle fire on the enemy. His coolness and courage saved a most critical situation.

Pemberton was killed in action at Sancourt.

AN ONLY SON'S DYING LAMENT

I'm not a soldier born and bred,
I hate the sound of guns,
I joined because they told me
England needed all her sons.

I love old England's country scenes,
The old cliffs by the sea,
The peaceful, mist-clad Devon moors,
'Tis there that I would be.

I love the gentle English girls,
I love their graceful ways,
I love to watch the sheep dog's work,
And the lazy cattle graze.

They used to give me all I asked
In those dear days of old,
They gave me wine, they gave me love,
And never asked for gold.

But now I do not ask for love,
For riches, wine, or song,
They tell me that I'll soon be well,
But I know they are wrong.

A stretcher party brought me here,
My left leg hurt like sin,
They sent my pay-book and my gold
Back to my next of kin.

It is not much for which I ask,
I know my knell has rung,
But they will not give me anything
To cool my burning tongue.

TO WINGLES TOWER

I sit and gaze at Wingles
As the fading sunlight mingles
With the smoke that hangs o'er Hersin and Béthune.
For a moment Loos reposes
As another long day closes
And awaits the rising of another moon.

In the background Fosse's towers
Through the long and weary hours
Like a sentinel on guard above the mine,
And surveys the field of battle
Silent now save for the rattle
Of the wheels of transport going up the line.

On the right the long white trenches,
Waterlogged and full of stenches
Crawl like snakes across the Lens - La Bassée road,
Where the trees all bent and battered,
Seared with scars where shrapnel spattered,
Bow like aged men beneath a heavy load.

Silver clouds hang soft and dreamy
O'er the distant ridge of Vimy
Where the ruined hamlets snuggle down to rest.
Through the golden autumn glimmer
In the trees there steals the shimmer
Of the sun that sinks in flame into the west.

I have gazed on Wingles Tower
Hour after weary hour,
Till my heavy eyes ceased watching for a while,
And sometimes I fell to wondering
If I'd not been sorely blundering
When I thought I knew the meaning of your smile.

WAR MEDITATIONS

When the snow lies crisp and sparkling o'er
    the frozen sea of mud
Which lies round Combles and Péronne;
When your veins are full of icicles instead of
    warm red blood,
And your circulation's absolutely gone;
When your fingers get so numb your glasses
    won't stay near your eyes,
And you're tired of watching movement in
    Bapaume,
Don't you sometimes feel you'd like to have
    a really damned good cry,
When your thoughts begin to turn towards
    your home.

When your D111s out of order and the dug-
    out's cold and damp,
And your best telephonists are sick with
    "flue",
When you find that you've forgotten on
    which point you were to clamp,
And you know you have to register at two.
When the watch that you had synchronised
    an hour ago has stopped,
And the Major wants the F.O.O.'s report,
When you haven't got the faintest notion
    where the first round dropped,
And the infantry report rounds falling short.

When you're passing Ginchy corner and the
    Hun begins to strafe,
And you want to throw yourself down in the
    mud,

But you daren't because you know that the
    telephonists would laugh,
So you can but hope the next will be a dud,
When you get to your O.P. and find you've
    worked your factors wrong,
And you're well within the hundred per cent
    zone,
Have you never felt that feeling when your
    whole soul seems to long
For home, a dog, or wife to call your own.

LIEUTENANT WILFRED EDWARD SALTER OWEN M.C.

2nd Battalion Manchester Regiment.
Born: 18th March 1893. Oswestry, Shropshire.
Educated: Birkenhead Institute.
        Shrewsbury Technical School.
Killed: 4th November 1918. Aged 25 years.
Ors Village Communal Cemetery, France.

Wilfred Owen, the eldest of four children, was the son of a railway official. Both his parents were of Welsh ancestry and he was particularly close to his mother; his Celtic fore-elders and his mother's evangelical christianity greatly influenced his poetry.

The family moved from Oswestry to Birkenhead in 1897 and to Shrewsbury in 1907. In September 1911, at the age of eighteen, Owen passed the University of London Matriculation Examination. The following month he went as an unpaid assistant to the Vicar of Dunsden, near Reading. During the sixteen months at the Vicarage he continued his studies and worked with kindness and sympathy amongst the poor and sick in the parish, but found he had doubts about orthodox religion and 'pulpit professionals'.

Wilfred Owen arrived home in February 1913 in a distressed state. He was then ill with congestion of the lungs, and his brother Harold later wrote:

> ... How dreadfully he was in need of peace of mind; but he could not find it. In this way, his bodily succumbing to the physical illness which seized him immediately after he had returned home acted as a safety-valve; it came just in time to prevent a nervous breakdown...

After his recuperation Owen failed to win a scholarship to Reading University, became ill again, and encouraged by his family and doctor decided to work in the south of France. He arrived in Bordeaux in September 1913 and taught English in the Berlitz School for the next ten months. War was declared five days after Owen left Bordeaux to become tutor to the Leger family at Bagnères-de-Bigorre in the High Pyrenees. His letters home for the next few weeks describe his 'perfect (holiday) existence' and his meeting with the French poet and pacifist, Laurent Tailhade. On 28th August 1914, he wrote to his mother:

... The war affects me less than it ought. But I can do no service to anybody by agitating for news or making dole over the slaughter... I feel my own life all the more precious and more dear in the presence of this deflowering of Europe. While it is true that the guns will effect a little useful weeding, I am furious with chagrin to think that the Minds which were to have excelled the civilization of ten thousand years, are being annihilated - and bodies, the product of aeons of Natural Selection, melted down to pay for political statues...

In June 1915 Owen wrote to his mother from Merignac, Bordeaux, that he now 'intensely' wanted to fight and ten days later asked her to find the address of the Artists' Rifles, 'the Corps which offers commissions to gentlemen returning from abroad'. He arrived home in the middle of September 1915 and joined the Artists' Rifles a few weeks later.

After initial training at Hare Hall in Romford, Essex, Owen was commissioned in the 5th Battalion Manchester Regiment at the beginning of June 1916 and further training followed. On 30th December 1916 he arrived at the Base Camp at Etaples; two days later he joined the 2nd Battalion in billets behind the lines at Pernois-Lès-Halloy near Doullens, where the men were resting after suffering heavy losses in November fighting at Beaumont Hamel. He was given command of 3 Platoon, 'A' Company. On 6th January 1917 the Battalion marched in bitterly cold weather to Beauval and on 8th January it moved further up the line to billets at Courcelles. On 12th January Owen and his platoon spent four days in a front line dug-out in the Beaumont Hamel area and he wrote to his mother on 16th January:

... I can see no excuse for deceiving you about these last 4 days. I have suffered seventh hell.
I have not been at the front.
I have been in front of it.
I held an advanced post, that is, a 'dug-out' in the middle of No Man's Land.
We had a march of 3 miles over shelled road then nearly 3 along a flooded trench. After that we came to where the trenches had been blown flat out and had to go over the top. It was of course dark, too dark, and the ground was not mud, not sloppy mud, but an octopus of sucking clay, 3, 4, and 5 feet deep, relieved only by craters full of water. Men have been known to drown in them. Many stuck in the mud & only got on by leaving their waders, equipment, and in some cases their clothes.
High explosives were dropping all around, and machine guns

spluttered every few minutes. But it was so dark that even the German flares did not reveal us.

Three quarters dead, I mean each of us 3/4 dead, we reached the dug-out, and relieved the wretches therein. I then had to go forth and find another dug-out for a still more advanced post where I left 18 bombers. I was responsible for other posts on the left but there was a junior officer in charge.

My dug-out held 25 men tight packed. Water filled it to a depth of 1 or 2 feet, leaving say 4 feet of air.

One entrance had been blown in & blocked.

So far, the other remained.

The Germans knew we were staying there and decided we shouldn't.

Those fifty hours were the agony of my happy life.

Every ten minutes on Sunday afternoon seemed an hour.

I nearly broke down and let myself drown in the water that was now slowly rising over my knees.

Towards 6 o'clock, when, I suppose, you would be going to church, the shelling grew less intense and less accurate: so that I was mercifully helped to do my duty and crawl, wade, climb and flounder over No Man's Land to visit my other post. It took me half an hour to move about 150 yards...

In the Platoon on my left the sentries over the dug-out were blown to nothing. One of these poor fellows was my first servant whom I rejected. If I had kept him he would have lived, for servants don't do Sentry Duty. I kept my own sentries half way down the stairs during the more terrific bombardment. In spite of this one lad was blown down and, I am afraid, blinded...

THE SENTRY

We'd found an old Boche dug-out, and he knew,
And gave us hell, for shell on frantic shell
Hammered on top, but never quite burst through.
Rain, guttering down in waterfalls of slime
Kept slush waist-high that, rising hour by hour,
 Choked up the steps too thick with clay to climb.
What murk of air remained stank old, and sour
With fumes of whizz-bangs, and the smell of men
Who'd lived there years, and left their curse in the den,
If not their corpses...
                      There we herded from the blast
Of whizz-bangs, but one found our door at last,-
Buffeting eyes and breath, snuffing the candles.
And thud! flump! thud! down the steep steps came thumping

And splashing in the flood, deluging muck -
The sentry's body; then, his rifle, handles
Of old Boche bombs, and mud in ruck on ruck.
We dredged him up, for killed, until he whined
"O sir, my eyes - I'm blind - I'm blind, I'm blind!"
Coaxing, I held a flame against his lids
And said if he could see the least blurred light
He was not blind; in time he'd get all right.
"I can't," he sobbed. Eyeballs, huge-bulged like squids',
Watch my dreams still; but I forgot him there
In posting next for duty, and sending a scout
To beg a stretcher somewhere, and floundering about
To other posts under the shrieking air.

. . . .

Those other wretches, how they bled and spewed,
And one who would have drowned himself for good, -
I try not to remember these things now.
Let dread hark back for one word only: how
Half listening to that sentry's moans and jumps,
And the wild chattering of his broken teeth,
Renewed most horribly whenever crumps
Pummelled the roof and slogged the air beneath -
Through the dense din, I say, we heard him shout
"I see your lights!" But ours had long died out.

From billets at Courcelles, Owen wrote on 19th January:

...Last night indeed I had to 'go up' with a party. We got lost in the
snow. I went on ahead to scout - foolishly alone - and when, half a
mile away from the party, got overtaken by

GAS

It was only tear-gas from a shell, and I got safely back (to the party) in
my helmet, with nothing worse than a severe fright! And a few tears,
some natural, some unnatural...
They want to call No Man's Land 'England' because we keep
supremacy there.
It is like the eternal place of gnashing of teeth; the Slough of Despond
could be contained in one of its crater-holes; the fires of Sodom and
Gomorrah could not light a candle to it - to find the way to Babylon
the Fallen.
It is pock-marked like a body of foulest disease and its odour is the
breath of cancer.
I have not seen any dead. I have done worse. In the dank air I have
perceived it, and in the darkness, felt....

No Man's Land under snow is like the face of the moon chaotic, crater-ridden, uninhabitable, awful, the abode of madness...

Owen was soon in the Front Line again and wrote to his mother when he returned to his billets:

4th February 1917... I have no mind to describe all the horrors of this last Tour. But it was almost wusser than the first, because in this place my Platoon had no Dug-Outs, but had to lie in the snow under the deadly wind. By day it was impossible to stand up or even crawl about because we were behind only a little ridge screening us from the Bosches' periscope.
We had 5 Tommy's cookers between the Platoon, but they did not suffice to melt the ice in the water-cans. So we suffered cruelly from thirst.
The marvel is that we did not all die of cold. As a matter of fact, only one of my party actually froze to death before he could be got back, but I am not able to tell how many have ended in hospital. I had no real casualties from shelling, though for 10 minutes every hour whizz-bangs fell a few yards short of us. Showers of soil rained on us, but no fragments of shell could find us...
We were marooned on a frozen desert.
There is not a sign of life on the horizon and a thousand signs of death.
Not a blade of grass, not an insect; once or twice a day the shadow of big hawk, scenting carrion...
I suppose I can endure cold, and fatigue, and the face-to-face death, as well as another; but extra for me there is the universal pervasion of Ugliness. Hideous landscapes, vile noises, foul language and nothing but foul, even from one's own mouth (for all are devil ridden), everything unnatural, broken, blasted; the distortion of the dead, whose unburiable bodies sit outside the dug-outs all day, all night, the most execrable sights on earth. In poetry we call them the most glorious. But to sit with them all day, all night... and a week later to come back and find them still sitting there, in motionless groups, THAT is what saps the 'soldierly spirit'...

EXPOSURE

Our brains ache, in the merciless iced east winds that knive us...
Wearied we keep awake because the night is silent...
Low, drooping flares confuse our memory of the salient...
Worried by silence, sentries whisper, curious, nervous,
        But nothing happens.

Watching, we hear the mad gusts tugging on the wire,
Like twitching agonies of men among its brambles.
Northward, incessantly, the flickering gunnery rumbles,
Far off, like a dull rumour of some other war.
       What are we doing here?

The poignant misery of dawn begins to grow...
We only know war lasts, rain soaks, and clouds sag stormy.
Dawn massing in the east her melancholy army
Attacks once more in ranks on shivering ranks of gray,
       But nothing happens.

Sudden successive flights of bullets streak the silence.
Less deadly than the air that shudders black with snow,
With sidelong flowing flakes that flock, pause, and renew,
We watch them wandering up and down the wind's nonchalance,
       But nothing happens.

Pale flakes with fingering stealth come feeling for our faces -
We cringe in holes, back on forgotten dreams, and stare, snow-
dazed,
Deep into grassier ditches. So we drowse, sun-dozed,
Littered with blossoms trickling where the blackbird fusses.
       Is it that we are dying?

Slowly our ghosts drag home: glimpsing the sunk fires, glozed
With crusted dark-red jewels; crickets jingle there;
For hours the innocent mice rejoice: the house is theirs;
Shutters and doors, all closed: on us the doors are closed, -
       We turn back to our dying.

Since we believe not otherwise can kind fires burn;
Nor ever suns smile true on child, or field, or fruit.
For God's invincible spring our love is made afraid;
Therefore, not loath, we lie out here; therefore were born,
       For love of God seems dying.

To-night, His frost will fasten on this mud and us,
Shrivelling many hands, puckering foreheads crisp.
The burying-party, picks and shovels in their shaking grasp,
Pause over half-known faces. All their eyes are ice,
       But nothing happens.

Wilfred Owen was sent on a three week Transport Course at Abbeville in early February. On 1st March he rejoined the Battalion near Fresnoy-lès-Roye where as part of the 14th Brigade, it had taken over the line from the French. Billets were at Beaufort-en-Santerre and "most comfortable dug-outs, grass fields, woods, sunshine, quiet" at Bouchoir, on the Amiens - Roye road. He was posted to 'B' Company and on 11th March he was sent to Le Quesnoy-en-Santerre, a small village nearer the line, in charge of a party of 'Dug-Out Diggers':

> ... It is a soft job. I take the men up sometimes by day, sometimes by night, so that (as today) I lie snug in my blankets until lunchtime. We are 4 officers living in this cellar; our servants cook for us. It is a relief to be away from the Battalion for a while. How I hope it will last. It <u>may</u> spin out 3 weeks...

On the night of 13th/14th March Owen went to see a man suffering from exhaustion. In the pitch dark Owen fell into a "kind of well, only about 15ft" and caught the back of his neck as he fell. He suffered from a headache for 3 days but continued to go up to the front until he "developed a high fever, vomitted strenuously, and long, and was seized with muscular pains..."

Owen was taken to the Military Hospital at Nesle and then to 13th Casualty Clearing Station at Gailly, on the banks of the Somme canal. He wrote to his mother on the 18th March saying that he thought he had fallen into a deep cellar and the next day he told his brother that he "lost count of days in that cellar, and even missed the passing of night & daylight, because my only light was a candle."

Owen was kept at the Casualty Clearing Station for two weeks and on 4th April rejoined the Battalion at Selency. It had just been involved in an attack on Savy Wood. 'A' Company had suffered heavily but had captured six machine-guns and advanced to the outskirts of St. Quentin. He wrote to his mother:

> ... I shall no doubt be in time for the <u>Counter Attack</u>. I have bought an automatic pistol in the town... <u>By the time you get this we'll be out of the line again</u>... My long rest has shaken my nerve. But after all <u>I hate old age</u>, and there is only one way to avoid it!...

From billets in Beauvois-en-Vermandois, a few miles west of St. Quentin, Wilfred Owen wrote on 8th April 1917:

... When I turned up I went back to A Coy, where Captain Green was hanging on with only one officer. We stuck to our line 4 days (and 4 nights) without relief, in the open, and in the snow. Not an hour passed without a shell amongst us. I never went off to sleep for those days, because the others were far more fagged after several days of fighting than I fresh from bed. We lay in wet snow. I kept alive on brandy, the fear of death, and the glorious prospect of the cathedral Town [St. Quentin] just below us, glittering with the morning... It was unknown where exactly the Bosche was lying in front of us. The job of finding out fell upon me. I started out at midnight with 2 corporals & 6 picked men; warning other Regiments on our flanks not to make any mistake about us. It was not very long before the Hun sent up his verilights, but the ground was favourable to us, and I and my Corporal prowled on until we clearly heard voices and the noises of carrying & digging. When I had seen them quite clearly moving about, and marked the line of their entrenchment it might seem my job was done; but my orders were to discover the force of the enemy. So then I took an inch or two of cover and made a noise like a platoon. Instantly we had at least two machine guns turned on us, and a few odd rifles. Then we made a scramble for 'home'...

On 12th April the Battalion was sent back to Savy Wood to take part in another attack by the French on St. Quentin. The Battalion's objective was to occupy Faubourg St. Martin ready to deal with a counter attack in the direction of Fayet. Fayet was taken on April 14th and the Battalion was ordered the next day to take over the main line of defence in front of Savy Wood. Owen later wrote to his mother:

... Twice in one day we went over the top, gaining both our objectives. Our A Company led the Attack, and of course lost a certain number of men. I had some extraordinary escapes from shells & bullets. Fortunately there was no bayonet work, since the Hun ran before we got up to his trench... Never before has the Battalion encountered such intense shelling as rained on us as we advanced in the open... The reward we got for all this was to remain in the Line 12 days. For twelve days I did not wash my face, nor take off my boots, nor sleep a deep sleep. For twelve days we lay in holes, where at any moment a shell might put us out. I think the worst incident was one wet night when we lay up against a railway embankment. A big shell lit on the top of the bank, just 2 yards from my head. Before I awoke, I was blown in the air right away from the bank! I passed most of the following days in a railway cutting, in a hole just big enough to lie in, and covered with corrugated iron. My brother officer of B Coy, 2/Lt. Gaukroger lay opposite in a similar hole. But he was covered with earth, and no relief will ever relieve him, nor will his Rest be a 9 days-

Rest. I think that the terribly long time we stayed unrelieved was unavoidable; yet it makes us feel bitterly towards those in England who might relieve us, and will not...

SPRING OFFENSIVE

Halted against the shade of a last hill,
They fed, and, lying easy, were at ease
And, finding comfortable chests and knees,
Carelessly slept. But many there stood still
To face the stark, blank sky beyond the ridge,
Knowing their feet had come to the end of the world.

Marvelling they stood, and watched the long grass swirled
By the May breeze, murmurous with wasp and midge,
For though the summer oozed into their veins
Like an injected drug for their bodies' pains,
Sharp on their souls hung the imminent line of grass,
Fearfully flashed the sky's mysterious glass.

Hour after hour they ponder the warm field -
And the far valley behind, where the buttercup
Had blessed with gold their slow boots coming up,
Where even the little brambles would not yield,
But clutched and clung to them like sorrowing hands;
They breathe like trees unstirred.

Till like a cold gust thrills the little word
At which each body and its soul begird
And tighten them for battle. No alarms
Of bugles, no high flags, no clamorous haste -
Only a lift and flare of eyes that faced
The sun, like a friend with whom their love is done.
O larger shone that smile against the sun, -
Mightier than his whose bounty these have spurned.

So, soon they topped the hill, and raced together
Over an open stretch of herb and heather
Exposed. And instantly the whole sky burned
With fury against them; earth set sudden cups
In thousands for their blood; and the green slope
Chasmed and steepened sheer to infinite space.

. . . . . .

Of them who running on that last high place
Leapt to swift unseen bullets, or went up
On the hot blast and fury of hell's upsurge,
Or plunged and fell away past this world's verge,
Some say God caught them even before they fell.

But what say such as from existence' brink
Ventured but drave too swift to sink.
The few who rushed in the body to enter hell,
And there out-fiending all its fiends and flames
With superhuman inhumanities,
Long-famous glories, immemorial shames -
And crawling slowly back, have by degrees
Regained cool peaceful air in wonder -
Why speak not they of comrades that went under?

The Battalion was relieved on 21st April, and from his cellar quarters at Quivières Owen wrote:

LE CHRISTIANISME

So the church Christ was hit and buried
    Under its rubbish and its rubble.
In cellars, packed-up saints lie serried,
    Well out of hearing of our trouble.

One Virgin still immaculate
    Smiles on for war to flatter her.
She's halo'd with an old tin hat,
    But a piece of hell will batter her.

On 2nd May Owen was back in the 13th Casualty Clearing Station, "labelled neurasthenia." A few days later he wrote to his mother:

... I am more and more Christian as I walk the unchristian ways of Christendom. Already I have comprehended a light which never will filter into the dogma of any national church: namely that one of Christ's essential commands was: Passivity at any price! Suffer dishonour and disgrace; but never resort to arms. Be bullied, be outraged, be killed; but do not kill. It may be a chimerical and an ignominious principle, but there it is. It can only be ignored: and I think pulpit professionals are ignoring it very skilfully and successfully indeed...

And am I not myself a conscientious objector with a very seared conscience?...

Christ is literally in no man's land. There men often hear His voice: Greater love hath no man than this, that a man lay down his life - for a friend.

Is it spoken in English only and French?

I do not believe so.

Thus you see how pure Christianity will not fit in with pure patriotism...

Wilfred Owen reached the Welsh Hospital, Netley in Hampshire on 16th June where it was "pleasant to be among the Welsh - doctors, sisters, orderlies. And nurses." He was examined by a Medical Board and pronounced unfit for General Service for six months. He arrived at Craiglockhart War Hospital in Edinburgh on the 25th June 1917.

Under sympathetic and enlightened medical care Owen's days were full but at night he continued to suffer from vivid and terrifying nightmares. In August 1917 Siegfried Sassoon was sent to Craiglockhart; his public statement of protest at the continuation of the war had embarrassed and angered the authorities but the intervention of friends, pleading his shell-shock, saved him from a court-martial. Gradually, with Sassoon's encouragement, Owen took the brave and therapeutic step towards his recovery by writing about his war experiences.

Owen enclosed a copy of 'Anthem for Doomed Youth' in a letter to his mother on 25th September 1917 saying "Sassoon supplied the title 'Anthem': just what I meant it to be..."

ANTHEM FOR DOOMED YOUTH

What passing-bells for these who die as cattle?
- Only the monstrous anger of the guns.
Only the stuttering rifles' rapid rattle
Can patter out their hasty orisons.
No mockeries now for them; no prayers nor bells;
Nor any voice of mourning save the choirs, -
The shrill, demented choirs of wailing shells;
And bugles calling for them from sad shires.

What candles may be held to speed them all?
    Not in the hands of boys, but in their eyes
Shall shine the holy glimmers of good-byes.
    The pallor of girls' brows shall be their pall;
Their flowers the tenderness of patient minds,
And each slow dusk a drawing-down of blinds.

On 16th October Owen wrote to his mother:

... Here is a gas poem done yesterday... The famous Latin tag means of course It is sweet and meet to die for one's country. Sweet! And decorous!...

DULCE ET DECORUM EST

Bent double, like old beggars under sacks,
Knock-kneed, coughing like hags, we cursed through sludge,
Till on the haunting flares we turned our backs
And towards our distant rest began to trudge.
Men marched asleep. Many had lost their boots
But limped on, blood-shod. All went lame; all blind;
Drunk with fatigue; deaf even to the hoots
Of tired, outstripped Five-Nines that dropped behind.

Gas! GAS! Quick, boys! - An ecstasy of fumbling,
Fitting the clumsy helmets just in time·
But someone still was yelling out and stumbling,
And flound'ring like a man in fire or lime...
Dim, through the misty panes and thick green light,
As under a green sea, I saw him drowning.

In all my dreams, before my helpless sight,
He plunges at me, guttering, choking, drowning.

If in some smothering dreams you too could pace
Behind the wagon that we flung him in,
And watch the white eyes writhing in his face,
His hanging face, like a devil's sick of sin;
If you could hear, at every jolt, the blood
Come gargling from the froth-corrupted lungs,
Obscene as cancer, bitter as the cud
Of vile, incurable sores on innocent tongues, -
My friend, you would not tell with such high zest

To children ardent for some desperate glory,
The old Lie: Dulce et decorum est
Pro patria mori.

After he left Craiglockhart at the end of October 1917 Wilfred
Owen had three weeks leave and then joined the 5th (Reserve)
Battalion Manchester Regiment at Scarborough. He wrote to his
mother on New Year's Eve 1917:

> ... I am not dissatisfied with my years. Everything has been done in
> bouts:
> Bouts of awful labour at Shrewsbury & Bordeaux; bouts of amazing
> pleasure in the Pyrenees, and play at Craiglockhart; bouts of religion
> at Dunsden; bouts of horrible danger on the Somme; bouts of poetry
> always; of your affection always; of sympathy for the oppressed
> always.
> I go out of this year a Poet, my dear Mother, as which I did not enter
> it. I am held peer by the Georgians; I am a poet's poet.
> I am started. The tugs have left me; I feel the great swelling of the
> open sea taking my galleon...

In March 1918 Owen was transferred to Ripon and he took a
room in a cottage, near the camp. During the few weeks in his attic
retreat he settled to write whenever he had the opportunity. He
revised and rewrote many poems drafted or written previously, and
wrote new ones.

On 4th June 1918 Owen was passed fit by the Medical Board
and returned to Scarborough. During July he began to gather
poems for a book; he had probably already drafted his Preface:

> This book is not about heroes. English Poetry is not yet fit to speak of
> them.
> Nor is it about deeds, or lands, nor anything about glory, honour,
> might, majesty, dominion, or power, except War.
> Above all I am not concerned with Poetry.
> My subject is War, and the pity of War.
> The Poetry is in the pity.
> Yet these elegies are to this generation in no sense consolatory. They
> may be to the next. All a poet can do today is warn. That is why the
> true Poets must be truthful.
> (If I thought the letter of this book would last, I might have used
> proper names; but if the spirit of it survives - survives Prussia - my
> ambition and those names will have achieved themselves fresher
> fields than Flanders...)

After he heard that Siegfried Sassoon had been wounded, and invalided home at the end of July, Owen wrote: "Now must I throw my little candle on his torch, and go out again."

Owen arrived at the Base Camp at Etaples on 1st September and on 9th September he was at a Reception Depot in shell-torn Amiens. He rejoined the 2nd Battalion on the 15th at La Neuville, east of Corbie; Owen was posted to 'D' Company and made Bombing Officer. The second-in-command of the Battalion was Major J.N. Marshall, M.C., who had recently received his tenth wound.

On 28th September the Battalion, part of the 96th Brigade, marched to Vendelles. At 2.30 p.m. the next day it continued further east towards the front line. The Battalion crossed the St. Quentin Canal at about 8.30 p.m. and stayed the night in old German trenches about 3 kilometres beyond the canal near the village of Bellenglise. On the 30th, under shell-fire, it moved to positions east of Magny-la-Fosse with the Battalion Headquarters on the outskirts of the village. A brigade attack was planned on Joncourt and the Beaurevoir-Fonsommes Line round Chataignies Wood. The attack started at 4.00 p.m. on 1st October; the Battalion broke through the line, reached Joncourt and, after fierce hand-to-hand fighting, drove the Germans out of Swiss Cottage trench and gained all it's objectives; the operation cost the Manchesters over ninety casualties, but they took more than two hundred prisoners. The Germans made repeated counter-attacks throughout the following night but the Battalion held its ground.

On the 3rd October the Battalion was relieved and went to dug-outs near Le Haucourt, on the banks of the St. Quentin Canal; and two days later, after suffering more casualties from shell-fire, it was sent further back to Hancourt, seven miles south east of Péronne. From here Owen wrote his mother two accounts:

... I can find no word to qualify my experiences except the word SHEER (Curiously enough I find the papers talk about sheer fighting!) It passed the limits of my Abhorrence. I lost all my earthly faculties, and fought like an angel.
If I started into detail of our engagement I should disturb the censor and my own Rest.
You will guess what has happened when I say I am now Commanding the Company, and in the line had a boy lance-corporal as my Sergeant-Major.
With this corporal who stuck to me and shadowed me like your prayers I captured a German Machine Gun and scores of prisoners.

I'll tell you exactly how another time. I only shot one man with my revolver (at about 30 yards!); The rest I took with a smile. The same thing happened with other parties all along the line we entered.

I have been recommended for the Military Cross; and have recommended every single N.C.O. who was with me!

My nerves are in perfect order.

I came out in order to help these boys - directly by leading them as well as an officer can; indirectly, by watching their sufferings that I may speak of them as well as a pleader can. I have done the first.

Of whose blood lies yet crimson on my shoulder where his head was - and where so lately yours was - I must not now write.

It is all over for a long time. We are marching steadily <u>back</u>.

Moreover

The War is nearing an end...

8th October 1918... You will understand I could not write - when you think of us for days all but surrounded by the enemy. All one day (after the battle) we could not move from a small trench, though hour by hour the wounded were groaning just outside. Three stretcher-bearers who got up were hit, one after one. I had to order no one to show himself after that, but remembering my own duty, and remembering also my forefathers the agile Welshmen of the Mountains I scrambled out myself & felt an exhilaration in baffling the Machine Guns by quick bounds from cover to cover. After the shells we had been through, and the gas, bullets were like the gentle rain from heaven...

Owen was awarded the Military Cross. The citation ran:

For conspicuous gallantry and devotion to duty in the attack on the Fonsomme Line on 1st/2nd October 1918. On the Company Commander becoming a casualty, he assumed command and showed fine leadership and resisted a heavy counter-attack. He personally captured an enemy Machine Gun in an isolated position and took a number of prisoners. Throughout he behaved most gallantly.

STRANGE MEETING

It seemed that out of battle I escaped
Down some profound dull tunnel, long since scooped
Through granites which titanic wars had groined.
Yet also there encumbered sleepers groaned,
Too fast in thought or death to be bestirred.
Then, as I probed them, one sprang up, and stared

With piteous recognition in fixed eyes,
Lifting distressful hands as if to bless.
And by his smile, I knew that sullen hall,
By his dead smile I knew we stood in Hell.
With a thousand pains that vision's face was grained;
Yet no blood reached there from the upper ground,
And no guns thumped, or down the flues made moan.
"Strange friend," I said, "here is no cause to mourn."
"None," said the other, "save the undone years,
The hopelessness. Whatever hope is yours,
Was my life also; I went hunting wild
After the wildest beauty in the world,
Which lies not calm in eyes, or braided hair,
But mocks the steady running of the hour,
And if it grieves, grieves richlier than here.
For by my glee might many men have laughed,
And of my weeping something had been left,
Which must die now. I mean the truth untold,
The pity of war, the pity war distilled.
Now men will go content with what we spoiled.
Or, discontent, boil bloody, and be spilled.
They will be swift with swiftness of the tigress,
None will break ranks, though nations trek from progress.
Courage was mine, and I had mystery,
Wisdom was mine, and I had mastery;
To miss the march of this retreating world
Into vain citadels that are not walled.
Then, when much blood had clogged their chariot-wheels
I would go up and wash them from sweet wells,
Even with truths that lie too deep for taint.
I would have poured my spirit without stint
But not through wounds; not on the cess of war.
Foreheads of men have bled where no wounds were.
I am the enemy you killed, my friend.
I knew you in this dark; for so you frowned
Yesterday through me as you jabbed and killed.
I parried; but my hands were loath and cold.
Let us sleep now..."

After thirteen days in his 'Corrugated Iron & Red Tent Billet' Owen and the men of the 2nd Battalion marched back towards the front line via Bohain to Busigny. On the 29th October the Battalion moved into the line at St. Souplet and on the 31st it took over the line west of the Sambre-Oise Canal north of the village of Ors in readiness for an attack over and beyond the canal.

From 'The Smoky Cellar of the Forester's House' Wilfred Owen wrote to his mother at 6.15 p.m. on 31st October:

... So thick is the smoke in this cellar that I can hardly see by a candle 12 ins. away, and so thick are the inmates that I can hardly write for pokes, nudges & jolts... It is a great life...
... There is no danger down here, or if any, it will be well over before you read these lines.
I hope you are as warm as I am; as serene in your room as I am here...
Of this I am certain you could not be visited by a band of friends half so fine as surround me here.

On the night of 3rd/4th November the assault troops were gathered in rain-sodden fields some 300 yards short of the Sambre Canal. At 5.45 a.m., Zero Hour, on bridges carried by the Royal Engineers, the Manchesters had first to cross a 3 ft deep ditch which ran parallel to the canal and then the canal itself, beyond the towpath. The Artillery Support Fire Plan for the assault of the Sambre canal allowed for a creeping barrage to start a short distance beyond the canal bank. It failed to account for the German machine gun defences behind the parapet of the east bank. Five minutes after Zero Hour the barrage lifted and the Germans on the far side manned their machine-guns and fired relentlessly on the line of troops as they scrambled on planks over the flooded ditch and reached the towpath. At the same time the men of the Royal Engineers struggled to assemble their pontoon bridge. The bridge was destroyed and under heavy fire the Engineers attempted to repair it. When only two men remained standing, Second Lieutenant James Kirk who was attached to the 2nd Battalion, took a Lewis gun and under heavy machine gun fire paddled out on a raft half-way across the canal. He opened fire forcing the enemy to take cover; he held them down long enough for the bridge to be mended and for two platoons to scramble across before it was broken again as he fell shot through the head.

On the Battalion's right, Acting Lieutenant-Colonel Marshall, commanding the 16th Lancashire Fusiliers, organised and encouraged parties of volunteers to repair another broken bridge. The first party were all killed or wounded. Standing on the canal bank under intense fire he called for more volunteers and helped the men in their work until they had succeeded. Marshall led his men across the bridge but was mortally wounded as he reached the other side. For their gallantry both Kirk and Marshall were awarded a posthumous Victoria Cross.

Wilfred Owen was on the canal bank working with his platoon when he was hit and killed. A few hours later a diminished Battalion crossed the canal south of Ors, on a floating bridge.

As the bells announcing the Armistice rang out in Shrewsbury seven days later, Wilfred Owen's parents received the telegram telling them of his death.

LIST OF SOLDIER-POETS AND POEMS

*There is some doubt about the authorship of the poem 'Trenches: St Eloi'. This was orginally published before Hulme's death, under the initials 'TEH', in the 'Catholic Anthology: 1914-1915', edited by Ezra Pound and entitled 'Poem: Abbreviated from the Conversation of Mr. TEH'. However, Pound probably wrote the poem after talking to Hulme about this specific incident in 1915, and then put it under Hulme's name in the Catholic Anthology. The poem was reprinted by Pound as his own poem, without Hulme's initials, in 'Umbra' (1920) and is still in print in Ezra Pound's Collected Early Poems.

**'The Sentry'; 'Exposure'; 'Spring Offensive'; and 'Strange Meeting', are placed in the text after the letter giving details of the incident or action to which they refer. These poems were not, however, completed until a later date.

A Brief Chronology of the Major Battles
in Northern France and Flanders, 1914-1918

1914

4 August	Britain declares war on Germany	
23 August	Battle of Mons	⎫ The Retreat
26 August	The counter attack at Le Cateau	⎪ from Mons
3-9 September	First Battle of the Marne	⎬ and the Defence
13-28 September	First Battle of the Aisne	⎭ of Paris
19 October– 21 November	First Battle of Ypres	

1915

10-13 March — Battle of Neuve Chapelle
22 April-24 May — Second Battle of Ypres
9 May — Battle of Aubers Ridge
15-25 May — Battle of Festubert
25 September–
  15 October — Battle of Loos

1916

21 February–
  18 December — Battle of Verdun
1 July–
  18 November — Battle of the Somme

1917

9 April-16 May — Battle of Arras
  (Canadians take Vimy Ridge)
16 April-16 May — Second Battle of the Aisne
7-14 June — Battle of Messines
31 July–
  12 November — Third Battle of Ypres (Passchendaele)
20 November–
  9 December — Battle of Cambrai

1918

21 March– 5 April	German Spring Offensive (Second Battle of the Somme)	
9-29 April	Battle of the Lys	
27 May– 2 June	Third Battle of the Aisne	
9-13 June	Battle of Noyon-Montidier	
15 July– 5 August	Second Battle of the Marne	
8 August– 3 September	Battle of Amiens	⎫ Final Allied ⎪ Offensive on
12 September	Battle of St Mihiel	⎬ the Western
11 November	Armistice Day	⎭ Front

MAP SHOWING LOCATIONS OF CEMETERIES OF YPRES GROUP

Cemeteries thus: ✝

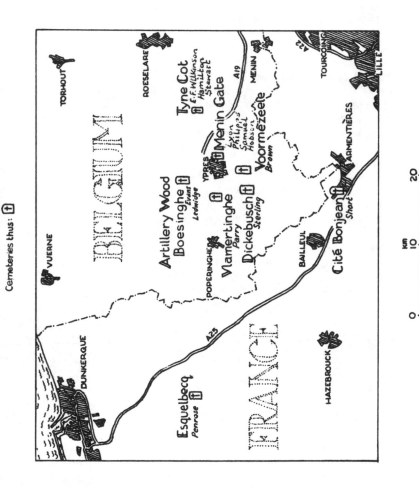

YPRES REGION

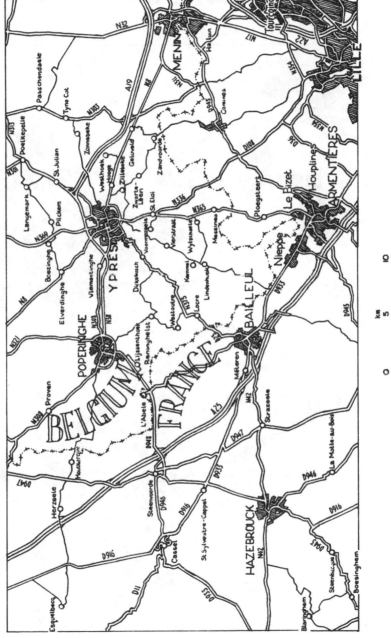

MAP OF NORTH-EAST FRANCE SHOWING
LOCATIONS OF CEMETERIES OF ARRAS GROUP

Cemeteries thus : ⛪

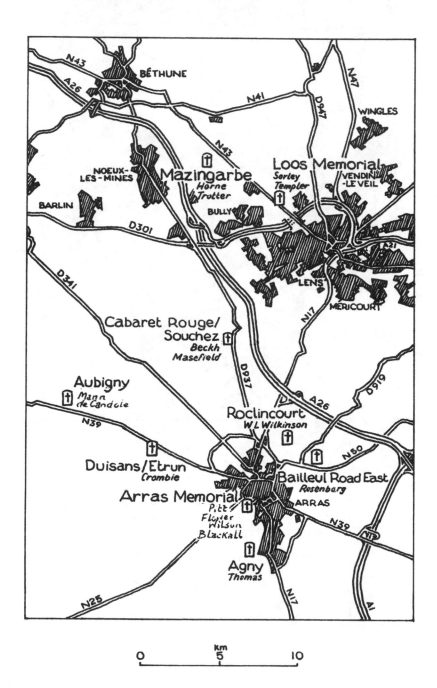

ARRAS REGION

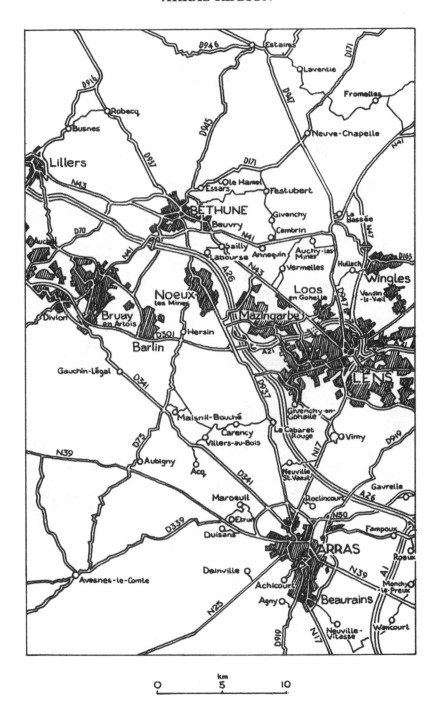

MAP OF OF NORTH-EAST FRANCE SHOWING
LOCATIONS OF CEMETERIES OF SOMME
GROUP NORTH AND SOUTH

Cemeteries thus :

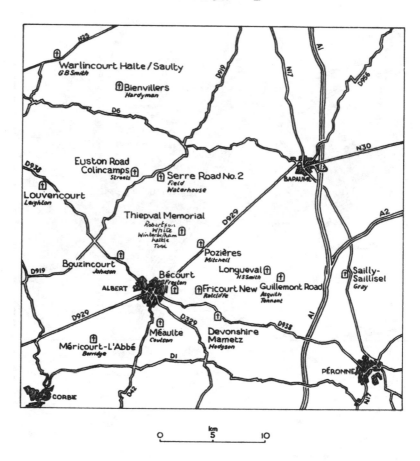

SOMME REGION

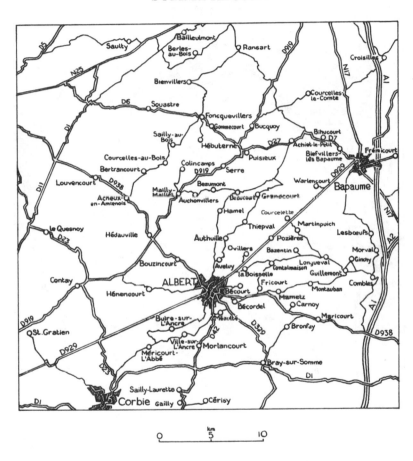

Bailleulmont
Sauity
Berles-au-Bois
Ransart
Croisilles
N17
Bienvillers
Courcelles-le-Comte
D6
Souastre
Foncquevillers
Gommecourt
Bucquoy
Bihucourt
Sailly-au-Bois
D27
Achiet-le-Petit
D7
Frémicourt
Hébuterne
Puisieux
Biefvillers-lès Bapaume
Courcelles-au-Bois
Colincamps
Serre
D919
Bertrancourt
Warlencourt
Bapaume
Louvencourt
D938
Mailly-Maillet
Beaumont
Acheux-en-Amienois
Auchonvillers
Beaucourt
Grandcourt
Hamel
Courcelette
le Quesnoy
Hédauville
Thiepval
Martinpuich
Lesbœufs
D23
Authuille
Pozières
Morval
Ovillers
Bazentin
Ginchy
Bouzincourt
Aveluy
Longueval
la Boisselle
Contalmaison
Guillemont
Combles
Contay
ALBERT
Fricourt
Montauban
Hénencourt
Bécourt
Mametz
Bécordel
Carnoy
St.Gratien
Buire-sur-L'Ancre
Méaulte
Méricourt
Bronfay
D919
D42
D329
D938
Ville-sur-L'Ancre
Morlancourt
D929
Méricourt-L'Abbé
D23
Bray-sur-Somme
D1
Sailly-Laurette
D1
Corbie
Gailly
Cérisy

km
0   5   10

MAP OF NORTH-EAST FRANCE SHOWING
LOCATIONS OF CEMETERIES OF CAMBRAI GROUP

Cemeteries thus : ⊞

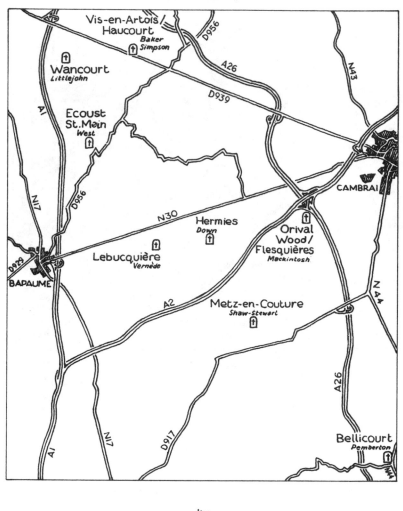

CAMBRAI REGION

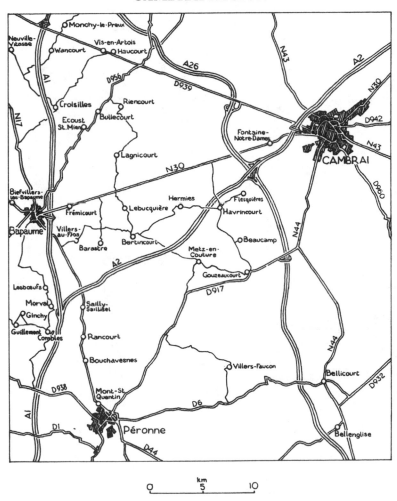

km
0   5   10

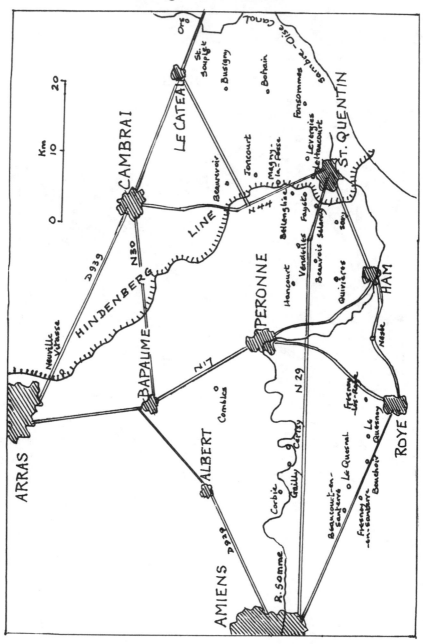

Appendix A

LIST OF REGIMENTS

Argyll & Sutherland Highlanders, 1st/8th Bn	Wilkinson, Walter.
Argyll & Sutherland Highlanders, 2nd Bn	Smith, Hugh
Black Watch, 8th Bn	Mann, Hamish
Border Regiment, 8th Bn	Stewart, John
Border Regiment, 10th Bn	Pitt, Bernard
Coldstream Guards	Hamilton, William
Devonshire Regiment, 9th Bn	Hodgson, William Noel
East Yorkshire Regiment, 12th Bn	Beckh, Robert
Essex Regiment, 2nd Bn	Waterhouse, Gilbert
Gloucestershire Regiment, 1st Bn	Templer, Claude
Gloucestershire Regiment, 1st/5th Bn	Winterbotham, Cyril
Gordon Highlanders, 4th Bn	Crombie, Eugene
Grenadier Guards, 3rd Bn	Asquith, Raymond
Grenadier Guards, 4th Bn	Tennant, Edward Wyndham
Guards Machine Gun Regiment, 4th Bn	Hamilton, William
King's Own Royal Lancaster Regiment, 1st Bn	Rosenberg, Isaac
King's Own Royal Lancaster Regiment, 11th Bn	Rosenberg, Isaac
King's Own Scottish Borderers, 7th Bn	Horne, Cyril
King's Royal Rifle Corps, 17th Bn	Parry, Harold.
Lancashire Fusiliers, 1st Bn	Simpson, Henry
Lancashire Fusiliers, 19th Bn	Smith, Geoffrey
Leicestershire Regiment, 11th Bn	Trotter, Bernard
London Regiment, 1st/12th Bn	Todd, Nicholas
London Regiment, 2nd/20th Bn	Baker, John
London Regiment, 2nd Bn	Coulson, Leslie
London Regiment, 7th Bn	Baker, John
London Regiment, 12th Bn	Coulson, Leslie
Loyal North Lancashire Regt, 10th Bn	Dennys, Richard
Machine Gun Corps, 49th Coy	de Candole, Alec
Machine Gun Corps, 116th Coy	Hobson, John
Manchester Regiment, 2nd Bn	Johnson, Donald
Manchester Regiment, 2nd Bn	Owen, Wilfred
Middlesex Regiment, 1st/7th Bn	Littlejohn, William
Middlesex Regiment, 16th Public Schools Bn	West, Arthur Graeme
North Staffordshire Regiment, 1st/5th Bn	Masefield, Charles
Northumberland Fusiliers, 20th Bn	White, Bernard
Oxfordshire & Buckinghamshire Light Infantry, 6th Bn	West, Arthur Graeme
Rifle Brigade, 3rd Bn	Mitchell, Colin
Rifle Brigade, 3rd Bn	Vernède, Robert
Rifle Brigade, 8th Bn	Mitchell, Colin

Rifle Brigade, 12th Bn	Vernède, Robert
Royal Berkshire Regiment, 2nd Bn	Gray, John
Royal Berkshire Regiment, 3rd Bn	Freston, Rex
Royal Berkshire Regiment, 4th Bn	Down, Oliphant
Royal Berkshire Regiment, 6th Bn	Freston, Rex
Royal Dragoons, 1st Bn	Grenfell, Julian
Royal Dublin Fusiliers, 9th Bn	Kettle, Tom
Royal Field Artillery, 14th Bde	Short, William
Royal Field Artillery, 242nd Bde	Flower, Clifford
Royal Field Artillery, 286th Bde	Short, William
Royal Flying Corps	Morris, Vincent
Royal Garrison Artillery	Pemberton, Vivian
Royal Garrison Artillery, 244th Siege Bty	Thomas, Edward
Royal Garrison Artillery, 245th Siege Bty	Penrose, Claude
Royal Horse Guards	Philipps, Colwyn
Royal Inniskilling Fusiliers, 1st Bn	Ledwidge, Francis
Royal Inniskilling Fusiliers, 5th Bn	Ledwidge, Francis
Royal Marine Artillery, Naval Siege Bty	Hulme, Thomas Ernest
Royal Naval Division, Hood Bn	Shaw-Stewart, Patrick
Royal Scots, 9th Bn	Brown, John
Royal Scots, 9th Bn	Lyon, Walter
Royal Scots Fusiliers, 1st Bn	Sterling, Robert
Royal Warwickshire Regiment, 6th Bn	Field, Henry
Royal Welch Fusiliers, 15th Bn	Evans, Ellis
Royal West Kent Regiment, 10th Bn	Samuel, Gerald
Seaforth Highlanders, 4th Bn	Mackintosh, Alan
Seaforth Highlanders, 5th Bn	Mackintosh, Alan
Seaforth Highlanders, 9th Bn	Brown, John
Sherwood Foresters, 3rd Bn	Morris, Vincent
Sherwood Foresters, 10th Bn	Wilson, Cameron
Somerset Light Infantry, 6th Bn	Berridge, Eric
Somerset Light Infantry, 8th Bn	Hardyman, John
South Staffordshire Regiment, 4th Bn	Blackall, Charles
South Staffordshire Regiment, 4th Bn	Stewart, John
Suffolk Regiment, 7th Bn	Sorley, Charles
Suffolk Regiment, 12th Bn	Rosenberg, Isaac
Warwickshire Regiment, 2nd Bn	Flower, Clifford
West Yorkshire Regiment, 8th Bn	Wilkinson, Eric
West Yorkshire Regiment, 10th Bn	Ratcliffe, Alfred
Wiltshire Regiment, 4th Bn	de Candole, Alec
Worcestershire Regiment, 1st/7th Bn	Leighton, Roland
York & Lancaster Regiment, 12th Bn	Robertson, Alexander
York & Lancaster Regiment, 12th Bn	Streets, John

Appendix B

LIST OF CEMETERIES AND MEMORIALS

Belgium

Artillery Wood Cemetery, Boesinghe	Evans, Ellis
Artillery Wood Cemetery, Boesinghe	Ledwidge, Francis
Coxyde Military Cemetery	Hulme, Thomas Ernest
Dickebusch New Military Cemetery	Sterling, Robert
Menin Gate Memorial, Ypres	Hobson, John
Menin Gate Memorial, Ypres	Lyon, Walter
Menin Gate Memorial, Ypres	Philipps, Colwyn
Menin Gate Memorial, Ypres	Samuel, Gerald
Tyne Cot Memorial, Passchendaele	Hamilton, William
Tyne Cot Memorial, Passchendaele	Stewart, John
Tyne Cot Memorial, Passchendaele	Wilkinson, Eric
Vlamertinghe Military Cemetery	Parry, Harold
Voormezeele Enclosure No 3	Brown, John

France

Agny Military Cemetery	Thomas, Edward
Arras Memorial, Faubourg d'Amiens	Blackall, Charles
Arras Memorial, Faubourg d'Amiens	Flower, Clifford
Arras Memorial, Faubourg d'Amiens	Pitt, Bernard
Arras Memorial, Faubourg d'Amiens	Wilson, Cameron
Aubigny-en-Artois Communal Cemetery Extension	Mann, Hamish
Aubigny-en-Artois Communal Cemetery Extension	de Candole, Alec
Bailleul Road East Cemetery, St Laurent-Blangy	Rosenberg, Isaac
Bécourt Military Cemetery, Bécordel-Bécourt	Freston, Rex
Bellicourt British Cemetery	Pemberton, Vivian
Bienvillers Military Cemetery	Hardyman, John
Boulogne Eastern Cemetery	Grenfell, Julian
Bouzincourt Communal Cemetery Extension	Johnson, Donald
Cabaret-Rouge British Cemetery, Souchez	Beckh, Robert
Cabaret-Rouge British Cemetery, Souchez	Masefield, Charles
Caterpillar Valley Cemetery, Longueval	Smith, Hugh
Cité Bonjean Military Cemetery, Armentières	Short, William
Devonshire Cemetery, Mansel Copse, Mametz	Hodgson, William Noel
Duisans British Cemetery, Etrun	Crombie, Eugene
Esquelbecq Military Cemetery	Penrose, Claude
Euston Road Cemetery, Colincamps	Streets, John
Fricort New Military Cemetery	Ratcliffe, Alfred
Grove Town Cemetery, Méaulte	Coulson, Leslie

Guillemont Road Cemetery	Asquith, Raymond
Guillemont Road Cemetery	Tennant, Edward Wyndham
HAC Cemetery, Ecoust-St Mein	West, Arthur Graeme
Heilly Station Cemetery, Méricourt L'Abbé	Berridge, Eric
Hermies Hill British Cemetery	Down, Oliphant
Highland Cemetery, Roclincourt	Wilkinson, Walter
Lebucquière Communal Cemetery Extension	Vernède, Robert
Loos Memorial to the Missing	Sorley, Charles
Loos Memorial to the Missing	Templer, Claude
Louvencourt Military Cemetery	Leighton, Roland
Mazingarbe Communal Cemetery	Horne, Cyril
Mazingarbe Communal Cemetery, Extension	Trotter, Bernard
Metz-en-Couture Communal Cemetery British Extn	Shaw-Stewart, Patrick
Orival Wood Cemetery, Flesquières	Mackintosh, Alan
Ors Village Communal Cemetery	Owen, Wilfred
Pozières Memorial, Ovillers-la-Boisselle	Mitchell, Colin
Sailly-Saillesel British Cemetery	Gray, John
Serre Road No 2, Beaumont Hamel and Hébuterne	Field, Henry
Serre Road No 2, Beaumont Hamel and Hébuterne	Waterhouse, Gilbert
St Sever Cemetery, Rouen	Dennys, Richard
St Sever Cemetery, Rouen	Morris, Vincent
Thiepval Memorial, Nr Albert	Kettle, Tom
Thiepval Memorial, Nr Albert	Robertson, Alexander
Thiepval Memorial, Nr Albert	Todd, Nicholas
Thiepval Memorial, Nr Albert	White, Bernard
Thiepval Memorial, Nr Albert	Winterbotham, Cyril
Vis-en-Artois Memorial, Haucourt	Baker, John
Vis-en-Artois Memorial, Haucourt	Simpson, Henry
Wancourt British Cemetery	Littlejohn, William
Warlincourt Halte British Cemetcry, Saulty	Smith, Geoffrey

ACKNOWLEDGEMENTS

I would like to thank the following who have kindly given permission to reprint copyright material:

Mr. Winston S. Churchill, M.P., for an extract from a letter from his Grandfather, Sir Winston Churchill, to Katherine Asquith; Messrs. Faber and Faber Ltd., on behalf of the Ezra Pound Literary Property Trust, for 'Trenches: St. Eloi' reprinted from Ezra Pound's *Collected Early Poems*; Mr. Dominic Hibberd and Messrs. Chatto and Windus for permission to quote 'Anthem for Doomed Youth' and 'Dulce et Decorum Est' from *Wilfred Owen War Poems and Others*, Edited with an Introduction and Notes by Dominic Hibberd, Chatto and Windus 1973; and for permission to quote 'Anthem for Doomed Youth' and 'Dulce et Decorum Est' by Wilfred Owen from *The Collected Poems of Wilfred Owen*, Copyright 1963, by Chatto and Windus, Ltd. Reprinted by permission of New Directions Publishing Cor; The Hon. John Jolliffe for extracts from his book *Raymond Asquith Life and Letters*, Collins 1980; Mr. David Leighton for four peoms by Roland Leighton; Mr. Martin Middlebrook for an extract about Private Harry Streets, from *The First Day on the Somme*, Allen Lane 1971; The University of Minnesota Press and Professor Samuel Hynes for extracts from T.E. Hulme's 'Diary from the Trenches' from *Further Speculations: T.E. Hulme* Edited by Sam Hynes, University of Minnesota Press, 1955; Lord Norwich and Mr. Michael Shaw-Stewart for an extract from a letter from Patrick Shaw-Stewart to Lady Diana Manners; Dr. Conor Cruise O'Brien for the last letter Tom Kettle wrote to his wife; The Earl of Oxford and Asquith for his father's Belgian Railway verses; Oxford University Press for extracts from *Wilfred Owen Collected Letters*: Edited by Harold Owen and John Bell, OUP, 1967; Messrs. Peters Fraser & Dunlop on behalf of the Julian Grenfell Estate for three extracts from *Julian Grenfell his life and the times of his death 1888–1915* by Nicholas Mosley, Weidenfeld and Nicolson, 1976; Mr. Tomos Roberts, Archivist, University College of North Wales, Bangor, for extracts from his article on 'Hedd Wyn' published in *Barddas*; Mrs. Myfanwy Thomas and The National Library of Wales for extracts from the 1917 Edward Thomas letters; Mrs. Myfanwy Thomas and the Edward Thomas Collection, University of Wales College, Cardiff, for an extract from a letter written by Edward Thomas to his daughter, Myfanwy.

The Vera Brittain material from her World War I Diary, *Chronicle of Youth* is included with the permission of her literary executors and Victor Gollancz, publisher.

I am deeply grateful to the following for research on my behalf and for their help and kindness in various ways:

Rosemary Barker; Glenda Carr, Academic Translator, University College of North Wales, Bangor; Wendy Chandley, Archivist, Tameside Archive Service; The staff of the Commonwealth War Graves Commission and in particular, Norman Christie and the Tracing Team;

Jenny Hazell, Publicity Section; Bernard McGee; Beverley Webb, Information Officer; and all the gardeners we have met during cemetery visits; Mr. Trevor Craker; Mr. Roger Custance, Archivist, Winchester College; Mr. C. Dean, Archivist, St Paul's School; The Reverend Charles de Candole; Mrs. Audrey de Candole; Mrs. M.E. Griffiths, Archivist and Librarian, Sedbergh School; the staff of the Guildhall Library Aldermanbury, London; Anne Harvey; Mrs. Elspeth Harvey, Librarian Haileybury College; Mr. Daniel Huws, The National Library of Wales; the staff of the Imperial War Museum, particularly from the Printed Books and Documents Departments; Mr. Michael Meredith, Eton College; Mrs. Ann Morris, Trawsfynydd; Mrs. Enid Morris, Trawsfynydd; Major John Porter-Wright; the staff of the Public Records Office, Kew; Brigadier Norman Routledge; the late Viscount St. Davids; Mr. George Simons; Lt. Col. R.J.M. Sinnett; Mr. Andrew Stanley; The Venerable Michael Till, Archdeacon of Canterbury; Mr. Brian Turner; Mr. D.R.C. West, Hon. Archivist, Marlborough College; Mr. Ellis Williams, Trawsfynydd; Dr. Jean Moorcroft Wilson and Mr. Cecil Woolf.

I am also very grateful to the following Archivists, Curators and Regimental Secretaries for providing helpful information:

Colonel (Rtd.) The Hon. W.D. Arbuthnott, MBE, The Black Watch (Royal Highland Regiment); Colonel J.R. Baker (Rtd.), The Royal Green Jackets; Brigadier J.K. Chater, The Royal Regiment of Fusiliers; Major (Rtd.) R.A. Creamer, The Worcestershire and Sherwood Foresters Regiment; Brigadier (Rtd.) J.M. Cubiss, CBE, MC, The Prince of Wales's Own Regiment of Yorkshire; Lieutenant Colonel (Rtd.) A.A. Fairrie, Queen's Own Highlanders (Seaforth and Camerons); Colonel J.W. Francis, The Queen's Regiment; Lieutenant Colonel (Rtd.) A.M. Gabb, OBE, The Worcestershire and Sherwood Foresters Regiment; Major (Rtd.) J. McQ. Hallam, The Royal Regiment of Fusiliers (Lancashire); Captain (Rtd.) C. Harrison, The Gordon Highlanders; Mr. Ian Hook, Keeper of the Essex Regiment Museum; Major A.W. Kersting, Household Cavalry Museum; Mr. R.D. Lippiatt, Secretary, Machine Gun Corps Old Comrades Association; Colonel I.H. McCausland (Rtd.), The Royal Green Jackets; Major R.D.W. McLean, The Staffordshire Regiment; Lieutenant Colonel R.K. May, FMA, Border Regiment and The King's Own Royal Border Regiment; Major (Rtd.) N.J. Perkins, The Queen's Lancashire Regiment; Major (Rtd.) J.H. Peters, MBE, The Duke of Edinburgh's Royal Regiment (Berkshire and Wiltshire); Lieutenant Colonel W.G. Pettifar, MBE, Royal Regiment of Fusiliers (City of London); Lieutenant Colonel (Rtd.) H.L.T. Radice, MBE, The Gloucestershire Regiment; Mr. John Scott, The York and Lancaster Regiment; Lieutenant Colonel A.W. Scott Elliot, Argyll and Sutherland Highlanders; Captain J.H. Sedgwick, Coldstream Guards; Major W. Shaw, MBE (Rtd.), The Royal Highland Fusiliers; Major H.C.L. Tennent, The Queen's Regiment; Brigadier K.A. Timbers, The Royal

Artillery Institution; Mrs. Jean Tsushima, Honourable Artillery Company; Major (Rtd.) A.E.F. Waldron, MBE, Middlesex Regiment; Lieutenant Colonel D.C.R. Ward, the King's Own Scottish Borderers; Colonel K.N. Wilkins, OBE, Royal Marines Museum; Lieutenant Colonel J.L. Wilson, DL, Royal Tigers' Association, The Royal Leicestershire Regiment; Lieutenant J.L. Wilson Smith, OBE, The Royal Scots; Lieutenant Colonel R.G. Woodhouse, DL, Somerset Light Infantry.

I am especially indebted to the following for a variety of reasons; for pointing me in the right direction, for advice, support, and friendship:

Dr. Christopher Dowling, The Imperial War Museum; Christine Lingard, Language and Literature Library, Manchester Central Library; Mr. Alan Martin; Mr. Martin Taylor, The Imperial War Museum; Pam Williams, Arts Language and Literature Birmingham Library Services; and particularly to Catherine Reilly, for her superb Bibliography, which has been a guiding light; and Mr. John Kinnane, for printing my original article, *A Slate Rubbed Clean*, in the Antiquarian Book Monthly Review in 1986.

My final thanks are to my family without whose cheerfulness, encouragement, understanding and love this book would never have been completed. To my three children for sparing precious time in their already full lives; Jonathan for hours of research at the Public Records Office and for solving problems on the computer; Rupert for tracking down many rare books, and for the very exacting task of proof-reading; Lucinda for tireless work on the computer, proof-reading and for taking on all the publicity side.

I can never thank Jeremy enough for his unwavering commitment to the idea of *A Deep Cry* from the start; for the work he has undertaken towards its production with never-failing stamina and good humour; and for his infinite patience and loving care which has sustained me throughout.

SELECT BIBLIOGRAPHY
MAIN SOURCES

ASQUITH, Raymond. *Life and Letters* by John Jolliffe. Collins, 1980.

BAKER, Jack. *Memories of the Line*. Privately Printed, [1917].

BATTALION WAR DIARIES. Relevant War Diaries consulted in the Public Records Office, Kew.

BECKH, Robert Harold. *Swallows in Storm and Sunlight*. Chapman & Hall Ltd., 1917.

BERRIDGE, William Eric. *Verses by WEB*. Privately Printed, [1917].

BLACKALL, C.W. *Songs from the Trenches*. Bodley Head, 1915.

BROWN, John. *Letters, essays and verses*. Elliot, Edinburgh, 1921.

COOMBS, Rose, E.B. *Before Endeavours Fade: A Guide to the Battlefields of the First World War*. After the Battle Publication, 1990.

COULSON, Leslie. *From an Outpost and other Poems*. Erskine Macdonald, 1917.

CRAWFORD, Fred D. *British Poets of the Great War*. Associated University Presses, 1988.

de CANDOLE, Alec. *Poems*. Privately Printed at the Cambridge University Press, 1919.
The Faith of a Subaltern: Essays on Religion and Life. Cambridge at the University Press, 1919.

DENNYS, Richard. *There is no Death: Poems*. With a Foreword by Desmond Coke. Bodley Head, 1917.

DOWN, Oliphant. *Poems*. Gowans and Gray, 1921.

EVANS, Ellis Humphrey (Hedd Wyn). Translation from the Welsh of an article written by Tomos Roberts for 'Barddas', (Nos. 128-9. Dec/Jan 1987/88).

FIELD, H.L. *Poems and Drawings*. Cornish Brothers, Birmingham University, 1917.

FLOWER, Clifford. *Memoir and Poems*. Printed Stockport, [1917].

FRESTON, H. Rex. *The Quest of Beauty and other Poems*. Blackwell, Oxford, 1915.
The Quest of Truth and other Poems. Blackwell, Oxford, 1916.
The Poetry of H. Rex Freston: A Paper by Russell Markland. N. Ling & Co., 1916.

GRAY, John. *A Souvenir of the War: Four Poems*. Privately Printed, 1917.

GRENFELL, Julian. *Pages from a Family Journal: 1888-1915*. Privately Printed, Eton College, 1916.
Julian Grenfell by Viola Meynell. Burns & Oates Ltd., [1919].
Julian Grenfell his life and times of his death 1888-1915 by Nicholas Mosley Weidenfeld & Nicolson, 1976.

HAMILTON, William. *Modern Poems*. Blackwell, Oxford, 1917.

HARDYMAN, Maitland. *A Challenge*. Allen & Unwin, 1919.

HOBSON, John Collinson. *Poems, Etc*. With Biographical Note and Memoir by John Murray. Blackwell, Oxford, 1920.

HODGSON, William Noel ["Edward Melbourne"]. *Verse and Prose in Peace and War*. Smith, Elder & Co., 1916.

HORNE, Cyril Morton. *Songs of the Shrapnel Shell and other Verse*. Harper & Brothers, New York and London, 1918.

HULME, T.E. *Speculations: Essays on Humanism and the Philosophy of Art*. Edited by Herbert Read. Kegan, Paul, Trench etc., 1936 (Second Edition).
The Life and Opinions of T.E. Hulme by Alun R. Jones. Gollancz, 1960.
Further Speculations: T.E. Hulme. Edited by Sam Hynes. University of Nebraska Press, 1962.
T.E. Hulme by Michael Roberts. With an Introduction by Anthony Quinton. Carcanet New Press, 1982.

JOHNSON, Donald F. Goold. *Poems*. With a Prefatory Note by P. Giles. Cambridge University Press, 1919.

KETTLE, T.M. *Poems & Parodies*. Duckworth & Co., 1916.
The Ways of War: With a Memoir by his wife, Mary S. Kettle. Talbot Press, Dublin, 1917.
The Enigma of Tom Kettle: Irish Patriot, Essayist, Poet, British Soldier 1880-1916 by J.B. Lyons. Glendale Press, Dublin 1983.

LEDWIDGE, Francis. *The Complete Poems of Francis Ledwidge: With Introductions* by Lord Dunsany. Herbert Jenkins, 1919.
  Francis Ledwidge: A Life of the Poet (1887-1917) by Alice Curtayne. Martin Brian & O'Keeffe, 1972.
  The Complete Poems of Francis Ledwidge. Newly Edited and with a Foreword by Alice Curtayne. Martin Brian & O'Keeffe, 1974.
LEIGHTON, Roland. *Chronicle of Youth: Vera Brittain's War Diary 1913-1917.* Edited by Alan Bishop with Terry Smart. Foreword by Clare Leighton. Gollancz, 1981.
  Poems. Privately Printed by David Leighton.
LYON, W.S.S. *Easter at Ypres 1915, and other Poems.* Maclehose, Glasgow, 1916.
MACKENZIE, Jeanne. *The Children of the Souls: A Tragedy of the First World War* Chatto & Windus, 1986.
MACKINTOSH, E.A. *A Highland Regiment.* Bodley Head, 1917.
  War, The Liberator and other Pieces. With a Memoir by John Murray. Bodley Head, 1918.
MANN, Hamish. *A Subaltern's Musings.* John Long Ltd., 1918.
MASEFIELD, Charles J.B. *Poems.* Blackwell, Oxford, 1919.
MITCHELL, Colin. *Trampled Clay* [Poems]. Erskine Macdonald, 1917.
MORRIS, Francis St. Vincent. *Poems.* Blackwell, Oxford, 1917.
OWEN, Wilfred. *Poems.* With an Introduction by Siegfried Sassoon. Chatto & Windus, 1920.
  The Poems of Wilfred Owen. A new edition including many pieces now first published, and notices of his life and work by Edmund Blunden. Chatto & Windus, 1931.
  Wilfred Owen: A Critical Study by D.S.R. Welland. Chatto & Windus, 1960.
  Journey from Obscurity: Wilfred Owen 1893-1918: Memoirs of the Owen Family. 3 Volumes. Oxford University Press, 1963, 1964 and 1965.
  Wilfred Owen: Collected Letters. Edited by Harold Owen and John Bell. Oxford University Press, 1967.
  Wilfred Owen: A Biography by Jon Stallworthy. Oxford University Press and Chatto & Windus, 1974.
  Wilfred Owen War Poems and Others. Edited with an Introduction and Notes by Dominic Hibberd. Chatto & Windus, 1974.
  Owen the Poet by Dominic Hibberd. Macmillan, 1986.
  Wilfred Owen: The Last Year by Dominic Hibberd. Constable, 1992.
PARRY, Harold. *In Memoriam* [Poems and Letters]. Printed W.H. Smith & Son, London [1918].
PEMBERTON, V.T. *Reflections in Verse.* Grant Richards, 1919.
PENROSE, Claude, L. *Poems.* With a Biographical Preface. Harrison and Sons, London, 1919.
PHILIPPS, Colwyn Erasmus Arnold. *Verses: Prose Fragments: Letters from the Front.* Smith, Elder & Co. 1916.
PITT, Bernard. *Essays, Poems, Letters.* Francis Edwards, London, 1917.
REILLY, Catherine W. *English Poetry of the First World War: A Bibliography.* George Prior Publishers, 1978.
ROBERTSON, Alexander. *Comrades.* Elkin Mathews, 1916.
  Last Poems. Preface by P. Hume Brown. Elkin Mathews, 1918.
ROSENBERG, Isaac. *Poems.* Selected and Edited by Gordon Bottomley. With an Introductory Memoir by Laurence Binyon. Heinemann, 1922.
  Collected Works. Poetry, Prose, Letters, and Some Drawings. Edited by Gordon Bottomley and Denys Harding. With a foreword by Siegfried Sassoon. Chatto & Windus, 1937.
  Journey to the Trenches: The Life of Isaac Rosenberg 1890-1918 by Joseph Cohen. Robson Books, 1975.
  Isaac Rosenberg: The Half Used Life by Jean Liddiard. Gollancz, 1975.
  Isaac Rosenberg: Poet and Painter. A Biography by Jean Moorcroft Wilson. Cecil Woolf, 1975.

The Collected Works of Isaac Rosenberg. Poetry: Prose: Letters: Paintings: and Drawings. With a Foreword by Siegfried Sassoon. Edited with an Introduction and Notes by Ian Parsons, Chatto & Windus, 1979.

SAMUEL, Gerald George. *Poems.* Arthur Humphreys, 1917.

SHAW-STEWART, Patrick. [Biography and Letters] by Ronald Knox. Collins, 1920.

SHORT, William Ambrose. *Poems.* Arthur Humphreys, 1918.

SIMPSON, Henry Lamont. *Moods and Tenses.* Erskine Macdonald, 1919.

SMITH, Geoffrey Bache. *A Spring Harvest* Erskine Macdonald, 1918.

SMITH, H.S.S. *Verses.* [1917].

SORLEY, Charles Hamilton. *Marlborough and Other Poems.* Cambridge University Press, 1916. (1st and 2nd Editions).
The Letters of Charles Sorley: With a chapter of Biography. Cambridge University Press, 1919.
Charles Hamilton Sorley: A Biography by Jean Moorcroft Wilson. Cecil Woolf, 1985.
The Collected Poems of Charles Hamilton Sorley. Edited by Jean Moorcroft Wilson. Cecil Woolf, 1985.
The Collected Letters of Charles Hamilton Sorley. Edited by Jean Moorcroft Wilson. Cecil Woolf, 1990.

STERLING, Robert. W. *Poems.* Oxford University Press, 1916.

STEWART, J.E. *Grapes of Thorns.* Erskine Macdonald, 1917.

STREETS, J.W. *The Undying Splendour.* Erskine Macdonald, 1917.

TEMPLER, Captain. *Poems and Imaginings.* Editions Bossard, Paris, 1920.

TENNANT, Edward Wyndham. *Worple Flit and other Poems*, Blackwell, Oxford, 1916.
Wheels: An Anthology of Verse. Blackwell, Oxford, 1917.
A Memoir by his Mother, Pamela Glenconner. Bodley Head, 1920.
Bim: A Tribute to Lieutenant, The Honourable Edward Wyndham Tennant by Anne Powell, 1990.

THOMAS, Edward. *Collected Poems.* With a Foreword by Walter de la Mare. Selwyn and Blount, 1920.
The Life and Letters of Edward Thomas by John Moore. Heinemann, 1939.
As It Was and World Without End by Helen Thomas. Faber combined edition, 1956.
Diary of Edward Thomas: 1 January-8 April 1917. Introduced by R. George Thomas. Anglo-Welsh Review, 1971.
Edward Thomas: A Poet for his Country by Jan Marsh. Elek Books, 1978.
The Childhood of Edward Thomas. Faber, 1983.
Edward Thomas: A Portrait by R. George Thomas. Oxford University Press, 1985.

TODD, Nicholas, H. *Poems and Plays.* Jackson & Son, Sedbergh, 1917.

TROTTER, Bernard Freeman. *A Canadian Twilight and other Poems of War and of Peace.* Toronto, 1917.

VERNEDE, R.E. *War Poems and other Verses.* With an Introductory Note by Edmund Gosse, CB. Heinemann, 1917.
Letters to his Wife. Collins, 1917.

WATERHOUSE, Gilbert. *Rail-head, and other Poems.* Erskine Macdonald, 1916.

WEST, Arthur Graeme. *The Diary of a Dead Officer: Being the Posthumous Papers of Arthur Graeme West.* Allen & Unwin, [1918].
The Diary of a Dead Officer: Being the Posthumous Papers of Arthur Graeme West. With a new Introduction by Dominic Hibberd. Imperial War Musuem, 1991 (Arts and Literature Series Number 3).

WHITE, Bernard Charles de Boismaison. *Remembrance, and other Verses.* Edited with a Memoir by De V. Payen-Payne. Selwyn & Blount, 1917.

WILKINSON, Eric Fitzwater. *Sunrise dreams and other poems.* Erskine Macdonald, 1916.

WILSON, T.P. Cameron. *Magpies in Picardy.* The Poetry Bookshop, 1919.

WINTERBOTHAM, Cyril William. *Poems.* Privately Printed [1917].

ANTHOLOGIES

An Anthology of War Poems. Compiled by Frederick Brereton. With an Introduction by Edmund Blunden. Collins, 1930.

A Treasury of War Poetry: British and American Poems of The World War, 1914-1919. Edited, with Introduction and Notes, by George Herbert Clarke. Hodder and Stoughton, 1917.

For Remembrance: Soldier Poets Who Have Fallen in the War by A. St. John Adcock Revised and Enlarged Edition. Hodder and Stoughton [1920].

Poetry of the Great War: An Anthology. Edited by Dominic Hibberd and John Onions. With an Introduction, Notes and Biographical Outlines. Macmillan, 1986.

Soldier Poets: Songs of the Fighting Men. Preface by Galloway Kyle. Erskine Macdonald, 1916.

Soldier Poets: Second Series: More Songs by the Fighting Men. Preface by Galloway Kyle. Erskine Macdonald, 1917.

The Muse in Arms: A Collection of War Poems, For the most part written in the Field of Action, By Seamen, Soldiers and Flying Men who are Serving, or have Served, in the Great War. Edited, with an introduction, by E.B. Osborn. Murray, 1917.

Up the Line to Death: The War Poets 1914-18: An Anthology selected and arranged, with an introduction and notes by Brian Gardner. Foreword by Edmund Blunden. Methuen & Co., 1964.

War Letters of Fallen Englishmen. Edited by Laurence Housman. Gollancz, 1930.

SECONDARY SOURCES

ABDY, Jane & Charlotte Gere. *The Souls: An Elite in English Society 1885-1930* Sidgwick and Jackson, 1984.

BALLIOL COLLEGE WAR MEMORIAL BOOK 1914-1919. 2 Volumes. Maclehose, University Press, Glasgow, 1924.

BERGONZI, Bernard. *Heroes' Twilight: A Study of the Literature of the Great War.* Constable, 1965.

ENGLISH LITERATURE OF THE GREAT WAR REVISITED. Proceedings of the Symposium on the British Literature of the First World War. Edited by Michel Roucoux. University of Picardy, 1986.

FUSSELL, Paul. *The Great War and Modern Memory.* Oxford University Press, 1975.

GRAHAM, Desmond. *The Truth of War:* Owen; Blunden and Rosenberg, Carcanet Press, 1984.

HIBBERD, Dominic [Editor]. *Poetry of The First World War: A Casebook.* Macmillan, 1981.

HYNES, Samuel. *A War Imagined: The First World War and English Culture.* Bodley Head, 1990.

JOHNSTON, John, H. *English Poetry of the First World War: A Study in the Evolution of the Lyric and Narrative Form.* Princeton University Press, 1964.

LAMBERT, Angela. *Unquiet Souls: The Indian Summer of the British Aristocracy.* Macmillan, 1984.

LEHMANN, John. *The English Poets of the First World War.* Thames and Hudson, 1981.

LONGWORTH, Philip. *The Unending Vigil.* Leo Cooper, 1985.

MIDDLEBROOK, Martin. *The First Day on the Somme: 1 July 1916.* Allen Lane, 1971.

MIDDLEBROOK, Martin & Mary. *The Somme Battlefields: A Comprehensive Guide From Crecy to the Two World Wars.* Viking, 1991.

OSBORN, E.B. *The New Elizabethans: A First Selection of the Lives of Young Men who have Fallen in the Great War.* Bodley Head, 1919.

POUND, Reginald. *The Lost Generation.* Constable, 1964.

RAW, David. *"It's Only Me": A life of The Reverend Theodore Bayley Hardy, VC, DSO, MC, 1863-1918.* Frank Peters Publishing, 1988.

SILKIN, Jon. *Out of Battle: The Poetry of the Great War*. Oxford University Press, 1972.
SPEAR, Hilda, D. *Remembering, We Forget*. A Background Study to the Poetry of the First World War. Davis-Poynter Ltd., 1979.
WOHL, Robert. *The Generation of 1914*. Weidenfeld and Nicolson, 1980.

ANTHOLOGIES

In Time of War. Edited by Anne Harvey. Blackie and Son, 1987 and Penguin Books, 1989.
Lads: Love Poetry of the Trenches by Martin Taylor. Constable, 1989.
Men Who March Away: Poems of the First World War: An Anthology. Edited with an Introduction by I.M. Parsons. Chatto & Windus, 1965.
Never Such Innocence: A New Anthology of Great War Verse. Edited and Introduced by Martin Stephen. Buchan & Enright, 1988.
Poems of the War and the Peace. Collected with a Foreword and Notes, by Sterling Andrus Leonard. New York, 1921.
The Lost Voices of World War I. An International Anthology of Writers, Poets and Playwrights. Edited by Tim Cross. Bloomsbury, 1988.
The Malory Verse Book: A Collection of Contemporary Poetry for School and General Use. Compiled by Editha Jenkinson. Erskine Macdonald, 1919.
The Penguin Book of First World War Poetry. Edited by Jon Silkin, Penguin Books, 1979.

SELECT BIBLIOGRAPHY OF REGIMENTAL HISTORIES.

A Short History of the Gloucestershire Regiment, Gale and Polden Ltd., 1920; History of the 1/6th Battalion Royal Warwickshire Regiment; Cornish Bros. Ltd., 1922; History of the Manchester Regiment (Late the 63rd and 96th Foot), Compiled by Colonel H.C. Wylly, CB (Vol. 2). Forster and Groom & Co. Ltd., 1923-25; History of the Grenadier Guards (1656-1949), Abridged by Captain F. Martin, Gale & Polden Ltd., 1951; History of the Somerset Light Infantry (Prince Albert's) 1914-1919 by Everard Wyrall, Methuen, 1927; A Short History of the Prince of Wales's (North Staffordshire Regiment), Gale & Polden, 1920; A Short History of the South Staffordshire Regiment; The Border Regiment in the Great War by Colonel H.C. Wylly, Gale & Polden, 1924; The Grenadier Guards in the Great War of 1914-1918 by Lt. Col. the Rt. Hon. Sir F. Ponsonby, Macmillan, 1920; The Loyal North Lancashire Regiment by Col. H.C. Wylly, 1933; The Rangers Historical Records from 1859 to the conclusion of the Great War, edited by Captain A.V. Wheeler-Holohan and Captain G.M.C. Wyatt, Harrison & Son, 1921; The Royal Fusiliers in the Great War by H.C. O'Neill, Heinemann, 1922; The Gordon Highlanders in the First World War 1914-1919 by Cyril Falls, Aberdeen University Press, 1958; The War Services of the 1/4th Royal Berkshire Regiment (T.F.) by C.R.M.F. Cruttwell, Blackwell, 1922; The Queen's Own Royal West Kent Regiment 1914-1919 by C.T. Atkinson, Simkin, Marshall, etc., 1924; Regimental Records of the Royal Welch Fusiliers (late the 23rd Foot) Vol. III. Forster, Groom & Co., Ltd., 1921; War Diary of the 5th Seaforth Highlanders by Captain D. Sutherland, Bodley Head 1920; The Royal Naval Division by Douglas Jerrold, Hutchinson, 1927; The History of The Royal Scots Fusiliers (1678-1918) by John Buchan, Nelson & Sons, Ltd., [1925]; The Royal Scots, 1914-1919 by Major John Ewing, Edinburgh, 1925; The History of the Suffolk Regiment, 1914-1927 by Lieut. Col. C.C.R. Murphy, Hutchinson & Co. Ltd., 1928; The Coldstream Guards, 1914-1918 by Lieut. Col. Sir John Ross-of-Bladensburg, OUP, 1928; History of the 7th (City of London) Battalion, The London Regiment, compiled by C. Digby Planck, London 1946; The K.O.S.B. in the Great War by Captain Stair Gillon, Nelson [1930]; The Essex Regiment by John Wm. Burrows (Essex Units in the War, 1914-1919); The York and Lancaster Regiment, 1758-1919 by Col. H.C. Wylly, 1930; The Worcestershire Regiment in the Great War by Captain H. Fitz-M. Stacke, Cheshire & Sons Ltd., 1929; and various other relevant Regimental and Military histories.

INDEX

Eastaway, Edward, (pseudonym of
  Edward Thomas), 202
East Tyrone, 130
East Yorkshire Regt., 12th Bn., 115
Easter Rising, 283
Ebrington Barracks, Derry, 284
Ecoust-St. Mein, 183
Edgbaston, 87
Edinburgh, 75, 228, 393, 421
Edinburgh University, 6, 75, 393
Egypt, 69, 75, 170, 390
Eiffel Tower Restaurant, 291
Emmanuel College, Cambridge, 106
Ems, River, 380
Esquelbecq Military Cemetery, 383
Essarts, 175
Essex Regt., 2nd Bn., 81
Essex Yeomanry, 12
Etaples, 329, 412, 424
Eton Chronicle, 15
Eton College, 10, 15, 121, 257, 322-3
Etrun, 237
Euston Road Cemetery, 69
EVANS, Ellis (Hedd Wyn), 276-8
Evans, Evan, 276
Evans, Mary, 276
Exeter College, Oxford, 48, 244

Fampoux, 360
Fantassins, 145
Farjeon, Eleanor, 201
Faubourg d'Amiens, 58, 208, 233,
  336, 345
Faubourg Ranville, 209
Faubourg St. Martin, 418
Fayet, 418
Feilding, General, G.P.T., 159
Felsted School, 165
Festubert, 98, 380
Fettes College, 393
Field Ambulance Units, 73
FIELD, Henry, 87-9
Fife, 362
Flanders, 118, 166, 258-9, 291, 323,
  381, 393-4, 403, 423
Flat Iron Copse Cemetery, xiii
Flechin, 276-7
Flesquières, 312
Flodden Field, 6
Florence, 110
Florida, 383
FLOWER, Clifford, 233-4
Fonquevillers, 88, 170, 397
Fonsommes, 424-5
Fontaine Notre-Dame, 320

Fosse, 408
Frémicourt, 349
French, Field-Marshal Sir John, 12,
  37-8, 384
Fresnoy-lès-Roye, 417
FRESTON, Hugh (Rex), 48-9, 52,
  190, 244
Freyberg, Lt-Colonel Bernard, V.C.,
  323, 329
Fricourt, 96, 100, 124, 150, 161
Fricourt New Military Cemetery, 96
Fricourt Wood, 368
Fritz Trench, 182
Frohen-le-Grand, 396
Fromelles, 181
Frost, Robert, 201, 203
Fry, Carol Howard, 215

Gailly, 417
Gallipoli, 170, 231, 282, 327, 329
Gaukroger, 2nd Lt., 418
Gavrelle, 329
Geddes Detachment, 5
Gemmenich, 145
George Watson's College, Edinburgh,
  75, 228
Gershot, 145
Gertler, Mark, 351
Ghent, 144-5
Gibson, Wilfrid, 201
Gillingham, Dorset, 254
Ginchy, 136, 139, 150, 409
Givenchy, 68, 273
Givenchy-en-Gohelle, 199
Gladstone, W.G.C., 345
Glasgow, 2, 372
Glasgow Academy, 2
Glasgow University, 372
Glenconner, Baron, 152
Glenconner, Lady, 152, 162
Glencourse Wood, 6, 7, 365
Gloucester Gazette, 5th, 127
Gloucester Regt., 1st Bn., 378, 380
Gloucester Regt., 1st/5th Bn., 126
Godley, Private S.F., V.C., ix
Gogarty, Oliver, 130
Gommecourt, 265
Gordon Highlanders, 4th Bn., 237-8,
  241
Gorre, 380
Gough, General Sir H., 333
Gouzeaucourt, 356
Gower, 200
Grantham, 270
Grantully Castle, 323-5

Mudd, Rifleman, 304
Munich Trench, 81, 88
Musée de Guerre, Mons, ix
Muttra, 15

Namur, 146
National Eisteddfod, 276, 278
Nationist, The, 130
Needham, Private, 142, 151
Neeld, Henry, 234
Nepal Trench, 232
Nesle, 417
Netley Hospital, Hampshire, 421
Neuve Chapelle, 141, 384
Neuve Chapelle, Battle of, 178-81
Neuville-St-Vaast, 234
New Age, 290, 301
Newcastle Scholarship, 322
Newcastle-under-Lyme, 290
New College, Oxford, 121
Newdigate Prize, 2, 371
Newfoundland, 140
Newfoundland Park, xi, xiii
New Numbers, 201
New Zealand, 316
Nieppe, 31-2, 372
Nieuport, 302, 307
Nigeria, 118
Nimy, ix
Nivelle, General, 199
Nixon, Lt., F., 95
Norfolk Regt., 4th Bn., 40
Norrent Fontes, 141
North Staffordshire Regt, 1st/5th Bn.,
  264-5, 267-8
'North Staffs', 301
Northumberland Fusiliers, 20th Bn.,
  90, 92, 94

Obourg Station, ix
Occold, Suffolk, 165
Odyssey, The, 28
Oise, River, 427
'Old Contemptibles', x
Oost Duinkerke Bains, 302
Orchard Trench, 223
Orival Wood Cemetery, 312
Ors, 427-8
Ors Village Communal Cemetery, 411
Ostend, 145
Oswestry, 260, 411
Ottignies, 146
Outsider, The, 15, 322
Ovillers, 108, 128, 197, 237, 255, 332,
  374

Owen, Harold, 411
OWEN, Wilfred, 204, 411-2, 414-5,
  417, 420-28
Oxford, 2, 6, 15, 28, 40, 48-50, 75, 98,
  118, 121, 126, 140, 165, 174, 183,
  190, 200, 215, 224, 244, 250, 270,
  312, 322, 362
Oxfordshire and Buckinghamshire
  Light Infantry, 6th Bn., 183, 187,
  191, 194-6

Palace Camp, 403
Pallas Trench, 182
Parnell, Charles, 130
Paris, 24
PARRY, Harold, 244-6, 248
Passchendaele, ix, xii, 304, 308, 310,
  372
Passchendaele Ridge, 308
Pauline, The, 312
PEMBERTON, Vivian, 407
Pembroke College, Cambridge, 399
Pembroke College, Oxford, 2
Penfield, Lt., 57
PENROSE, Claude, 383-5, 387-8
Pepham Down, 183
Pepinster, 146
Pernois-Lès-Halloy, 412
Péronne, 234, 388, 409, 424
PHILIPPS, The Hon. Colwyn, 10-14
Phillips, Colonel, 385
Picardy, 119, 255-6, 340-1
Piccadilly Farm, 371
Picquigny, 284, 396
Pierrerie, 145
Pigeon Ravine Cemetery, xiii
Pilckem, 277
Pilckem Ridge, 277, 289
PITT, Bernard, 58-9, 65-7
Ploegsteert Wood, 33, 35, 38, 43, 219,
  233, 262-3, 372-4, 376
Plumer, Lord, 258
Poetry Bookshop, 341
Poets' Club, 290-1
Polygon Wood, 5
Ponsonby, Sir John, 159
'Pop', 15
Poperinghe, 4, 158-60, 364
Portesham, Dorset, 304
Port Said, 323
Portsmouth, 302
Posen Crater, 134
Potijze, 9, 366-7
Powell, Kenneth, 298
Pozières Memorial, 332

Vis-en-Artois Memorial to the
Missing, 389
Vlamertinghe, 11, 25, 147, 217, 274,
365-6, 368
Vlamertinghe Military Cemetery, 244
Voormezeele, 258, 363
Voormezeele Enclosure No. 3, 362

Waley, Captain Frank, 356
Wallner, 2nd Lt., 5
Wancourt British Cemetery, 231
Ward-Price Lt., 13
Ware, Fabian, xii
Wareham, Dorset, 189, 394
Warlincourt Halte British Cemetery,
174
Warwickshire Regt., 2nd Bn., 233
WATERHOUSE, Gilbert, 81
Watou, 24
Watts, Arthur, 31, 34, 37-8
Welkenraedt, 145-6
Wellington College, 378
Welsh Guards, 139
Welsh Ridge, 330
WEST, Arthur Graeme, 183-4, 186-91,
195-6
Westhoek, 6
Westminster Gazette, The, 343
Westminster School, 270
Westoutre, 298, 364
West Yorkshire Regt., 8th Bn., 304-5,
307-8
West Yorkshire Regt., 10th Bn., 96
Whitchurch, Oxfordshire, 118
Whitwell, Derbyshire, 69
WHITE, Bernard, 90, 95
Whitechapel Group, 351
Wieltje, 366
WILKINSON, Eric, 304-5, 307-8
WILKINSON, Walter, 197-9
WILSON, Cameron, 336-7, 339, 341,
343-4
Wiltshire, 152, 200, 406
Wiltshire Regt., 1st Bn., 376
Wiltshire Regt., 4th Bn., 403, 406

Wimereux, 26
Winchester College, 110, 140, 152,
237, 260-1
Winchester Road, 156
Windmill Trench, 369
Windy Corner, 212
Wingles Tower, 408-9
Winsten, Samuel, 351
WINTERBOTHAM, Cyril, 126-9
Wireless News, 90
Wismar, 39
Wolverhampton, 264
Woodland Life, The, 200
Wood-Martyn, Colonel, 258
Woodstock College, Ontario, 249
Woolwich, R.M.A., 383
Worcestershire Regt., 1st/7th Bn., 40,
44
Working Men's College, St Pancras,
58
Wyn, Hedd (Bardic name of Ellis
Evans), 276-8
Wyndham, Sir Henry, 163
Wytschaete, 17, 371

York and Lancaster Regt., 11th Bn., 92
York and Lancaster Regt., 12th Bn.,
69, 73, 75
Yorkshire, 39, 62
Yorkshire Post, The, 100
Ypres, ix, xiii, 3-6, 10, 12-14, 24-6,
158, 160, 248, 257, 270, 272-3, 277,
286, 307, 362, 365-6, 368, 391, 399,
405
Ypres, First Battle of, 17
Ypres, Second Battle of, 5, 7, 11, 24
Ypres, Third Battle of, 271, 277, 287,
289
Ypres Salient, xii, 5, 10-11, 17, 22,
145, 148, 215, 219, 362

Zandvoorde, 17
Zillebeke, 20, 22
Zonnebeke, xii, 5, 12
Zwarte-Leen, 10